y Country at the start of The Race to Dubai

The European Tour International Schedule embraces the world. In total no fewer than 37 countries have hosted competition on The European Tour and players from no fewer than 35 countries have become Tour champions. The year of 1971 officially marked the birth of The European Tour and leading into the inaugural Race to Dubai in November, 2008, there had been in total 359 champions.

30 TAIWAN
Number of wins: 1
Number of winners: 1
Leading performer: Yeh Wei-Tze (1).

31 THAILAND
Number of wins: 4
Number of winners: 3
Leading performers: Thongchai Jaidee (2); Chapchai Nirat, Thaworn Wiratchant (1).

32 TRINIDAD and TOBAGO
Number of wins: 2
Number of winners: 1
Leading performer: Stephen Ames (2).

19 KOREA
Number of wins: 3
Number of winners: 3
Leading performers: KJ Choi, Charlie Wi, Y E Yang (1).

20 HOLLAND
Number of wins: 4
Number of winners: 3
Leading performers: Robert-Jan Derksen (2); Maarten Lafeber, Rolf Muntz (1).

21 NEW ZEALAND
Number of wins: 24
Number of winners: 6
Leading performers: Michael Campbell (8); Frank Nobilo (5); Bob Charles, Greg Turner (4).

26 SOUTH AFRICA
Number of wins: 86
Number of winners: 26
Leading performers: Ernie Els (24); Retief Goosen (14); Hugh Baiocchi (6).

MOST VICTORIES BY COUNTRY THE TOP TEN

1.	England	239
2.	Spain	147
3.	Scotland	125
4.	USA	111
5.	Australia	99
6.	South Africa	86
7.	Sweden	78
8.	Germany	54
9.	Ireland	45
10.	Wales	43

22 NORTHERN IRELAND
Number of wins: 32
Number of winners: 5
Leading performers: Darren Clarke (12); Ronan Rafferty (7); David Feherty (5).

23 PORTUGAL
Number of wins: 1
Number of winners: 1
Leading performer: Daniel Silva (1).

24 SCOTLAND
Number of wins: 125
Number of winners: 20
Leading performers: Colin Montgomerie (31); Sam Torrance (21); Sandy Lyle (18).

25 SINGAPORE
Number of wins: 1
Number of winners: 1
Leading performer: Mardan Mamat (1).

27 SPAIN
Number of wins: 147
Number of winners: 27
Leading performers: Seve Ballesteros (50); José Maria Olazábal (23); Miguel Angel Jiménez (15).

28 SWEDEN
Number of wins: 78
Number of winners: 24
Leading performers: Robert Karlsson (9); Niclas Fasth, Anders Forsbrand, Per-Ulrik Johansson, Henrik Stenson (6).

29 SWITZERLAND
Number of wins: 1
Number of winners: 1
Leading performer: André Bossert (1).

33 USA
Number of wins: 111
Number of winners: 49
Leading performers: Tiger Woods (36); Tom Watson (5); Bob Byman, Phil Mickelson, Mark O'Meara (4).

W0010090

35 ZIMBABWE
Number of wins: 29
Number of winners: 3
Leading performers: Mark McNulty (16); Nick Price (7); Tony Johnstone (6).

The European Tour
Yearbook 2009

OFFICIAL PUBLICATION

Introduction from The European Tour

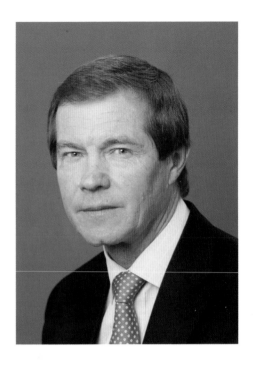

P adraig Harrington's remarkable accomplishment in successfully defending The Open Championship then completing 21 days later a unique double by capturing the US PGA Championship quite rightly earned for him The European Tour Golfer of the Year Award and from many observers the accolade of the "Greatest Sportsman in Ireland's History."

I know, however, that Padraig and each and every player and supporter of golf and all sports worldwide would agree that while competition continued our hearts and focus were directed in October onwards towards the La Paz Hospital in Madrid where Severiano Ballesteros courageously faced the most formidable challenge of his life and, as we all know, life itself following surgery for a brain tumour.

Seve's courage and charisma, invention and intensity, from the moment he stepped on the first tee elevated golf to another dimension and five Major Championships – three Open Championships and two Masters Tournaments – and 87 tournament wins worldwide between the ages of 17 and 38 provide ample statistical evidence of his peerless ability.

Seve captivated audiences in a way in which very few golfers have done in the history of the game. He flexed his muscles and with explosive power snatched triumph from disaster. All felt privileged to watch him play and, while the premature end of his competitive days denied future generations the opportunity to witness his extraordinary talent, we look forward to Seve continuing his strong links with The European Tour both in an ambassadorial role and also with The Seve Trophy.

There are many compelling achievements recognised in this the 21st edition of The European Tour Yearbook including Trevor Immelman's thrilling victory in the Masters Tournament; Robert Karlsson's rise to Number One for which he received the coveted Harry Vardon Trophy; Sergio Garcia's achievement in being The Players Champion in the United States where he also finished runner-up in the US PGA Championship and Tour Championship in addition in Europe to winning the CASTELLÓ MASTERS Costa Azahar on his home course at Club de Campo del Mediterráneo; and the passionate Major Championship challenges of Ian Poulter (The Open Championship), Henrik Stenson (The Open Championship and the US PGA Championship) and Lee Westwood (US Open Championship).

Pride of place, however, must go to Harrington. His story is told not only in a chapter specially devoted to him and written by Dermot Gilleece, the doyen of Irish golf writers, but also in those chapters dedicated to The 137th Open Championship and the 90th US PGA Championship which together define Harrington's high-octane summer.

It was in the spring amongst the azaleas and the dogwood at the famed Augusta National Golf Club that Immelman, having

fought back from ill health and returned to the fairways, enjoyed his finest hour when he followed in the footsteps of one of his great idols and compatriots, Gary Player, by receiving the celebrated Green Jacket for winning the Masters Tournament which, unquestionably, is one of the finest legacies Bobby Jones left for the game to appreciate.

The Royal and Ancient game recognises the Major Championships as a true barometer of greatness. Nevertheless the roll call of recipients of the Harry Vardon Trophy, first awarded in 1937, reads like a "Who's Who" of golf and with every season the challenge to be The European Tour Number One heightens in anticipation as the season unfolds.

This was the case in 2008 when Karlsson became the first Swedish golfer to secure Number One honours, ahead of Harrington, Westwood and the indefatigable Miguel Angel Jiménez, during a season in which he won the Mercedes-Benz Championship and the Alfred Dunhill Links Championship in addition to recording no fewer than 12 top tens which included finishing tied eighth in the Masters Tournament, tied fourth in the US Open Championship, tied seventh in The Open Championship and tied 20th in the US PGA Championship.

What is more we feel assured that in 2009 the pursuit of the Harry Vardon Trophy will stretch to a new level of excitement with the advent of The Race to Dubai which replaces the Order of Merit. The arrival of The Race to Dubai is described in full in a chapter of this Yearbook. Suffice to say that we regard the milestone signing of the unique agreement between The European Tour and Leisurecorp as another indication of our desire to grow and showcase this great game globally. This we intend to continue to achieve fuelled by the loyalty of our Members whose genius and flare provides entertainment of the highest level for spectators and television viewers in every corner of the globe.

This Yearbook recognises their talent and dedication by tracing the story every step of the way of another enthralling twelve months in the history of The European Tour. We also acknowledge through our tournament by tournament journey, vividly recorded in words and pictures, all the victories by Tour Members, recognising that the players are the stars of the show, and that the stage on which to play would not be there without the staunch support we continue to receive from all our sponsors, promoters and host venues.

Our Members regard the winning of each and every tournament as a title to cherish and in 2008 no fewer than seven enjoyed the thrill of winning on two occasions – Darren Clarke (BMW Asian Open; The KLM Open), Richard Finch (Michael Hill New Zealand Open; The Irish Open), Miguel Angel Jiménez (UBS Hong Kong Open; BMW PGA Championship), Martin Kaymer (Abu Dhabi Golf Championship; BMW International Open) and Graeme McDowell (Ballantine's Championship; The Barclays Scottish Open) in addition to Harrington and Karlsson. We congratulate them all as we do Tiger Woods, winner three times on The 2008 European Tour International Schedule, and we look forward to his return in 2009 following surgery.

In 2008 there were also no fewer than 13 first time winners – Felipe Aguilar (Enjoy Jakarta Astro Indonesia Open), Mark Brown (Johnnie Walker Classic), S S P Chowrasia (EMAAR-MGF Indian Masters), David Dixon (SAINT-OMER Open presented by Neuflize OBC), Richard Finch, Martin Kaymer, James Kingston (South African Airways Open), Peter Lawrie (Open de España), Jean-François Lucquin (Omega European Masters), Damien McGrane (Volvo China Open), Hennie Otto (Methorios Capital Italian Open) and Scott Strange (The Celtic Manor Wales Open) in addition to Pablo Larrazabal (Open de France ALSTOM) whom we congratulate on being named the Sir Henry Cotton Rookie of the Year.

The Race to Dubai will be on the agenda of all our new champions as it will be for the 20 graduates who earned their places from the 2008 European Challenge Tour and we further congratulate England's David Horsey on finishing Number One as we do Ian Woosnam on leading the way on the European Senior Tour. Incidentally the European Senior Tour has now produced 95 champions who previously accounted for no fewer than 273 victories on The European Tour and Ian has now played in no fewer than 530 European Tour events at all levels with 37 wins.

David Davies, Golf Correspondent of The Guardian, authored some of the finest essays in the history of golf writing and his work has also been enjoyed in many European Tour Yearbooks. His name is missing this year. Dai lost his courageous battle with serious illness during 2008 as did Barry Willett whom for many years was "Mr Mizuno" in the equipment facility that has become a fixture on the practice range. We remember all our friends in golf whom we have lost over the last year and recognise the challenges that remain on the horizon for others on and off the fairways.

George O'Grady

George O'Grady
Chief Executive
The European Tour

Acknowledgements

Executive Editor
Mitchell Platts

Deputy Executive Editor
Scott Crockett

Production Editor
Frances Jennings

Editorial Consultant
Chris Plumridge

Picture Editors
Andrew Redington
Rob Harborne

Art Direction
Tim Leney
Andrew Wright
TC Communications Ltd

Print Managed by
Peter Dane
Mark Baldwin
The Print House Ltd

The European Tour Yearbook 2009 is published by The PGA European Tour, Wentworth Drive, Virginia Water, Surrey GU25 4LX.
Distributed through Aurum Press Ltd.
7 Greenland Street
London NW1 0ND

© PGA European Tour.

BREAK THE INNOVATION BARRIER.
FREE IT.

No longer can IT be considered "the cost of doing business." IT modernization can drive your organization forward with greater strength, innovation and agility. Our approach leverages existing investments with solutions and services to realize early savings that are, in turn, reinvested in innovation projects until we achieve your optimal IT model — at your pace. In short, modernization pays for itself. From consulting to systems integration to outsourcing, Unisys Secure Business Operations don't simply modernize IT, they unleash your full potential.

Security unleashed. **UNISYS**

Secure Business Operations. imagine it. done.

www.securityunleashed.com/FreeIT

Contents

Padraig Harrington - A Celebration	6
The European Tour Order of Merit Winner	16
The Year In Retrospect	22
The Race to Dubai	28
HSBC Champions	36
UBS Hong Kong Open	42
MasterCard Masters	46
Michael Hill New Zealand Open	50
Alfred Dunhill Championship	54
South African Airways Open	58
Joburg Open	62
Abu Dhabi Golf Championship	66
Commercialbank Qatar Masters presented by Dolphin Energy	72
Dubai Desert Classic	78
EMAAR-MGF Indian Masters	82
Enjoy Jakarta Astro Indonesia Open	86
WGC - Accenture Match Play	90
Johnnie Walker Classic	94
Maybank Malaysian Open	98
Ballantine's Championship	102
Madeira Islands Open BPI - Portugal	108
WGC - CA Championship	112
MAPFRE Open de Andalucía by Valle Romano	116
Estoril Open de Portugal	120
Masters Tournament	124
Volvo China Open	130
BMW Asian Open	134
Open de España	138
Methorios Capital Italian Open	142
The Irish Open	146
BMW PGA Championship	152
The Celtic Manor Wales Open	164
Bank Austria GolfOpen presented by Telekom Austria	170
SAINT-OMER OPEN presented by Neuflize OBC	174
US Open Championship	178
BMW International Open	184
Open de France ALSTOM	190
The European Open	196
The Barclays Scottish Open	202
The 137th Open Championship	208
Inteco Russian Open Golf Championship 2008	216
WGC - Bridgestone Invitational	220
US PGA Championship	224
SAS Masters	228
The KLM Open	232
Johnnie Walker Championship at Gleneagles	236
Omega European Masters	242
Mercedes-Benz Championship	248
The 2008 Ryder Cup	254
The Quinn Insurance British Masters	274
Alfred Dunhill Links Championship	280
Madrid Masters	286
Portugal Masters	290
CASTELLÓ MASTERS Costa Azahar	296
Volvo Masters	302
Omega Mission Hills World Cup	308
The European Tour Qualifying School	314
Wins Around The World	316
European Senior Tour	324
European Challenge Tour	338
The European Tour Golfer of the Month Awards	352
The European Tour Shot of the Month Awards	353
Genworth Financial Statistics	354
The European Tour Order of Merit	356
The European Tour International Schedule 2008	358
Credits	360

Extraordinary Dividend

Padraig Harrington at Dublin Castle in October following the announcement he had extended his contract with Wilson Golf

I n a conversation I had with Paddy Harrington six weeks before his death in July 2005, he recalled a winter's day when his teenage son, Padraig, pleaded to join him at Stackstown Golf Club even though the ground was covered in a thick blanket of snow. "When we went up there, he cleared away snow from one of the tees and began hitting balls into a sea of white," said Paddy. "The thought of missing a day's practice would have killed him."

Congratulated by John O'Leary after his victory in The 2007 Irish Open. O'Leary had been the last Irishman to win the tournament back in 1982

With fellow Irishmen Darren Clarke (left) and Paul McGinley (centre) after Europe's Ryder Cup victory at The K Club in 2006

This was the club, now boasting a membership of 1,166, where Paddy was a founder member when it was launched in 1975. Indeed he, and his fellow policemen in An Garda Siochana, literally dug the course out of an awkward, elevated site in the south west suburbs of Dublin. In the process, Stackstown became a cherished playground where the five Harrington boys, including Padraig, took their first, tentative swings at the Royal and Ancient game.

As it happened, a devoted father never witnessed the ultimate rewards which admirable dedication would bring his youngest son. But he did not need to. With nine victories on The European Tour International Schedule by mid 2005, along with success in the United States and a high placement on the Official World Golf Ranking, the Dubliner's competitive future seemed secure. All that remained was a breakthrough at Major Championship level.

Now, 13 years after coming through the Qualifying School Final Stage at San Roque, Harrington's European Tour successes number 14 and include three Major titles – back-to-back Open Championships and the first victory by a European native in the US PGA Championship since Tommy Armour back in 1930. Those cold, bleak days on Stackstown's hilly perch, have delivered a truly extraordinary dividend.

Meanwhile, one of the two Bobs in his life could readily see the value of a solid family base in the player's development. "Padraig has a wonderful spirit; a wonderful soul," said American sports psychologist, Dr Bob Rotella. "His parents brought him up right and he was smart enough to listen to them."

The other Bob is the grizzled Scot who has completed ten years as Harrington's coach from the time they first came together after the US Open Championship at the Olympic Club in San Francisco in 1998. It was there, after finishing in a share of 32nd place while playing to the best of his ability, Harrington concluded he lacked the necessary technique to compete successfully at that level of the game.

Bob Torrance is understandably proud of his star pupil. "We have yet to see the best of Padraig," he said recently. Would that include taking on Tiger Woods for the top spot in the professional game? The Scots burr emanating from a deep bed of gravel, became even deeper than usual. "Maybe Tiger will be setting his sights on him!" exclaimed the man from Largs.

He then revealed that, within a few days of Harrington's stunning victory in the US PGA Championship at Oakland Hills in August, they had already talked twice in transatlantic phone calls to discuss "some problems with his game."

Left to right: Honorary Secretary Larry McCormack, Lady Captain Muriel O'Shea and Club President Eddie Ryan lead the celebrations at Stackstown Golf Club in south Dublin, after fellow member Padraig Harrington's Open Championship win

"I had seen from the television that his address position wasn't good during the final round, which is why his driving was poor," said the coach.

"He always discusses things with me while he's away; things to work on before his next tournament, and winning his second Major in three weeks didn't change that." So, could we take it that Torrance considered it a fruitful summer? "Oh yes," he replied. "His performance in the Open at Royal Birkdale was unbelievable, especially the back nine which was as good as I've ever seen from anyone."

Which led, almost inevitably, to the reason Torrance now speaks of Harrington and Woods in the same breath. His assessment was crushingly simple. "What Padraig did at Oakland Hills, getting up and down brilliantly over the finishing holes, Woods does all the time," he said. "That's why he's so good. But they're both wonderfully dedicated. And that doesn't mean hitting a few balls on the practice range in the morning and leaving. It means hitting balls all day. Then on to the short game, bunker play, putting, every day of your life. I've been with Padraig when we've done 12 hour days together, and before his injury, Tiger never stopped working. While we know about Gary Player and Ben Hogan, I can also tell you that Sam Snead practised every day of his life."

The decidedly modest position which Harrington occupied in the game 20 years ago, was light years removed from these great names. Yet those who travelled the 30 miles from Dublin to watch the Leinster Boys' Championship at Royal Tara, were rewarded with a precious glimpse into the future. On July 21, 1988, the 16 year old scratch player from Stackstown captured the title by a crushing 11 strokes. Among those in his wake on that

Life's a beach: Relaxing at Carnoustie after his Open Championship triumph in 2007

With partner JP McManus after the pair won the team contest in the 2006 Alfred Dunhill Links Championship at St Andrews. Padraig also won the individual title that year

International Team – Nairn, 1989.
Boys' Home International Championship.

The Irish team for the 1989 Boys Home Internationals at Nairn featuring Padraig (back row, fourth from right), alongside his fellow European Tour professional Gary Murphy (back row, fifth from right)

Australian Peter Thomson (right), five times winner of The Open Championship, was a guest at Royal Birkdale for the annual AGW Dinner at which Lewine Mair (left), the AGW Chairman, presented Padraig Harrington (centre) with the Golf Writers' Trophy

Irish Taoiseach Bertie Ahern (left) welcomes Padraig and wife Caroline to a civic reception at the Government Buildings in Dublin in July 2007 following his Open Championship victory at Carnoustie

tournaments I was involved in. So, unlike most kids who eagerly followed the performances of great players like Seve Ballesteros and Nick Faldo, I didn't have an idol. For instance, the real star of 1989 for me, was Scotland's Colin Fraser (now a teaching professional with the Roland Stafford Golf Schools in America), who beat me at Number One in a Boys' International match at Nairn."

He went on: "There were important ways in which those amateur days shaped my career. After going close to winning, only to be disappointed on quite a few occasions, I was patient enough to hang around in the belief that things would change. Later, when I became frustrated at all my second place finishes as a professional; I kept telling myself that things would turn around, just as they had done in my amateur days. Gradually, the concept of winning appeared to get easier until eventually, some really amazing things began to happen."

occasion was Gary Murphy, who went on to join him on The European Tour where they remain close friends and colleagues.

Interestingly, at the time, Harrington did not have heroes from the big, international stage. "To be honest, I was very insular," he recalled. "I was more concerned with my peers, the guys I was trying to beat in the various amateur

As a teenager, Harrington learned golf by observation, with the odd tip from his father who played off single figures. It was not until he became part of the Golfing Union of Ireland's national panel in his late teens that he was exposed to professional tuition. In the event, he adopted Irish national coach, Howard Bennett, as his tutor and they remained together until the player took up with Torrance in 1998.

The winning Great Britain and Ireland Walker Cup team at Royal Porthcawl in 1995. Alongside Padraig (back row, third from left) are his fellow European Tour professionals Mark Foster (back row, second from left), David Howell (back row, third from right), Lee James (back row, second from right) and Stephen Gallacher (front row, extreme right)

In November 2006, two days after beating no less a figure than Woods in a play-off for the Dunlop Phoenix Tournament in Japan, Harrington was at the Royal Dublin Society in the Irish capital for a rather special ceremony. Topped by a fetching, pancake hat, he was attired in robes comprising two shades of blue separated by a narrow green stripe while being conferred with an Honorary Fellowship by Dublin Business School, in association with Liverpool's John Moores University.

This was Harrington the accountant, a world removed from the international golf circuits he has trod with such distinction. Yet the contrasting qualifications seemed to sit easily on his athletic frame to the extent that he considered his accountancy studies invaluable towards developing competitive skills at the highest level of his chosen sporting pursuit.

"Passing the finals of the Association of Chartered Certified Accountants examination at 23 was memorable for me so it was a terrific honour to be invited back to the Dublin Business School to receive the Fellowship," he said. Typically precise, he went on to explain that, not having done his articles, he would need about three years work experience before being entitled to practice as a fully-fledged accountant. He took obvious pride, however, in a qualification which is recognised worldwide.

"I started accountancy when I was 18 because I had no idea what I wanted to do when I left school," he went on. "It struck me as a good, general business degree and that's essentially what it is. Half the course has to do with what people would term accountancy and the other half is mostly business stuff including business law.

"My original plan was to get a job in the golf industry via accountancy but halfway through the exams, I decided to become a tournament professional and try my luck on The European Tour. So from that point onwards, whenever I applied myself to studying, golf was always in back of my mind which eased the exam pressure.

"The interesting thing is that when I was competing at golf, I could reassure myself that there was always the accountancy to fall back on if things didn't go as I hoped. In this way, my academic pursuit eased the stress on my sporting ambitions, and vice versa.

"Meanwhile, accountancy also gave me the discipline to manage my time properly. Nobody likes doing exams and it takes a bit of effort and commitment to get through them, especially with other options in your life. But I acquired the organisational discipline to manage these things, to commit to something and see it through to a satisfactory conclusion."

His accountancy qualification played no part in the decision to join forces with the International Management Group. "I joined them essentially because of their impressive reputation, which has proved to be well founded," he said.

With the same, Yorkshire born manager, Adrian Mitchell, and the same accountant, Philip Barker, from the outset, a 13 year journey together has brought some amazing things. When victory was secured in the US PGA Championship at Oakland Hills, I witnessed a jubilant Harrington with Mitchell at his side. "It's hard to believe," were the only words a normally loquacious player could find. "It's hard to believe, Mitch."

But one could easily imagine his father visualising such magic, from those early, snow-clad days at Stackstown.

Dermot Gilleece
Sunday Independent

Padraig lifts the Wanamaker Trophy following his victory in the 90th US PGA Championship

TEAM HARRINGTON

Padraig with his two Bobs: Bob Rotella (left) and Bob Torrance and The Open Championship Trophy

Bob Torrance - Coach

Torrance loves golfers who are prepared to work long hours to chase perfection, and in Harrington he found a soulmate. "You'll never reach perfection, but if you stop trying, then you can put your clubs away," says Torrance. They have been together since 1998.

Dr Bob Rotella - Sports Psychologist

An internationally renowned Sports Psychologist whose brand of mind mastery in relation to golf developed Harrington's already formidable mental prowess from 2002 onwards.

Ronan Flood - Caddie

Already a good friend and a scratch golfer before he took on the job of carrying the bag in 2004, Flood is now Harrington's brother-in-law, and has played a key role in helping Harrington maintain his equilibrium in the white heat of Carnoustie, Royal Birkdale and Oakland Hills.

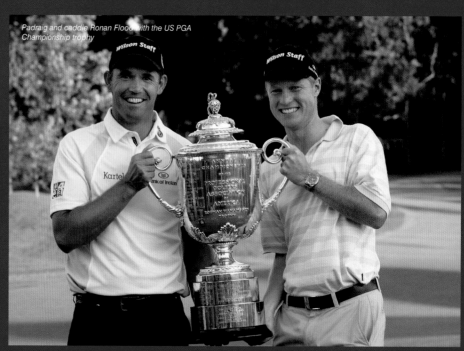

Padraig and caddie Ronan Flood with the US PGA Championship trophy

Top left Dr Liam Hennessy

Top right Dr Dale Richardson

Above left Dr Paul Hurrion

Above right Adrian Mitchell

Right Katie Powell

The Harrington family: Padraig with sons Paddy (centre) and Ciaran with wife Caroline

Dr Liam Hennessy - Sports Physiologist

An expert in Sports Physiology. Has woked with Padraig for over ten years now and in addition to spending years of developing the blend of strength, power and speed and suppleness in Harrington's body, he has designed programmes to guard against injury and optimise the player's food and drink intake on and off the course.

Dr Dale Richardson - SportsChiropractor

A doctor of chiropractic medicine, Richardson was crucial to keeping Harrington going despite a neck problem at Carnoustie in 2007 and a wrist injury at Royal Birkdale in 2008. Dr Richardson has been a member of the last three European Ryder Cup Medical teams and currently works with a number of top players in the Official World Golf Ranking.

Dr Paul Hurrion – Biomechanist

A leading international Biomechanist who has specialised in developing research and analysis of putting. He uses Hi-speed cameras, force platforms and Quintic computer software to assist golfers in learning the ultimate techniques in relation to putting.

Adrian Mitchell - Manager

Harrington's Manager since the golfer turned professional and signed with the International Management Group (IMG) in 1995, overseeing all aspects of his commercial and business interests.

Katie Powell - Assistant

Takes care of Harrington's day-to-day scheduling needs, including travel and sponsor liaison.

Family

Wife Caroline (nee Gregan) has been invaluable to Padraig's success, and sons Paddy and Ciaran are a great source of delight to the Champion. His mother Breda and the other members of the Harrington, Gregan and Flood clans are an integral element of Harrington's support base.

Higher and Higher

With wife Ebba during The 2008 Ryder Cup in Kentucky

S ometimes a man must wait a long time before he finds himself. For Robert Karlsson, this wait has been longer than most and certainly more complicated. It has, however, been worth the patient effort even if at times the chief demons, anger and frustration, have flown wickedly around his head.

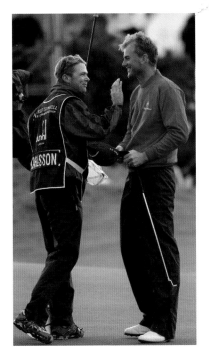

With his trusty caddie, Gareth Lord

On the verge of his first victory in 2008 - the Mercedes-Benz Championship in Cologne

As he strides into 2009 and into what, for The European Tour is a brave, new and, potentially, hugely lucrative world, this tall, introspective, yet well mannered and sociable Swede does so as the freshly anointed winner of the Harry Vardon Trophy. Traditionally, at this stage of proceedings, one would contract this high honour into the simple statistic: Europe's Number One player.

Yet, however, in a year when a Ryder Cup team-mate won two Major Championships, such a title would fly in the face of logic. This is not only my opinion, it is Robert's. As he pointed out: "Padraig has had the better season. He's the one with The Open and the US PGA Championship."

Quite so. Still, it says much for Karlsson's own glittering campaign that it took such prodigious trophy gathering by the Irishman for the Swede's sensational season to be headed in the home straight.

No-one, after all, has been more consistent and it is this high-level graph of relentless achievement that marks him out so vividly from everyone else. Historically, he is the final Order of Merit winner now that The Race to Dubai takes over and, judged however you may wish, he is among the worthiest of victors of this prestigious accolade.

No fewer than 12 top ten finishes – including back-to-back victories in the Mercedes-Benz Championship and the Alfred Dunhill Links Championship – bear eloquent statistical testimony to his play, while his performances in the year's four Major Championships also demand the highest respect.

He was, after all, tied eighth in the Masters Tournament, tied fourth in the US Open Championship, tied seventh in The Open Championship and tied 20th in the US PGA Championship. That is some drum roll of achievement especially if one factors in the thought that it was only his second trip to Augusta National, his fifth US Open and his seventh US PGA. It also bears mentioning that – prior to this year – in the 15 Open Championships in which he has competed since turning professional, he had failed to qualify four times and missed the halfway cut on nine other occasions.

What this tends to suggest is that the Swede is one hell of an improved golfer. This is partly down to improved technical competence but mostly it is because, at 39 years of age, he at last appears to be at ease with himself. Until relatively recently the better acquainted he became privately with golf's finer details, the worse he performed publicly. For a man playing the game for a living, this is not the best of news.

When this happened he turned to various sources to try to work out the who, what, why, where and when questions. It is now irretrievably attached to his curriculum vitae that, apart from psychology, he experimented with some of the fringe outlets open to a man with an inquiring mind and a spiritual sense of self. Yes, he ingested some volcanic ash, yes he spent some time deep in the woods and at retreats lost in silence and, yes, he fasted for days on end. Other stuff, too.

LEADERS

HOLE		+·PAR
17	KARLSSON	−13
17	MOLINARI	−11
18	JIMENEZ	−9
18	FISHER R	−9
18	CAMPBELL	−9
18	FINCH	−7

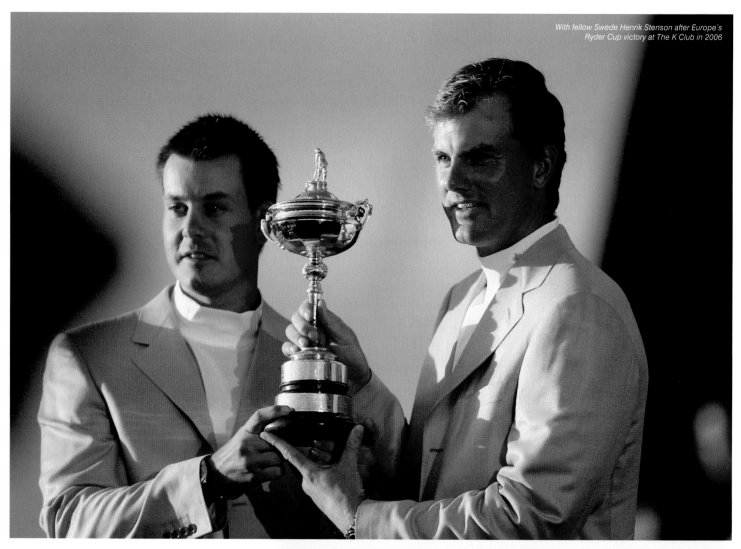

With fellow Swede Henrik Stenson after Europe's Ryder Cup victory at The K Club in 2006

He has talked openly about all these things but prefers now to leave these experiences in the background having learned the hard way that such honesty can encourage ridicule from certain quarters. "Many people think I am crazy," he has said. "But I try not to care too much." It is, of course, the perfectly correct attitude.

Born the son of a greenkeeper at Katrineholms Golfklubb some 75 miles south of Stockholm, his childhood home was a pretty house to the side of the fourth fairway. By 13 he was practically unbeatable by any of the members and it was around the same age that he announced he needed to learn English well because, he was "going to be a golf pro."

He turned professional in 1989 by which time his handicap was plus three and earned his Tour card the following year at the Qualifying School Final Stage. He has never been back. His first European Tour win came in the Turespaña Open Mediterrania in Spain in 1995

Celebrating as part of the winning Continental Europe team in the Seve Trophy at Sunningdale Golf Club, England, in 2000

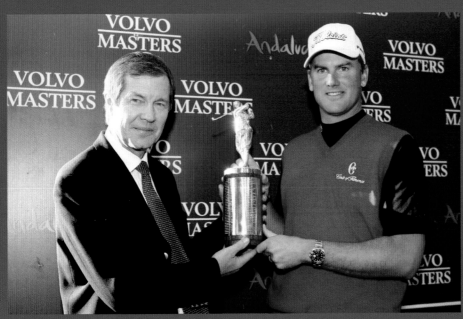

Robert Karlsson (right) receives the Harry Vardon Trophy from George O'Grady, Chief Executive The European Tour, for finishing Number One in the 2008 Order of Merit

Celebrating after winning the 2001 Via Digital Open de España

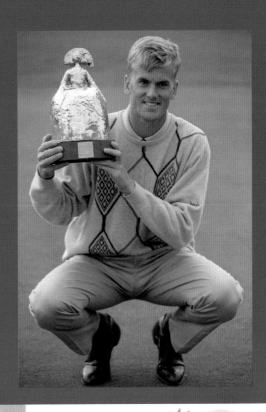

Right After his maiden European Tour triumph in the Turespaña Open Mediterrania in 1995

and he has now captured nine European Tour titles, a flurry of success that makes him Sweden's most successful golfer although, not yet, as successful as he desires.

His father was an accomplished pistol shooter but lost much of his appetite for the sport when he realised he could not be the best and it is this genetic default position, this ambition to achieve overwhelming excellence, that has eaten away so much at Karlsson over the years. Now it appears, rather ironically, that having accepted that he cannot always be right at the top of his game, he actually mostly is.

"I tried too much to force results, tried to make it happen instead of just going out and playing. I didn't play my game; instead I sort of went out and tried to play someone else's," he explained. So he has learned to be himself, to fly through life with the wings he was born with.

Also, as it happens, he has learned the secret of putting or at least how to remain sane on the

greens. "I used to get too tense, to grip too tight when I was putting," he said. "Now I know that after I've worked out the line I need to relax and that if I make it, I make it and if I miss it, I miss it."

Mostly this year he has made it and when he is in that mood, in that zone, then he is irrepressible. So tall he can look awkward sometimes as he stands over a shot, he now has the ability to go with the flow of his game. Most of all, he has learned to trust his instinct and to accept, with a smile, the occasional setbacks fate throws his way.

After all that soul-searching he has reached a place that offers contentment. "All I found out is that there is nothing to look for," he grins. This, however, is the same wisdom that comes when realisation dawns that it is not the answer that is important but the sagacity of the question in the first place.

Annchristine Lindstrom has helped him hugely to reach this conclusion. She is, he says, his coach

Executing a watery escape on his way to victory in the 1997 BMW International Open

Receiving the Red Jacket and the 2002 Omega European Masters trophy from supermodel Cindy Crawford

for "everything except golf." He likes to retreat to her village in the Swedish wilderness to recharge his body and mind while living a simpler life and sharing in the chores. His golfing success helps to fund this general lifestyle just as his charitable foundation aims to improve the future for challenged children.

His wife, Ebba, says that she knew he was different right from the start. "My first impression of Robert was that he knew something I didn't know. He was a bit mysterious and he had a lot of charisma." It is a compelling combination.

What it means is that, in a world often populated by the tediously one-dimensional, Karlsson's multi-faceted, deeply-questioning approach to the conundrum that is life, never mind golf, shines very brightly indeed. The other thought is that no-one ever has worked harder or longer to win the Order of Merit.

Top man. Top Title. Number One in fact.

Bill Elliott
The Observer

*On his way to victory in The 2006
Celtic Manor Wales Open*

21

Historic and Significant

The Year In Retrospect

There are a beguiling posse of adjectives available to describe the 2008 season on The European Tour International Schedule. Only one of these, however, is truly apt. That word is historic. Close second is unbelievable while unprecedented has legitimate claims of its own.

History, of a sort, is made all the time of course. Mostly, however, it is banal, forgettable stuff. However, there is nothing banal about Padraig Harrington's imprint on 2008.

It really is historically significant to have successfully defended an Open Championship – as he did at Royal Birkdale Golf Club, Southport, Lancashire, England, in July – while his victory in the US PGA Championship just three weeks later at Oakland Hills Country Club, Bloomfield Township, Michigan, USA, was the first such triumph by a European since Scotland's Tommy Armour won in 1930. Back then, of course, it was a match play event so, in that sense at least, this achievement is truly an historic first.

What is also relevant here, of course, is the fact that Ireland's greatest ever golfer – some historic claim in itself – has honed his game on the worldwide European Tour, a fact celebrated by an in-depth look at this extraordinary Dubliner's career elsewhere in this publication.

While 2008 will always be remembered as Harrington's year on a global stage, there are others who also deserve to be selected for a place in the limelight and the attendant applause. Principal among these is Order of Merit winner Robert Karlsson whose season was highlighted by victories in the Mercedes-Benz Championship at Golf Club Gut Lärchenhof, Cologne, Germany, and the Alfred Dunhill Links Championship at the Old Course, St Andrews, Carnoustie and Kingsbarns, Scotland.

These victories were back-to-back successes, the former coming immediately before The Ryder Cup at Valhalla Golf Club, Louisville, Kentucky, USA, with the latter a fortnight later. But then Karlsson could have won several more titles with just a smidgeon of luck, such was his consistency throughout the 2008 season, a fact outlined in a detailed chapter on the Swede also within these pages.

Certainly he can recall The Ryder Cup with great personal satisfaction for even though Europe lost to the United States by 16 ½ - 11 ½, Karlsson performed heroically. The important thing to remember about this Ryder Cup is

The Three Capitanos! Ian Woosnam, Bernhard Langer and Sam Torrance, Europe's winning Ryder Cup Captains in 2006, 2004 and 2002 respectively, were all champions on the 2008 European Senior Tour - with Woosnam finishing Number One in his rookie season, Langer Number One on the Champions Tour and Torrance claiming the OKI Castellón Open España – Senior Tour Championship

Trevor Immelman, Padraig Harrington and Retief Goosen, all members of The European Tour, joined Jim Furyk in the PGA Grand Slam of Golf held in Bermuda

Top right Genworth Financial, Official Sponsor of The European Tour Statistics, held their annual awards ceremony during the week of the season ending Volvo Masters. Left to right: Alvaro Quiros, winner of the Driving Distance category for the second successive year, Peter Barrett, Senior Vice President of Genworth Financial and Robert Karlsson, who topped the Stroke Average category

Right Robert-Jan Derksen 'drives' off in Moscow's Red Square

not so much the fact that the United States emerged deservedly victorious, but that once again the biennial encounter produced brilliant golf and a compelling narrative that twisted this way and that until deep into the final afternoon. The Celtic Manor Resort and the whole of Wales must be quivering with anticipation as the 2010 contest approaches.

That, however, is for then. For now we must celebrate the rest of the 2008 season and the

many examples of derring-do that occurred during it. As ever we need to cast an eye firstly over the remaining Major Championships.

South Africa's Trevor Immelman set the early pace when he won the Masters Tournament at Augusta National, Georgia, USA, in April, holding his nerve brilliantly during a final day that saw Tiger Woods chasing but coming up just short.

The World Number One looked like coming up short again in the US Open Championship two months later over the brilliant Torrey Pines Golf Club in La Jolla, California, USA. But for Woods' wonderful, snaking birdie putt on the 72nd green, the honours would have gone to Rocco Mediate, an amiable American whose career has been resurrected following surgery to his back. Woods, of course, went on to win the play-off and then shocked us all by revealing he had done so on a dodgy knee complete with a a shredded cruciate ligament. "He's not normal," said Mediate, admirably smiling as he spoke.

There was a lot more smiling going on elsewhere, nowhere more obviously than the grin offered by Miguel Angel Jiménez when he won the Tour's flagship event, the BMW PGA Championship at Wentworth Club, Surrey, England. Before the cheerful Spaniard headed into what was to turn out to a brilliant last round I had asked him how he was going to prepare for one of the biggest days of his career. His answer was pleasing. "I will have breakfast and then a large espresso and a cigar," he said. Maybe not for everyone but this caffeine-fuelled, laid-back approach certainly worked for him although he had to defeat England's Oliver Wilson in a play-off to achieve it.

Jiménez also won the UBS Hong Kong Open at the Hong Kong Golf Club, Fanling, Hong Kong, to underline his continuing ability as he works his way through his forties. Other multiple winners included Northern Ireland's Darren Clarke who returned to winning ways in the BMW Asian Open at the Tomson Shanghai Pudong Golf Club, Shanghai, China, before triumphing in The KLM Open at Kennemer Golf and Country Club, Zandvoort, The Netherlands; England's Richard Finch who claimed the Michael Hill New Zealand Open at The Hills Golf Club, Queenstown, New Zealand, and The Irish Open at Adare Manor Hotel and Golf Resort, Co. Limerick, Ireland; talented young German Martin Kaymer who took the Abu Dhabi Golf Championship at the

25

Abu Dhabi Golf Club, Abu Dhabi, UAE, and the BMW International Open in front of adoring home spectators at Golfclub München Eichenried, Germany, and in doing so became the first German player to win the tournament in this, its 20th anniversary year; Northern Ireland's Graeme McDowell who won the inaugural Ballantine's Championship at Pinx Golf Club, Jeju Island, South Korea, and The Barclays Scottish Open at Loch Lomond Golf Club, Glasgow, Scotland; and Tiger Woods, who won the Dubai Desert Classic at the Emirates Golf Club, Dubai, UAE, and the World Golf Championships - Accenture Match Play at The Gallery Golf Club, Tucson, Arizona, USA before his heroics in the US Open Championship four months later.

Englishman Finch's double success was particularly impressive given that the New Zealand triumph was his first European Tour title and that only a few weeks earlier he had narrowly clambered into the safety of the top 115 players on the final 2007 Order of Merit. Kaymer, too, had not won before 2008.

Other maiden victors from this season included, chronologically: South Africa's James Kingston in the South African Airways Open at the Pearl Valley Golf Estates, Paarl, Western Cape, South Africa; India's S S P Chowrasia in the EMAAR-MGF Indian Masters at Delhi Golf Club, New Delhi, India; Chile's Felipe Aguilar in the Enjoy Jakarta Astro Indonesia Open at the Cengkareng Golf Club, Jakarta, Indonesia; New Zealand's Mark Brown in the Johnnie Walker Classic at the DLF Golf and Country Club, New Delhi, India; Ireland's Damien McGrane in the Volvo China Open at Beijing CBD International Golf Club, Beijing, China; Ireland's Peter Lawrie in the Open de España at Real Club de Golf de Sevilla, Seville, Spain; South Africa's Hennie Otto in the Methorios Capital Italian Open at Castello di Tolcinasco Golf and Country Club, Milan, Italy; Australia's Scott Strange in The Celtic Manor Wales Open at The Celtic Manor Resort, Newport, South Wales; England's David Dixon in the SAINT-OMER Open presented by Neuflize OBC at the Aa Saint Omer Golf Club, Lumbres, France; Spain's Pablo Larrazabal in the Open de France ALSTOM at Le Golf National, Paris, France; and Frenchman Jean-François Lucquin in the Omega European Masters at Crans-sur-Sierre, Crans Montana, Switzerland.

Some other winners had to work even harder for their first prizes. There were 15 play-offs during the 2008 season, a record for these nail-biting

occasions. The template for this was laid down in the opening event, the HSBC Champions at Sheshan International Golf Club, Shanghai, China, which was won by the then World Number Two Phil Mickelson against the English duo of Ross Fisher and Lee Westwood.

A fortnight later it was extra time again. On this occasion Australia's Aaron Baddeley needed four additional holes to win the MasterCard Masters at the Huntingdale Golf Club, Melbourne, Australia, and so it went on. Local hero Richard Sterne won the Joburg Open at Royal Johannesburg and Kensington Golf Club, South Africa; India's Arjun Atwal won the Maybank Malaysian Open at the Kota Permai Golf and Country Club, Kuala Lumpur, Malaysia; Scotland's Alastair Forsyth won the Madeira Islands Open BPI – Portugal at Santo da Serra, Madeira, Portugal; France's Thomas Levet was eventually victorious in the MAPFRE Open de Andalucia by Valle Romano at the Aloha Golf Club, Andalucia, Spain; Grégory Bourdy took the Estoril Open de Portugal, at Oitavos Dunes, Estoril, Portugal; and Spain's Gonzalo Fernandez-Castaño triumphed in The Quinn Insurance British Masters at The Belfry, Sutton Coldfield, West Midlands, England.

No play-offs were needed when England's John Bickerton won the Alfred Dunhill Championship at Leopard Creek, Mpumalanga, South Africa; or when the ever-impressive Jeev Milkha Singh of India

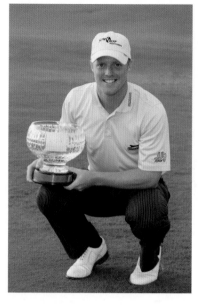

David Horsey of England finished Number One on the Euroepean Challenge Tour in 2008 with record earnings of €144,118. The leading 20 players from the Challenge Tour Rankings qualified to play in The Race to Dubai on The 2009 European Tour International Schedule

The 21st and final Volvo Masters was played at Club de Golf Valderrama in November. Volvo continue their support of The European Tour in 2009, becoming title sponsors of the World Match Play Championship to be played at Cortesín Golf Club near Malaga in the Andalucia region of Spain. Left to right: Per Ericsson, President & CEO, Volvo Event Management, Robert Karlsson with the Harry Vardon Trophy, Søren Kjeldsen with the Volvo Masters trophy

Tommy Horton MBE (right), won eight times on The European Tour and 23 times on the European Senior Tour and after a 51 year playing career he has retired. He won the European Senior Tour Order of Merit in 1993 and four years in succession from 1996, receiving each time from John Jacobs OBE (left), The John Jacobs Trophy

Pablo Larrazabal – the 2008 Sir Henry Cotton Rookie of the Year

Masters at the Oceânico Victoria Golf Course, Vilamoura, Portugal, before Sergio Garcia rather fittingly won the first tournament he and his father Victor have hosted in tandem, the CASTELLÓ MASTERS Costa Azahar at Club de Campo del Mediterráneo, Castellón, Spain.

In between times, and completing the year's Roll of Honour in terms of the World Golf Championships; Australia's Geoff Ogilvy won the WGA-CA Championship at the Doral Golf Resort and Spa, Doral, Florida, USA; while the WGC – Bridgestone Invitational at the Firestone Country Club, Akron, Ohio, USA was taken by Vijay Singh as the Fijian found some serious late season form.

And so to the season-ending Volvo Masters at the magnificent Club de Golf Valderrama, Sotogrande, Spain, and the final jousting for the last Order of Merit title available before The Race to Dubai. Denmark's Søren Kjeldsen won the tournament but the big prize, of course, went to Karlsson. It was an appropriate end to 21 years of the Volvo Masters and a fond farewell to a truly great golf course. Owner Jaime Ortiz-Patiño deserves much applause, as does the popular Tommy Horton, who announced his retirement during a year when Ian Woosnam won the European Senior Tour Order of Merit, following an immense career.

Back to 2008 and, some tasty statistics to consider. There were 28 holes in one during the season and four albatrosses. The lowest cut was four under par in the Maybank Malaysian Open; the highest, nine over par, came at The Open Championship. In total, 24 players either equalled or set new course records while Robert Karlsson and Lee Westwood had the most top five finishes with nine each. England's Nick Dougherty had the most consecutive birdies with seven, again in Malaysia, while Australian Kane Webber was the only player to enjoy two consecutive eagles, on holes nine and ten, during the Ballantine's Championship in South Korea.

Much to savour then and much to digest. A lot of what happened during the season will figure in someone's history book but the big, most relevant pages in the game's serious tomes are reserved for Padraig Harrington. No ladybirds for the Irishman in 2008 but lots of bouquets. It was terrific to watch.

Bill Elliott
The Observer

won the 54 hole Bank Austria GolfOpen presented by Telekom Austria at the Fontana Golf Club, Vienna, Austria; or when Australia's Adam Scott set the year's low final round when he conjured up 11 birdies during a final round 61 as he won the Commercialbank Qatar Masters presented by Dolphin Energy at Doha Golf Club, Qatar.

Elsewhere during the course of the season, England's Ross Fisher led on his own from start to finish as he dominated The European Open at The London Golf Club, Kent, England, to finish some 20 strokes under par. Sweden's Mikael Lundberg went one better, actually one fewer, with his 21 under par total of 267 that won the Inteco Russian Open Golf Championship 2008 at Le Méridien Moscow Country Club, Russia, while another Swede, Peter Hanson, won the SAS Masters in his home country at Arlandastad Golf, Stockholm, Sweden, with a more conservative nine under par total of 271. Meanwhile, at the end of August, Grégory Havret kept the Auld Alliance between France and Scotland alive by winning the Johnnie Walker Championship at Gleneagles at The Gleneagles Hotel, Perthshire, Scotland.

As the season gathered pace towards its climax, South Africa's Charl Schwartzel won the Madrid Masters at Club de Campo Villa de Madrid, Spain; Spain's Alvaro Quiros triumphed in the Portugal

New World
Odyssey

Alan Rogers, Group CEO of Leisurecorp (left) and George O'Grady, Chief Executive of The European Tour, on the helipad of the Burj Al Arab hotel in November 2007 following the announcement of a wide ranging partnership in Dubai

When, on November 19, 2007, George O'Grady, Chief Executive of The European Tour, unveiled the most significant development in world golf by announcing the £100,000,000 partnership with Leisurecorp, he immediately transformed the landscape of the game.

For the crown jewels in the landmark agreement provided for a restyled season-long competition entitled The European Tour Race to Dubai. It would be played on the fairways of the world, culminating with the Number One to 60 players teeing-up in the Dubai World Championship at Jumeirah Golf Estates, Dubai, UAE, from November 19-22, 2009.

As O'Grady outlined the additional benefits the partnership would bring, including a European Tour International Headquarters in Dubai, so it was also natural that the media gathered in the suitably ethereal setting of the Burj Al Arab – reaching 321 metres above the Arabian Gulf – should first take note of the seriously increased riches available to the players.

In essence, the inaugural European Tour Race to Dubai has a US$10,000,000 bonus pool and with the Dubai World Championship also having a prize fund of US$10,000,000 it could transpire that a player will stand over the last putt of the season with a staggering US$3,666,660 at stake as well as a seven year European Tour exemption.

All of which provided China, following the success of the Olympic Games in Beijing, with another opportunity to be the focus for world sport when the first shot in The Race to Dubai was struck by Sweden's Robert Karlsson at the HSBC Champions tournament at Sheshan International Golf Club in Shanghai on November 6, 2008, where Spain's Sergio Garcia triumphed.

That shot ignited a new, enthralling odyssey for the leading golfers in the world as the inaugural Race to Dubai was set to visit 27 destinations on The 2009 European Tour International Schedule, with players from no fewer than 40 countries vying to be the first to face the most lucrative putt in golfing history.

The 2009 European Tour Race to Dubai would take 382 days to unfold but in reality it took only five weeks to conceive because, soon after touching base at the KPMG Golf Conference in Budapest, The European Tour and Leisurecorp, the company developing Dubai's leading residential golf community at Jumeirah Golf Estates, met at the BMW International Open in Munich in June 2007.

There, David Spencer, Chief Executive Officer – Golf, Leisurecorp, unveiled Leisurecorp's plan. Negotiations immediately commenced, lawyers were instructed and the second significant meeting, including the signing of a Memorandum of Understanding, took place at The Players' Championship of Europe in Hamburg in late July between, for The European Tour, George O'Grady, Keith Waters, Director of International Policy, and Jonathan Orr, Financial Director; and for Leisurecorp, David Spencer and Alan Rogers, Group Chief Executive.

The decision as to when to make the announcement was an easy one, albeit keeping it under wraps was a challenge, as it seemed only natural to unveil the partnership exactly two years ahead of when the world's media would return for the Dubai World Championship on the Earth Course at Jumeirah Golf Estates from November 19-22, 2009. The venue, too, was swiftly selected since the iconic seven-star Burj Al Arab looks over Dubai which many observers regard as the most vibrant city in the world.

In reality it spawned a venture so spectacular that, as O'Grady and Rogers spoke, so their words resonated around the world. For the wide-ranging partnership not only substantially raised the profile of The European Tour, it also further enhanced the business plan instigated by O'Grady when he took command as Chief Executive on January 1, 2005.

The first five years of the partnership - there is an option for a further five years – will see the relationship cemented through the establishment in Dubai of a new, purpose-built International Headquarters for The European Tour including a 'Performance Institute'; Leisurecorp support for a number of tournaments on The Race to Dubai; funding of The European Tour Physio Unit and the creation of a global property company through a joint initiative designed to develop new tournament venues around the world.

Leisurecorp was established by Dubai World, one of the world's largest holding companies that supervise a portfolio of business and projects across more than 100 countries, in July 2006, to identify, acquire and develop leisure and lifestyle related investments in Dubai and across the world.

Its portfolio includes Jumeirah Golf Estates, Dubai's premier residential golf community,

The Dubai World Championship Top 20 Prize Money		The Race to Dubai Bonus Pool	
1.	US$ 1,666,660	1.	US$ 2,000,000
2.	US$ 1,111,110	2.	US$ 1,500,000
3.	US$ 650,000	3.	US$ 1,000,000
4.	US$ 500,000	4.	US$ 800,000
5.	US$ 400,000	5.	US$ 700,000
6.	US$ 325,230	6.	US$ 600,000
7.	US$ 290,000	7.	US$ 550,000
8.	US$ 270,000	8.	US$ 500,000
9.	US$ 250,000	9.	US$ 450,000
10.	US$ 230,000	10.	US$ 400,000
11.	US$ 210,000	11.	US$ 350,000
12.	US$ 200,000	12.	US$ 325,000
13.	US$ 190,000	13.	US$ 300,000
14.	US$ 180,000	14.	US$ 275,000
15.	US$ 170,000	15.	US$ 250,000
16.	US$ 160,000		
17.	US$ 150,000		
18.	US$ 140,000		
19.	US$ 130,000		
20.	US$ 120,000		

and Pearl Valley Golf Estates, South Africa's leading residential which hosts the South African Open Championship. Jumeirah Golf Estates has brought together Sergio Garcia, Greg Norman, Vijay Singh, and "the father of modern golf course design" Pete Dye, to create one of the most distinctive golf developments. The four courses – Fire, Earth, Water and Wind – will be surrounded by the most desirable residential communities in Dubai and it is on the Greg Norman-designed Earth Course that the inaugural Dubai World Championship will be played.

It is, of course, the fairways of the world that are providing the influential shop window for The European Tour as the players chase that coveted Number One spot which, through The Race to Dubai, links tradition and the future through the instantly recognisable Harry Vardon Trophy.

Robert Karlsson climbed to Number One in 2008 71 years on from when Charles Whitcombe won the inaugural Harry Vardon Trophy in 1937 and in so doing continued a tradition won by such luminaries as Seve Ballesteros, Henry Cotton, Ernie Els, Nick Faldo, Retief Goosen, Padraig Harrington, Bernhard Langer, Bobby Locke, Sandy Lyle, Greg Norman, Ian Woosnam, and record eight time winner Colin Montgomerie.

Karlsson said: "The Race to Dubai is a tremendously exciting development for everyone involved with The European Tour and European golf as a whole and something which has made the whole world of golf sit up and take notice."

Justin Rose, Number One in 2007, said: "To be Number One, to follow in the footsteps of so many great players, is an awesome feeling and it was huge for me to receive the Harry Vardon Trophy. It's like the Premiership – a season long challenge that tests all your skills and demands consistency."

Padraig Harrington, Number One in 2006, commented: "It certainly meant a lot to me to win the Harry Vardon Trophy. It's a good mark to success in a career. I had been a professional for more than ten years and it underlined how far I had come. I had been runner-up twice so it was good to win it. It took me to a new level and winning The Open

Championship in 2007, and of course two Major Championships in 2008, raised the bar again. In fact 2007 was a great year for me personally and for The European Tour, ending with the announcement of The Race to Dubai and the Dubai World Championship. It is a great concept and looks like The European Tour have found the right formula."

Garcia, the first winner on The Race to Dubai, said: "Winning the opening event, and making such a great start to The Race to Dubai, was very important. The Race to Dubai represents a real statement of intent by The European Tour and by Dubai. The Tour has clearly moved up a gear in the ability to attract the world's best players and Dubai has reinforced its position as a centre of world golf."

The move to the globalisation of golf by The European Tour began with the Tunisian Open in 1982. Fast forward a quarter of a century and the infrastructure was in place at its Wentworth Headquarters to attract a partner such as Leisurecorp as The European Tour brand held a strengthening hand in countries all round the world.

On The 2008 European Tour International Schedule there were 52 events played in 28 different destinations. In addition the 2008 European Challenge Tour had 33 in 25 and the 2008 European Seniors Tour had 18 in 14. In total The European Tour has now visited no fewer than 68 destinations and the victory by Felipe Aguilar in the Enjoy

Jakarta Astro Indonesia Open in February, 2008, brought to 35 the number of countries to have provided champion golfers on The European Tour International Schedule.

O'Grady outlined the future when he told The Golf Channel, which delivers more than 65 million subscribers in the USA, Canada and Japan, on the eve of signing the Leisurecorp agreement: "Our global strategy provides the flexibility to play whenever possible in really good climates and where the money is available. The key is to create clusters of tournaments that are increasingly attractive to our global players so ensuring they focus whenever possible on The European Tour. We are providing a wide ranging choice so that they do not have to go to America if they don't want to."

O'Grady went further following the announcement with Leisurecorp in Dubai. He explained: "We are pushing the boundaries to be the best that we can and looking ahead The European Tour, which is increasingly a business of influence, will develop sustainable growth throughout all sections of the business in order that we are not at the mercy of the markets in terms of economic cycles. The announcement with Leisurecorp came, coincidentally, at a time when as we all now know the world would face a serious challenge as far as the global financial markets are concerned.

Left to right: Thomas Björn, Chairman of The European Tour's Tournament Committee, George O'Grady, Chief Executive of The European Tour, David Spencer, Leisurecorp CEO-Golf, and Gonzalo Fernandez-Castaño at the unveiling of the improved and re-branded European Tour Physiotherapy Unit, during the MAPFRE Open de Andalucia by Valle Romano at Aloha Golf Club in Spain in March 2008

"The Leisurecorp announcement unquestionably endorsed our desire to partner with excellence through endeavour and to cultivate perfection. Across the globe interest in golf is intensifying. We have our ideals and our aspirations. The support of companies such as Leisurecorp, not to mention our many other blue chip sponsors including Alfred Dunhill, ALSTOM, Ballantine's, Barclays, BMW, HSBC, Johnnie Walker, KLM, MasterCard, Mercedes-Benz, Omega, Rolex, UBS and Volvo, will see that we use our skills, our insight and our creativity to develop the game and grow our brand.

"What we never forget is that the key to this is the skills and loyalty of the players. They remain the bedrock of our industry and therefore it is our role to achieve our ideals and our aspirations by being dedicated to providing a unique global experience for the players to enjoy and which will excite and entertain the spectators."

Many observers indicated, as Leisurecorp came to the forefront, that in The European Tour they were gaining a partner with immense cachet and prestige. The European Tour players – referred to as the Membership – are as charismatic as they are cosmopolitan. One golf writer described them as "some of the most exciting sportsmen on the planet – people want to go and see them play."

O'Grady added: "The Race to Dubai will take us on a wonderful week by week, tournament by tournament odyssey around the world. Then it is all about the Number One to 60 players coming together at the end of the season for the Dubai World Championship. Our players are in demand; The Race to Dubai and the Dubai World Championship will attract their attention. They are talented and we have responded to their ability, willingness and preparedness to travel."

The first five years of the partnership between the two organisations officially started in January, 2008, and from 2010 The Race to Dubai will commence in January and the Dubai World Championship will complete the season in November. O'Grady added:

"The biggest thing is to get a co-ordinated schedule which has the right focus at the right time of the year and keeps all the parties, including the players and the sponsors, happy. We are looking at a six week off season towards the end of the year beginning in 2009 and we hope this will give a real definition to the Tour."

The relationship between The European Tour and Leisurecorp is being further cemented by the creation of a new International Headquarters with the organisation having a base and operating from a purpose-built facility within Jumeirah Golf Estates. The European Tour Centre will be a focal point of the Jumeirah Golf Estates Fire and Earth neighbourhoods incorporating golf lodges, boutique stores and shops and restaurants including the exclusive Greg Norman Grill.

The European Tour Performance Institute will provide a unique base exclusively for European Tour players to practice and train at any time of the year, utilising state-of-the-art facilities including a fitness centre,

Left to right: David Spencer, Leisurecorp CEO-Golf; Alan Rogers, Group CEO of Leisurecorp; George O'Grady, Chief Executive of The European Tour; Robert Karlsson; Giles Morgan, Group Head of Sponsorship HSBC; Zhang Xiaoning, Director of Multi-ball Games Administration Centre, General Administration of Sport in China, Managing Deputy Chairman and General Secretary of China Golf Association and Richard Cheung, Chairman of Sheshan International Golf Club, on the first tee prior to the start of The Race to Dubai at the HSBC Champions at Sheshan International Golf Club, Shanghai, China

COME HOME TO A LEGEND

Vijay Singh, Course Designer

Greg Norman, Course Designer

Sergio Garcia, Course Designer

JUMEIRAH
GOLF ESTATES

bio-mechanic swing studios, putting laboratory, physiotherapy services and a medical centre. It will also provide for a dedicated Jumeirah Golf Estates Golf Academy and swing bays for students and residents to improve their skills. The Golf Academy will offer personalised instruction using the latest technology and training knowledge to deliver real improvement to every part of the student's game.

The state-of-the-art fitness centre at The European Tour International Headquarters will also reflect Leisurecorp's sponsorship of The European Tour Physio Unit which provides Tour Members with outstanding facilities on The Race to Dubai.

Sultan Ahmed bin Sulayem, Chairman of Dubai World, the parent company of Leisurecorp, said: "At Jumeirah Golf Estates we are creating the world's leading residential golf community based around four of the world's leading courses. It is absolutely fitting therefore that we should welcome the world's leading tournament.

"This deal is yet another step in Dubai's evolution as one of the most important golf centres anywhere in the world. From golf tourism to world-beating golf communities to world-class tournaments we can claim to offer it all. It also marks an important step forward in extending the Leisurecorp brand across the globe. Leisurecorp already has assets around the world, and it will become an ever more important name in the golf and wider leisure industries in the coming years."

O'Grady added: "This is so much more than a tournament sponsorship. It is a long term partnership which will see The European Tour and Dubai joining together to significantly enhance the game worldwide and take golf to a new level for spectators everywhere. The scale of this agreement is testament to the vision of Dubai and its ruler His Highness Sheikh Mohammed bin Rashid Al Maktoum who has recognised the dynamic role golf can play in developing the global profile of this amazing city. It is also testament to Sultan Ahmed bin Sulayem, who has been instrumental in turning that vision into reality.

"The Race to Dubai will bring a new dimension to The European Tour, creating great drama

and theatre throughout the year as all the best players in the world are given the opportunity to compete in the world's richest tournament – the Dubai World Championship. With the combined prize funds of the Dubai World Championship and The Race to Dubai we then have that fabulous prospect of a player standing over a shot worth US$3,666,660.

"Moreover as The European Tour has become ever-more global in its outlook, it has become increasingly important to us to have an international base in a strategically placed location. Dubai is a massively important and growing hub, with

outstanding air links to all our locations, and the perfect place for us to offer a tailor-made service to all our Members through the Performance Institute at The European Tour International Headquarters. Furthermore, it provides a central meeting place for sponsors and promoters from all tournaments on The European Tour International Schedule."

Spencer added: "The partnership agreement we reached with The European Tour is great news for Leisurecorp, great news for Dubai – and it's also great news for The European Tour. We look forward to extending this relationship well into the future."

Sergio Garcia at Turnberry at the Media launch of The Race to Dubai and (below) holing the first winning putt on The Race to Dubai - making a birdie at the second extra hole against Oliver Wilson to claim the HSBC Champions title in Shanghai

Earth Course - 16th Hole

This will be further achieved through the creation of a global property company, in a joint initiative with Leisurecorp, providing The European Tour with the opportunity to develop new tournament venues around the world with a partner whose commitment in this sphere was demonstrated during the BMW PGA Championship at Wentworth Club in May 2008. There, Dubai World, the state-controlled investment firm that owns the QE2 and Tilbury and Southampton docks, announced that through Leisurecorp, it had agreed to acquire Turnberry – the historic Scottish golf resort which will host The 138th Open Championship on the Ailsa Course in July 2009 – for £55million.

O'Grady pointed out: "The Middle East has become a vital component of The European Tour. All the events, be it the Dubai Desert Classic, or the tournaments in Abu Dhabi and Qatar, are fantastic, high quality events, very well organised and played on courses in very good condition. Leisurecorp's sponsorship is giving us great confidence for the future – the fact that they have shown confidence in The European Tour and the product. Their development plans for Dubai, and for other parts of the world, including their purchase of Turnberry, shows they are very serious, very determined."

Dubai World's developments include The World, comprising more than 300 man-made islands strategically positioned to form a world map, and the Palm Jumeirah development where the QE2 will be moored and transformed into a floating hotel and leisure attraction.

Even so, from November 19-22, 2009, the focus on Leisurecorp's US$7billion of developments will be trained firmly on the

Earth Course, a Greg Norman signature course, at the Jumeirah Golf Estates when the inaugural Dubai World Championship will be played. The decision to host the first Dubai World Championship on the Earth Course was taken after Norman, who enjoyed an emotional revival in The 137th Open Championship at Royal Birkdale where he tied for third, visited the site early in 2008 to monitor progress and make final design enhancements.

Earth Course - 12th Hole

Norman said: "As a golf course architect, it is both rewarding and challenging to know that this course will be hosting the Dubai World Championship. I've been fortunate to have a number of PGA Tour events played on courses I have designed. Of course, Jumeirah Golf Estates will be showcased on a global basis and as the golf course designer, I'm proud to be a part of such a significant event.

"I think the entire course has a great balance, but the finish will really stand out. The last four holes will measure exactly a mile, 1760 yards. I expect it will be considered one of the most challenging and exciting miles of golf, in terms of risk and reward.

"The 'final four' will be comprised of a short par four, long par four, a great par three and a medium to long par five, so a lot of things can happen on the home stretch. There could be a two or three shot swing which will cater to the best players, and of course will be a defining moment for spectators and the television audience alike.

"The challenge is that the wind switches so much. So the variety of this golf course is going to change dramatically from ten o'clock in the morning to two o'clock in the afternoon – and that's why we need to be meticulous in the way we designed the course. There are going to be guys that will get through this golf course teeing off at 11 o'clock one way and then finishing off a totally different way. So they could really get the brunt of all the hard holes into the wind and that's where this golf course could really change things."

Thomas Björn, Chairman of The European Tour Tournament Committee, hailed the development at Jumeirah Golf Estates on a visit to view progress of the course for the first Dubai World Championship. The Dane said: "This development is really sensational. You instantly get a feel for what it will be like. The players are really going to enjoy the tournament. Every sporting season should have a climax and that's what the Dubai World Championship will give us. It's a finalé which will mean all eyes focus on Dubai for a really exciting four days."

Meanwhile the Norman Clubhouse, designed by and named after the Australian golf legend, will serve both the Fire and Earth

Greg Norman, designer of the Earth Course

Courses and will be complimented by an ultra-modern practice facility. A landmark of elegance and style, the Mediterranean-influenced Norman Clubhouse will offer a range of options for both formal and casual dining, a Wellness Centre with a variety of massage and spa treatments, a Sports Centre, a nearby Tennis Academy, two tennis courts and a coaching facility and The European Tour Performance Institute with adjoining Golf Academy.

Spencer said: "This is a big course, with a big tournament and big designer, in Greg Norman. It deserves a big clubhouse – and that's what it's getting. This is going to be a stunning facility, somewhere which will attract golfers and non-golfers alike. Greg has designed the best golf courses in the Middle East here at Jumeirah Golf Estates, along with the best homes, at his Fireside by Greg Norman development. He's added the best clubhouse to that roll of honour and, as always, we thank him for his time, his commitment and his talent."

The Clubhouse's Sports Centre will also cater for a variety of leisure activities, featuring a fully-equipped gymnasium, swimming pools, exercise studio, yoga and pilates studio, a leisure-focused lagoon, a lounge area and a Spa and Wellness Centre with several treatment rooms.

A number of dining and entertainment options will be situated within the Clubhouse including fine dining, a Grille, a rooftop lounge,

a wine cellar themed restaurant and a juice and health bar. Another feature of the Norman Clubhouse will be a stunning rock waterfall backdrop to the 18th greens of both the Fire and Earth courses.

The change to a strict calendar year programme for The European Tour International Schedule will further enhance the partnership as the 2010 season – and the second edition of The Race to Dubai – will start with the South African Open Championship at Pearl Valley Golf Estates, in January of that year and close with The Dubai World Championship in November.

That, however, is looking ahead. All the world's leading golfers will tee-up on the inaugural Race to Dubai which will take 382 days from Shanghai to Dubai – 382 days which, unquestionably, will showcase the supreme talents of the greatest golfers in the game.

Mitchell Platts

Wide Eyed
Wonderment

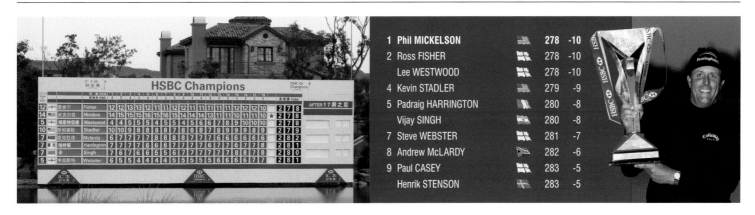

1	Phil MICKELSON		278	-10
2	Ross FISHER		278	-10
	Lee WESTWOOD		278	-10
4	Kevin STADLER		279	-9
5	Padraig HARRINGTON		280	-8
	Vijay SINGH		280	-8
7	Steve WEBSTER		281	-7
8	Andrew McLARDY		282	-6
9	Paul CASEY		283	-5
	Henrik STENSON		283	-5

The HSBC Champions in Shanghai could hardly be described as having started from humble beginnings. Yet it is still remarkable how, three years since its inception, this marvellous event has established itself in the eyes of many of the world's top golfers as a 'must-play' tournament.

Lee Westwood

Steve Webster

It is little wonder, however, that with HSBC, The European Tour and the Asian Tour joining forces for a three-pronged approach – namely to stage a top-class event and thus aid the development of the game in this part of the world – that China's emergence onto golf's world stage should be gathering such momentum.

If evidence were needed that the tournament had captured the imagination of the game's elite, then you needed to look no further than the field that assembled at the immaculately presented Sheshan International Golf Club for the opening event of The 2008 European Tour International Schedule.

Vijay Singh described the line-up as the strongest ever to have gathered in Asia and, with the inclusion of six Major Champions and ten of the world's top 20 players, who could argue?

As well as Phil Mickelson, the World Number Two and, until then, a reluctant traveller, there were Angel Cabrera and Padraig Harrington, respectively the US Open and Open Champions, Ernie Els, Retief Goosen and Singh. Add to that, players of the ilk of Paul Casey, Sergio Garcia, Colin Montgomerie, Henrik Stenson and Lee Westwood and it was easy to understand the excitement that such a gathering had managed to generate.

Inevitably, much of the local attention centred on Mickelson, who rarely plays outside the United States, but had decided to take advantage of a shortened season on the US PGA Tour. With his family in tow, the three time Major Champion spoke glowingly all week about the hospitality he had received and, while not quite the innocent abroad, he was nevertheless wide eyed with wonderment at his first experience of China.

In what proved a perfect mix of business and pleasure, the Mickelsons had flown to Beijing to visit the Great Wall and the Forbidden City before the tournament got underway and then made the most of all that Shanghai had to offer. But, trips to the Bund and the Circus notwithstanding, there was still work to be done and although Mickelson started as narrow favourite, he knew that competition was going to be fierce.

By midway through the final day, however, the thousands that lined the fairways looked more likely to witness the American's procession than a chase for the line. With 11 holes to play, he had opened up a five shot lead over his playing partner Ross Fisher and appeared to be cruising to victory. That he then proceeded to drop shot after shot until he was walking off the 15th green trailing the Englishman by two, simply defied belief.

Local Rules

PROTECTIVE FENCES AROUND GREENS
a) A protective fence around a green is an Immovable Obstruction(Rule 24-2 applies)
b)If a ball strikes any part of a protective fence around a green the player MAY disregard that stroke, abandon the ball and play another ball as nearly as possible at the spot from which the original ball was played in accordance with Rule 20-5 (playing next stroke from where previous ball played).

BRORA
GOLF CLUB
SCOTLAND

Different golf courses have different rules. How wonderful.

Yet in the most dramatic of finishes, Mickelson was thrown a lifeline when Fisher double bogeyed the final hole. It meant a sudden-death play-off that included an equally stunned Westwood, who had started the day nine shots off the lead but had picked up six birdies in seven holes from the tenth in a round of 67. Mickelson, however, did not need a second invitation to grab victory, eventually securing it, and the €575,445 (£400,240) first prize, with a birdie at the second extra hole.

In regulation play, Mickelson had in his last round four birdies, six bogeys and one double bogey. He had driven out of bounds at the eighth, found water at the sixth, 13th and 18th, and came home in 40 in a round of 76. It brought new meaning to the phrase, 'Winning Ugly'.

"I can't believe that I'm sitting here as the champion," he said. "I had a good lead and then played some horrendous golf for the last 11 holes, but was able to eke out a victory. For all the tournaments I've given away on the last hole, it was nice to get one to go my way."

Of equal significance for Mickelson was that he had succeeded where World Number One Tiger Woods, his greatest rival, had previously come up short. "It's nice to win a tournament that Tiger has tried unsuccessfully to win the last couple of years," he said.

So, what of Fisher? As he approached his 27th birthday, he was able to look back on a calendar year in which he had played tremendously well alongside Ernie Els and Tiger Woods in Dubai, had led the BMW PGA Championship at Wentworth Club going into the final round and had claimed his maiden victory at The KLM Open in the Netherlands.

A calm player with a sound temperament, there is every reason to suspect that the Englishman – who got married later that week – would lick his wounds and come back stronger for the experience. "I've pushed the World Number Two all the way and finished ahead of some very highly ranked, top-quality players," he said. "I'm disappointed not to walk away with the trophy, but it has still been a great week."

Peter Dixon
The Times

Angel Cabrera

Ross Fisher

Padraig Harrington (left) and Retief Goosen

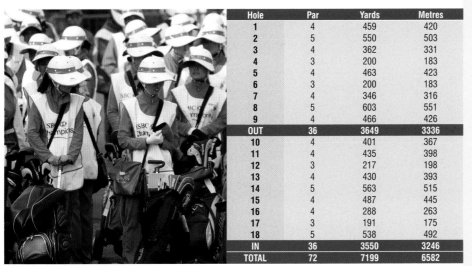

Hole	Par	Yards	Metres
1	4	459	420
2	5	550	503
3	4	362	331
4	3	200	183
5	4	463	423
6	3	200	183
7	4	346	316
8	5	603	551
9	4	466	426
OUT	**36**	**3649**	**3336**
10	4	401	367
11	4	435	398
12	3	217	198
13	4	430	393
14	5	563	515
15	4	487	445
16	4	288	263
17	3	191	175
18	5	538	492
IN	**36**	**3550**	**3246**
TOTAL	**72**	**7199**	**6582**

Phil Mickelson (right), is presented with the trophy by Vincent Cheng, Chairman, Hongkong and Shanghai Banking Corporation Limited

Louis Oosthuizen

Phil Mickelson's triumph in the HSBC Champions was only the American's second victory outside the United States in his 16 year professional career. His first triumph came in the Tournoi Perrier Paris event on the European Challenge Tour in 1993.

Sheshan International Golf Club

Final Results

Pos	Name		Rd1	Rd2	Rd3	Rd4	Total		€	£
1	Phil MICKELSON	USA	68	66	68	76	278	-10	575,445.27	400,240.15
2	Lee WESTWOOD	ENG	70	74	67	67	278	-10	299,893.79	208,585.49
	Ross FISHER	ENG	68	68	68	74	278	-10	299,893.79	208,585.49
4	Kevin STADLER	USA	64	69	73	73	279	-9	172,640.49	120,076.85
5	Padraig HARRINGTON	IRL	68	72	69	71	280	-8	133,969.02	93,179.63
	Vijay SINGH	FIJ	67	70	72	71	280	-8	133,969.02	93,179.63
7	Steve WEBSTER	ENG	69	70	72	70	281	-7	103,584.29	72,046.11
8	Andrew MCLARDY	RSA	68	69	72	73	282	-6	86,320.24	60,038.42
9	Henrik STENSON	SWE	70	70	71	72	283	-5	73,199.57	50,912.58
	Paul CASEY	ENG	68	71	66	78	283	-5	73,199.57	50,912.58
11	Louis OOSTHUIZEN	RSA	71	68	72	73	284	-4	63,531.70	44,188.28
12	Angel CABRERA	ARG	68	72	72	73	285	-3	59,388.33	41,306.44
13	Simon YATES	SCO	70	66	75	75	286	-2	54,209.11	37,704.13
	Nick DOUGHERTY	ENG	71	70	74	71	286	-2	54,209.11	37,704.13
15	Mikko ILONEN	FIN	74	69	72	72	287	-1	48,477.45	33,717.58
	Søren KJELDSEN	DEN	71	72	73	71	287	-1	48,477.45	33,717.58
	Chapchai NIRAT	THA	69	73	73	72	287	-1	48,477.45	33,717.58
18	Grégory HAVRET	FRA	72	75	72	69	288	0	42,584.65	29,618.96
	Retief GOOSEN	RSA	69	74	71	74	288	0	42,584.65	29,618.96
	Nathan GREEN	AUS	73	68	69	78	288	0	42,584.65	29,618.96
21	Bradley DREDGE	WAL	73	73	72	71	289	1	38,671.47	26,897.21
	Markus BRIER	AUT	69	73	73	74	289	1	38,671.47	26,897.21
	Ernie ELS	RSA	75	69	74	75	289	1	38,671.47	26,897.21
24	Richard STERNE	RSA	68	72	69	81	290	2	35,563.94	24,735.83
	Wen-tang LIN	TPE	71	72	74	73	290	2	35,563.94	24,735.83
	Kyung-Tae KIM	KOR	71	73	74	72	290	2	35,563.94	24,735.83
27	Scott STERLING	AUS	69	73	74	75	291	3	30,902.65	21,493.76
	Scott HEND	AUS	69	74	75	73	291	3	30,902.65	21,493.76
	Niclas FASTH	SWE	64	75	74	78	291	3	30,902.65	21,493.76
	Daniel VANCSIK	ARG	70	75	74	72	291	3	30,902.65	21,493.76
	José Manuel LARA	ESP	70	72	70	79	291	3	30,902.65	21,493.76
	John SENDEN	AUS	73	72	75	71	291	3	30,902.65	21,493.76
33	Peter HANSON	SWE	72	75	71	74	292	4	25,723.43	17,891.45
	Frankie MINOZA	PHI	69	70	75	78	292	4	25,723.43	17,891.45
	Jason KNUTZON	USA	71	72	71	77	292	4	25,723.43	17,891.45
	Brett RUMFORD	AUS	69	71	75	77	292	4	25,723.43	17,891.45
37	Anders HANSEN	DEN	70	72	77	74	293	5	23,479.11	16,330.45
38	Lian-wei ZHANG	CHN	70	74	82	68	294	6	20,371.58	14,169.07
	Ian POULTER	ENG	70	78	74	72	294	6	20,371.58	14,169.07
	Gonzalo FDEZ-CASTAÑO	ESP	71	75	73	75	294	6	20,371.58	14,169.07
	Wen-chong LIANG	CHN	69	72	74	79	294	6	20,371.58	14,169.07
	Mads VIBE-HASTRUP	DEN	75	73	73	73	294	6	20,371.58	14,169.07
	Michael LORENZO-VERA	FRA	73	72	73	76	294	6	20,371.58	14,169.07
	Marc LEISHMAN	AUS	74	72	75	73	294	6	20,371.58	14,169.07
	Sung LEE	KOR	73	76	71	74	294	6	20,371.58	14,169.07
46	Sergio GARCIA	ESP	73	72	76	74	295	7	16,918.77	11,767.53
	Darren FICHARDT	RSA	70	78	73	74	295	7	16,918.77	11,767.53
48	Raphaël JACQUELIN	FRA	71	75	79	71	296	8	15,537.64	10,806.92
	Charl SCHWARTZEL	RSA	73	72	78	73	296	8	15,537.64	10,806.92
50	K J CHOI	KOR	68	77	76	76	297	9	13,811.24	9,606.15
	Nick O'HERN	AUS	74	74	73	76	297	9	13,811.24	9,606.15
	Rodney PAMPLING	AUS	73	73	72	79	297	9	13,811.24	9,606.15
53	Hennie OTTO	RSA	74	71	70	83	298	10	12,084.83	8,405.38
	Thongchai JAIDEE	THA	74	74	77	73	298	10	12,084.83	8,405.38
55	Grégory BOURDY	FRA	77	71	77	74	299	11	10,703.71	7,444.76
	Gaurav GHEI	IND	70	75	81	73	299	11	10,703.71	7,444.76
57	Andres ROMERO	ARG	69	77	76	78	300	12	9,667.87	6,724.30
58	Bradford VAUGHAN	RSA	74	72	74	81	301	13	8,286.74	5,763.69
	Jyoti RANDHAWA	IND	70	74	78	79	301	13	8,286.74	5,763.69
	Søren HANSEN	DEN	73	75	77	76	301	13	8,286.74	5,763.69
61	Thaworn WIRATCHANT	THA	75	72	80	75	302	14	6,732.98	4,683.00
	Anton HAIG	RSA	77	69	74	82	302	14	6,732.98	4,683.00
63	Paul SHEEHAN	AUS	74	75	78	78	305	17	5,869.78	4,082.61
	Peter HEDBLOM	SWE	73	75	72	85	305	17	5,869.78	4,082.61
	Juvic PAGUNSAN	PHI	71	78	82	74	305	17	5,869.78	4,082.61
66	Pablo MARTIN	ESP	73	76	78	83	310	22	5,179.21	3,602.31

Total Prize Fund
€3,450,255 £2,399,759

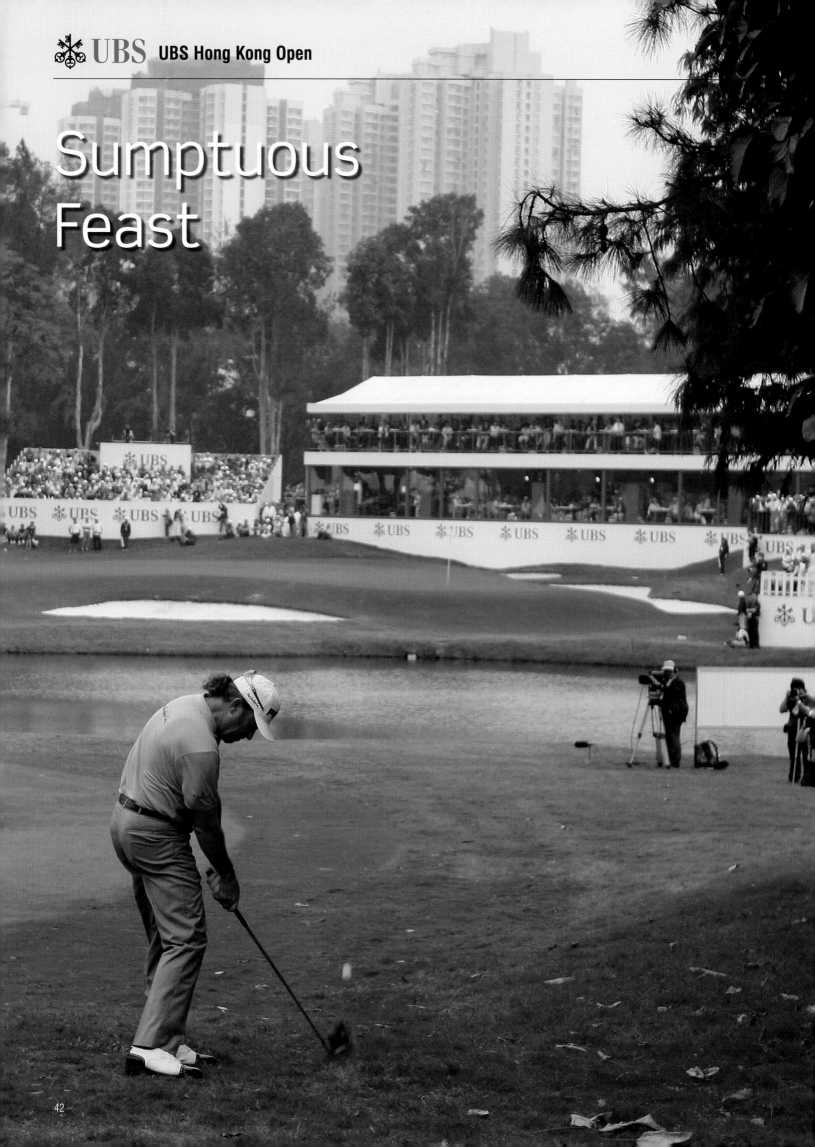

Sumptuous Feast

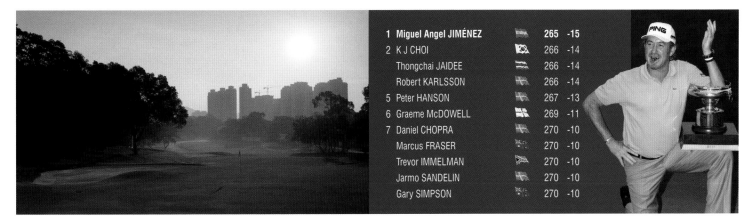

1	Miguel Angel JIMÉNEZ		265	-15
2	K J CHOI		266	-14
	Thongchai JAIDEE		266	-14
	Robert KARLSSON		266	-14
5	Peter HANSON		267	-13
6	Graeme McDOWELL		269	-11
7	Daniel CHOPRA		270	-10
	Marcus FRASER		270	-10
	Trevor IMMELMAN		270	-10
	Jarmo SANDELIN		270	-10
	Gary SIMPSON		270	-10

W hen Miguel Angel Jiménez celebrated his second victory in the UBS Hong Kong Open by lighting up his trademark cigar in the Media Centre interview room directly beneath a large No Smoking sign, it was a somehow fitting end to what had been a bizarre few days both on and off the course.

Thongchai Jaidee

Gary Murphy

The week had begun, in the self same room, with an entertaining chat with Stuart Appleby. The Australian was making a rare appearance in the tournament and as well as talking about golf, he also threw in amusing anecdotes of cows, lush grass and fences for good measure.

As he was raised on a dairy farm and, according to popular belief, hit balls from one paddock to another in his early years, it perhaps should not have come as a surprise. But this time his analogy was aimed directly at his indolent US PGA Tour colleagues. "If you are a cow sitting in a lush field, it becomes difficult to want to go and chew grass somewhere else when you have plenty in your own paddock," he opined.

It was not a new topic for Appleby who once confounded America by declaring: "Americans travel like prawns on a hot day " – meaning the country's golfers have pretty much everything so why would they cross the world to play?

But there are signs that times are changing. Tiger Woods continues to play globally while Phil Mickelson stuck his head 'through the fence' and went to China for the first time and won the HSBC Champions tournament the week before.

Canadian Mike Weir was also tempted to pastures new by coming to the Hong Kong Golf Club on his way to the Omega Mission Hills World Cup. "I have always wanted to play a bit more internationally and my kids are now at an age which allows me to do that," said the left-hander, who eventually finished in a share of 12th place.

Six weeks earlier, Weir had given his home supporters at the Royal Montreal Golf Club something to cheer when he beat Woods in the singles during the United States triumph in the Presidents Cup, but it was another of Weir's International Team colleagues – Korea's K J Choi – who stole the limelight on the opening day in Hong Kong.

The winner of the Memorial Tournament and the AT&T National tournament on the 2007 US PGA Tour momentarily threatened the Fanling course record of 61 before finally settling for an opening eight under par 62.

A 72 the following day saw him removed from pole position and replaced by Sweden's Robert Karlsson who maintained his four shot lead at the end of the third round thanks to virtually flawless golf for cards of 64-64-66. But lurking, menacingly, was Jiménez, the winner of the tournament in The European Tour's 2005 season.

No one was more surprised to be leading into the final round than Karlsson himself. "I've actually tried to avoid this tournament in the past because I've done so badly," he admitted. "I just couldn't see how, with my game the way it was, that I could get round this golf course," he added, recalling two previous trips to Fanling in 1993 and 2005. "My caddie said, 'If I'm going to come with you to that course again, we are going to have to change something radically.

"I played both Pro-Ams to see if we could figure out how to get round a bit better. You have to be conservative in the way you select your club, but aggressive in the shot you hit."

The Swede won both The Celtic Manor Wales Open and The Deutsche Bank Players' Championship of Europe in 2006 when he led after the second round and never looked back, but this time the danger was right beside him – Jiménez. The two traded blows during the third round and it ended in a 66-66 draw. However the Spaniard knew a four shot lead was not bombproof.

Three years previously Jiménez had a front row seat as he watched South African James Kingston implode on the famous 18th hole and gift wrap him the title. Now it was Karlsson's turn. Level coming down the last, the Swede came up short of the green, fluffed his chip and ended up with a double bogey six. Despite three putting for a bogey five, the victory was the Spaniard's.

However, there was no celebration overkill, Jiménez instead empathising with the man who was consigned to second place alongside the fast-finishing Thongchai Jaidee and Choi; golf once again proving to be the most gentlemanly and honourable of sports.

"I felt for Robert, the way he finished," he said. "Someone has to win. I feel happy for that, but sorry for him. I must say though that I like this golf course very much and I like it hot – I am like a fish in water when it's hot."

Fish, cows, prawns and a tasty finish: the UBS Hong Kong Open certainly provided a sumptuous golfing feast.

Noel Prentice
South China Morning Post

Robert Karlsson

K J Choi

Marcus Fraser

Shiv Kapur

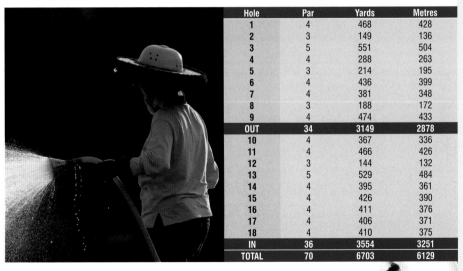

Miguel Angel Jiménez is presented with the trophy by Kathryn Shih, Chief Executive, UBS Hong Kong Branch

Hole	Par	Yards	Metres
1	4	468	428
2	3	149	136
3	5	551	504
4	4	288	263
5	3	214	195
6	4	436	399
7	4	381	348
8	3	188	172
9	4	474	433
OUT	34	3149	2878
10	4	367	336
11	4	466	426
12	3	144	132
13	5	529	484
14	4	395	361
15	4	426	390
16	4	411	376
17	4	406	371
18	4	410	375
IN	36	3554	3251
TOTAL	70	6703	6129

i Miguel Angel Jiménez extended his current record of most European Tour victories by a player over 40 to seven, courtesy of this latest triumph in the UBS Hong Kong Open.

Hong Kong Golf Club

Final Results

Pos	Name		Rd1	Rd2	Rd3	Rd4	Total		€	£
1	Miguel Angel JIMÉNEZ	ESP	65	67	66	67	265	-15	255,710.51	179,331.45
2	K J CHOI	KOR	62	72	65	67	266	-14	114,410.57	80,236.88
	Robert KARLSSON	SWE	64	64	66	72	266	-14	114,410.57	80,236.88
	Thongchai JAIDEE	THA	66	67	68	65	266	-14	114,410.57	80,236.88
5	Peter HANSON	SWE	68	66	65	68	267	-13	65,052.75	45,621.92
6	Graeme MCDOWELL	NIR	67	66	68	68	269	-11	53,699.21	37,659.61
7	Gary SIMPSON	AUS	69	67	65	69	270	-10	35,533.53	24,919.90
	Marcus FRASER	AUS	67	68	64	71	270	-10	35,533.53	24,919.90
	Trevor IMMELMAN	RSA	71	62	70	67	270	-10	35,533.53	24,919.90
	Jarmo SANDELIN	SWE	69	64	68	69	270	-10	35,533.53	24,919.90
	Daniel CHOPRA	SWE	66	68	66	70	270	-10	35,533.53	24,919.90
12	Mike WEIR	CAN	69	64	67	71	271	-9	24,855.06	17,431.02
	Scott STRANGE	AUS	66	68	66	71	271	-9	24,855.06	17,431.02
	Shiv KAPUR	IND	67	67	65	72	271	-9	24,855.06	17,431.02
15	Wen-chong LIANG	CHN	68	66	68	70	272	-8	20,743.24	14,547.37
	Simon DYSON	ENG	68	65	70	69	272	-8	20,743.24	14,547.37
	Garry HOUSTON	WAL	63	71	71	67	272	-8	20,743.24	14,547.37
	Robert-Jan DERKSEN	NED	72	67	68	65	272	-8	20,743.24	14,547.37
	Thaworn WIRATCHANT	THA	69	68	66	69	272	-8	20,743.24	14,547.37
20	Christian CÉVAËR	FRA	70	65	68	70	273	-7	17,132.60	12,015.21
	Charlie WI	KOR	67	68	67	71	273	-7	17,132.60	12,015.21
	Damien MCGRANE	IRL	69	66	67	71	273	-7	17,132.60	12,015.21
	Anders HANSEN	DEN	67	70	68	68	273	-7	17,132.60	12,015.21
	Retief GOOSEN	RSA	69	66	68	70	273	-7	17,132.60	12,015.21
	Prom MEESAWAT	THA	68	70	67	68	273	-7	17,132.60	12,015.21
26	Maarten LAFEBER	NED	68	67	68	71	274	-6	15,035.78	10,544.69
	Gary MURPHY	IRL	66	70	66	72	274	-6	15,035.78	10,544.69
	Wook-soon KANG	KOR	65	70	71	68	274	-6	15,035.78	10,544.69
29	Søren KJELDSEN	DEN	70	65	68	72	275	-5	13,654.94	9,576.30
	Francesco MOLINARI	ITA	68	69	69	69	275	-5	13,654.94	9,576.30
	Markus BRIER	AUT	68	68	69	70	275	-5	13,654.94	9,576.30
32	Peter HEDBLOM	SWE	71	67	64	74	276	-4	12,082.32	8,473.41
	Mathias GRÖNBERG	SWE	66	71	68	71	276	-4	12,082.32	8,473.41
	Chawalit PLAPHOL	THA	67	68	71	70	276	-4	12,082.32	8,473.41
	S S P CHOWRASIA	IND	69	67	70	70	276	-4	12,082.32	8,473.41
36	Jamie DONALDSON	WAL	69	68	68	72	277	-3	10,739.84	7,531.92
	Carlos RODILES	ESP	72	67	70	68	277	-3	10,739.84	7,531.92
	Keith HORNE	RSA	67	68	68	74	277	-3	10,739.84	7,531.92
	Ter-chang WANG	TPE	70	68	71	68	277	-3	10,739.84	7,531.92
40	Michael JONZON	SWE	70	68	68	72	278	-2	9,359.01	6,563.53
	Fredrik ANDERSSON HED	SWE	64	71	71	72	278	-2	9,359.01	6,563.53
	Gary ORR	SCO	67	68	70	73	278	-2	9,359.01	6,563.53
	Frankie MINOZA	PHI	69	69	70	70	278	-2	9,359.01	6,563.53
	Mahal PEARCE	NZL	68	70	66	74	278	-2	9,359.01	6,563.53
45	Bryan SALTUS	USA	68	65	72	74	279	-1	8,285.02	5,810.34
	Mardan MAMAT	SIN	69	68	71	71	279	-1	8,285.02	5,810.34
47	Sung LEE	KOR	66	71	73	70	280	0	7,517.89	5,272.34
	Antonio LASCUNA	PHI	68	69	68	75	280	0	7,517.89	5,272.34
	Daniel VANCSIK	ARG	66	71	73	70	280	0	7,517.89	5,272.34
50	Juvic PAGUNSAN	PHI	70	67	71	73	281	1	6,290.48	4,411.55
	Wei-chih LU	TPE	68	71	67	75	281	1	6,290.48	4,411.55
	Lian-wei ZHANG	CHN	70	68	71	72	281	1	6,290.48	4,411.55
	Martin ERLANDSSON	SWE	68	65	70	78	281	1	6,290.48	4,411.55
	Paul MCGINLEY	IRL	68	70	72	71	281	1	6,290.48	4,411.55
55	Thomas BJÖRN	DEN	68	71	71	72	282	2	4,848.27	3,400.12
	Jean-François LUCQUIN	FRA	68	66	73	75	282	2	4,848.27	3,400.12
	Anthony KANG	USA	66	70	74	72	282	2	4,848.27	3,400.12
	Clay DEVERS	USA	70	68	73	71	282	2	4,848.27	3,400.12
	Jason KNUTZON	USA	67	69	74	72	282	2	4,848.27	3,400.12
60	Adam GROOM	AUS	70	69	67	77	283	3	4,065.80	2,851.37
	Rahil GANGJEE	IND	71	68	69	75	283	3	4,065.80	2,851.37
	Nick FALDO	ENG	68	71	72	72	283	3	4,065.80	2,851.37
	Ricardo GONZALEZ	ARG	67	70	70	76	283	3	4,065.80	2,851.37
64	Grégory HAVRET	FRA	66	73	72	73	284	4	3,682.23	2,582.37
65	Barry HUME	SCO	65	68	74	78	285	5	3,528.81	2,474.77
66	David HOWELL	ENG	72	66	74	74	286	6	3,375.38	2,367.18
67	Gerald ROSALES	PHI	73	66	71	77	287	7	3,145.24	2,205.78
	BAE SANG-MOON	KOR	71	68	70	78	287	7	3,145.24	2,205.78
69	Chapchai NIRAT	THA	66	73	76	73	288	8	2,670.62	1,872.93
	Marc WARREN	SCO	67	71	76	74	288	8	2,670.62	1,872.93
	Panuwat MUENLEK	THA	68	67	72	81	288	8	2,670.62	1,872.93
72	Jong-yul SUK	KOR	71	67	72	79	289	9	2,298.00	1,611.60
73	José-Filipe LIMA	POR	68	69	78	75	290	10	2,295.00	1,609.50

Total Prize Fund

€1,541,157 £1,080,823

First Past the Post

1	**Aaron BADDELEY**		275	-13
2	Daniel CHOPRA		275	-13
3	Stuart APPLEBY		277	-11
4	Peter O'MALLEY		278	-10
5	Dave HORSEY		279	-9
	Peter LONARD		279	-9
	Rodney PAMPLING		279	-9
8	Kurt BARNES		280	-8
	Steven JEFFRESS		280	-8
10	Robert ALLENBY		281	-7
	Richard FINCH		281	-7
	Marcus FRASER		281	-7
	Anthony SUMMERS		281	-7
	Andrew TAMPION		281	-7

Australians love a punt and it is a good bet that several rejoiced with a few extra dollars in their back pockets when one of their own – Aaron Baddeley – beat Sweden's Daniel Chopra in a play-off to win the MasterCard Masters. Even at 10/1 favourite before the tournament started, the 26 year old represented good value.

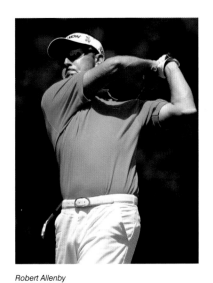

Robert Allenby

Stuart Appleby

Those with more adventurous betting tendencies, however, might have fancied a flutter on young Irishman Rory McIlroy, especially after former Open Champion Ian Baker-Finch singled out the 18 year old as worthy of a wager.

McIlroy might have been teeing-up in only his sixth event as a professional but the record books indicated that he did have previous form at the Huntingdale Golf Club in Melbourne. For, in 2005 when still an amateur, he played in the MasterCard Masters and made the cut for the first time in a professional tournament.

McIlroy also gave those taking Baker-Finch's advice plenty to analyse when he insisted: "It's good coming back to Melbourne. I played nicely that week in 2005 and this is a course that I feel suits my game because if you are hitting the ball well you can also lay back and still shoot a good score."

Baker-Finch had singled out McIlroy for praise when he hosted a 'Meet the Players' function prior to the tournament, but the irony was that the guy seated next to the young Ulsterman just happened to be Baddeley!

Although off the mark on this occasion, Baker-Finch's credentials as a tipster were sound when he heralded Baddeley's own sensational victory in 1999 when he held off the challenges of players such as Colin Montgomerie and Greg Norman to become the first amateur to win the Australian Open since Bruce Devlin in 1960.

Daniel Chopra

At the time, Baker-Finch said: "I've never seen an 18 year old who is so level-headed and well behaved. To use the old cliché, he has an old head on young shoulders. He has all the ingredients to be an Australian Tiger Woods."

Coincidentally on turning professional Baddeley declared: "Yes, definitely, I want to be better than Tiger Woods. Tiger is the best in the world and I want to be the best in the world. Tiger is Number One, so I have to be better than him."

Baddeley, of course, is not alone in finding that to be 'Mission Impossible' at present. Nevertheless he was right to set his targets high although throughout his career, blessed with an endearing modesty, he has kept his feet firmly on the ground. Furthermore he has found success in a sport that seemed the least likely to attract him as a youngster.

Neither of his parents – his father, Ron, was briefly a mechanic in Mario Andretti's IndyCar team in the United States where Aaron was born – played golf. Baddeley was good at all sports, but initially he wanted to play cricket for Australia.

That changed when his grandmother, Jean, invited him to swing a club at the Dorset Golf Club in East Melbourne. At 13, he was playing in Under 21 matches while at 14 he won the Croydon Club Championship and received a letter from Jack Nicklaus wishing him well. At 15, he was off scratch – and the rest is history.

A successful defence of the Australian Open – as a professional – in 2000 was followed by his first European Tour – Australian Tour co-sanctioned victory in the 2001 Greg Norman Holden International. The Major Championships have so far remained out of reach but after victories on the US PGA Tour in both 2006 and 2007 he further underlined his claim to be a strong contender for those coveted titles in 2008 with his success in Melbourne.

Compatriot Robert Allenby initially set the pace with an opening 67 with Baddeley and McIlroy both scoring 70s. Allenby added a 68 and Baddeley a 66 but as they partnered each other on the third day, so Chopra surged ahead with a 65, registering only 23 putts on the slick Huntingdale greens on Melbourne's sand-belt.

McIlroy, as close as third place after two rounds, would slip back to eventually finish in a share of 15th place, but in an epic finish Baddeley carded a 70 to Chopra's 71 to force a sudden-death play-off.

It took four attempts on the 18th hole to separate the pair in a marathon extra holes session after which Baddeley slipped into the winner's Gold Jacket. With some justification he could be forgiven for thinking about one day wearing something similar, only in green.

Mitchell Platts

Peter O'Malley

Aaron Baddeley (right) is presented with his winner's cheque by Leigh Clapham, Executive Vice President Australasia MasterCard Worldwide

Rory McIlroy

Hole	Par	Yards	Metres
1	4	428	391
2	4	352	322
3	3	185	169
4	4	396	362
5	3	211	193
6	5	580	530
7	5	536	490
8	4	343	314
9	4	413	378
OUT	36	3444	3149
10	5	495	453
11	4	437	400
12	3	176	161
13	4	348	318
14	5	607	555
15	3	176	161
16	4	384	351
17	4	465	425
18	4	448	410
IN	36	3536	3234
TOTAL	72	6980	6383

Scott Strange

i This was Australian Aaron Baddeley's second European Tour title, both having come in his home country. The first was the 2001 Greg Norman Holden International which, ironically, he also claimed in a play-off, beating Sergio Garcia in extra holes in Sydney seven years ago.

Huntingdale Golf Club

Final Results

Pos	Name		Rd1	Rd2	Rd3	Rd4	Total		€	£
1	Aaron BADDELEY	AUS	70	66	69	70	275	-13	172,811.09	123,634.30
2	Daniel CHOPRA	SWE	69	70	65	71	275	-13	97,926.29	70,059.44
3	Stuart APPLEBY	AUS	69	71	68	69	277	-11	64,804.16	46,362.87
4	Peter O'MALLEY	AUS	72	72	67	67	278	-10	46,082.96	32,969.15
5	Rodney PAMPLING	AUS	69	71	67	72	279	-9	34,562.22	24,726.86
	Peter LONARD	AUS	70	71	68	70	279	-9	34,562.22	24,726.86
	Dave HORSEY	ENG	77	65	72	65	279	-9	34,562.22	24,726.86
8	Steven JEFFRESS	AUS	73	72	69	66	280	-8	26,881.72	19,232.00
	Kurt BARNES	AUS	69	71	65	75	280	-8	26,881.72	19,232.00
10	Andrew TAMPION	AUS	70	74	68	69	281	-7	19,585.26	14,011.89
	Marcus FRASER	AUS	72	69	70	70	281	-7	19,585.26	14,011.89
	Anthony SUMMERS	AUS	71	72	67	71	281	-7	19,585.26	14,011.89
	Robert ALLENBY	AUS	67	68	73	73	281	-7	19,585.26	14,011.89
	Richard FINCH	ENG	70	71	67	73	281	-7	19,585.26	14,011.89
15	Simon KHAN	ENG	75	69	72	66	282	-6	12,048.77	8,620.06
	John SENDEN	AUS	73	69	71	69	282	-6	12,048.77	8,620.06
	Martin ERLANDSSON	SWE	73	72	70	67	282	-6	12,048.77	8,620.06
	Terry PILKADARIS	AUS	71	68	72	71	282	-6	12,048.77	8,620.06
	Scott STRANGE	AUS	70	69	72	71	282	-6	12,048.77	8,620.06
	Ross McGOWAN	ENG	74	71	68	69	282	-6	12,048.77	8,620.06
	Rory MCILROY	NIR	70	69	70	73	282	-6	12,048.77	8,620.06
22	Peter SENIOR	AUS	72	70	71	70	283	-5	9,408.60	6,731.20
	Adam CRAWFORD	AUS	72	69	71	71	283	-5	9,408.60	6,731.20
24	Jarmo SANDELIN	SWE	74	70	71	69	284	-4	7,872.50	5,632.23
	Damien MCGRANE	IRL	72	71	69	72	284	-4	7,872.50	5,632.23
	Stephen LEANEY	AUS	70	72	68	74	284	-4	7,872.50	5,632.23
	Michael LONG	NZL	69	74	68	73	284	-4	7,872.50	5,632.23
	Ewan PORTER	AUS	70	73	67	74	284	-4	7,872.50	5,632.23
	Rick KULACZ	AUS	70	69	72	73	284	-4	7,872.50	5,632.23
30	Heath REED	AUS	73	71	68	73	285	-3	5,787.80	4,140.77
	Adam BLAND	AUS	75	70	69	71	285	-3	5,787.80	4,140.77
	Robert DINWIDDIE	ENG	74	71	68	72	285	-3	5,787.80	4,140.77
	Aaron BLACK	AUS	70	72	73	70	285	-3	5,787.80	4,140.77
	Peter BAKER	ENG	68	72	74	71	285	-3	5,787.80	4,140.77
	Edward RUSH	ENG	71	73	73	68	285	-3	5,787.80	4,140.77
	Alexander NOREN	SWE	72	72	71	70	285	-3	5,787.80	4,140.77
37	Peter WHITEFORD	SCO	73	71	72	70	286	-2	4,704.30	3,365.60
	Paul MARANTZ	AUS	69	75	74	68	286	-2	4,704.30	3,365.60
	Peter WILSON	AUS	72	73	72	69	286	-2	4,704.30	3,365.60
	Shane BAXTER	AUS	72	70	70	74	286	-2	4,704.30	3,365.60
41	Ashley HALL	AUS	77	68	73	69	287	-1	3,552.23	2,541.37
	Tim WOOD	AUS	71	73	73	70	287	-1	3,552.23	2,541.37
	Matthew ECOB	AUS	70	75	68	74	287	-1	3,552.23	2,541.37
	Marcus CAIN	AUS	75	70	70	72	287	-1	3,552.23	2,541.37
	David BRANSDON	AUS	79	66	71	71	287	-1	3,552.23	2,541.37
	Paul SHEEHAN	AUS	72	73	71	71	287	-1	3,552.23	2,541.37
	Fredrik ANDERSSON HED	SWE	68	75	74	70	287	-1	3,552.23	2,541.37
	Matthew ZIONS	AUS	70	70	71	76	287	-1	3,552.23	2,541.37
49	Terry PRICE	AUS	72	72	72	72	288	0	2,496.16	1,785.83
	Richard GREEN	AUS	72	73	69	74	288	0	2,496.16	1,785.83
	Josh CARMICHAEL	AUS	72	70	74	72	288	0	2,496.16	1,785.83
52	Scott LAYCOCK	AUS	75	70	72	72	289	1	1,860.12	1,330.79
	Anthony BROWN	AUS	74	71	73	71	289	1	1,860.12	1,330.79
	Michael WRIGHT	AUS	74	71	71	73	289	1	1,860.12	1,330.79
	Chris DOWNES	AUS	72	72	70	75	289	1	1,860.12	1,330.79
56	Mahal PEARCE	NZL	71	74	73	72	290	2	1,593.70	1,140.18
	Nick FLANAGAN	AUS	70	73	74	73	290	2	1,593.70	1,140.18
	Simon FURNEAUX	AUS	70	71	73	76	290	2	1,593.70	1,140.18
59	Rhys DAVIES	WAL	70	75	72	74	291	3	1,526.50	1,092.10
	Peter FOWLER	AUS	74	71	73	73	291	3	1,526.50	1,092.10
	Didier DE VOOGHT	BEL	74	70	73	74	291	3	1,526.50	1,092.10
62	Ryan HAMMOND	AUS	74	70	76	72	292	4	1,488.10	1,064.63
63	Alistair PRESNELL	AUS	71	70	79	73	293	5	1,459.29	1,044.02
	Stuart MANLEY	WAL	71	73	76	73	293	5	1,459.29	1,044.02
65	Paul SPARGO	AUS	71	72	75	76	294	6	1,420.89	1,016.55
	Luke HICKMOTT	AUS	70	71	75	78	294	6	1,420.89	1,016.55
67	Michael CURTAIN	RSA	74	71	71	79	295	7	1,372.89	982.21
	Jarrod MOSELEY	AUS	74	71	76	74	295	7	1,372.89	982.21

Total Prize Fund
€909,428 £650,632

Unlikely Heroes

1	**Richard FINCH**		**274**	**-14**
2	Steven BOWDITCH		277	-11
	Paul SHEEHAN		277	-11
4	Steven JEFFRESS		278	-10
	Matthew MILLAR		278	-10
	Alexander NOREN		278	-10
	Craig PARRY		278	-10
8	Peter FOWLER		279	-9
9	Oliver FISHER		280	-8
	Matthew ZIONS		280	-8

F ilm Director Peter Jackson has won worldwide acclaim for his work on epic adventures such as Lord of the Rings and King Kong but should the New Zealander ever venture away from fantasy and fiction and turn his attention to real-life drama, the story of his own national Open would be worthy of a Hollywood blockbuster.

Steven Bowditch

The plot would outline a struggling tournament rescued by a home-grown benefactor for its centenary; the action played out on a spectacular stage as an unlikely hero emerges from the shadows, while a wise old sage defies the years to upstage the young pretenders.

The New Zealand Open celebrated 100 years of existence with significant changes implemented to help restore the tournament to its former glory, the first being the new venue of The Hills Golf Club.

New Zealand's South Island, renowned for its scenic beauty, had not hosted the national Open since 1985, but the move to the Queenstown venue, with The Remarkables mountain range providing a stunning backdrop, meant the centenary would take place in one of the most breathtaking settings on The European Tour International Schedule.

The course is owned by New Zealand businessman Michael Hill, a resident of Queenstown, and, as host and sponsor, he breathed new life into the event jointly sanctioned by The European Tour and the PGA Tour of Australasia.

So, the stage was set, but what of the cast? Here, the scriptwriters chose an Englishman to play the lead role, identifying a player who would demonstrate courage on his way to the summit. Step forward Richard Finch.

A few weeks earlier Finch had been fighting for survival. As the 2007 season drew to a close, the 30 year old was struggling to retain his playing privileges for another year.

But he saved himself in the final counting event with a courageous joint seventh place in the

Mallorca Classic. Having endured the nail-biting end to the season, just three events later he experienced the elation of his maiden European Tour title.

Finch started the week slowly with an opening 73 but set the tournament alight with a second round seven under par 65 which he bettered by one the following day to open up a three stroke lead. Despite a slight wobble over the closing stages, he went on to claim his breakthrough win with a level par 72 and a 14 under par total of 274, three strokes better than the Australian pair of Steven Bowditch and Paul Sheehan.

However, we cannot overlook the exploits of the Grand Master, adding a wonderful twist to the tale. Finch may have walked away with the trophy but in many ways the tournament belonged to Sir Bob Charles, the legendary New Zealander who rewrote the record books.

In the second round, at the age of 71 years and 261 days, Charles became the oldest player to make a cut on any of golf's major tours. His second round 68 - three shots better than his age, which was another record – gave him a one under par aggregate of 143 and ensured he would be the first septuagenarian to compete over the weekend of a European Tour event.

His record surpassed that of the great American Sam Snead, who was 67, two months and 21 days old when he survived the halfway cut in the 1979 Manufactures Hanover Westchester Classic on the US PGA Tour, and shattered The European Tour record held by Ireland's Christy O'Connor who was a mere 64 and 184 days when he made the cut in the 1989 Carroll's Irish Open.

The fact that Charles, who in 1963 became the first left-hander and New Zealander to win a Major Championship when he won The Open at Royal Lytham & St Annes, went on to match his age in a third round of 71 before bettering it again in the final round with a 70 underlined his undoubted class and longevity. His four under par total of 284 put him in a share of 23rd place and he would have been the highest placed New Zealand golfer for the week had he not double bogeyed the last hole.

Charles had retired from the New Zealand Open in 2004 but was persuaded to tee it up once again for the centenary and he admitted his performance had prompted a rethink on retirement from his national Open in the future.

After all, he will be level par 72 for the sequel.

Roddy Williams

Sir Bob Charles

Richard Finch (left) is presented with the trophy by Michael Hill, Title sponsor and course owner

Peter Fowler

Hole	Par	Yards	Metres
1	5	519	475
2	4	406	371
3	4	386	353
4	3	257	235
5	4	337	308
6	4	432	395
7	3	206	189
8	4	509	465
9	5	595	544
OUT	36	3647	3335
10	3	163	149
11	4	434	397
12	4	424	388
13	5	572	525
14	4	447	392
15	4	329	301
16	3	182	167
17	5	553	506
18	4	492	450
IN	36	3596	3275
TOTAL	72	7243	6610

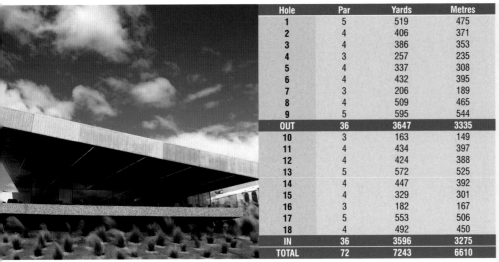

Oliver Fisher

Richard Finch claimed his maiden European Tour title at the Michael Hill New Zealand Open in his 90th appearance. He also had the honour of becoming the first Englishman to win New Zealand's national crown.

The Hills Golf Club

Final Results

Pos	Name		Rd1	Rd2	Rd3	Rd4	Total		€	£
1	Richard FINCH	ENG	73	65	64	72	274	-14	144,895.33	104,457.68
2	Paul SHEEHAN	AUS	68	67	73	69	277	-11	68,221.55	49,182.16
	Steven BOWDITCH	AUS	69	65	71	72	277	-11	68,221.55	49,182.16
4	Alexander NOREN	SWE	76	69	67	66	278	-10	31,393.99	22,632.50
	Craig PARRY	AUS	68	74	70	66	278	-10	31,393.99	22,632.50
	Matthew MILLAR	AUS	72	71	68	67	278	-10	31,393.99	22,632.50
	Steven JEFFRESS	AUS	71	68	72	67	278	-10	31,393.99	22,632.50
8	Peter FOWLER	AUS	69	75	62	73	279	-9	23,344.25	16,829.29
9	Oliver FISHER	ENG	70	69	72	69	280	-8	20,929.32	15,088.33
	Matthew ZIONS	AUS	72	73	66	69	280	-8	20,929.32	15,088.33
11	Robert DINWIDDIE	ENG	72	72	66	71	281	-7	17,709.43	12,767.05
12	Michael CURTAIN	AUS	71	70	70	71	282	-6	14,288.29	10,300.69
	Josh GEARY	NZL	75	67	70	70	282	-6	14,288.29	10,300.69
	Adam BLAND	AUS	71	74	67	70	282	-6	14,288.29	10,300.69
	Gary SIMPSON	AUS	69	69	76	68	282	-6	14,288.29	10,300.69
16	Andrew TSCHUDIN	AUS	70	71	70	72	283	-5	9,412.45	6,785.60
	Scott GARDINER	AUS	72	72	67	72	283	-5	9,412.45	6,785.60
	Kyron SULLIVAN	WAL	72	68	69	74	283	-5	9,412.45	6,785.60
	Gareth PADDISON	NZL	70	72	71	70	283	-5	9,412.45	6,785.60
	Anthony BROWN	AUS	71	70	72	70	283	-5	9,412.45	6,785.60
	Matthew BALLARD	AUS	72	70	70	71	283	-5	9,412.45	6,785.60
	Rick KULACZ	AUS	71	69	68	75	283	-5	9,412.45	6,785.60
23	Doug HOLLOWAY	NZL	72	71	74	67	284	-4	6,761.78	4,874.69
	Marc LEISHMAN	AUS	69	70	71	74	284	-4	6,761.78	4,874.69
	Ewan PORTER	AUS	72	66	70	76	284	-4	6,761.78	4,874.69
	Michael WRIGHT	AUS	71	69	72	72	284	-4	6,761.78	4,874.69
	Peter WHITEFORD	SCO	70	68	75	71	284	-4	6,761.78	4,874.69
	Bob CHARLES	NZL	75	68	71	70	284	-4	6,761.78	4,874.69
	Tony CHRISTIE	NZL	71	73	71	69	284	-4	6,761.78	4,874.69
30	Anthony SUMMERS	AUS	73	71	70	71	285	-3	4,937.17	3,559.30
	Terry PILKADARIS	AUS	77	68	69	71	285	-3	4,937.17	3,559.30
	Marcus FRASER	AUS	73	69	73	70	285	-3	4,937.17	3,559.30
	Aaron TOWNSEND	AUS	74	71	67	73	285	-3	4,937.17	3,559.30
	Dave HORSEY	ENG	74	70	70	71	285	-3	4,937.17	3,559.30
	Shane BAXTER	AUS	71	73	73	68	285	-3	4,937.17	3,559.30
36	Paul SPARGO	AUS	75	70	71	70	286	-2	3,944.37	2,843.57
	Mahal PEARCE	NZL	71	70	69	76	286	-2	3,944.37	2,843.57
	Matthew WOODS	ENG	68	74	73	71	286	-2	3,944.37	2,843.57
	Didier DE VOOGHT	BEL	73	70	72	71	286	-2	3,944.37	2,843.57
	Damien MCGRANE	IRL	72	72	69	73	286	-2	3,944.37	2,843.57
	Brendan STUART	NZL	69	73	70	74	286	-2	3,944.37	2,843.57
42	Michael LONG	NZL	69	67	76	75	287	-1	3,300.39	2,379.31
	Jamie DONALDSON	WAL	70	74	77	66	287	-1	3,300.39	2,379.31
44	Kim FELTON	AUS	71	73	70	74	288	0	2,656.41	1,915.06
	Martin DOYLE	AUS	71	72	78	67	288	0	2,656.41	1,915.06
	Andrew MCKENZIE	AUS	71	69	72	76	288	0	2,656.41	1,915.06
	Jamie LITTLE	ENG	72	73	71	72	288	0	2,656.41	1,915.06
	Alvaro VELASCO	ESP	73	70	72	73	288	0	2,656.41	1,915.06
	Danny LEE (AM)	NZL	73	71	75	69	288	0		0.
	Josh CARMICHAEL	NZL	77	67	70	74	288	0	2,656.41	1,915.06
51	Rodney BOOTH	AUS	69	73	72	75	289	1	1,851.44	1,334.74
	Adam BLYTH	AUS	75	68	73	73	289	1	1,851.44	1,334.74
	Daniel CHOPRA	SWE	70	71	70	78	289	1	1,851.44	1,334.74
	Marco SOFFIETTI	ITA	75	70	73	71	289	1	1,851.44	1,334.74
55	David BRANSDON	AUS	69	73	75	73	290	2	1,388.58	1,001.05
	Ally MELLOR	ENG	72	73	71	74	290	2	1,388.58	1,001.05
	Michael SIM	AUS	69	76	72	73	290	2	1,388.58	1,001.05
	Ben WHARTON	AUS	70	74	74	72	290	2	1,388.58	1,001.05
	Nick GILLESPIE (AM)	NZL	78	67	72	73	290	2		
60	Steven JONES	AUS	70	73	76	72	291	3	1,263.81	911.10
	Craig SCOTT	AUS	75	67	73	76	291	3	1,263.81	911.10
	Peter NOLAN	AUS	71	74	74	72	291	3	1,263.81	911.10
	Scott STRANGE	AUS	75	70	73	73	291	3	1,263.81	911.10
	Steven JEPPESEN	SWE	72	72	73	74	291	3	1,263.81	911.10
	Richard LEE	NZL	70	71	78	72	291	3	1,263.81	911.10
	Paul MARANTZ	AUS	69	76	72	74	291	3	1,263.81	911.10
67	Philip TATAURANGI	NZL	74	71	68	79	292	4	1,191.36	858.87
	Luke HICKMOTT	AUS	70	73	75	74	292	4	1,191.36	858.87
69	Jarrod MOSELEY	AUS	73	71	75	74	293	5	1,151.11	829.86
	Terry PRICE	AUS	73	71	70	79	293	5	1,151.11	829.86
71	Ricky SCHMIDT	AUS	75	70	75	74	294	6	1,102.82	795.04
	David HUTTON	ENG	75	69	76	74	294	6	1,102.82	795.04
73	Lucas PARSONS	AUS	73	71	74	78	296	8	1,091.00	786.52
74	Lee HUNT	AUS	76	69	79	73	297	9	1,088.00	784.36
75	Henry EPSTEIN	AUS	74	69	74	82	299	11	1,085.00	782.20

Total Prize Fund

€767,989   £553,657

53

Delight and Despair

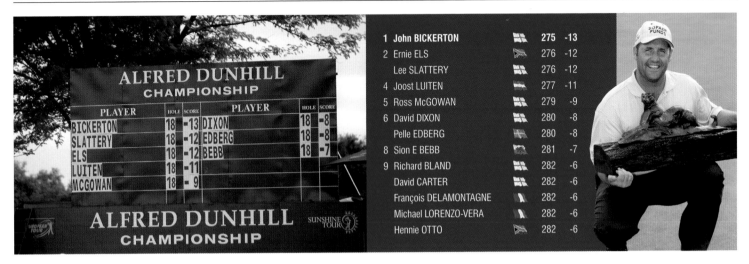

	PLAYER		SCORE	
1	John BICKERTON		275	-13
2	Ernie ELS		276	-12
	Lee SLATTERY		276	-12
4	Joost LUITEN		277	-11
5	Ross McGOWAN		279	-9
6	David DIXON		280	-8
	Pelle EDBERG		280	-8
8	Sion E BEBB		281	-7
9	Richard BLAND		282	-6
	David CARTER		282	-6
	François DELAMONTAGNE		282	-6
	Michael LORENZO-VERA		282	-6
	Hennie OTTO		282	-6

S port is exhilarating and can produce moments of sheer delight unrivalled in any other sphere of life. Just ask any player who has lifted a trophy high above his head or any supporter who has cheered from the stands watching him do it and they will vouch for this fact.

Lee Slattery

Joost Luiten

However, by its very nature, sport can often produce the exact opposite, moments of such deep despair that often the spectator cannot bear to look; moments when, inexplicably, a victory which seems a certainty is cruelly wrenched asunder.

In horse racing folklore, the perfect example came in the 1956 Grand National. After a flawless performance over the previous four miles, Devon Loch, the horse belonging to Her Majesty Queen Elizabeth the Queen Mother and ridden by Dick Francis, was 50 yards from the line and a memorable victory.

Suddenly, however, the horse appeared to jump over nothing and collapsed to the ground leaving the chasing E.S.B. and rider Dave Dick to canter first past the post. Reports suggested

everything from cramp in its hindquarters to a shadow from the adjacent water jump to be the problem, although Francis' later assertion that the huge cheer from the grandstands to herald a Royal victory had spooked the horse seems a more likely explanation.

Watching in his native Yorkshire at the time, little did Rugby League stalwart Don Fox realise that, 12 years later, he would produce a sporting moment which would see him forever linked with Devon Loch.

Having played so well during the 1968 Rugby League Challenge Cup Final for Wakefield Trinity, he had already been awarded the Lance Todd Trophy for Man of the Match when, with only seconds remaining, he was faced with a conversion in front of the posts which would give his team victory over Leeds.

It was such a straightforward kick that the Trinity supporters in the 87,100 crowd were already celebrating when, inexplicably, Fox miskicked and sliced the ball wide of the upright before slumping to the ground with his head in his hands as the referee blew for full time to signal an 11-10 Leeds victory.

That the moment is seared into the sporting public's consciousness is due in no small part to the late, great commentator Eddie Waring, whose take on the scene was, simply: "He's a poor lad."

Had the irrepressible Mr Waring been alive today and watching the 72nd hole of the Alfred Dunhill Championship at Leopard Creek, he might well have been moved to offer the same description of Ernie Els after an ending equally as dramatic as those events at Aintree and Wembley.

Having – like Devon Loch and Don Fox – dominated proceedings up to that point, Els stood in the middle of the 18th fairway with a two shot lead in the tournament and a mere 190 yards to the pin on the par five hole after a drive which could only be described as perfect.

Like the Queen Mother and the Wakefield Trinity supporters before them, the massed ranks of Els fans in the gallery around the green prepared to celebrate his quarter century of European Tour International Schedule titles, before it all went horribly wrong.

Having come off his six iron approach, the ball flew into the water as did his next shot, a pulled pitching wedge. Having finally found the green in six, he two putted for a triple bogey eight to hand the title to an astonished John Bickerton; the Englishman so convinced that second was his best hope that he was packing his bags outside the clubhouse when given the news by a television producer who required him for the winner's interview.

To his credit, although naturally delighted to have claimed his third European Tour title, Bickerton, one of the most genuine men on Tour, preferred to direct his comments in sympathy towards Els. "I have to be honest, disbelief is the main thing I feel right now," he said. "Sometimes the game jumps up and bites you and sometimes it goes for you as it did for me today. But I have to say I feel very sorry for Ernie."

Reflecting on events the following morning, Els admitted: "In this game you have to take the rough with the smooth but yesterday was about the most disappointed I've ever felt walking off a golf course. I was gutted. But hey, let's keep things in proportion. This is sport – it's not like anyone died out there. I just have to take it on the chin and move on."

It is reported that, in the aftermath of Devon Loch's collapse, the Queen Mother stoically said: "Never mind, that's racing." If the grand old lady had been alive today, it is a fair bet she would have said to the big South African, "Never mind, that's golf."

Scott Crockett

John Bickerton is awarded the trophy by Gaynor Rupert, wife of Johann Rupert, Chairman of Richemont International

Sion Bebb

Ernie Els

ALFRED DUNHILL
CHAMPIONSHIP

10
432 yds 395 mtrs
Par 4

ALFRED DUNHILL ALFRED DUNHI
CHAMPIONSHIP CHAMPIONSHIP

Hole	Par	Yards	Metres
1	4	419	383
2	5	542	496
3	4	448	410
4	4	427	390
5	3	164	150
6	4	319	292
7	3	215	197
8	4	480	439
9	4	476	435
OUT	**35**	**3490**	**3192**
10	4	432	395
11	4	375	343
12	3	192	176
13	5	552	505
14	4	413	378
15	5	598	547
16	3	208	190
17	4	448	410
18	5	541	495
IN	**37**	**3759**	**3439**
TOTAL	**72**	**7249**	**6631**

Richard Sterne (left) and Darren Clarke

Leopard Creek

Final Results

Pos	Name		Rd1	Rd2	Rd3	Rd4	Total		€	£
1	John BICKERTON	ENG	70	69	68	68	275	-13	158,500.00	113,193.26
2	Ernie ELS	RSA	70	69	64	73	276	-12	92,100.00	65,773.50
	Lee SLATTERY	ENG	73	65	67	71	276	-12	92,100.00	65,773.50
4	Joost LUITEN	NED	75	71	64	67	277	-11	49,100.00	35,064.92
5	Ross McGOWAN	ENG	71	69	67	72	279	-9	41,300.00	29,494.52
6	David DIXON	ENG	72	72	67	69	280	-8	32,450.00	23,174.27
	Pelle EDBERG	SWE	74	66	73	67	280	-8	32,450.00	23,174.27
8	Sion E BEBB	WAL	67	72	74	68	281	-7	24,600.00	17,568.17
9	David CARTER	ENG	72	71	70	69	282	-6	18,300.00	13,069.00
	Hennie OTTO	RSA	75	69	68	70	282	-6	18,300.00	13,069.00
	Richard BLAND	ENG	69	70	73	70	282	-6	18,300.00	13,069.00
	François DELAMONTAGNE	FRA	77	67	70	68	282	-6	18,300.00	13,069.00
	Michael LORENZO-VERA	FRA	72	70	73	67	282	-6	18,300.00	13,069.00
14	Robert ROCK	ENG	73	72	69	69	283	-5	13,950.00	9,962.44
	Omar SANDYS	RSA	68	68	74	73	283	-5	13,950.00	9,962.44
	Keith HORNE	RSA	74	70	68	71	283	-5	13,950.00	9,962.44
	Trevor FISHER	RSA	74	72	68	69	283	-5	13,950.00	9,962.44
18	Titch MOORE	RSA	71	68	72	73	284	-4	11,500.00	8,212.76
	Andrew MCLARDY	RSA	72	73	71	68	284	-4	11,500.00	8,212.76
	Martin WIEGELE	AUT	74	71	73	66	284	-4	11,500.00	8,212.76
	Craig LEE	SCO	68	71	72	73	284	-4	11,500.00	8,212.76
	Richard STERNE	RSA	74	70	70	70	284	-4	11,500.00	8,212.76
	George COETZEE	RSA	69	72	75	68	284	-4	11,500.00	8,212.76
	Chris SWANEPOEL	RSA	73	73	70	68	284	-4	11,500.00	8,212.76
25	Oliver WILSON	ENG	73	71	68	73	285	-3	9,900.00	7,070.12
	Rafael CABRERA BELLO	ESP	70	75	68	72	285	-3	9,900.00	7,070.12
	Marc CAYEUX	ZIM	75	71	68	71	285	-3	9,900.00	7,070.12
28	David DRYSDALE	SCO	73	72	74	67	286	-2	8,760.00	6,255.98
	Klas ERIKSSON	SWE	74	71	69	72	286	-2	8,760.00	6,255.98
	Edoardo MOLINARI	ITA	75	71	71	69	286	-2	8,760.00	6,255.98
	Simon DYSON	ENG	75	68	74	69	286	-2	8,760.00	6,255.98
	Alvaro VELASCO	ESP	70	74	71	71	286	-2	8,760.00	6,255.98
33	Gary BOYD	ENG	72	71	72	72	287	-1	7,500.00	5,356.15
	Alan MICHELL	RSA	72	73	72	70	287	-1	7,500.00	5,356.15
	Magnus A CARLSSON	SWE	72	71	74	70	287	-1	7,500.00	5,356.15
	Stuart MANLEY	WAL	71	72	75	69	287	-1	7,500.00	5,356.15
	Ross FISHER	ENG	76	70	73	68	287	-1	7,500.00	5,356.15
	Chris WILLIAMS	RSA	74	69	75	69	287	-1	7,500.00	5,356.15
	Darren CLARKE	NIR	73	69	70	75	287	-1	7,500.00	5,356.15
40	Philip GOLDING	ENG	72	72	73	71	288	0	6,300.00	4,499.16
	Alessandro TADINI	ITA	72	73	69	74	288	0	6,300.00	4,499.16
	Wallie COETSEE	RSA	72	71	71	74	288	0	6,300.00	4,499.16
	Grant VEENSTRA	RSA	73	70	72	73	288	0	6,300.00	4,499.16
	Pablo LARRAZABAL	ESP	70	70	74	74	288	0	6,300.00	4,499.16
45	Julio ZAPATA	ARG	77	69	69	74	289	1	5,400.00	3,856.43
	Sven STRÜVER	GER	72	73	76	68	289	1	5,400.00	3,856.43
	Joakim BÄCKSTRÖM	SWE	77	67	77	68	289	1	5,400.00	3,856.43
	Benn BARHAM	ENG	72	71	73	73	289	1	5,400.00	3,856.43
49	Dion FOURIE	RSA	72	71	75	72	290	2	4,700.00	3,356.52
	Anton HAIG	RSA	71	71	74	74	290	2	4,700.00	3,356.52
	Steven JEPPESEN	SWE	75	69	73	73	290	2	4,700.00	3,356.52
52	Stephen BROWNE	IRL	70	71	77	73	291	3	3,900.00	2,785.20
	Michiel BOTHMA	RSA	78	67	76	70	291	3	3,900.00	2,785.20
	Adilson DA SILVA	BRA	73	73	71	74	291	3	3,900.00	2,785.20
	James KINGSTON	RSA	71	74	77	69	291	3	3,900.00	2,785.20
	Tyrone VAN ASWEGEN	RSA	75	70	77	69	291	3	3,900.00	2,785.20
57	Alan MCLEAN	SCO	75	71	73	73	292	4	3,100.00	2,213.87
	Luis CLAVERIE	ESP	74	70	71	77	292	4	3,100.00	2,213.87
	Mikael LUNDBERG	SWE	76	67	73	76	292	4	3,100.00	2,213.87
	Jaco VAN ZYL	RSA	75	70	72	75	292	4	3,100.00	2,213.87
	Thomas AIKEN	RSA	74	70	74	74	292	4	3,100.00	2,213.87
62	Peter WHITEFORD	SCO	71	72	77	73	293	5	2,800.00	1,999.63
63	Gary CLARK	ENG	71	72	74	78	295	7	2,700.00	1,928.21
64	Doug McGUIGAN	RSA	74	67	75	80	296	8	2,600.00	1,856.80
65	Kevin STONE	RSA	73	71	81	76	301	13	2,500.00	1,785.38
66	Rossouw LOUBSER	RSA	74	71	80	77	302	14	2,400.00	1,713.97

i The Alfred Dunhill Championship made history by becoming the first European Tour event to be co-sanctioned with another Tour in 1995. The tournament was played at the Wanderers Club and won by Ernie Els who finished tied second behind John Bickerton this year.

Total Prize Fund

€991,600   £708,154

Slaying the Demon

	Player		Score	
1	James KINGSTON		284	-4
2	Oliver WILSON		285	-3
3	Darren CLARKE		287	-1
	Garth MULROY		287	-1
	Louis OOSTHUIZEN		287	-1
	Kyron SULLIVAN		287	-1
7	Nic HENNING		288	0
	Craig LILE		288	0
	Greg NORMAN		288	0
	Robert ROCK		288	0

Even on the face of it, James Kingston's victory at the South African Airways Open is a glorious story. The fact that his first European Tour victory in 20 years as a professional came in his national Open is a fairytale in itself, but perhaps the most engrossing element to the story is in the troubled history from where he emerged to slay his sporting demons en route to ultimate triumph at the Pearl Valley Golf Estates in Paarl, Western Cape.

Greg Norman

The demons in this particular story take the form of one of a golfer's most devastating nightmares – the 72nd hole collapse. There cannot be many more crushing blows for any professional than that of getting to within one hole of your ultimate goal, only to throw it all away.

What could be worse than that? Doing it twice, perhaps?

It was in December 2005, at the Omega Hong Kong Open, when Kingston was first haunted. Standing on the 72nd tee, the South African was level with Miguel Angel Jiménez but hooked his drive against a fence to hand the Spaniard the title.

Twelve months later, the Hong Kong Open had a new sponsor in UBS, but it had the same leader as the final round drew to a close. With three holes to play, Kingston, who had played gallantly for most of his round, led by two strokes before disaster struck again.

He three putted the 16th for bogey and then double bogeyed the 18th after, this time,

finding trouble to the right of the fairway from the tee, a mistake which allowed Scotland's Colin Montgomerie to triumph.

The 42 year old South African knew if he wanted to experience the joy of being a European Tour champion he was going to have overcome the final hole jitters, and where better to accomplish that than in the familiar surroundings of his homeland.

By the end of round two Kingston led the field by a stroke, with many of the game's biggest names trailing in his wake, amongst them the 2007 US Open Champion Angel Cabrera, Ryder Cup hero Darren Clarke, three time Major winner Ernie Els, double US Open Champion Retief Goosen, and former World Number One Greg Norman.

After a third round 67, England's Oliver Wilson appeared to be Kingston's main rival and so it proved to be as, after a dramatic final round in which the pair traded blows throughout, the duo arrived at the par five 72nd hole. Wilson, trailing by one, sent his drive into the distance and made way for Kingston on the tee. His moment had arrived – could he exorcise the ghosts of Hong Kong?

To his utmost credit, Kingston's focus was unnerving as he reached into his bag and drove straight through the heart of any self doubt in one perfect swing as his ball split the fairway in two.

With both players subsequently laying up, Wilson put his third shot on the green, some 20 feet from the cup. Kingston followed the Englishman's lead, his ball stopping 12 feet short of the hole, sparking a roar from the home crowd packed around the 18th green. Wilson's birdie attempt stayed above ground allowing Kingston two putts for the title, which he duly accepted before being overcome with emotion.

"That was the toughest day I have ever had," he said, both exhilarated and exhausted moments after signing his card. "I have had chances before and not made the most of those chances but, for once, I've clinched it. It's taken me 20 years to do it, but right now I feel it's all been worth the wait.

"I'm going to be joining some of our country's greatest names on the trophy and for me, winning South Africa's important title in front of my own people makes me very proud indeed."

The South African Airways Open has been a part of The European Tour International Schedule since 1997 although the tournament itself dates back to 1893. It is a fair bet that there may never have been a more thrilled, and relieved, champion in those 115 years.

Michael Gibbons

James Kingston (left), is presented with the trophy by Khaya Ngqula, President & CEO of South African Airways

Robert Rock

Oliver Wilson

Right *Andrew McLardy*

Below *Chris Evert*

Pearl Valley Golf Estates

Final Results

Pos	Name		Rd1	Rd2	Rd3	Rd4	Total		€	£
1	James KINGSTON	RSA	73	69	71	71	284	-4	158,500.00	114,557.06
2	Oliver WILSON	ENG	76	69	67	73	285	-3	115,000.00	83,117.11
3	Louis OOSTHUIZEN	RSA	78	72	66	71	287	-1	48,750.00	35,234.43
	Garth MULROY	RSA	80	70	64	73	287	-1	48,750.00	35,234.43
	Kyron SULLIVAN	WAL	72	71	73	71	287	-1	48,750.00	35,234.43
	Darren CLARKE	NIR	72	73	74	68	287	-1	48,750.00	35,234.43
7	Nic HENNING	RSA	74	71	70	73	288	0	23,825.00	17,219.70
	Greg NORMAN	AUS	75	70	72	71	288	0	23,825.00	17,219.70
	Craig LILE	RSA	73	73	72	70	288	0	23,825.00	17,219.70
	Robert ROCK	ENG	70	75	71	72	288	0	23,825.00	17,219.70
11	Alan MICHELL	RSA	76	74	68	71	289	1	16,766.67	12,118.23
	Simon DYSON	ENG	75	76	71	67	289	1	16,766.67	12,118.23
	Andrew MCLARDY	RSA	72	71	73	73	289	1	16,766.67	12,118.23
14	Garry HOUSTON	WAL	76	73	68	73	290	2	14,700.00	10,624.53
15	Edoardo MOLINARI	ITA	75	74	72	71	292	4	14,200.00	10,263.16
16	Richard STERNE	RSA	74	72	75	72	293	5	12,720.00	9,193.47
	Charl SCHWARTZEL	RSA	71	76	71	75	293	5	12,720.00	9,193.47
	Joakim BÄCKSTRÖM	SWE	76	74	71	72	293	5	12,720.00	9,193.47
	Retief GOOSEN	RSA	74	74	70	75	293	5	12,720.00	9,193.47
	Ernie ELS	RSA	77	70	77	69	293	5	12,720.00	9,193.47
21	Miles TUNNICLIFF	ENG	77	74	69	74	294	6	10,500.00	7,588.95
	Alan MCLEAN	SCO	80	71	69	74	294	6	10,500.00	7,588.95
	Hennie OTTO	RSA	77	74	72	71	294	6	10,500.00	7,588.95
	Peter LAWRIE	IRL	74	75	71	74	294	6	10,500.00	7,588.95
	Magnus A CARLSSON	SWE	76	73	74	71	294	6	10,500.00	7,588.95
	François DELAMONTAGNE	FRA	75	74	71	74	294	6	10,500.00	7,588.95
	Fabrizio ZANOTTI	PAR	80	71	71	72	294	6	10,500.00	7,588.95
28	Gary BOYD	ENG	72	76	74	73	295	7	8,760.00	6,331.36
	Anton HAIG	RSA	75	74	72	74	295	7	8,760.00	6,331.36
	Andrew MCARTHUR	SCO	72	74	75	74	295	7	8,760.00	6,331.36
	Ulrich VAN DEN BERG	RSA	71	73	71	80	295	7	8,760.00	6,331.36
	Angel CABRERA	ARG	80	73	72	70	295	7	8,760.00	6,331.36
33	Luis CLAVERIE	ESP	79	74	69	74	296	8	7,800.00	5,637.51
	Lee S JAMES	ENG	76	75	73	72	296	8	7,800.00	5,637.51
	David FROST	RSA	73	80	75	68	296	8	7,800.00	5,637.51
	Joost LUITEN	NED	82	67	75	72	296	8	7,800.00	5,637.51
37	Thomas AIKEN	RSA	76	75	78	68	297	9	7,000.00	5,059.30
	Peter WHITEFORD	SCO	81	70	76	70	297	9	7,000.00	5,059.30
	Warren ABERY	RSA	76	74	71	76	297	9	7,000.00	5,059.30
	Neil SCHIETEKAT	RSA	72	73	81	71	297	9	7,000.00	5,059.30
41	David DIXON	ENG	76	75	73	74	298	10	6,300.00	4,553.37
	Tim CLARK	RSA	75	74	74	75	298	10	6,300.00	4,553.37
	Paul WARING	ENG	73	76	73	76	298	10	6,300.00	4,553.37
44	George COETZEE	RSA	73	76	75	75	299	11	5,566.67	4,023.35
	Michiel BOTHMA	RSA	85	68	73	73	299	11	5,566.67	4,023.35
	Patrik SJÖLAND	SWE	79	71	73	76	299	11	5,566.67	4,023.35
	Adilson DA SILVA	BRA	77	74	73	75	299	11	5,566.67	4,023.35
	Jean HUGO	RSA	78	75	75	71	299	11	5,566.67	4,023.35
	Keith HORNE	RSA	77	75	74	73	299	11	5,566.67	4,023.35
50	Richard BLAND	ENG	76	77	77	70	300	12	4,100.00	2,963.31
	Euan LITTLE	SCO	72	72	78	78	300	12	4,100.00	2,963.31
	Brett LIDDLE	RSA	77	71	78	74	300	12	4,100.00	2,963.31
	Birgir HAFTHORSSON	ISL	79	73	75	73	300	12	4,100.00	2,963.31
	Alvaro VELASCO	ESP	75	78	72	75	300	12	4,100.00	2,963.31
	Ryan TIPPING	RSA	74	75	70	81	300	12	4,100.00	2,963.31
	Alex HAINDL	RSA	71	78	71	80	300	12	4,100.00	2,963.31
57	Jaco VAN ZYL	RSA	74	77	71	79	301	13	3,200.00	2,312.82
	Mattias ELIASSON	SWE	79	73	72	77	301	13	3,200.00	2,312.82
	Marc CAYEUX	ZIM	78	73	74	76	301	13	3,200.00	2,312.82
60	Sam WALKER	ENG	80	73	76	73	302	14	2,850.00	2,059.86
	Mikael LUNDBERG	SWE	80	73	74	75	302	14	2,850.00	2,059.86
	Michael LORENZO-VERA	FRA	75	71	78	78	302	14	2,850.00	2,059.86
	Pablo LARRAZABAL	ESP	79	72	75	76	302	14	2,850.00	2,059.86
64	Chris WILLIAMS	RSA	77	74	73	79	303	15	2,600.00	1,879.17
65	Mathias GRÖNBERG	SWE	79	74	74	77	304	16	2,500.00	1,806.89
66	Grant MULLER	RSA	78	75	73	79	305	17	2,350.00	1,698.48
	Ross WELLINGTON	RSA	76	72	76	81	305	17	2,350.00	1,698.48
68	Lee SLATTERY	ENG	76	76	78	79	309	21	2,200.00	1,590.07
69	Steven JEPPESEN	SWE	74	78	75	87	314	26	2,100.00	1,517.79

Hole	Par	Yards	Metres
1	4	427	390
2	4	427	390
3	5	623	570
4	3	224	205
5	5	530	485
6	4	363	332
7	4	427	390
8	3	229	209
9	4	471	431
OUT	**36**	**3721**	**3402**
10	4	386	353
11	4	441	403
12	3	200	183
13	5	581	531
14	4	389	356
15	3	214	196
16	4	462	422
17	4	443	405
18	5	601	550
IN	**36**	**3717**	**3399**
TOTAL	**72**	**7438**	**6801**

James Kingston became the sixth different South African to win the South African Airways Open since the event became part of The European Tour International Schedule in 1997. He followed Ernie Els (1998 and 2007), David Frost (1999), Tim Clark (2002), Trevor Immelman (2003 and 2004) and Retief Goosen (2006).

Total Prize Fund

€999,200   £722,179

Little Man, Big Heart

PLAYER	HOLE	SCORE	PLAYER	HOLE	SCO
MULROY	18	-13	MOOLMAN	18	-
STERNE	18	-13	MURLESS	18	-
CARLSSON	18	-13	FERREIRA	18	-
CLARKE	18	-11			
WILLIAMS	18	- 9			

1	Richard STERNE		271	-13
2	Magnus A CARLSSON		271	-13
	Garth MULROY		271	-13
4	Darren CLARKE		273	-11
5	Louis MOOLMAN		275	-9
	Mark MURLESS		275	-9
	Chris WILLIAMS		275	-9
8	Tyrone FERREIRA		276	-8
9	Ariel CANETE		277	-7
	Ian GARBUTT		277	-7
	Dawie VAN DER WALT		277	-7
	Sven STRÜVER		277	-7
	Paul WARING		277	-7

S ize matters, or so sporting folklore would appear to indicate. A cursory glance around the globe and everywhere there seems to be some towering athletic titan with silverware clutched in his huge hands. In this world there would appear to be little room for the vertically challenged – well, try telling that to Richard Sterne.

Garth Mulroy

Mark Murless

At only five feet seven inches tall in his socks and a mere 150 pounds dripping wet, the man from the city of Pretoria in Gauteng Province, some 50 kilometres north of Johannesburg, is the classic example of Little Man, Big Heart.

Sterne, by coincidence, shares the same vital statistics as another of his fellow South Africans, no less a figure than 'The Black Knight' himself, Gary Player. Lack of physical stature did little to impede Player's rise to iconic status in the golfing world, and Sterne displays all the signs of following the same path.

True, Player had laid claim to a Masters Tournament Green Jacket and a Claret Jug as Open Champion by the same age, but it could be argued that the competition in the upper echelons of professional golf has never been stiffer than is apparent nowadays.

Sterne has often looked like a superstar in waiting. With a compact, powerful swing, a low centre of gravity and forearms akin to Craig 'Popeye' Parry of Australia, the 26 year old can beat the golf ball enormous distances.

It was that raw power which served him well in his homeland, as he collected the Joburg Open trophy at Royal Johannesburg and Kensington Golf Club – his third European Tour title.

Over the past four seasons on The European Tour International Schedule, he has averaged between 288 yards and 302 yards in Driving Distance on the Genworth Financial Statistics. That deceptive strength lurking beneath a wiry frame came into play more than once over the 7590 yard, par 71 East Course, the course used for three of the four rounds.

As the tournament reached a crescendo, Sterne revealed a combination of guile, nerve and muscle to get into contention. Rounds of 71-68-67 had left him four shots adrift of 54 hole leader, fellow countryman Mark Murless, while a resurgent Darren Clarke of Northern Ireland was one of ten players ahead of him.

Sterne, though, picked his way through the field like a Grand National jockey plotting a route around Aintree. He birdied both the 17th and the 18th for a 65 to set the clubhouse target of 13 under par 271. After Sweden's Magnus A Carlsson and another South African, Garth Mulroy, tied that total, it was back to the 18th tee. Sterne, a reserved and laid back

individual, then shone like a beacon in the Johannesburg night.

After catching a fairway bunker from the tee, he proceeded to pummel a four iron from the sand some 216 yards to 15 feet above the hole. Two putts and two fine up and downs by his rivals ensured a return for them all to the 18th tee.

This time, Sterne's rippling forearms helped propel a drive in excess of 315 yards down the middle. A mid-iron approach and two putts later it was all over, a second birdie four neither Carlsson nor Mulroy could match.

"It was close all day so it required some special things to win," said Sterne, whose calm persona was illustrated after signing his card at the end of regulation play. While Carlsson headed to the putting green, Sterne chose to put his feet up on the clubhouse veranda until Mulroy – a

Durban native based in the United States – had completed his round.

Reflecting on his play-off bunker shot, he admitted: "That was pretty impressive, even if I say so myself. I thought about laying up, but it was a play-off and the shot was 50-50 in terms of getting it right. However I thought it was on, and I went for it."

Fortune, on this occasion, favoured the brave. Carlsson and Mulroy could be proud of their week's work but if Sterne follows the Player mantra – 'The harder I practise, the luckier I get' – then this unassuming South African has the scope to join the list of his country's Major Champions.

Gordon Simpson

Richard Sterne (left), is presented with the trophy by Councillor Amos Masondo, the Executive Mayor of Johannesburg

Magnus A Carlsson

Joburg Open

5

Par 3
177 Yards
162 Metres

WEST COURSE			
Hole	Par	Yards	Metres
1	4	409	374
2	5	536	490
3	4	465	425
4	4	386	353
5	3	121	111
6	4	408	373
7	4	492	450
8	3	234	214
9	5	554	507
OUT	36	3605	3297
10	4	422	386
11	4	372	340
12	4	451	412
13	3	206	188
14	4	475	434
15	5	535	489
16	3	178	163
17	4	381	348
18	4	494	452
IN	35	3514	3212
TOTAL	71	7119	6509

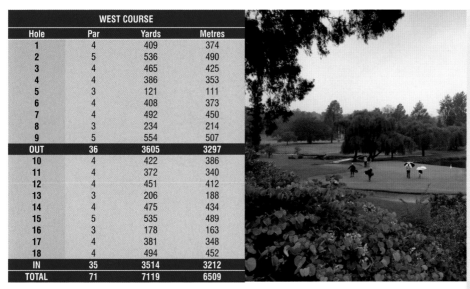

Darren Clarke

EAST COURSE			
Hole	Par	Yards	Metres
1	4	516	472
2	3	253	231
3	4	475	434
4	4	476	435
5	3	177	162
6	5	580	530
7	4	420	384
8	5	553	506
9	4	425	389
OUT	36	3875	3543
10	4	518	474
11	4	500	457
12	3	198	181
13	4	420	384
14	4	452	413
15	4	481	440
16	3	208	190
17	4	387	354
18	5	551	504
IN	35	3715	3397
TOTAL	71	7590	6940

Richard Sterne's third European Tour victory at the Joburg Open was the 83rd victory in total by South African players in European Tour history.

Royal Johannesburg and Kensington Golf Club
(East Course and West Course)

Final Results

Pos	Name		Rd1	Rd2	Rd3	Rd4	Total		€	£
1	Richard STERNE	RSA	71	68	67	65	271	-13	174,350.00	130,482.94
2	Magnus A CARLSSON	SWE	70	66	69	66	271	-13	101,310.00	75,820.06
	Garth MULROY	RSA	67	72	66	66	271	-13	101,310.00	75,820.06
4	Darren CLARKE	NIR	73	65	67	68	273	-11	54,010.00	40,420.90
5	Mark MURLESS	RSA	65	68	69	73	275	-9	38,940.00	29,142.56
	Chris WILLIAMS	RSA	73	65	67	70	275	-9	38,940.00	29,142.56
	Louis MOOLMAN	RSA	68	69	69	69	275	-9	38,940.00	29,142.56
8	Tyrone FERREIRA	RSA	65	70	69	72	276	-8	27,060.00	20,251.61
9	Dawie VAN DER WALT	RSA	74	65	68	70	277	-7	20,130.00	15,065.22
	Paul WARING	ENG	69	67	69	72	277	-7	20,130.00	15,065.22
	Sven STRÜVER	GER	67	71	66	73	277	-7	20,130.00	15,065.22
	Ian GARBUTT	ENG	71	69	68	69	277	-7	20,130.00	15,065.22
	Ariel CANETE	ARG	70	70	67	70	277	-7	20,130.00	15,065.22
14	Charl SCHWARTZEL	RSA	70	69	70	69	278	-6	14,535.71	10,878.48
	Justin WALTERS	ENG	73	67	69	69	278	-6	14,535.71	10,878.48
	Warren ABERY	RSA	70	65	71	72	278	-6	14,535.71	10,878.48
	Iain PYMAN	ENG	68	68	73	69	278	-6	14,535.71	10,878.48
	Andrew MCLARDY	RSA	68	73	67	70	278	-6	14,535.71	10,878.48
	Jake ROOS	RSA	71	71	67	69	278	-6	14,535.71	10,878.48
	Ross McGOWAN	ENG	66	75	64	73	278	-6	14,535.71	10,878.48
21	James KAMTE	RSA	68	71	70	70	279	-5	12,045.00	9,014.44
	Pablo LARRAZABAL	ESP	66	68	70	75	279	-5	12,045.00	9,014.44
	Chris GANE	ENG	73	69	70	67	279	-5	12,045.00	9,014.44
	Lee S JAMES	ENG	72	68	68	71	279	-5	12,045.00	9,014.44
25	Stephen GALLACHER	SCO	70	70	70	70	280	-4	10,245.71	7,667.85
	Kyron SULLIVAN	WAL	74	67	67	72	280	-4	10,245.71	7,667.85
	Gary LOCKERBIE	ENG	67	71	70	72	280	-4	10,245.71	7,667.85
	Craig LEE	SCO	74	68	68	70	280	-4	10,245.71	7,667.85
	Liam BOND	WAL	71	71	70	69	280	-4	10,245.71	7,667.85
	Dave HORSEY	ENG	72	69	69	70	280	-4	10,245.71	7,667.85
	Trevor FISHER JNR	RSA	68	73	71	68	280	-4	10,245.71	7,667.85
32	Gary BOYD	ENG	68	69	70	74	281	-3	8,250.00	6,174.27
	Marcel SIEM	GER	68	71	70	72	281	-3	8,250.00	6,174.27
	Hendrik BUHRMANN	RSA	70	71	68	72	281	-3	8,250.00	6,174.27
	Raphaël JACQUELIN	FRA	72	70	68	71	281	-3	8,250.00	6,174.27
	Klas ERIKSSON	SWE	70	72	71	68	281	-3	8,250.00	6,174.27
	Louis OOSTHUIZEN	RSA	68	74	69	70	281	-3	8,250.00	6,174.27
	John MELLOR	ENG	69	71	69	72	281	-3	8,250.00	6,174.27
	Martin WIEGELE	AUT	71	68	71	71	281	-3	8,250.00	6,174.27
	Robert ROCK	ENG	74	65	68	74	281	-3	8,250.00	6,174.27
41	André CRUSE	RSA	69	68	72	73	282	-2	6,710.00	5,021.74
	James KINGSTON	RSA	68	73	72	69	282	-2	6,710.00	5,021.74
	Jbe' KRUGER	RSA	72	70	68	72	282	-2	6,710.00	5,021.74
	Oliver BEKKER	RSA	67	74	69	72	282	-2	6,710.00	5,021.74
	Charl COETZEE	RSA	68	67	72	75	282	-2	6,710.00	5,021.74
46	Alex HAINDL	RSA	68	68	76	71	283	-1	5,170.00	3,869.21
	Marcus HIGLEY	ENG	68	72	69	74	283	-1	5,170.00	3,869.21
	Richard BLAND	ENG	68	74	68	73	283	-1	5,170.00	3,869.21
	Joakim BÄCKSTRÖM	SWE	68	68	72	75	283	-1	5,170.00	3,869.21
	Ben MASON	ENG	70	72	69	72	283	-1	5,170.00	3,869.21
	Brandon PIETERS	RSA	70	68	69	76	283	-1	5,170.00	3,869.21
	Craig LILE	RSA	70	72	71	70	283	-1	5,170.00	3,869.21
	Jeppe HULDAHL	DEN	71	71	72	69	283	-1	5,170.00	3,869.21
	Andrew MCARTHUR	SCO	73	69	68	73	283	-1	5,170.00	3,869.21
55	Florian PRAEGANT	AUT	74	65	74	71	284	0	3,767.50	2,819.58
	Jaco VAN ZYL	RSA	70	74	68	72	284	0	3,767.50	2,819.58
	Edward RUSH	ENG	70	69	73	72	284	0	3,767.50	2,819.58
	Marco SOFFIETTI	ITA	70	72	71	71	284	0	3,767.50	2,819.58
59	Sion E BEBB	WAL	66	73	73	73	285	1	3,245.00	2,428.55
	Marco RUIZ	PAR	67	71	76	71	285	1	3,245.00	2,428.55
	Juan ABBATE	ARG	76	66	73	70	285	1	3,245.00	2,428.55
	Benoit TEILLERIA	FRA	71	70	69	75	285	1	3,245.00	2,428.55
63	François DELAMONTAGNE	FRA	70	71	73	72	286	2	2,805.00	2,099.25
	David DRYSDALE	SCO	67	73	73	73	286	2	2,805.00	2,099.25
	Deane PAPPAS	RSA	72	69	73	72	286	2	2,805.00	2,099.25
	Branden GRACE	RSA	76	65	71	74	286	2	2,805.00	2,099.25
67	Prinavin NELSON	RSA	68	72	77	70	287	3	2,420.00	1,811.12
	Brett LIDDLE	RSA	74	66	74	73	287	3	2,420.00	1,811.12
	Edoardo MOLINARI	ITA	70	72	72	73	287	3	2,420.00	1,811.12
70	Jan-Are LARSEN	NOR	73	69	70	76	288	4	1,832.33	1,371.31
	Ryan REID	RSA	67	75	71	75	288	4	1,832.33	1,371.31
	Werner GEYER	RSA	70	72	72	74	288	4	1,832.33	1,371.31
73	Doug McGUIGAN	RSA	71	71	72	75	289	5	1,642.50	1,229.24
	Jamie DONALDSON	WAL	70	71	72	76	289	5	1,642.50	1,229.24
75	Warren BENNETT	ENG	69	72	73	76	290	6	1,638.00	1,225.87
76	Henk ALBERTS	RSA	71	71	74	75	291	7	1,632.00	1,221.38
	Patrik SJÖLAND	SWE	75	67	75	74	291	7	1,632.00	1,221.38
	Teboho SEFATSA	RSA	68	74	77	72	291	7	1,632.00	1,221.38
79	Bobby LINCOLN	RSA	71	71	78	72	292	8	1,626.00	1,216.89
80	Gary EMERSON	ENG	69	72	74	78	293	9	1,623.00	1,214.65

Total Prize Fund

€1,116,585 £835,648

Technically Correct

1	**Martin KAYMER**		273	-15
2	Henrik STENSON		277	-11
	Lee WESTWOOD		277	-11
4	Richard FINCH		278	-10
	Ignacio GARRIDO		278	-10
	Peter HEDBLOM		278	-10
7	James KINGSTON		279	-9
	Scott STRANGE		279	-9
9	Paul McGINLEY		280	-8
	Ian POULTER		280	-8

Abu Dhabi Golf Championship

When you are in your second season as a professional, not yet 24, and arrive at a tournament where eight of the world's top 25 are also competing, you do not expect much notice to be taken of you - even if you were The Sir Henry Cotton Rookie of the Year the previous season.

On the other hand when you lead a tournament from start to finish, take a six stroke lead after 36 holes and then withstand the challenges of several of the world's best players who are older and more experienced, you have every right to expect people to sit up and take notice.

That is precisely what happened to Martin Kaymer over the space of four days in the desert in January. The young German arrived as a contender for the Abu Dhabi Golf Championship and left as the champion. It was a remarkable performance and it suggested that a new star had arisen on The European Tour.

When Kaymer took the lead on Thursday with a 66 he grabbed our attention, not only because six under par was a very good score on a difficult golf course, but also because of the quality of players who were left in his wake.

To be honest, though, there was a suspicion he would soon begin to slither down the leaderboard. We knew he was a powerful hitter with a tidy iron game who had eagled the first hole of the event, but once the top players got the measure of the course we fully expected them to reel him in.

It took less than 24 hours to realise this was not going to happen. Well before lunch on Friday, Kaymer appeared with a better score in the second round than his 66 in the first. Indeed, his 65 represented an early claim to be one of the rounds of the year.

From one stroke ahead after 18 holes, Kaymer was now six strokes clear at 13 under par 131, one stroke less than the record lead in a European Tour event at the halfway stage. "That is sensational golf," said Darren Clarke. "I have never played with him but he must be a very, very good player. I can't praise him highly enough because this course is tough, a fantastic test of golf."

At this stage the story was assuming the proportions of a fairytale. A young man, ranked 76th on the Official World Golf Ranking, enters his first tournament of the year after a month long lay-off and goes about spread-eagling the field. He is asked how he feels and admits it is all a bit of a surprise but then remembers he had rounds of 59 and 60 on the third level EPD Tour in his native Germany before joining the European Challenge Tour, and a 61 in the inaugural Portugal Masters on The European

Left to right: HRH The Duke of York, Martin Kaymer and His Highness Sheikh Sultan Bin Tahnoon Al Nahyan, Chairman, Abu Dhabi Tourism Authority

Ignacio Garrido

Peter Hedblom

Richard Finch

Rory McIlroy

Tour in October 2007. Suddenly, perhaps, it is not such a surprise after all.

Saturday's third round of 68 might have been his highest of the week to date but his lead still remained at six strokes. Just as the professionals say that the hardest shot in golf is a long bunker shot, so they also say how hard it is to defend a lead. Could Kaymer hold on? Indeed he could.

Though Lee Westwood got to within two strokes after 12 holes, Kaymer birdied the 72nd to finish at 15 under par 273, four strokes ahead of the Englishman and Sweden's Henrik Stenson.

After that there arose a feeling that a special player had emerged. "He looks a real talent," said Westwood. "I have seen him on the practice ground and he is technically very correct."

If it had been premature to talk about Kaymer and The Ryder Cup at the end of his first round, it got less and less the longer the event went on. At 23 years and 24 days old he became the youngest German winner in the history of The European Tour, beating Bernhard Langer who

had been 23 years and 38 days when he won the 1980 Dunlop Masters.

Kaymer had ended the 2007 season well, not finishing outside the top 25 in any of his last six events, including the Volvo Masters where he finished in a tie for sixth place on his first look at Club de Golf Valderrama.

In Abu Dhabi he had said he wanted a good finish to give his World Ranking a boost and he certainly achieved that, moving from 76th to 34th place which, apart from anything else, secured his debut in a World Golf Championship event as he booked his place in the starting line-up for the WGC – Accenture Match Play in Arizona the following month.

We may not have known much about him before the start of the week, but it appears we will be hearing a lot more about Martin Kaymer in the future.

John Hopkins
The Times

The official sponsor of the European Tour Statistics

think it possible.com℠

Genworth℗
Financial

Paul McGinley

Abu Dhabi Golf Club

Final Results

Pos	Name		Rd1	Rd2	Rd3	Rd4	Total		€	£
1	Martin KAYMER	GER	66	65	68	74	273	-15	225,421.38	170,135.76
2	Henrik STENSON	SWE	67	70	69	71	277	-11	117,475.02	88,663.74
	Lee WESTWOOD	ENG	69	73	65	70	277	-11	117,475.02	88,663.74
4	Ignacio GARRIDO	ESP	69	70	70	69	278	-10	57,437.94	43,351.02
	Peter HEDBLOM	SWE	69	70	69	70	278	-10	57,437.94	43,351.02
	Richard FINCH	ENG	71	70	69	68	278	-10	57,437.94	43,351.02
7	Scott STRANGE	AUS	72	71	66	70	279	-9	37,194.90	28,072.68
	James KINGSTON	RSA	71	68	72	68	279	-9	37,194.90	28,072.68
9	Paul MCGINLEY	IRL	72	71	66	71	280	-8	28,673.89	21,641.49
	Ian POULTER	ENG	70	70	73	67	280	-8	28,673.89	21,641.49
11	Padraig HARRINGTON	IRL	72	72	69	68	281	-7	21,595.58	16,299.17
	Robert KARLSSON	SWE	68	72	70	71	281	-7	21,595.58	16,299.17
	Rory MCILROY	NIR	73	71	69	68	281	-7	21,595.58	16,299.17
	Oliver FISHER	ENG	72	71	69	69	281	-7	21,595.58	16,299.17
	Alexander NOREN	SWE	70	72	69	70	281	-7	21,595.58	16,299.17
	Luke DONALD	ENG	71	73	67	70	281	-7	21,595.58	16,299.17
17	Alvaro QUIROS	ESP	73	69	68	72	282	-6	16,613.72	12,539.13
	Ricardo GONZALEZ	ARG	71	70	72	69	282	-6	16,613.72	12,539.13
	Steve WEBSTER	ENG	70	68	71	73	282	-6	16,613.72	12,539.13
	Richard GREEN	AUS	75	68	73	66	282	-6	16,613.72	12,539.13
	Anthony WALL	ENG	71	69	65	77	282	-6	16,613.72	12,539.13
	Peter LAWRIE	IRL	73	70	70	69	282	-6	16,613.72	12,539.13
23	Andrew MCLARDY	RSA	71	72	69	71	283	-5	13,660.67	10,310.33
	Colin MONTGOMERIE	SCO	72	72	68	71	283	-5	13,660.67	10,310.33
	Thomas LEVET	FRA	70	72	68	73	283	-5	13,660.67	10,310.33
	Maarten LAFEBER	NED	74	69	68	72	283	-5	13,660.67	10,310.33
	Simon DYSON	ENG	73	71	68	71	283	-5	13,660.67	10,310.33
	Adam SCOTT	AUS	68	74	71	70	283	-5	13,660.67	10,310.33
	Jamie DONALDSON	WAL	70	71	71	71	283	-5	13,660.67	10,310.33
30	Daniel VANCSIK	ARG	71	71	73	69	284	-4	11,428.98	8,625.97
	Leif WESTERBERG	SWE	72	73	69	70	284	-4	11,428.98	8,625.97
	Phillip ARCHER	ENG	71	68	73	72	284	-4	11,428.98	8,625.97
	Paul LAWRIE	SCO	70	73	71	70	284	-4	11,428.98	8,625.97
34	Søren HANSEN	DEN	71	71	74	69	285	-3	9,873.56	7,452.02
	Mark FOSTER	ENG	70	70	69	76	285	-3	9,873.56	7,452.02
	Thongchai JAIDEE	THA	71	74	68	72	285	-3	9,873.56	7,452.02
	Paul SHEEHAN	AUS	73	72	70	70	285	-3	9,873.56	7,452.02
	Charl SCHWARTZEL	RSA	70	70	72	73	285	-3	9,873.56	7,452.02
39	Mikko ILONEN	FIN	70	74	70	72	286	-2	8,656.27	6,533.28
	Rhys DAVIES	WAL	73	71	72	70	286	-2	8,656.27	6,533.28
	Francesco MOLINARI	ITA	73	71	71	71	286	-2	8,656.27	6,533.28
	John BICKERTON	ENG	71	70	71	74	286	-2	8,656.27	6,533.28
43	Fredrik ANDERSSON HED	SWE	71	72	73	71	287	-1	7,168.47	5,410.37
	Johan EDFORS	SWE	73	71	70	73	287	-1	7,168.47	5,410.37
	Sam LITTLE	ENG	75	69	71	72	287	-1	7,168.47	5,410.37
	Miguel Angel JIMÉNEZ	ESP	74	69	73	71	287	-1	7,168.47	5,410.37
	Paul BROADHURST	ENG	72	72	68	75	287	-1	7,168.47	5,410.37
	Peter HANSON	SWE	74	70	69	74	287	-1	7,168.47	5,410.37
	Gonzalo FDEZ-CASTAÑO	ESP	70	68	76	73	287	-1	7,168.47	5,410.37
50	Nick DOUGHERTY	ENG	72	71	69	76	288	0	5,545.42	4,185.38
	Chapchai NIRAT	THA	73	72	73	70	288	0	5,545.42	4,185.38
	Jean-François LUCQUIN	FRA	71	72	71	74	288	0	5,545.42	4,185.38
	Henrik NYSTRÖM	SWE	73	71	73	71	288	0	5,545.42	4,185.38
	David LYNN	ENG	74	70	73	71	288	0	5,545.42	4,185.38
55	Michael LORENZO-VERA	FRA	71	73	73	72	289	1	4,463.39	3,368.72
	Matt WEIBRING	USA	74	70	75	70	289	1	4,463.39	3,368.72
	Thomas AIKEN	RSA	70	75	69	75	289	1	4,463.39	3,368.72
58	Jean-Baptiste GONNET	FRA	74	71	70	75	290	2	3,922.37	2,960.39
	Martin ERLANDSSON	SWE	75	70	70	75	290	2	3,922.37	2,960.39
	Damien MCGRANE	IRL	70	72	73	75	290	2	3,922.37	2,960.39
61	Darren CLARKE	NIR	72	72	74	73	291	3	3,584.24	2,705.19
	Simon WAKEFIELD	ENG	72	71	73	75	291	3	3,584.24	2,705.19
63	Benn BARHAM	ENG	74	71	75	72	292	4	3,313.73	2,501.02
	José-Filipe LIMA	POR	71	73	74	74	292	4	3,313.73	2,501.02
65	Louis OOSTHUIZEN	RSA	72	73	73	76	294	6	3,043.22	2,296.86
	Phillip PRICE	WAL	73	71	75	75	294	6	3,043.22	2,296.86
67	Thomas BJÖRN	DEN	73	70	72	80	295	7	2,772.71	2,092.69
	Rafa ECHENIQUE	ARG	75	68	76	76	295	7	2,772.71	2,092.69

Total Prize Fund

€1,347,504 £1,017,022

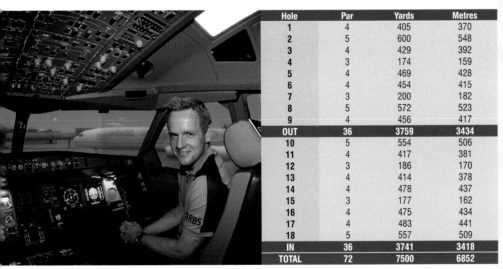

Hole	Par	Yards	Metres
1	4	405	370
2	5	600	548
3	4	429	392
4	3	174	159
5	4	469	428
6	4	454	415
7	3	200	182
8	5	572	523
9	4	456	417
OUT	36	3759	3434
10	5	554	506
11	4	417	381
12	3	186	170
13	4	414	378
14	4	478	437
15	3	177	162
16	4	475	434
17	4	483	441
18	5	557	509
IN	36	3741	3418
TOTAL	72	7500	6852

Luke Donald

In winning the Abu Dhabi Golf Championship, Martin Kaymer became the first wire-to-wire winner of the 2008 season. He was also the sixth different German to enter the winners' enclosure, following Alex Cejka, Tobias Dier, Bernhard Langer, Marcel Siem and Sven Strüver.

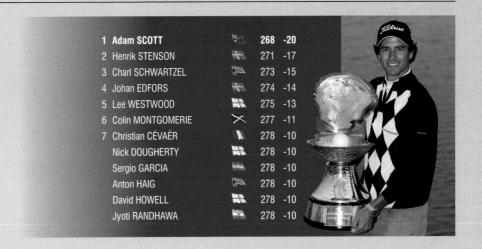

1	Adam SCOTT		268	-20
2	Henrik STENSON		271	-17
3	Charl SCHWARTZEL		273	-15
4	Johan EDFORS		274	-14
5	Lee WESTWOOD		275	-13
6	Colin MONTGOMERIE		277	-11
7	Christian CÉVAËR		278	-10
	Nick DOUGHERTY		278	-10
	Sergio GARCIA		278	-10
	Anton HAIG		278	-10
	David HOWELL		278	-10
	Jyoti RANDHAWA		278	-10

Sublime Control

Compiled from results over a rolling two year period, the Official World Golf Ranking is a fairly accurate guide to ability. So when Australian Adam Scott arrived in Qatar with the highest ranking in the field of eighth, his place among the pre-tournament favourites was assured.

Furthermore, having won the tournament on his only previous visit to Doha Golf Club in 2002, he brought a proven track record with him to the 2008 Commercialbank Qatar Masters presented by Dolphin Energy. Thus Scott's eventual three shot victory could never be construed as a surprise.

One factor which did fit into that category, however, was the weather. Cold and overcast with outbreaks of rain, it caught several players on the hop who had travelled with only tee shirts and suntan lotion for company and led to the Club shop experiencing a heavy and unprecedented departure of pullovers and fleeces from its shelves throughout the week.

On the expansive practice ground with its new sheltered bays, ironically designed for protection against the burning sun, there was almost universal agreement about the direction in which the tournament would head.

A lack of water in the weeks leading up to the event had restricted the growth of the rough which normally protects the 7,388 yard layout and, without the normal premium placed upon accuracy, it was generally felt the course would be at the mercy of the field's bigger hitters.

One of the sponsors had generously offered a BMW 6 Series to any player who could break Doha Golf Club's course record of 63 set by Robert Karlsson and Mark Pilkington in 2001, and few players expected the car to still be in place by the end of the week. None, however, could have predicted the spectacular way the record was eventually toppled.

A strong wind for the first two days kept the scoring within bounds, although the opening 67s served up by South Africa's Anton Haig, maximizing the power within his towering frame, and England's Lee Westwood, who had spent the winter improving his upper body strength, gave a hint of events to follow.

But the two sides to the power game and the driver friendly nature of the course was perhaps best illustrated in some of the detail of the second round 68 carded by David Howell. After signing his card the Englishman described how,

at the 16th, his wayward drive had landed in scrubland between two sizeable boulders but, once he had moved them aside, he was able to chip and make birdie.

The third round saw a welcome return to form for Scotsman Andrew Coltart who lost his playing privileges at the end of the 2007 season and who was hoping his 65, which moved him into second place behind Sweden's

HOLE	PLAYER	PAR
18	SCOTT	-20
18	STENSON	-17
18	SCHWARTZEL	-15
18	EDFORS	-14
18	WESTWOOD	-13
18	MONTGOMERIE	-11
MATCH NO	AFTER 17	SCORE

Colin Montgomerie

Left to right: Andrew Stevens, Group CEO Commercialbank, Adam Scott and Hassan Al-Naimi, President of the Qatar Golf Association

Henrik Stenson

Lee Westwood

Johan Edfors, would be a platform from which to relaunch his career.

The Scot eventually finished in a creditable share of 13th place but it was in another Saturday pairing that seeds for the eventual outcome of the tournament were sown. Playing alongside the Ulster teenager Rory McIlroy, who himself was six under for the day, Scott recovered from dropping a shot to par overall in the second round to post a fine 65.

It set the stage for an intriguing final round as the class of players such as Henrik Stenson, who had moved into a share of third place after a Saturday 67, mixed with the youthful experience of McIlroy, the raw power of Haig and Edfors, and the experience of Coltart and Scott in the shake up.

Stenson, after finishing joint second in the Abu Dhabi Golf Championship the previous week, rose to the challenge with a closing seven under par 65 which on almost every other Sunday would have taken the honours. But not in Qatar.

Instead it was Scott who swept to victory with an 11 under par 61 that was a sublime display of controlled golf. Starting with five straight birdies to immediately put pressure on the overnight leaders, he only missed two fairways in total, hit every green in regulation and holed more than a half a dozen putts in the crucial ten to 20 foot range on his way to a 20 under par total of 268.

Scott's victory, however, was welcomed not just because of the superb quality of his golf. When the tournament was over he also confirmed that, after spending five years based primarily on the US PGA Tour, he would, in future, be returning more to The European Tour and would hope to compete for the Order of Merit this season and the Race to Dubai from 2009 onwards.

On the evidence of an amazing Sunday afternoon in Qatar, the whole European golf scene will be all the richer for his decision.

Graham Otway

Commercialbank has played a part in the growth and prosperity of Qatar since 1975, financing the very infrastructure of the country and providing banking services of established value. We will always conduct our business here with ethics and integrity, reaching out to every aspect of Qatari life, in celebration of the place that we call home. Why? Because each and every one of us at Commercialbank lives here too. We are proud to be inspired by Qatar.

قطر مصدر الهامنا

Supporting Qatar since 1975

Johan Edfors

Below *Jane Seymour, one of the many stars who played in the Pro-Am*

Doha Golf Club

Final Results

Pos	Name		Rd1	Rd2	Rd3	Rd4	Total		€	£
1	Adam SCOTT	AUS	69	73	65	61	268	-20	285,071.48	213,354.50
2	Henrik STENSON	SWE	69	70	67	65	271	-17	190,045.37	142,234.62
3	Charl SCHWARTZEL	RSA	70	67	69	67	273	-15	107,074.56	80,137.23
4	Johan EDFORS	SWE	69	66	69	70	274	-14	85,522.81	64,007.37
5	Lee WESTWOOD	ENG	67	70	73	65	275	-13	72,523.34	54,278.25
6	Colin MONTGOMERIE	SCO	71	68	69	69	277	-11	59,865.97	44,805.16
7	David HOWELL	ENG	70	68	71	69	278	-10	37,915.11	28,376.60
	Sergio GARCIA	ESP	69	75	67	67	278	-10	37,915.11	28,376.60
	Jyoti RANDHAWA	IND	70	70	72	66	278	-10	37,915.11	28,376.60
	Christian CÉVAËR	FRA	71	69	68	70	278	-10	37,915.11	28,376.60
	Nick DOUGHERTY	ENG	72	67	70	69	278	-10	37,915.11	28,376.60
	Anton HAIG	RSA	67	71	69	71	278	-10	37,915.11	28,376.60
13	Ross McGOWAN	ENG	70	68	69	72	279	-9	24,190.74	18,104.94
	Andrew COLTART	SCO	70	70	65	74	279	-9	24,190.74	18,104.94
	Alexander NOREN	SWE	69	69	72	69	279	-9	24,190.74	18,104.94
	Jean-Baptiste GONNET	FRA	71	72	68	68	279	-9	24,190.74	18,104.94
	Marc WARREN	SCO	74	70	67	68	279	-9	24,190.74	18,104.94
	Emanuele CANONICA	ITA	73	68	70	68	279	-9	24,190.74	18,104.94
	Steve WEBSTER	ENG	72	70	67	70	279	-9	24,190.74	18,104.94
20	Søren KJELDSEN	DEN	70	72	69	69	280	-8	19,362.36	14,491.27
	Raphaël JACQUELIN	FRA	71	72	69	68	280	-8	19,362.36	14,491.27
	José Manuel LARA	ESP	71	72	68	69	280	-8	19,362.36	14,491.27
	Graeme MCDOWELL	NIR	70	71	70	69	280	-8	19,362.36	14,491.27
	Oliver WILSON	ENG	72	68	70	70	280	-8	19,362.36	14,491.27
25	Ross FISHER	ENG	74	71	68	68	281	-7	15,992.77	11,969.38
	Oliver FISHER	ENG	72	73	67	69	281	-7	15,992.77	11,969.38
	Thongchai JAIDEE	THA	71	71	70	69	281	-7	15,992.77	11,969.38
	Louis OOSTHUIZEN	RSA	72	70	71	68	281	-7	15,992.77	11,969.38
	Luke DONALD	ENG	70	72	68	71	281	-7	15,992.77	11,969.38
	Anthony WALL	ENG	71	69	70	71	281	-7	15,992.77	11,969.38
	Paul LAWRIE	SCO	73	70	66	72	281	-7	15,992.77	11,969.38
	Francesco MOLINARI	ITA	71	70	70	70	281	-7	15,992.77	11,969.38
33	Grégory HAVRET	FRA	73	70	68	71	282	-6	12,163.24	9,103.27
	Thomas BJÖRN	DEN	72	72	68	70	282	-6	12,163.24	9,103.27
	Phillip ARCHER	ENG	71	70	69	72	282	-6	12,163.24	9,103.27
	Barry LANE	ENG	73	71	69	69	282	-6	12,163.24	9,103.27
	Damien MCGRANE	IRL	72	71	66	73	282	-6	12,163.24	9,103.27
	Grégory BOURDY	FRA	70	71	68	73	282	-6	12,163.24	9,103.27
	Gonzalo FDEZ-CASTAÑO	ESP	70	70	74	68	282	-6	12,163.24	9,103.27
	Scott STRANGE	AUS	71	73	69	69	282	-6	12,163.24	9,103.27
	Rory MCILROY	NIR	71	71	66	74	282	-6	12,163.24	9,103.27
42	Richard FINCH	ENG	72	73	71	67	283	-5	9,749.60	7,296.84
	Simon DYSON	ENG	72	70	71	70	283	-5	9,749.60	7,296.84
	Peter O'MALLEY	AUS	72	70	74	67	283	-5	9,749.60	7,296.84
	Søren HANSEN	DEN	72	69	73	69	283	-5	9,749.60	7,296.84
	Marcel SIEM	GER	69	72	71	71	283	-5	9,749.60	7,296.84
47	Jean-François LUCQUIN	FRA	71	71	71	71	284	-4	8,210.19	6,144.71
	Rolf MUNTZ	NED	73	71	72	68	284	-4	8,210.19	6,144.71
	Niclas FASTH	SWE	74	71	72	67	284	-4	8,210.19	6,144.71
	Shiv KAPUR	IND	73	68	74	69	284	-4	8,210.19	6,144.71
51	Phillip PRICE	WAL	73	72	70	70	285	-3	6,670.78	4,992.58
	Bradley DREDGE	WAL	73	72	71	69	285	-3	6,670.78	4,992.58
	Peter HANSON	SWE	75	70	69	71	285	-3	6,670.78	4,992.58
	Thomas LEVET	FRA	74	67	71	73	285	-3	6,670.78	4,992.58
	Martin ERLANDSSON	SWE	72	72	73	68	285	-3	6,670.78	4,992.58
56	Robert-Jan DERKSEN	NED	74	70	72	70	286	-2	5,259.65	3,936.45
	Jeev Milkha SINGH	IND	74	71	73	68	286	-2	5,259.65	3,936.45
	José-Filipe LIMA	POR	73	71	73	69	286	-2	5,259.65	3,936.45
	Sam WALKER	ENG	70	73	70	73	286	-2	5,259.65	3,936.45
60	Richard GREEN	AUS	75	70	71	71	287	-1	4,532.71	3,392.39
	Carlos RODILES	ESP	74	70	70	73	287	-1	4,532.71	3,392.39
	Simon KHAN	ENG	73	72	71	71	287	-1	4,532.71	3,392.39
	Robert KARLSSON	SWE	71	74	70	72	287	-1	4,532.71	3,392.39
64	Miles TUNNICLIFF	ENG	73	71	72	72	288	0	3,934.05	2,944.34
	Peter LAWRIE	IRL	73	72	74	69	288	0	3,934.05	2,944.34
	Seve BENSON	ENG	72	70	74	72	288	0	3,934.05	2,944.34
67	Pelle EDBERG	SWE	71	73	76	69	289	1	3,420.91	2,560.29
	Miguel Angel JIMÉNEZ	ESP	74	71	69	75	289	1	3,420.91	2,560.29
	Ricardo GONZALEZ	ARG	74	71	73	71	289	1	3,420.91	2,560.29
70	Michael CAMPBELL	NZL	73	71	74	72	290	2	3,126.71	2,340.11
71	Jean-François REMESY	FRA	72	73	76	75	296	8	2,566.00	1,920.46

Total Prize Fund

€1,713,022 £1,282,067

Hole	Par	Yards	Metres
1	5	591	540
2	4	433	396
3	3	235	215
4	4	379	347
5	4	452	413
6	4	488	446
7	4	391	358
8	3	195	178
9	5	639	584
OUT	**36**	**3803**	**3477**
10	5	548	501
11	4	474	433
12	4	429	392
13	3	203	186
14	4	410	375
15	4	470	430
16	4	307	281
17	3	155	142
18	5	589	539
IN	**36**	**3585**	**3279**
TOTAL	**72**	**7388**	**6756**

Adam Scott's record at Doha Golf Club now reads, played two, won two. Having triumphed in 2002, the Australian became the first player to record multiple victories in the event. For his eight rounds in the tournament he is a total of 39 under par – 19 under par in 2002 and 20 under par this year.

Pride and Passion

1	Tiger WOODS		274	-14
2	Martin KAYMER		275	-13
3	Ernie ELS		276	-12
	Louis OOSTHUIZEN		276	-12
5	Graeme McDOWELL		278	-10
6	Ricardo GONZALEZ		280	-8
	Søren HANSEN		280	-8
	Peter HEDBLOM		280	-8
	Henrik STENSON		280	-8
10	Niclas FASTH		281	-7
	Ross FISHER		281	-7
	Thomas LEVET		281	-7
	Lee WESTWOOD		281	-7

Scoreboard:

18	WOODS	-14
18	KAYMER	-13
18	OOSTHUIZEN	-12
18	ELS	-12
18	MCDOWELL	-10
18	STENSON	-8
18	GONZALEZ	-8
18	HEDBLOM	-8
18	SOREN HANSEN	-8

Show me a course with a storied history for pulsating finishes and I'll show you one with a magnificent risk/reward hole strategically placed over the closing stretch.

Sergio Garcia

Louis Oosthuizen

Invariably, its key element is a water hazard designed to fill the golfer's mind with images of terror. Think Augusta National, for example, which has not one but two such holes, the par fives 13th and 15th. Think the 18th hole at Carnoustie, and all the drama and havoc that the Barry Burn has wreaked over the years.

On the Majlis Course at the Emirates Golf Club in Dubai, it is also the 18th that falls into the collection of holes that have mesmerised both players and spectators. The vast majority of the 17 editions of the Dubai Desert Classic that have been staged there have been won or lost on its 564 nerve-wrenching yards.

Why is it such a great hole? Because it demands everything a player has got. It requires real steel to cut a sufficient amount off the corner to even have a chance of a stroke to the green, and what a shot it is; a long iron or metal wood to a target protected at the front by water, at the back by sand, and invariably played into a soft, swirling breeze.

Even the sanctuary of the putting surface is no cause for complacency. Bail out too far left in Sunday's final round, and you leave yourself a long putt so treacherous it only needs a fraction too much steam to undo all the good work and put your ball straight into the water you thought you had left behind.

All the possibilities and difficulties this hole has to offer were on show on a blessed last day of the 2008 tournament. First there was Ernie Els' protégé Louis Oosthuizen, who was threatening a round for the ages when he stood on the tee requiring a four for a 63, only to suffer a chastening six. Then there was the champion in Abu Dhabi two weeks earlier, Martin Kaymer, who more than doubled his take home pay by making a fabulous eagle three instead of a par five to finish runner-up instead of fifth.

But, most of all, there was Tiger Woods and Els himself.

If ever a man could be said to have played a hole in a manner that summed up a career it was the American on this 18th. He stood on the tee on the brink of a miraculous comeback, after five birdies in the space of eight holes. Now he needed a sixth to make the players behind really sit up and take notice.

On a day when he was having to use a driver he did not really like, after the face of a beloved one had cracked in practice, Woods unleashed

Niclas Fasth

Graeme McDowell

a mighty blow that brought the green within reach. A five wood that he had dropped into the water the previous day never left the flag on this occasion, allowing Woods to contemplate a 20 foot putt for an eagle. Or so he thought.

Trouble was, the ball had disappeared from his view. 'It must be in the back bunker,' he thought to himself when it was apparent it was not on the putting surface, which was not such a scary thought for a man with his gifts.

When he got to the green, however, everything changed. His caddie Steve Williams looked at the horrible lie, the ball sitting down in the rough adjacent to the bunker allowing no decent stance for a right hander, and mouthed a single word: "Damn!"

How many players would have railed against fate at that point, and subsequently botched up the hole? Not Woods. He had the resigned look of a man who knew this game was never meant to be fair. He was unlucky with the chip, too. It landed a yard short of perfection, and left him a slippery downhill 20 footer instead of a tap-in.

However, you do not win 13 Major Championships by looking up to the heavens and wondering: 'Why me?' Woods surveyed the putt

from all angles, one that history has shown few people have holed down the years, and knocked it straight in the middle. The passionate reaction said everything about the pride this man brings to every tournament he plays.

As Woods went to the players' dining area to wait, the enthralled spectators waited patiently for Els to enter the arena. What pleasure this Dubai regular has brought over the years to these parts. Now he needed a birdie to set up a repeat of his 2006 play-off against Woods.

The drive was fine but Els became yet another victim of the devious winds with his approach. His reaction when he struck the shot told you it was not a mishit, that he thought it was good. But it ballooned as it gathered momentum, right into the breeze which cruelly knocked it down into the water.

So Woods had won yet again, and when it was over, he said the words that are the sweetest music to any tournament promoter: "See you next year."

Derek Lawrenson
Daily Mail

Tiger Woods (left), is presented with the trophy by Shaikh Ahmed bin Mohammed bin Rashid Al Maktoum

Ernie Els

Emirates Golf Club
(Majlis Course)
Final Results

Pos	Name		Rd1	Rd2	Rd3	Rd4	Total		€	£
1	Tiger WOODS	USA	65	71	73	65	274	-14	283,965.09	210,413.09
2	Martin KAYMER	GER	67	73	69	66	275	-13	189,307.79	140,273.71
3	Louis OOSTHUIZEN	RSA	73	69	69	65	276	-12	95,924.94	71,078.68
	Ernie ELS	RSA	68	72	65	71	276	-12	95,924.94	71,078.68
5	Graeme MCDOWELL	NIR	67	72	69	70	278	-10	72,241.87	53,529.95
6	Ricardo GONZALEZ	ARG	72	71	72	65	280	-8	47,877.28	35,476.21
	Søren HANSEN	DEN	68	72	70	70	280	-8	47,877.28	35,476.21
	Peter HEDBLOM	SWE	69	70	70	71	280	-8	47,877.28	35,476.21
	Henrik STENSON	SWE	68	70	68	74	280	-8	47,877.28	35,476.21
10	Thomas LEVET	FRA	67	71	72	71	281	-7	30,540.93	22,630.29
	Niclas FASTH	SWE	72	71	70	68	281	-7	30,540.93	22,630.29
	Lee WESTWOOD	ENG	69	71	68	73	281	-7	30,540.93	22,630.29
	Ross FISHER	ENG	69	70	71	71	281	-7	30,540.93	22,630.29
14	Bradley DREDGE	WAL	73	72	68	69	282	-6	24,023.83	17,801.23
	Scott HEND	AUS	67	72	72	71	282	-6	24,023.83	17,801.23
	Jean-Baptiste GONNET	FRA	72	68	72	70	282	-6	24,023.83	17,801.23
	Paul MCGINLEY	IRL	71	72	69	70	282	-6	24,023.83	17,801.23
	Gary MURPHY	IRL	67	72	71	72	282	-6	24,023.83	17,801.23
19	Jeev Milkha SINGH	IND	67	76	69	71	283	-5	19,593.90	14,518.74
	Sergio GARCIA	ESP	68	71	70	74	283	-5	19,593.90	14,518.74
	Hennie OTTO	RSA	69	70	72	72	283	-5	19,593.90	14,518.74
	Anthony WALL	ENG	73	72	68	70	283	-5	19,593.90	14,518.74
	Robert KARLSSON	SWE	70	70	73	70	283	-5	19,593.90	14,518.74
	Thongchai JAIDEE	THA	69	73	70	71	283	-5	19,593.90	14,518.74
25	Simon DYSON	ENG	67	77	67	73	284	-4	16,697.41	12,372.49
	Brendan JONES	AUS	71	71	74	68	284	-4	16,697.41	12,372.49
	Shiv KAPUR	IND	68	72	69	75	284	-4	16,697.41	12,372.49
	David FROST	RSA	72	69	69	74	284	-4	16,697.41	12,372.49
	Paul BROADHURST	ENG	70	71	69	74	284	-4	16,697.41	12,372.49
30	Peter O'MALLEY	AUS	68	73	70	74	285	-3	14,652.83	10,857.49
	Gonzalo FDEZ-CASTAÑO	ESP	73	71	72	69	285	-3	14,652.83	10,857.49
	Ariel CANETE	ARG	68	75	72	70	285	-3	14,652.83	10,857.49
33	Richard STERNE	RSA	69	75	71	71	286	-2	12,636.65	9,363.53
	Marcus FRASER	AUS	69	75	70	72	286	-2	12,636.65	9,363.53
	Miles TUNNICLIFF	ENG	69	74	70	73	286	-2	12,636.65	9,363.53
	Johan EDFORS	SWE	71	70	73	72	286	-2	12,636.65	9,363.53
	Jyoti RANDHAWA	IND	67	74	75	70	286	-2	12,636.65	9,363.53
	Søren KJELDSEN	DEN	69	74	71	72	286	-2	12,636.65	9,363.53
39	Mark O'MEARA	USA	70	74	73	70	287	-1	10,734.05	7,953.74
	Ian POULTER	ENG	70	71	70	76	287	-1	10,734.05	7,953.74
	Andrew MCLARDY	RSA	67	74	73	73	287	-1	10,734.05	7,953.74
	Phillip ARCHER	ENG	72	72	74	69	287	-1	10,734.05	7,953.74
	Jean VAN DE VELDE	FRA	73	72	72	70	287	-1	10,734.05	7,953.74
44	Grégory HAVRET	FRA	72	71	72	73	288	0	8,178.33	6,059.99
	Pelle EDBERG	SWE	67	74	71	76	288	0	8,178.33	6,059.99
	Thomas BJÖRN	DEN	74	70	73	71	288	0	8,178.33	6,059.99
	James KINGSTON	RSA	68	74	75	71	288	0	8,178.33	6,059.99
	Damien MCGRANE	IRL	68	69	72	79	288	0	8,178.33	6,059.99
	Maarten LAFEBER	NED	71	72	74	71	288	0	8,178.33	6,059.99
	David HOWELL	ENG	68	75	72	73	288	0	8,178.33	6,059.99
	James KAMTE	RSA	74	71	71	72	288	0	8,178.33	6,059.99
	Mikko ILONEN	FIN	74	71	68	75	288	0	8,178.33	6,059.99
	Stephen GALLACHER	SCO	70	73	71	74	288	0	8,178.33	6,059.99
54	Simon KHAN	ENG	72	73	70	74	289	1	5,427.88	4,021.96
	Alexander NOREN	SWE	71	71	71	76	289	1	5,427.88	4,021.96
	José Manuel LARA	ESP	70	74	73	72	289	1	5,427.88	4,021.96
	Steve WEBSTER	ENG	73	71	71	74	289	1	5,427.88	4,021.96
	Robert-Jan DERKSEN	NED	68	75	71	75	289	1	5,427.88	4,021.96
	Martin ERLANDSSON	SWE	72	72	71	74	289	1	5,427.88	4,021.96
	Miguel Angel JIMÉNEZ	ESP	67	74	73	75	289	1	5,427.88	4,021.96
61	Anders HANSEN	DEN	70	74	72	74	290	2	4,600.31	3,408.75
62	Per-Ulrik JOHANSSON	SWE	71	74	74	72	291	3	4,259.54	3,156.25
	Benn BARHAM	ENG	70	72	74	75	291	3	4,259.54	3,156.25
	Graeme STORM	ENG	69	72	75	75	291	3	4,259.54	3,156.25
65	Andrew COLTART	SCO	69	71	72	80	292	4	3,833.59	2,840.62
	Colin MONTGOMERIE	SCO	72	72	73	75	292	4	3,833.59	2,840.62
67	Stephen DODD	WAL	73	72	73	77	295	7	3,578.02	2,651.25
68	Garry HOUSTON	WAL	77	78	73	296		8	3,407.64	2,525.00
69	Daniel VANCSIK	ARG	68	77	75	79	299	11	3,237.25	2,398.75
70	Richard GREEN	AUS	73	70	W/D		143	-1		

Total Prize Fund
€1,700,703 £1,260,190

Hole	Par	Yards	Metres
1	4	458	419
2	4	351	321
3	5	568	519
4	3	188	172
5	4	436	399
6	4	485	443
7	3	186	170
8	4	459	420
9	4	463	423
OUT	**35**	**3594**	**3286**
10	5	549	502
11	3	169	155
12	4	467	427
13	5	550	503
14	4	434	397
15	3	190	174
16	4	425	389
17	4	359	328
18	5	564	516
IN	**37**	**3707**	**3391**
TOTAL	**72**	**7301**	**6677**

Tiger Woods claimed his second Dubai Desert Classic title and joined Ernie Els (1994, 2002 and 2005) as the only multiple winner in the tournament's history. As a result of this victory, the World Number One has now recorded multiple victories in no fewer than ten European Tour International Schedule events.

Inspirational Figure

1	**SSP CHOWRASIA**		279	-9
2	Damien McGRANE		281	-7
3	José Manuel LARA		283	-5
4	Raphaël JACQUELIN		284	-4
	Digvijay SINGH		284	-4
6	Thomas BJÖRN		285	-3
	Ernie ELS		285	-3
	Gaurav GHEI		285	-3
	Maarten LAFEBER		285	-3
	Ross McGOWAN		285	-3

S hiv Shankar Prasad Chowrasia, the former caddie and son of a greenkeeper, may not have spent his formative years poring over schoolbooks but, in living behind Royal Calcutta's ninth hole, he certainly became a dab hand at reading greens – a skill readily exhibited during his stunning win in the EMAAR – MGF Indian Masters at Delhi Golf Club.

Raphaël Jacquelin

As a child, he would sneak in a couple of hours' of short game practice at first light and, at the end of a long day on the bag, he would be back, hard at work again. There were times when the members would send him packing but there is a common bond amongst golfers and it was not too long before Chowrasia's pursuers were proffering financial backing for his early forays on the Professional Golf Tour of India.

'S S P', as he is known, won ten times on his home circuit before graduating to the Asian Tour in 2006. Armed with $30,000 saved from his home circuit, he told Harji Malik, one of India's foremost golf writers: "If I can make money in my first year, I will stay. If I lose my $30,000, I will return to the Indian Tour."

He did nothing to write home about in the first half of his rookie season but all that changed in the latter stages as he made a handful of cuts and enough money to stick with his task for another year.

He notched six top 20 finishes in 2007 and, when it came to the start of 2008, the 29 year old had three top ten finishes to his name even before he arrived at Delhi Golf Club. It was there, incidentally, where he had finished second to Arjun Atwal in the 1999 Indian Open, a result which he had dismissed at the time as "a fluke".

Playing in his first co-sanctioned event between The European Tour and the Asian Tour, Chowrasia did not, for a minute, consider he might win. Indeed, if the truth be known, he was initially in awe at playing in the same field as Major Championship winners such as Ernie Els and Mark O'Meara.

However, after an opening 70 and a couple of 71s, he embarked on the final round well placed,

two shots behind Frenchman Raphaël Jacquelin and one adrift of Spain's José Manuel Lara and Irishmen Graeme McDowell and Damien McGrane.

As the leading groups got underway, Chowrasia immediately issued a series of Tiger-type Sunday messages to the field. He holed a 12 foot putt on the first green for birdie, chipped in from off the back of the third for another, before claiming a third birdie in four holes at the fourth to move clear of the field.

At this juncture he told himself, "I could go well ahead from here," and it was obvious that the crowd, peppered with local caddies, felt much the same as they poured after their rising star.

Out in 32, Chowrasia made a further birdie at the 11th before sticking rigidly to par for the rest of the way. He admitted to nerves on the 18th tee but they did not trouble him for long. The moment he bisected the fairway with a superb drive, they evaporated.

Sensibly, Chowrasia was not about to risk anything at a hole where, at the start of the week, Els had amassed a quadruple bogey nine via two visits to the trees. He played comfortably short of the cross bunkers in two, caught the fat of the green in three and signed off with a par which was good enough for a two shot victory over McGrane.

Some might have suggested his win was a one-off on a course he knew inside out, but Els and O'Meara, as well as European Tour Tournament Committee Chairman Thomas Björn, had given Delhi Golf Club a seal of approval. To them, it was a glorious old-fashioned course, one which asked many questions seldom posed today. "It certainly proves that a golf course doesn't need to be long to be difficult," said the Dane.

Chrowasia not only picked up the first prize of €280,561 (£211,642) and the magnificent trophy depicting India Gate, the famous war memorial in New Delhi, he also gained a priceless European Tour exemption until the end of the 2010 season.

However, his win could also, perhaps, make a wealth of difference for golf in his home country. As he said himself during his press conference: "Hopefully caddies from all over India will start playing the game now and have the feeling that they, too, can do well if they work at the game."

Lewine Mair
The Daily Telegraph

Damien McGrane

Thomas Björn

S S P Chowrasia (right), is presented with the trophy by Mr Siddharth Gupta, Executive Director, EMAAR-MGF Land Limited, India

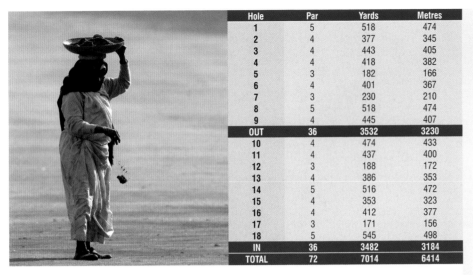

Hole	Par	Yards	Metres
1	5	518	474
2	4	377	345
3	4	443	405
4	4	418	382
5	3	182	166
6	4	401	367
7	3	230	210
8	5	518	474
9	4	445	407
OUT	**36**	**3532**	**3230**
10	4	474	433
11	4	437	400
12	3	188	172
13	4	386	353
14	5	516	472
15	4	353	323
16	4	412	377
17	3	171	156
18	5	545	498
IN	**36**	**3482**	**3184**
TOTAL	**72**	**7014**	**6414**

Maarten Lafeber

Delhi Golf Club

Final Results

Pos	Name		Rd1	Rd2	Rd3	Rd4	Total		€	£
1	S S P CHOWRASIA	IND	70	71	71	67	279	-9	280,561.35	211,642.19
2	Damien MCGRANE	IRL	67	69	75	70	281	-7	187,038.66	141,093.10
3	José Manuel LARA	ESP	68	72	71	72	283	-5	105,380.53	79,494.08
4	Raphaël JACQUELIN	FRA	69	69	72	74	284	-4	77,772.85	58,668.15
	Digvijay SINGH	IND	70	70	74	70	284	-4	77,772.85	58,668.15
6	Ross McGOWAN	ENG	72	71	70	72	285	-3	44,576.30	33,626.25
	Gaurav GHEI	IND	75	69	70	71	285	-3	44,576.30	33,626.25
	Maarten LAFEBER	NED	69	71	73	72	285	-3	44,576.30	33,626.25
	Ernie ELS	RSA	75	70	69	71	285	-3	44,576.30	33,626.25
	Thomas BJÖRN	DEN	68	72	74	71	285	-3	44,576.30	33,626.25
11	Søren KJELDSEN	DEN	74	71	75	66	286	-2	30,974.47	23,365.67
12	Hendrik BUHRMANN	RSA	69	69	75	74	287	-1	27,271.00	20,571.95
	Brendan JONES	AUS	74	68	76	69	287	-1	27,271.00	20,571.95
	Graeme MCDOWELL	NIR	69	69	73	76	287	-1	27,271.00	20,571.95
15	Jean-Baptiste GONNET	FRA	71	73	75	69	288	0	23,230.85	17,524.25
	Benn BARHAM	ENG	69	71	74	74	288	0	23,230.85	17,524.25
	Henrik NYSTRÖM	SWE	70	71	74	73	288	0	23,230.85	17,524.25
	Arjun ATWAL	IND	70	70	72	76	288	0	23,230.85	17,524.25
19	Mark O'MEARA	USA	69	73	74	73	289	1	20,200.74	15,238.48
	Scott HEND	AUS	71	74	73	71	289	1	20,200.74	15,238.48
	Martin WIEGELE	AUT	75	68	73	73	289	1	20,200.74	15,238.48
22	Christian CÉVAÉR	FRA	71	75	74	70	290	2	17,507.31	13,206.68
	David LYNN	ENG	69	75	74	72	290	2	17,507.31	13,206.68
	Ross BAIN	SCO	71	71	72	76	290	2	17,507.31	13,206.68
	Robert-Jan DERKSEN	NED	74	72	73	71	290	2	17,507.31	13,206.68
	Peter BAKER	ENG	73	71	74	72	290	2	17,507.31	13,206.68
	Jyoti RANDHAWA	IND	65	77	75	73	290	2	17,507.31	13,206.68
	Oliver FISHER	ENG	73	71	73	73	290	2	17,507.31	13,206.68
29	Adam GROOM	AUS	72	73	74	72	291	3	14,982.22	11,301.87
	Sam LITTLE	ENG	70	75	74	72	291	3	14,982.22	11,301.87
	Unho PARK	AUS	71	72	76	72	291	3	14,982.22	11,301.87
32	Mikael LUNDBERG	SWE	71	68	79	74	292	4	13,467.16	10,158.99
	Simon WAKEFIELD	ENG	74	68	78	72	292	4	13,467.16	10,158.99
	Simon YATES	SCO	70	74	72	76	292	4	13,467.16	10,158.99
35	Prayad MARKSAENG	THA	74	73	78	68	293	5	12,288.78	9,270.08
	Amandeep JOHL	IND	73	71	76	73	293	5	12,288.78	9,270.08
	Mark BROWN	NZL	71	75	71	76	293	5	12,288.78	9,270.08
38	Shiv KAPUR	IND	68	78	76	72	294	6	10,773.73	8,127.19
	Marcus FRASER	AUS	73	69	76	76	294	6	10,773.73	8,127.19
	Scott BARR	AUS	73	73	75	73	294	6	10,773.73	8,127.19
	Randhir Singh GHOTRA	IND	74	73	70	77	294	6	10,773.73	8,127.19
	Alexander NOREN	SWE	72	74	75	73	294	6	10,773.73	8,127.19
	Keith HORNE	RSA	70	73	80	71	294	6	10,773.73	8,127.19
44	Simon KHAN	ENG	70	75	73	77	295	7	9,090.33	6,857.32
	Chinnaswamy MUNIYAPPA	IND	69	77	77	72	295	7	9,090.33	6,857.32
	Prom MEESAWAT	THA	71	74	76	74	295	7	9,090.33	6,857.32
	Fabrizio ZANOTTI	PAR	71	76	77	71	295	7	9,090.33	6,857.32
48	Shamim KHAN	IND	73	74	76	73	296	8	7,238.60	5,460.46
	Jarmo SANDELIN	SWE	73	70	77	76	296	8	7,238.60	5,460.46
	Magnus A CARLSSON	SWE	70	76	75	75	296	8	7,238.60	5,460.46
	Stephen GALLACHER	SCO	71	72	74	79	296	8	7,238.60	5,460.46
	Leif WESTERBERG	SWE	73	71	75	77	296	8	7,238.60	5,460.46
	Joakim HAEGGMAN	SWE	74	69	73	80	296	8	7,238.60	5,460.46
	Phillip ARCHER	ENG	74	69	76	77	296	8	7,238.60	5,460.46
55	Andrew COLTART	SCO	76	69	71	81	297	9	5,723.54	4,317.57
	Ashok KUMAR	IND	72	73	75	77	297	9	5,723.54	4,317.57
57	Jong-yul SUK	KOR	70	74	80	74	298	10	5,050.19	3,809.62
	Adam BLYTH	AUS	74	71	71	82	298	10	5,050.19	3,809.62
	Carlos RODILES	ESP	74	70	81	73	298	10	5,050.19	3,809.62
60	José-Filipe LIMA	POR	72	71	79	77	299	11	4,713.51	3,555.65
61	Ali SHER	IND	77	70	78	75	300	12	4,545.17	3,428.66
62	Alvaro QUIROS	ESP	69	75	76	81	301	13	4,376.83	3,301.67
63	Darren CLARKE	NIR	72	69	79	82	302	14	4,208.49	3,174.68
64	Harmeet KAHLON	IND	70	75	83	75	303	15	3,955.98	2,984.20
	Richard FINCH	ENG	67	77	85	74	303	15	3,955.98	2,984.20
66	Airil RIZMAN	MAS	74	72	81	77	304	16	3,703.47	2,793.72
67	Rahul GANAPATHY	IND	76	71	78	84	309	21	3,535.13	2,666.73
68	Anthony KANG	USA	72	72	82	84	310	22	3,366.79	2,539.75
69	Sung LEE	KOR	75	72	75	89	311	23	3,198.45	2,412.76
70	Emanuele CANONICA	ITA	72	71	77	W/D	220	4		

i S S P Chowrasia made history when The European Tour played in India for the first time. Having joined as an Affiliate Member the week of the tournament he became the first Affiliate to win a European Tour event on his debut in that category.

Total Prize Fund

€1,680,318 £1,267,552

Speculate
to Accumulate

1	Felipe AGUILAR		262	-18
2	Jeev Milkha SINGH		263	-17
3	James KAMTE		264	-16
	Prom MEESAWAT		264	-16
5	Mark BROWN		265	-15
	Joost LUITEN		265	-15
7	Wen-chong LIANG		266	-14
	Jyoti RANDHAWA		266	-14
	Ter-chang WANG		266	-14
10	Arjun ATWAL		267	-13
	Sang-Moon BAE		267	-13
	Chris RODGERS		267	-13

H ow many Chief Executives, Company Presidents or Board Members would swap everything in their empires for the chance to be a professional golfer?

Joost Luiten

Prom Meesawat

The inextricable link between golf and business has always been an intriguing one. Indeed, it is often said that the majority of business deals the world over are concluded on the fairways and greens of golf clubs and country clubs.

Those who seem to have it all, however, always need a leveller and there are few things that can bring you down to earth better than 18 holes of golf. These captains of industry cannot buy golf out or take golf over and it is precisely this which makes the game so irresistible to them; allied to the fact they will never truly master it at the highest level.

Unless, of course, they are the 2008 Enjoy Jakarta Astro Indonesia Open champion, Felipe Aguilar of Chile.

Aguilar's journey to success on The European Tour International Schedule, which culminated in his thrilling one shot victory over India's Jeev Milkha Singh at the Cengkareng Golf Club, would have made most businessmen the world over green with envy.

The reason? He was once one of them.

The 33 year old ran his own construction company at home in Santiago but fantasised about life as a professional golfer. The difference between him and his fellow dreamers was that he had the ability and belief to put together a strategic plan which saw him speculate to accumulate success in the game.

Having graduated from a golf scholarship at the University of North Florida with a degree in Business Administration, Aguilar turned professional in 1999 but quickly realised that, with a family to care for, he had to provide as well as play. As a compromise, he kept practising but also went to work in his family's construction business, serving a year's apprenticeship before setting up his own company, manufacturing windows and doors.

With an engaging personality and keen business acumen, Aguilar's company quickly became a success and he established a firm foundation and quality of life for his family. He opened another business and assumed control of the family firm to cement his success, but the lure of professional golf was always at the back of his mind.

"I had to get support and sponsorship because I could not risk my family's money from the businesses," he explained. "But I was lucky because everything fell into place at the right time."

Aguilar's moment arrived on Sunday February 17, 2008. After excellent rounds of 65-62-67 to move to 16 under par after 54 holes, Aguilar led by two shots from China's Liang Wen-chong and Singh going into the final day. The former South American Amateur champion had played some beautiful golf over the first three rounds, displaying all of the shot making skills that had brought him two titles on the 2007 European Challenge Tour; reliable driving, a wicked short game and an assured putting stroke.

The final round provided a thrilling finale to Indonesia's National Open Championship. With eight players within five shots of Aguilar at the start of the day it was always going to be a close affair and indeed challengers such as James Kamte of South Africa and Thailand's Prom Meesawat made moves for the €137,883 (£102,706) first prize before eventually settling for a share of third place, leaving the destination of the trophy down to the battle between Aguilar and Singh.

The Indian strode to the 18th tee with a one stroke lead, thanks largely to an eagle three at the sixth and an eagle two at the 11th but, when his approach shot did not find the green, Aguilar sensed his moment and arrowed a brilliant nine iron to within eight feet of the hole.

Singh's chip to four feet allowed Aguilar to pile on the pressure by taking his birdie chance, leaving the winner of the 2006 Volvo Masters needing to hole his par putt to force a play-off. When the ball stayed above ground, Aguilar had won.

The man, who used to build offices and schools in his native Chile, had just constructed his first major golfing triumph.

Michael Gibbons

(left to right) Jero Wacik, Minister of Tourism and Culture, Felipe Aguilar and Dr. Ing H Fauzi Bowo, Governor of DKI Jakarta

(left to right) Indian golfers Arjun Atwal, Gaurav Ghei, Jeev Milkha Singh and Shiv Kapur

Liang Wen-chong

Hole	Par	Yards	Metres
1	4	501	461
2	4	448	410
3	4	347	317
4	3	141	129
5	4	447	409
6	5	545	498
7	4	381	348
8	3	201	184
9	5	524	479
OUT	36	3535	3235
10	4	402	368
11	4	324	296
12	3	243	222
13	4	459	420
14	4	477	436
15	4	440	402
16	4	425	389
17	3	178	163
18	4	416	380
IN	34	3364	3076
TOTAL	70	6899	6311

James Kamte

Cengkareng Golf Club

Final Results

Pos	Name		Rd1	Rd2	Rd3	Rd4	Total		€	£
1	Felipe AGUILAR	CHI	65	62	67	68	262	-18	137,883.22	102,706.31
2	Jeev Milkha SINGH	IND	65	66	65	67	263	-17	91,919.85	68,469.16
3	Prom MEESAWAT	THA	66	63	68	67	264	-16	46,576.95	34,694.19
	James KAMTE	RSA	62	67	68	67	264	-16	46,576.95	34,694.19
5	Joost LUITEN	NED	64	69	66	66	265	-15	32,016.48	23,848.41
	Mark BROWN	NZL	67	66	66	66	265	-15	32,016.48	23,848.41
7	Wen-chong LIANG	CHN	65	67	64	70	266	-14	21,344.32	15,898.94
	Jyoti RANDHAWA	IND	68	70	66	62	266	-14	21,344.32	15,898.94
	Ter-chang WANG	TPE	69	64	66	67	266	-14	21,344.32	15,898.94
10	Arjun ATWAL	IND	67	67	66	67	267	-13	15,332.61	11,420.94
	Chris RODGERS	ENG	68	68	67	64	267	-13	15,332.61	11,420.94
	Sang-Moon BAE	KOR	71	68	63	65	267	-13	15,332.61	11,420.94
13	Philip GOLDING	ENG	65	70	65	68	268	-12	12,988.60	9,674.93
	Mikael LUNDBERG	SWE	71	68	65	64	268	-12	12,988.60	9,674.93
15	Paul MCGINLEY	IRL	68	69	66	66	269	-11	11,416.73	8,504.08
	Simon YATES	SCO	70	68	68	63	269	-11	11,416.73	8,504.08
	Adam BLYTH	AUS	66	67	67	69	269	-11	11,416.73	8,504.08
	Jason KNUTZON	USA	68	68	67	66	269	-11	11,416.73	8,504.08
19	Gary SIMPSON	AUS	68	68	67	67	270	-10	10,093.05	7,518.10
	Tony CAROLAN	AUS	71	67	66	66	270	-10	10,093.05	7,518.10
21	Darren CLARKE	NIR	68	67	70	66	271	-9	9,224.39	6,871.05
	Prayad MARKSAENG	THA	65	65	69	72	271	-9	9,224.39	6,871.05
	Chinnarat PHADUNGSIL	THA	69	64	68	70	271	-9	9,224.39	6,871.05
	Chapchai NIRAT	THA	69	66	66	70	271	-9	9,224.39	6,871.05
25	Oliver FISHER	ENG	67	68	67	70	272	-8	7,487.06	5,576.95
	Rhys DAVIES	WAL	66	69	68	69	272	-8	7,487.06	5,576.95
	Scott STRANGE	AUS	66	72	66	68	272	-8	7,487.06	5,576.95
	Scott HEND	AUS	66	68	68	70	272	-8	7,487.06	5,576.95
	Peter WHITEFORD	SCO	68	67	69	68	272	-8	7,487.06	5,576.95
	Simon GRIFFITHS	ENG	68	68	68	68	272	-8	7,487.06	5,576.95
	Martin WIEGELE	AUT	65	65	70	72	272	-8	7,487.06	5,576.95
	Chris GANE	ENG	68	66	71	67	272	-8	7,487.06	5,576.95
	Jean VAN DE VELDE	FRA	67	71	67	67	272	-8	7,487.06	5,576.95
	Warren BENNETT	ENG	68	70	65	69	272	-8	7,487.06	5,576.95
35	Robert ROCK	ENG	68	68	70	67	273	-7	5,873.83	4,375.29
	Thomas AIKEN	RSA	66	70	68	69	273	-7	5,873.83	4,375.29
	Matthew MILLAR	AUS	70	69	68	66	273	-7	5,873.83	4,375.29
	Robert DINWIDDIE	ENG	69	66	67	71	273	-7	5,873.83	4,375.29
	Sung LEE	KOR	70	66	70	67	273	-7	5,873.83	4,375.29
40	Edoardo MOLINARI	ITA	66	73	67	68	274	-6	5,129.26	3,820.67
	Andrew COLTART	SCO	67	72	68	67	274	-6	5,129.26	3,820.67
	David BRANSDON	AUS	64	74	69	67	274	-6	5,129.26	3,820.67
	Gaurav GHEI	IND	71	67	67	69	274	-6	5,129.26	3,820.67
44	Sion E BEBB	WAL	69	68	68	70	275	-5	4,301.96	3,204.44
	Shiv KAPUR	IND	69	67	69	70	275	-5	4,301.96	3,204.44
	David HORSEY	ENG	70	68	69	68	275	-5	4,301.96	3,204.44
	Stuart MANLEY	WAL	69	66	69	71	275	-5	4,301.96	3,204.44
	Gerald ROSALES	PHI	67	68	72	68	275	-5	4,301.96	3,204.44
	Julio ZAPATA	ARG	69	70	67	69	275	-5	4,301.96	3,204.44
50	Kyron SULLIVAN	WAL	65	68	72	71	276	-4	3,309.20	2,464.95
	Mikko ILONEN	FIN	66	68	71	71	276	-4	3,309.20	2,464.95
	Scott BARR	AUS	66	71	71	68	276	-4	3,309.20	2,464.95
	Angelo QUE	PHI	67	67	70	72	276	-4	3,309.20	2,464.95
	Peter BAKER	ENG	68	71	69	68	276	-4	3,309.20	2,464.95
	Thaworn WIRATCHANT	THA	67	67	67	75	276	-4	3,309.20	2,464.95
56	Luis CLAVERIE	ESP	68	69	74	66	277	-3	2,368.14	1,763.98
	Wen-teh LU	TPE	70	69	69	69	277	-3	2,368.14	1,763.98
	Fabrizio ZANOTTI	PAR	65	74	66	72	277	-3	2,368.14	1,763.98
	Kane WEBBER	AUS	72	67	71	67	277	-3	2,368.14	1,763.98
	Unho PARK	AUS	67	72	73	65	277	-3	2,368.14	1,763.98
	Taichiro KIYOTA	JPN	71	67	71	68	277	-3	2,368.14	1,763.98
	Antonio LASCUNA	PHI	68	71	64	74	277	-3	2,368.14	1,763.98
	Maan NASIM	INA	68	70	70	69	277	-3	2,368.14	1,763.98
64	Steven JEPPESEN	SWE	71	66	71	70	278	-2	1,944.15	1,448.16
	Liam BOND	WAL	67	71	71	69	278	-2	1,944.15	1,448.16
66	Rafael CABRERA BELLO	ESP	69	69	73	68	279	-1	1,737.33	1,294.10
	David DIXON	ENG	69	68	72	70	279	-1	1,737.33	1,294.10
	Adam GROOM	AUS	69	70	71	69	279	-1	1,737.33	1,294.10
69	Eddie LEE	NZL	67	72	70	71	280	0	1,440.90	1,073.29
	Alan MCLEAN	SCO	72	67	73	68	280	0	1,440.90	1,073.29
	Iain STEEL	MAS	71	68	68	73	280	0	1,440.90	1,073.29
72	Richard BLAND	ENG	69	70	69	73	281	1	1,236.50	921.04
	Mitsuhiro TATEYAMA	JPN	70	69	76	66	281	1	1,236.50	921.04
74	Marcus BOTH	AUS	66	72	70	74	282	2	1,232.00	917.69
75	Airil RIZMAN	MAS	69	70	71	73	283	3	1,227.50	914.34
	Mattias ELIASSON	SWE	69	69	69	76	283	3	1,227.50	914.34
77	Ben MASON	ENG	70	68	72	74	284	4	1,223.00	910.99
	A SUPRAPTO (AM)	INA	67	71	68	78	284	4		
79	A ILYASSYAK	INA	71	66	75	73	285	5	1,220.00	908.75
80	Denny SUPRIADI	INA	67	70	77	73	287	7	1,217.00	906.52

Total Prize Fund

€838,360   £624,476

As a result of Felipe Aguilar's victory, Chile became the 35th different nation to provide a winner of a European Tour event. Chile was the first new country to do so since Mikko Ilonen won for Finland, coincidentally at this event 12 months earlier.

Magnificent Seven

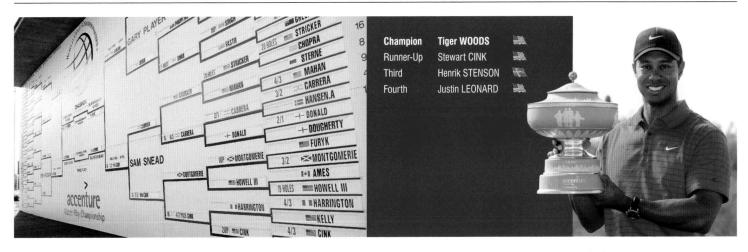

Champion	Tiger WOODS
Runner-Up	Stewart CINK
Third	Henrik STENSON
Fourth	Justin LEONARD

To the surprise of absolutely no-one – including the eventual runner up himself – Tiger Woods defeated Stewart Cink 8 and 7 in the final of the World Golf Championships – Accenture Match Play at The Gallery Golf Club in Tucson.

Angel Cabrera

Paul Casey

It was the World Number One's seventh victory in his previous eight starts on the US PGA Tour and The European Tour combined – leading back to the WGC – Bridgestone Invitational in August 2007 – and as Cink said on the eve of the 36 hole showdown: "I'm a golf fan, just like I'm a golf player, and I can say that Tiger is the best that's ever lived in golf. Just being able to get a front row seat and watch him play is fun."

Cink is a terrific player himself and unquestionably one of the game's gentlemen but some people, reading his words, were reminded of a Beatles fan in the 1960s being ushered into the presence of Paul McCartney. Understandably, they predicted a one-sided final and ultimately they were proved correct.

Both players birdied the opening hole and stepped on to the second tee all square. It was to prove parity's last dance as Woods won the second hole with a birdie. Further birdies at the fifth and seventh holes stretched his advantage and thereafter, realistically, it was not a question of 'if' he would win, but 'by how many?'

The first question was answered on the 11th green of their afternoon round, where the Number One seed hit his approach shot to within three feet of the pin. Cink conceded the birdie putt and with it the match. Woods' winning margin in the final was the biggest in the ten year history of the tournament and represented his 63rd US PGA Tour victory, one more than Arnold Palmer. "To be mentioned in the same breath as Arnold means you have had quite a career so I am very happy about that," he said, with a whiff of understatement.

The irony of the final outcome was that the overwhelming pre-tournament favourite was almost knocked out in the first round, but recovered from three down with five holes to play to beat his powerful compatriot J B Holmes. He was also involved in an epic third round struggle against Australia's Aaron Baddeley before winning on the second extra hole, and triumphed on the final green of his semi-final against Henrik Stenson.

The Swede had arrived in Tucson to defend a title he had won the previous year and had mounted a solid defence, dispatching Americans Woody Austin and Jonathan Byrd, Australian Robert Allenby and South African Trevor Immelman, the latter at the seventh extra hole, the extraordinary contest ending just as people were beginning to think the combatants

World Golf Championships – Accenture Match Play

Henrik Stenson

Vijay Singh

involved believed all matches in the competition, not just the final, were over 36 holes.

Stenson's performance was the highlight of the week from a European Tour perspective which saw, of the 31 Members who teed up on Wednesday morning, 16 make it to round two while five – Angel Cabrera, Paul Casey, Colin Montgomerie, Vijay Singh and Stenson – progressed to round three.

While that round signalled the end for Casey and Montgomerie, there was enough in their performance to cheer watching European golf fans both in the crowd and those tuning in on television back home.

Montgomerie had arrived in Tucson in the middle of a form slump that had seen him slip down and out of the top 50 in the Official World Golf Ranking and, therefore, out of the Masters Tournament the following month.

He needed a good week and started well by dispatching Americans Jim Furyk and Charles Howell III before a cold putter saw him sunk by Cink. However, like Casey, who was eventually

ousted on the home green by Korea's K J Choi, the Scot could look back on his week with pride, not to mention a bulging file of complimentary newspaper cuttings.

Cabrera and Singh both progressed one round further, to the quarter-finals, the duo showing the match play expertise that brought the Fijian the World Match Play title at Wentworth Club in 1997 and the Argentine only three losses in nine matches in two outings in the Presidents Cup.

Cabrera fought hard but came up against an inspired Cink in the last eight, the American eventually closing out the match 3 and 2, while Singh battled bravely to chip away at Justin Leonard's three hole lead after 11 holes in their match before eventually surrendering on the 18th green.

Lawrence Donegan
The Guardian

Hole	Par	Yards	Metres
1	5	588	538
2	4	467	427
3	3	225	206
4	4	495	453
5	5	635	581
6	4	450	411
7	4	314	287
8	3	171	156
9	4	448	410
OUT	36	3793	3469
10	5	534	488
11	4	402	368
12	4	336	307
13	4	495	452
14	3	192	176
15	4	435	398
16	3	178	163
17	5	601	550
18	4	447	409
IN	36	3620	3311
TOTAL	72	7413	6780

The Gallery at Dove Mountain

Total Prize Fund

€5,451,813 £4,078,927

	€	£
Champion:	919,993	688,319
Runner-up:	545,181	407,894
Third Place:	391,849	293,174
Fourth Place:	323,701	242,186
Quarter Finals:	177,184	132,565
Third Round:	88,592	66,282
Second Round:	61,333	45,888
First Round:	27,259	20,395

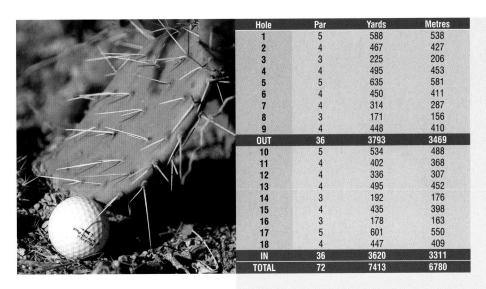

Tiger Woods (right), receives the trophy from William Green, Chairman & CEO, Accenture

Colin Montgomerie

Tiger Woods created World Golf Championships history after he claimed his third WGC – Accenture Match Play title. As a result of this latest triumph, he held all three WGC titles at once, having won the 2007 WGC – CA Championship and WGC – Bridgestone Invitational.

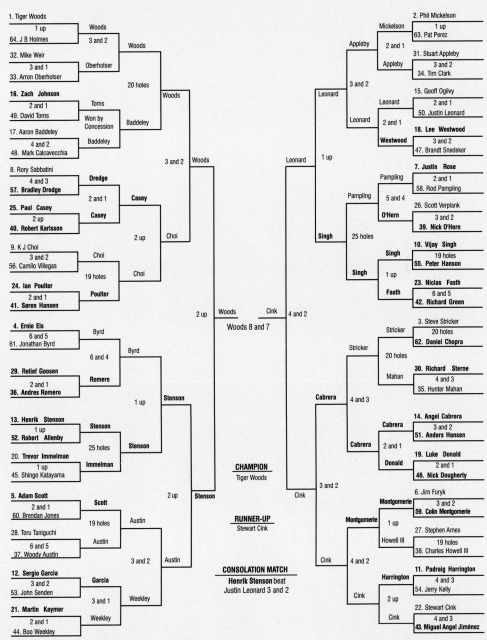

NB: Players in bold denote European Tour Members

Remarkable Turnaround

		1	Mark BROWN		270	-18
		2	Greg CHALMERS		273	-15
			Taichiro KIYOTA		273	-15
			Scott STRANGE		273	-15
		5	Johan EDFORS		274	-14
			Shiv KAPUR		274	-14
			Graeme STORM		274	-14
		8	Jyoti RANDHAWA		275	-13
		9	Prayad MARKSAENG		276	-12
			Daniel VANCSIK		276	-12

JOHNNIE WALKER LEADERS

HOLE	1	2	3	4	5	6	7	8	9	10	11	12	13	14	15	16	17	18	TOTAL
PAR	4	4	3	4	4	5	4	3	5	3	4	3	4	5	4	5	4	5	
13 BROWN	13	13	12	12	13	14	14	13	13	14	15	16	17	17	17	17	17	18	270
14 KIYOTA	14	14	15	15	15	16	17	17	17	17	16	16	16	16	16	15	15		273
13 RANDHAWA	13	13	14	14	12	12	11	11	11	11	11	12	12	12	12	12	13		275
11 STORM	11	12	12	12	11	11	11	12	13	13	13	12	13	12	13	14	14		277
8 SINGH J M	9	9	9	9	9	9	9	10	10	10	11	11	11	11					273
11 CHALMERS	11	12	12	12	13	12	12	12	12	12	12	12	12	14	14	14	14	14	274
7 EDFORS	7	7	8	9	10	11	12	12	14	14	14	14	14	14	14	13	11		276
10 VANCSIK	11	11	11	11	11	12	12	14	14	14	14	14	15	16	17	16	16	15	273
10 STRANGE	10	11	11	12	12	13	13	13	14	15	16	17	16	16	15				277
7 BARR	8	8	8	8	9	9	8	9	10	10	11	11	12	13	11	11			274

AFTER

MATCH NO.

They might have been playing golf in India for almost 180 years, but in all the time since that first tee shot at the Royal Calcutta Golf Club in 1829, the country had seen nothing to match the heady three week spell in February 2008 when The European Tour came to town.

Søren Hansen

Graeme Storm

The smile could not be wiped from the faces of local golfing aficionados as the Johnnie Walker Classic, won comfortably in the end by New Zealander Mark Brown, followed the inaugural EMAAR-MGF Indian Masters in bringing star names to New Delhi. In this cricket mad country, golf is currently proving the fastest growing sport.

"Two years ago we couldn't have even thought about this," admitted Ajai Gupta, Commissioner of the Professional Golf Tour of India. "To have two tournaments together so quickly just shows that India is a place to visit. The economy is growing and more and more of the world is looking at India as a destination."

Glamour and glitz were apparent throughout the week at the Arnold Palmer designed DLF Golf and Country Club as Johnnie Walker, past masters in putting on a golfing spectacle, ensured the tournament would gain maximum attention.

Stars including Miguel Angel Jiménez, Robert Karlsson, Paul McGinley, Colin Montgomerie, Adam Scott and Vijay Singh served behind a pre-tournament hotel bar populated with Bollywood's finest. Ian Poulter was typically flamboyantly dressed in garb depicting the blue, black and gold colours of the sponsor's whisky while, as play began, India held its breath in the hope that one of their own might emulate S S P Chowrasia's stunning win three weeks earlier in the EMAAR-MGF Indian Masters.

It very nearly happened. Arjun Atwal, Shiv Kapur, Jyoti Randhawa and Jeev Milkha Singh all enjoyed moments during the week to suggest the trophy might be headed their way. Indeed Kapur stirred home emotions with a closing 68 to grab a share of fifth place with Sweden's Johan Edfors and Graeme Storm of England while Randhawa finished eighth, Singh tied 11th and Atwal tied 17th. It was a huge week for the Indian players and most coped admirably, to suggest they will be contenders in tournaments all over the world from now on, and their influence was recognised.

"These players have become role models to the younger generation," said Gupta. "In the last five years we have seen a huge surge of youngsters taking up the game because of them. I honestly believe that India has the potential to be a golfing superpower, probably in ten years."

Montgomerie was quick to point out that India, with its ever expanding population and booming economy, could soon become one of the foremost golfing nations. "When golf does come over fully to places like India and China – and remember they make up half the world's population – it'll be exciting to see," he said. "In the future we, the players who are coming over at the moment, will be seen as the ambassadors and pioneers."

Unfortunately Montgomerie's first competitive visit to India as a professional ended after two indifferent days, leaving the Scot to reflect ruefully that the rounds he had served behind the bar a few nights earlier had been of a far higher quality.

Talking of quality brings us neatly to the golf played by the winner. Mark Brown surged to his maiden European Tour victory with a thrilling spell of four birdies in a row on the back nine of the final round to overhaul Japan's Taichiro Kiyota, who eventually shared second place with the Australian duo of Greg Chalmers and Scott Strange. Brown provided the romance to go with the glitz for, only the week before, he had recorded his first Asian Tour victory in the Sail Open Golf Championship at Jaypee Greens.

It was a remarkable turnaround for the 33 year old New Zealander who had given up competing entirely between 2003 and 2006. "Mentally I wasn't there, tee to green I wasn't there and my short game wasn't good enough," he admitted.

Brown, however, rededicated himself to the game and quickly found rich reward with a victory which opened up bountiful playing privileges on The European Tour International Schedule and won for him The European Tour Golfer of the Month for February.

Holding a two stroke advantage coming to the final hole, he knew the job was pretty much done. He then produced one of his best shots of the week, a drive straight down the middle, followed, ironically, by one of his worst. His six iron approach came out of the heel, barely making the green over the water, but the ball kindly settled rather than roll into what would have surely been a watery grave.

Nevertheless with three rounds in the 60s, including an equal best of the tournament 64 in the third round which took him to within one shot of the pacesetting Kiyota, this was a performance to be admired. Brown had played alongside Montgomerie in the first two rounds and confessed to being nervous. He should never feel that way again.

Iain Carter
BBC Radio Five Live

(left to right) Asif Adil, Managing Director, Diageo India, Mark Brown, and Bhupinder Singh Hooda, Honourable Chief Minister of the state of Haryana

Phillip Archer

Greg Chalmers

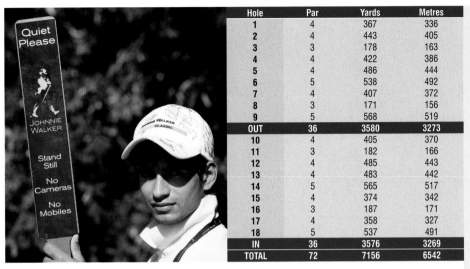

Hole	Par	Yards	Metres
1	4	367	336
2	4	443	405
3	3	178	163
4	4	422	386
5	4	486	444
6	5	538	492
7	4	407	372
8	3	171	156
9	5	568	519
OUT	36	3580	3273
10	4	405	370
11	3	182	166
12	4	485	443
13	4	483	442
14	5	565	517
15	4	374	342
16	3	187	171
17	4	358	327
18	5	537	491
IN	36	3576	3269
TOTAL	72	7156	6542

Daniel Vancsik

DLF Golf and Country Club

Final Results

Pos	Name		Rd1	Rd2	Rd3	Rd4	Total		€	£
1	Mark BROWN	NZL	71	68	64	67	270	-18	276,387.23	208,329.99
2	Taichiro KIYOTA	JPN	68	67	67	71	273	-15	123,659.84	93,210.00
	Greg CHALMERS	AUS	68	69	68	68	273	-15	123,659.84	93,210.00
	Scott STRANGE	AUS	71	67	68	67	273	-15	123,659.84	93,210.00
5	Shiv KAPUR	IND	69	65	72	68	274	-14	59,368.93	44,750.00
	Graeme STORM	ENG	70	66	69	69	274	-14	59,368.93	44,750.00
	Johan EDFORS	SWE	71	69	69	65	274	-14	59,368.93	44,750.00
8	Jyoti RANDHAWA	IND	70	65	68	72	275	-13	41,458.75	31,250.00
9	Daniel VANCSIK	ARG	67	71	68	70	276	-12	35,157.02	26,500.00
	Prayad MARKSAENG	THA	74	65	70	67	276	-12	35,157.02	26,500.00
11	Jeev Milkha SINGH	IND	68	70	70	69	277	-11	28,578.90	21,541.67
	José Manuel LARA	ESP	69	67	73	68	277	-11	28,578.90	21,541.67
	Scott BARR	AUS	71	70	67	69	277	-11	28,578.90	21,541.67
14	Søren HANSEN	DEN	69	69	71	69	278	-10	24,377.74	18,375.00
	Wen-tang LIN	TPE	70	67	72	69	278	-10	24,377.74	18,375.00
	Marcus FRASER	AUS	71	68	71	68	278	-10	24,377.74	18,375.00
17	Mark FOSTER	ENG	68	74	67	70	279	-9	19,775.82	14,906.25
	Arjun ATWAL	IND	69	72	67	71	279	-9	19,775.82	14,906.25
	Vijay SINGH	FIJ	70	68	69	72	279	-9	19,775.82	14,906.25
	Tony CAROLAN	AUS	71	69	68	71	279	-9	19,775.82	14,906.25
	Thaworn WIRATCHANT	THA	71	70	68	70	279	-9	19,775.82	14,906.25
	Phillip ARCHER	ENG	72	64	69	74	279	-9	19,775.82	14,906.25
	Scott LAYCOCK	AUS	72	68	68	71	279	-9	19,775.82	14,906.25
	Kane WEBBER	AUS	73	69	66	71	279	-9	19,775.82	14,906.25
25	Unho PARK	AUS	68	66	75	71	280	-8	16,251.83	12,250.00
	Adam BLAND	AUS	69	68	71	72	280	-8	16,251.83	12,250.00
	Chris RODGERS	ENG	72	67	70	71	280	-8	16,251.83	12,250.00
	Grégory HAVRET	FRA	72	68	70	70	280	-8	16,251.83	12,250.00
	Miguel Angel JIMÉNEZ	ESP	75	67	72	66	280	-8	16,251.83	12,250.00
30	Adam SCOTT	AUS	68	68	74	71	281	-7	14,013.06	10,562.50
	Paul SHEEHAN	AUS	68	70	70	73	281	-7	14,013.06	10,562.50
	Rahil GANGJEE	IND	68	71	70	72	281	-7	14,013.06	10,562.50
	Won Joon LEE	AUS	70	69	74	68	281	-7	14,013.06	10,562.50
34	James KAMTE	RSA	68	71	69	74	282	-6	12,271.79	9,250.00
	Robert KARLSSON	SWE	71	70	73	68	282	-6	12,271.79	9,250.00
	Raphaël JACQUELIN	FRA	72	68	67	75	282	-6	12,271.79	9,250.00
	Simon DYSON	ENG	73	69	71	69	282	-6	12,271.79	9,250.00
38	Robert-Jan DERKSEN	NED	68	72	72	71	283	-5	10,613.44	8,000.00
	Anthony SUMMERS	AUS	69	71	70	73	283	-5	10,613.44	8,000.00
	Wen-chong LIANG	CHN	69	71	71	72	283	-5	10,613.44	8,000.00
	Simon YATES	SCO	71	71	68	73	283	-5	10,613.44	8,000.00
	Peter LAWRIE	IRL	72	68	70	73	283	-5	10,613.44	8,000.00
	Joost LUITEN	NED	73	67	71	72	283	-5	10,613.44	8,000.00
44	Martin ERLANDSSON	SWE	70	72	72	70	284	-4	8,955.09	6,750.00
	Anton HAIG	RSA	71	71	69	73	284	-4	8,955.09	6,750.00
	David FROST	RSA	72	69	71	72	284	-4	8,955.09	6,750.00
	Mukesh KUMAR	IND	73	69	67	75	284	-4	8,955.09	6,750.00
48	Adam BLYTH	AUS	69	72	73	72	286	-2	7,462.57	5,625.00
	Iain STEEL	MAS	70	72	71	73	286	-2	7,462.57	5,625.00
	Richard FINCH	ENG	72	65	73	76	286	-2	7,462.57	5,625.00
	Oliver WILSON	ENG	72	68	71	75	286	-2	7,462.57	5,625.00
	Marc WARREN	SCO	73	69	72	72	286	-2	7,462.57	5,625.00
53	Arjun SINGH	IND	69	70	73	75	287	-1	5,804.22	4,375.00
	Michael LONG	NZL	70	69	73	75	287	-1	5,804.22	4,375.00
	Peter HEDBLOM	SWE	72	72	72	71	287	-1	5,804.22	4,375.00
	Gavin FLINT	AUS	73	68	68	78	287	-1	5,804.22	4,375.00
	Terry PILKADARIS	AUS	74	68	73	72	287	-1	5,804.22	4,375.00
58	Gaganjeet BHULLAR	IND	72	69	73	74	288	0	4,726.30	3,562.50
	Keith HORNE	RSA	72	70	72	74	288	0	4,726.30	3,562.50
	Sam WALKER	ENG	72	70	72	74	288	0	4,726.30	3,562.50
	Mikko ILONEN	FIN	72	70	72	74	288	0	4,726.30	3,562.50
62	Prom MEESAWAT	THA	70	72	73	75	290	2	4,311.71	3,250.00
63	Digvijay SINGH	IND	70	70	73	78	291	3	4,145.87	3,125.00
64	Rahul GANAPATHY	IND	73	69	74	77	293	5	3,980.04	3,000.00
65	Andrew TAMPION	AUS	72	70	76	85	303	15	3,814.20	2,875.00

Total Prize Fund

€1,641,713 £1,237,460

New Zealander Mark Brown won his maiden European Tour title in just his eighth start. He joined fellow Kiwi - Michael Campbell (2000) - in making the Johnnie Walker Classic his debut European Tour victory.

Silence is Golden

1	Arjun ATWAL			270	-18
2	Peter HEDBLOM			270	-18
3	Simon DYSON			271	-17
	Kane WEBBER			271	-17
5	Francesco MOLINARI			272	-16
6	David LYNN			273	-15
	Jyoti RANDHAWA			273	-15
	Charl SCHWARTZEL			273	-15
	Daniel VANCSIK			273	-15
10	Darren CLARKE			274	-14
	Johan EDFORS			274	-14

M ost golfers have a reason for turning professional which goes beyond an undisputed love for the game. Where the Indian contingent is concerned, S S P Chowrasia was a caddie who wanted to play his way out of poverty while Jeev Milkha Singh was not merely content to be the son of a famous father – the athlete nicknamed 'The Flying Sikh'- he wanted to be someone himself.

Nick Dougherty

Jyoti Randhawa

As for Arjun Atwal, who won his second Maybank Malaysian Open title after a play-off with defending champion Peter Hedblom, this offspring of an affluent Indian family needed to show that he could make his own way in life. In the general course of events, no-one would have spoken more eloquently in victory than Atwal. Yet, on this occasion, he could scarcely talk at all.

For months he had been worrying whether police in Florida would press charges in connection with a car accident some 12 months beforehand but now, in the space of one glorious fortnight, his life had taken a dramatic turn for the better. Firstly, he received notification that his name had been cleared by the authorities in the United States before, a week later, he picked up his first European Tour International Schedule title since his maiden Malaysian Open triumph in 2003. Little wonder his sense of relief was palpable.

The Kota Permai Golf and Country Club, a new venue for The European Tour, was showered not only with a couple of tropical downpours over the course of the week, but also with a never ending stream of compliments. To the players, it presented itself as a 'thinking man's course' in that it demanded rather more than one booming drive after another.

With the greens immaculate, the trees dappled in yellow bloom and the birds in full cry, the first day conditions resembled the pages from a PG Wodehouse novel, given the fact that all nature appeared to be crying 'fore'.

Nick Dougherty's golf contributed to the wondrous impression. Nine under par after 12 holes, the 25 year old Englishman holed from 35 feet across the fourth green – his 13th hole of the day – to move to ten under par.

Ten players – including Major Champions Seve Ballesteros, Mark O'Meara and Ian Woosnam – know what it feels like to make eight birdies in a row in a European Tour event and Dougherty, from the 16th to the fourth, had reeled off seven. As he strode to the fifth tee, he even had visions of carding the Tour's first 59.

"To get three birdies in the last five holes wasn't that tall an order," he said afterwards. His big chance came at the seventh, a 525 yard par five which he knew he could catch comfortably in two. However, to use his own cheerful choice of words, he "botched up", knocking his second right of the green on the way to collecting the third of five closing pars for a 62.

At that point, he led by two from his close friend and fellow Englishman Simon Dyson – who has built a reputation for himself as something of a warm weather specialist – and Australian Marcus Fraser.

Following a second round 70, Dougherty had to be content with a share of pole position with India's Jyoti Randhawa and home country favourite Danny Chia who had six birdies and exactly double that in cigarettes as he added a 67 to his opening 65. It was the excitement, he explained a little sheepishly, which had him smoking more than at any time in his life.

Into the weekend, the leading trio faded leaving Darren Clarke as the man to watch on Saturday as he strode up the leader board with an outward 29. As it so often does, however, the game put him back in his place with an inward 38 leaving Hedblom to come to the fore. The Swede posted a 65 which left him two shots clear of the field – and seven ahead of Atwal – and seemingly perfectly poised to make a successful defence of his title.

The last day was bisected by a storm of theatrical proportions and a lengthy break which did little to help the momentum of most. Hedblom, for example, could only extract two birdies from the course in a closing 71, good enough just to tie the fast-finishing Atwal who had bucked the general trend with a scintillating 64.

The first play-off hole – the 565 yard 18th – was halved in par fives after Hedblom found the water and Atwal encountered bunker trouble, before the Indian won it at the second – the 207 yard 17th – with a pitch and putt par three.

His exquisite chip was almost certainly a legacy of the short game work done over the winter alongside Tiger Woods in Florida. The World Number One had taught him to hit miniature draws and fades but, more than that, he had passed on a touch of his assumption of success.

Lewine Mair
The Daily Telegraph

Simon Dyson

(left to right) H.R.H Prince Abdul Majid Iskandar Tunku Bendahara Johor, President, Malaysian Golf Association, Arjun Atwal and Datuk Amirsham A Aziz President & CEO Maybank

Francesco Molinari

Peter Hedblom

Kota Permai Golf and Country Club

Final Results

Pos	Name		Rd1	Rd2	Rd3	Rd4	Total		€	£
1	Arjun ATWAL	IND	70	68	68	64	270	-18	219,483.65	167,806.09
2	Peter HEDBLOM	SWE	66	68	65	71	270	-18	146,322.43	111,870.72
3	Simon DYSON	ENG	64	71	67	69	271	-17	74,142.32	56,685.46
	Kane WEBBER	AUS	67	71	68	65	271	-17	74,142.32	56,685.46
5	Francesco MOLINARI	ITA	67	69	71	65	272	-16	55,837.20	42,690.29
6	Daniel VANCSIK	ARG	65	72	64	72	273	-15	37,005.31	28,292.39
	Jyoti RANDHAWA	IND	67	65	70	71	273	-15	37,005.31	28,292.39
	David LYNN	ENG	70	68	70	65	273	-15	37,005.31	28,292.39
	Charl SCHWARTZEL	RSA	71	66	67	69	273	-15	37,005.31	28,292.39
10	Darren CLARKE	NIR	69	68	67	70	274	-14	25,284.77	19,331.45
	Johan EDFORS	SWE	72	68	69	65	274	-14	25,284.77	19,331.45
12	Marcus FRASER	AUS	64	72	72	67	275	-13	20,385.85	15,585.99
	Keith HORNE	RSA	65	72	72	66	275	-13	20,385.85	15,585.99
	Carlos RODILES	ESP	66	69	71	69	275	-13	20,385.85	15,585.99
	Scott BARR	AUS	68	68	68	71	275	-13	20,385.85	15,585.99
	Graeme STORM	ENG	69	68	70	68	275	-13	20,385.85	15,585.99
17	Graeme MCDOWELL	NIR	66	68	71	71	276	-12	16,724.82	12,786.95
	Chinnarat PHADUNGSIL	THA	67	70	70	69	276	-12	16,724.82	12,786.95
	Raphaël JACQUELIN	FRA	68	69	69	70	276	-12	16,724.82	12,786.95
	Gary MURPHY	IRL	70	67	73	66	276	-12	16,724.82	12,786.95
21	Nick DOUGHERTY	ENG	62	70	72	73	277	-11	14,486.07	11,075.31
	Søren KJELDSEN	DEN	65	68	69	75	277	-11	14,486.07	11,075.31
	Scott STRANGE	AUS	66	71	72	68	277	-11	14,486.07	11,075.31
	Peter LAWRIE	IRL	69	67	72	69	277	-11	14,486.07	11,075.31
	David FROST	RSA	70	67	70	70	277	-11	14,486.07	11,075.31
26	Robert-Jan DERKSEN	NED	66	69	72	71	278	-10	12,115.62	9,262.99
	Mark BROWN	NZL	66	73	70	69	278	-10	12,115.62	9,262.99
	Lian-wei ZHANG	CHN	68	68	74	68	278	-10	12,115.62	9,262.99
	Artemio MURAKAMI	PHI	69	71	73	65	278	-10	12,115.62	9,262.99
	Felipe AGUILAR	CHI	70	70	67	71	278	-10	12,115.62	9,262.99
	Jean-François LUCQUIN	FRA	71	69	70	68	278	-10	12,115.62	9,262.99
	Scott DRUMMOND	SCO	72	66	72	68	278	-10	12,115.62	9,262.99
33	Anton HAIG	RSA	68	71	70	70	279	-9	10,041.48	7,677.21
	Iain STEEL	MAS	70	69	72	68	279	-9	10,041.48	7,677.21
	Richard LEE	NZL	70	70	70	69	279	-9	10,041.48	7,677.21
	Mardan MAMAT	SIN	72	65	70	72	279	-9	10,041.48	7,677.21
37	Gaurav GHEI	IND	67	71	72	70	280	-8	8,955.02	6,846.56
	Martin ERLANDSSON	SWE	69	67	71	73	280	-8	8,955.02	6,846.56
	Thomas BJÖRN	DEN	72	67	73	68	280	-8	8,955.02	6,846.56
	Sam LITTLE	ENG	73	67	68	72	280	-8	8,955.02	6,846.56
41	Danny CHIA	MAS	65	67	80	69	281	-7	7,769.80	5,940.39
	José Manuel LARA	ESP	68	67	76	70	281	-7	7,769.80	5,940.39
	Terry PILKADARIS	AUS	69	69	71	72	281	-7	7,769.80	5,940.39
	Jean VAN DE VELDE	FRA	71	68	72	70	281	-7	7,769.80	5,940.39
	Hendrik BUHRMANN	RSA	71	69	69	72	281	-7	7,769.80	5,940.39
46	S S P CHOWRASIA	IND	66	73	69	74	282	-6	6,321.19	4,832.86
	Bryan SALTUS	USA	67	71	71	73	282	-6	6,321.19	4,832.86
	Prayad MARKSAENG	THA	67	73	70	72	282	-6	6,321.19	4,832.86
	Angelo QUE	PHI	69	71	71	71	282	-6	6,321.19	4,832.86
	Ter-chang WANG	TPE	70	68	73	71	282	-6	6,321.19	4,832.86
	Grégory BOURDY	FRA	70	70	72	70	282	-6	6,321.19	4,832.86
52	Oliver WILSON	ENG	66	71	73	73	283	-5	4,740.89	3,624.65
	Mikko ILONEN	FIN	68	72	72	71	283	-5	4,740.89	3,624.65
	Young NAM	KOR	69	69	75	70	283	-5	4,740.89	3,624.65
	Shaaban HUSSEIN	MAS	69	71	70	73	283	-5	4,740.89	3,624.65
	Grégory HAVRET	FRA	70	68	70	75	283	-5	4,740.89	3,624.65
	Anthony KANG	USA	70	70	72	71	283	-5	4,740.89	3,624.65
58	Simon WAKEFIELD	ENG	69	69	72	74	284	-4	3,950.75	3,020.54
59	Oliver FISHER	ENG	68	71	72	74	285	-3	3,753.21	2,869.51
	Mads VIBE-HASTRUP	DEN	71	68	74	72	285	-3	3,753.21	2,869.51
61	Zane SCOTLAND	ENG	69	69	74	74	286	-2	3,489.82	2,668.14
	Zaw MOE	MYA	72	68	70	76	286	-2	3,489.82	2,668.14
63	Simon YATES	SCO	69	71	74	74	288	0	3,094.75	2,366.09
	José-Filipe LIMA	POR	69	71	76	72	288	0	3,094.75	2,366.09
	Ignacio GARRIDO	ESP	70	67	74	77	288	0	3,094.75	2,366.09
	S MURTHY	MAS	71	67	76	74	288	0	3,094.75	2,366.09
67	Rafa ECHENIQUE	ARG	66	68	78	78	290	2	2,699.68	2,064.04
	Marcus BOTH	AUS	67	72	75	76	290	2	2,699.68	2,064.04
69	Yasin ALI	ENG	73	67	82	76	298	10	2,502.14	1,913.01

Total Prize Fund
€1,314,512 £1,005,009

Hole	Par	Yards	Metres
1	5	544	497
2	4	362	331
3	4	411	376
4	3	191	175
5	4	387	354
6	3	212	194
7	5	525	480
8	4	441	403
9	4	419	383
OUT	**36**	**3492**	**3193**
10	4	408	373
11	4	368	337
12	5	525	480
13	4	419	383
14	3	165	151
15	4	446	408
16	4	384	351
17	3	207	189
18	5	565	517
IN	**36**	**3487**	**3189**
TOTAL	**72**	**6979**	**6382**

India's Arjun Atwal re-joined The European Tour in 2008 in the Past Champions category. With this victory he gained an exemption until the end of 2010. The Indian became the first from the Past Champions category to win on The European Tour since Per-Ulrik Johansson claimed the title at The Russian Open Golf Championship in 2007.

Celtic
Connection

1	Graeme McDOWELL		264	-24
2	Jeev Milkha SINGH		264	-24
3	Paul McGINLEY		271	-17
4	Shingo KATAYAMA		273	-15
5	Thomas BJÖRN		274	-14
	Johan EDFORS		274	-14
	Anthony KIM		274	-14
8	Oliver WILSON		275	-13
9	Phillip ARCHER		276	-12
	Kane WEBBER		276	-12

What is it like? More floridly perhaps, but Queen Elizabeth probably asked Walter Raleigh the same question on his return from the New World. A first visit to South Korea – a new world for The European Tour – and the question was inevitable.

Flying into Jeju – the country's holiday and honeymoon island – the first thought was that it looked similar to Mallorca. Seeing the volcanic rocks revised the opinion to, perhaps, the Canary Islands, while the drive to the Pinx Golf Club amid pines and firs with wintry wheat-coloured grasses turned thoughts to the Scottish Borders.

Given the fact it was the Ballantine's Championship, the link to Scotland was inevitable and was strengthened by the presence of a piper and promotions girls clad in blue tartan. Even the official starter had a kilt and sporran, while Sandy Lyle enjoyed a place in the spotlight during the week as the tournament's 'Official Ambassador'.

Just about the only thing Scotland did not give to the week was a winner, that being supplied by its Celtic cousin, Northern Ireland, in the shape of Graeme McDowell who eventually overcame India's Jeev Milkha Singh in a sudden-death play-off.

An information booklet in the clubhouse proclaimed that Jeju had three factors in abundance: wind, women and rocks. We will leave the women aside and come to the rocks later but the tourist brochure was spot on about the elements, perhaps helping to explain why a man reared on the windswept links of Royal Portrush prevailed.

Come Friday morning the flags were limbo dancing and in some cases removed, so as not to damage the holes themselves. Merely standing upright was an achievement, leaving many to force a wry smile at Korea's claim to be; 'Land of the Morning Calm'. Yet, aside from a two and a quarter hour delay that day, the Championship ran as smooth as a single malt.

Finland's Mikko Ilonen shared the first round lead with Tony Carolan of Australia who was not without his problems. He sacked his caddie early in the round after the troubled bagman clattered clubs as his partners putted, having earlier been forbidden to walk on the greens because of his spikes.

After a competent 68 on the opening day, McDowell's 64 saw him speed two shots clear on day two, an entirely appropriate description to use for the Ulsterman was one of many players seen running between shots to beat the klaxon and ensure they finished their second rounds on the appointed day.

McDowell was still two ahead until he had a close encounter with a Stone Grandfather on the final hole of the third day's play. Dol hareubang are figures carved from lava rock, reminiscent of the statues on Easter Island. They are found throughout Jeju, marking the founding myth when three divine men emerged from the ground of the uninhabited island.

Johan Edfors

Below left *Padraig Harrington*

Paul McGinley

Graeme McDowell (right) is presented with the trophy by Christian Porta, Chairman and CEO of Chivas

K J Choi

Presumably McDowell did not think them divine after their confrontation cost him a double bogey six which meant he and former Volvo Masters champion Singh were side by side into the final round, four shots clear of the field.

Paul McGinley – who eventually took third place – reckoned he won the tournament the rest of the field were playing but, at seven shots adrift, he was merely another observer among the thousands who thrilled to the closing day's duel in the wind. Singh's putter sang as he held sway through much of the day, but extra holes were needed after a strong finish from McDowell saw both men close with 66s.

Three times the duo returned to the 18th hole before the deadlock was broken in spectacular fashion. Singh had every right to be delighted with his approach shot to six feet but it paled into insignificance moments later when McDowell's seven iron finished a mere foot from the cup.

The Northern Irishman's guaranteed birdie three exerted additional pressure on the Indian's putt and when the ball stayed above ground, McDowell had his third European Tour International Schedule title, almost four years since his last victory in Italy in 2004.

A bonus was entry to the World Golf Championships – CA Championship in Florida the following week which meant he did not have much time to sample the sponsor's product.

That was a pity as he had won five bottles of whisky in total; a 17 year old for a birdie at the 17th on the first day; two 21 year olds for the lowest rounds of the day on Friday and Sunday; a 30 year old for the lowest round of the tournament; and one of only eight 40 year old Ballantine's in existence for winning their inaugural event.

It is a fair bet it was McDowell's only regret of the week.

Nick Dye
European Tour Radio

17 Years Old

LEAVE AN IMPRESSION

Ballantine's®

Pinx Golf Club

Final Results

Pos	Name		Rd1	Rd2	Rd3	Rd4	Total		€	£
1	Graeme MCDOWELL	NIR	68	64	66	66	264	-24	333,330.00	253,923.15
2	Jeev Milkha SINGH	IND	68	66	64	66	264	-24	222,220.00	169,282.10
3	Paul MCGINLEY	IRL	68	67	67	69	271	-17	125,200.00	95,374.49
4	Shingo KATAYAMA	JPN	68	70	68	67	273	-15	100,000.00	76,177.71
5	Anthony KIM	USA	68	68	69	69	274	-14	71,600.00	54,543.24
	Johan EDFORS	SWE	69	65	69	71	274	-14	71,600.00	54,543.24
	Thomas BJÖRN	DEN	70	66	70	68	274	-14	71,600.00	54,543.24
8	Oliver WILSON	ENG	70	69	67	69	275	-13	50,000.00	38,088.85
9	Kane WEBBER	AUS	71	68	65	72	276	-12	42,400.00	32,299.35
	Phillip ARCHER	ENG	71	70	67	68	276	-12	42,400.00	32,299.35
11	Jyoti RANDHAWA	IND	68	72	70	67	277	-11	34,466.67	26,255.92
	Terry PILKADARIS	AUS	71	66	71	69	277	-11	34,466.67	26,255.92
	Zane SCOTLAND	ENG	74	69	68	66	277	-11	34,466.67	26,255.92
14	Thaworn WIRATCHANT	THA	69	70	68	71	278	-10	28,800.00	21,939.18
	David FROST	RSA	69	71	70	68	278	-10	28,800.00	21,939.18
	Padraig HARRINGTON	IRL	71	65	68	74	278	-10	28,800.00	21,939.18
	Hyung-Sung KIM	KOR	72	70	66	70	278	-10	28,800.00	21,939.18
18	Adam BLYTH	AUS	69	72	70	68	279	-9	24,866.67	18,942.86
	Chris DIMARCO	USA	70	68	72	69	279	-9	24,866.67	18,942.86
	Sang-Moon BAE	KOR	71	71	69	68	279	-9	24,866.67	18,942.86
21	Hyung-Tae KIM	KOR	69	66	74	71	280	-8	22,600.00	17,216.16
	Ariel CANETE	ARG	70	68	67	75	280	-8	22,600.00	17,216.16
	David LYNN	ENG	71	71	68	70	280	-8	22,600.00	17,216.16
24	Mikko ILONEN	FIN	67	70	69	75	281	-7	19,300.00	14,702.30
	Prayad MARKSAENG	THA	68	71	71	71	281	-7	19,300.00	14,702.30
	Francesco MOLINARI	ITA	69	72	71	69	281	-7	19,300.00	14,702.30
	Anthony KANG	USA	70	71	69	71	281	-7	19,300.00	14,702.30
	K J CHOI	KOR	71	69	69	72	281	-7	19,300.00	14,702.30
	Damien MCGRANE	IRL	71	69	70	71	281	-7	19,300.00	14,702.30
	Maarten LAFEBER	NED	71	70	70	70	281	-7	19,300.00	14,702.30
	Wen-tang LIN	TPE	72	71	69	69	281	-7	19,300.00	14,702.30
32	Inn-Choon HWANG	KOR	68	69	73	72	282	-6	15,300.00	11,655.19
	Garry HOUSTON	WAL	69	74	69	70	282	-6	15,300.00	11,655.19
	Paul BROADHURST	ENG	70	72	70	70	282	-6	15,300.00	11,655.19
	Do-kyu PARK	KOR	71	72	67	72	282	-6	15,300.00	11,655.19
	Wook-soon KANG	KOR	73	70	68	71	282	-6	15,300.00	11,655.19
	Joong-kyung MO	KOR	74	70	70	68	282	-6	15,300.00	11,655.19
38	Marcus BOTH	AUS	74	70	71	68	283	-5	13,800.00	10,512.52
39	David GRIFFITHS	ENG	69	71	76	68	284	-4	12,800.00	9,750.75
	Martin ERLANDSSON	SWE	71	73	69	71	284	-4	12,800.00	9,750.75
	Thomas LEVET	FRA	71	73	72	68	284	-4	12,800.00	9,750.75
	José Manuel LARA	ESP	72	71	70	71	284	-4	12,800.00	9,750.75
43	Jong-yul SUK	KOR	71	70	71	73	285	-3	11,000.00	8,379.55
	Emanuele CANONICA	ITA	71	71	68	75	285	-3	11,000.00	8,379.55
	Thomas AIKEN	RSA	71	73	71	70	285	-3	11,000.00	8,379.55
	Yong-eun YANG	KOR	73	70	70	72	285	-3	11,000.00	8,379.55
	S K HO	KOR	74	67	70	74	285	-3	11,000.00	8,379.55
48	Scott BARR	AUS	70	70	74	72	286	-2	9,600.00	7,313.06
	Gary SIMPSON	AUS	70	70	74	72	286	-2	9,600.00	7,313.06
50	Tony CAROLAN	AUS	67	75	72	73	287	-1	7,800.00	5,941.86
	Carlos RODILES	ESP	69	71	75	72	287	-1	7,800.00	5,941.86
	Daniel VANCSIK	ARG	70	73	72	72	287	-1	7,800.00	5,941.86
	Juvic PAGUNSAN	PHI	70	73	73	71	287	-1	7,800.00	5,941.86
	David BRANSDON	AUS	72	70	73	72	287	-1	7,800.00	5,941.86
	Felipe AGUILAR	CHI	72	72	70	73	287	-1	7,800.00	5,941.86
	Mardan MAMAT	SIN	73	71	71	72	287	-1	7,800.00	5,941.86
57	Oliver FISHER	ENG	70	74	75	69	288	0	6,000.00	4,570.66
	Prom MEESAWAT	THA	71	71	76	70	288	0	6,000.00	4,570.66
	Gaurav GHEI	IND	72	72	74	70	288	0	6,000.00	4,570.66
60	Frankie MINOZA	PHI	75	69	76	69	289	1	5,600.00	4,265.95
61	Sang-Ki KIM	KOR	70	74	70	77	291	3	5,400.00	4,113.60
62	Tom WHITEHOUSE	ENG	70	70	77	75	292	4	5,000.00	3,808.89
	Gavin FLINT	AUS	72	72	74	74	292	4	5,000.00	3,808.89
	Kyung-Tae KIM	KOR	74	70	76	72	292	4	5,000.00	3,808.89
65	Jun TAE-HYUN	PKR	69	71	78	75	293	5	4,500.00	3,428.00
	Ter-chang WANG	TPE	71	73	72	77	293	5	4,500.00	3,428.00
67	Simon GRIFFITHS	ENG	68	74	80	73	295	7	4,200.00	3,199.46

Total Prize Fund

€1,988,550 £1,514,832

Hole	Par	Yards	Metres
1	4	385	352
2	3	187	171
3	4	381	349
4	5	543	497
5	3	202	185
6	4	460	421
7	4	468	428
8	4	423	387
9	5	557	510
OUT	**36**	**3606**	**3300**
10	5	543	497
11	4	421	385
12	4	463	424
13	4	408	373
14	3	201	184
15	4	436	399
16	5	563	515
17	3	214	196
18	4	490	448
IN	**36**	**3739**	**3421**
TOTAL	**72**	**7345**	**6721**

The visit to South Korea for the Ballantine's Championship was the first time The European Tour has played a tournament in this country. South Korea became the 38th different destination to host a European Tour International Schedule event.

Action Replay

1	**Alastair FORSYTH**		**273**	**-15**
2	Hennie OTTO		273	-15
3	Gary CLARK		277	-11
4	Sven STRÜVER		278	-10
5	John BICKERTON		279	-9
	Alvaro VELASCO		279	-9
	Fredrik WIDMARK		279	-9
8	Gary ORR		280	-8
9	Martin WIEGELE		281	-7
10	Sébastien DELAGRANGE		282	-6
	Ben EVANS		282	-6
	Peter GUSTAFSSON		282	-6
	Peter LAWRIE		282	-6
	Matthew MILLAR		282	-6

T he year was 1996, the venue Cardross in Scotland. Nerves were jangling for two young amateurs, home favourite Alastair Forsyth and South African Hennie Otto. After a cut and thrust tournament, the pair were locked together in the Scottish Amateur Open Stroke Play Championship. Amazingly, eight holes into a sudden-death play-off, there was still no winner.

Sven Strüver

Then, at the ninth hole, the local lad finally ended the deadlock as Otto made bogey; Forsyth's par good enough to see him claim his first significant title.

Fast forward a dozen years, the venue Santo da Serra in Madeira. Two seasoned professionals stand on the 18th tee preparing to engage in a sudden-death play-off for the Madeira Islands Open BPI – Portugal title. Incredibly, the duo are Alastair Forsyth and Hennie Otto.

Often, in dramatic situations, humour is a wonderful release for tension and the pair could not help but smile when the Scot – peering through the impenetrable mist shrouds which had already disrupted proceedings over a dramatic

final round – leaned down and whispered in the ear of the South African; "Don't worry Hennie, I don't think we can go nine holes today."

He was right. Almost before the play-off had begun, it was over. Both men had courageously birdied the 386 yard 18th in regulation play but on their return moments later, it was only Forsyth who could repeat the feat, Otto missing from eight feet before Forsyth did not from seven.

It proved a remarkable reversal of fortune for the Scot who did not trouble the bookmakers in the run-up to the tournament.

Indeed, when Forsyth's veteran caddie, Dave Renwick, a man who had accompanied both

José Maria Olazábal and Vijay Singh to Masters Tournament success and had been part of several European Ryder Cup victories, eyed the heavily undulating course for his first time, he was not optimistic, especially when statistics showed his man had missed the cut in all five tournaments he had played in 2008. Renwick, though, was in line for delivery of an unexpected windfall.

While the week ended in dramatic fashion, the focus at the beginning of the tournament centred on two deliveries of a very different kind.

The first arrived bang on time for Englishman Ian Garbutt in the shape of his second child, wife Zoe texting him in the early hours of Thursday morning from Doncaster Royal Infirmary to inform him of little Eva's safe entrance into the world.

Having lost his card at the end of the 2007 season, the 35 year old's playing opportunities had been limited in 2008 and, after discussing the situation with Zoe, he decided he had to take the opportunity offered to him to play in Madeira. Thankfully he held himself together well enough to make the cut, thus enabling him to put a "few bob" away for Eva's future.

The second delivery – the suitcase containing all of Hennie Otto's clothes for the week – sadly, did not appear on time. There is, however, a silver lining in every cloud and the absence of the South African's entire wardrobe enabled club officials to kit him out in polo shirts and jumpers bedecked with the Santo da Serra logo.

It gave the club priceless advertising, with Otto's picture appearing in every newspaper and on every website as he held sway for the majority of the week, eventually, it seemed, having rediscovered the game which took him to the top of the leader board after the first round of The 132nd Open Championship at Royal St George's.

Three consecutive rounds of 67 gave him a five shot lead over Forsyth going into the final afternoon but his advantage quickly began to erode, until a major turning point arrived at the fifth where the Scot's stunning approach shot to six inches gave him a birdie three as Otto made bogey five.

The momentum was now with the pursuer who kept up the chase until he finally overcame Otto on the 73rd hole.

It was an admirable bid by the South African to regain his full European Tour card but one which came up just short. For Forsyth though, it continued his exemplary play-off record, having beaten Stephen Leaney in sudden-death for his first European Tour win in the Malaysian Open in 2002.

Norman Dabell

Hennie Otto

Alastair Forsyth (left), is presented with the trophy by João Cunha e Silva, The Vice President of Madeira

John Bickerton

Hole	Par	Yards	Metres
1	4	398	364
2	4	441	403
3	5	521	476
4	3	202	185
5	4	412	377
6	4	364	333
7	5	538	492
8	3	168	154
9	4	385	352
OUT	36	3429	3136
10	4	395	361
11	5	572	523
12	4	315	288
13	4	462	422
14	4	358	327
15	3	187	171
16	5	556	508
17	3	166	152
18	4	386	353
IN	36	3397	3105
TOTAL	72	6826	6241

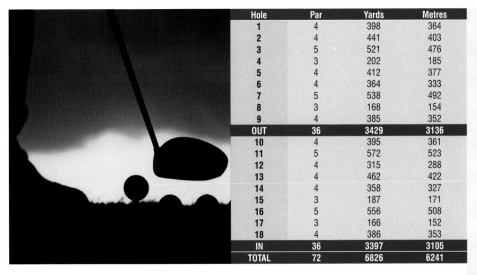

Gary Clark

Fredrik Widmark

madeira island

TURISMO DE
PORTUGAL

Santo da Serra

Final Results

Pos	Name		Rd1	Rd2	Rd3	Rd4	Total		€	£
1	Alastair FORSYTH	SCO	70	70	66	67	273	-15	116,660.00	89,699.82
2	Hennie OTTO	RSA	67	67	67	72	273	-15	77,770.00	59,797.32
3	Gary CLARK	ENG	72	71	64	70	277	-11	43,820.00	33,693.18
4	Sven STRÜVER	GER	66	72	71	69	278	-10	35,000.00	26,911.48
5	Fredrik WIDMARK	SWE	68	70	70	71	279	-9	25,060.00	19,268.62
	John BICKERTON	ENG	69	72	68	70	279	-9	25,060.00	19,268.62
	Alvaro VELASCO	ESP	73	70	68	68	279	-9	25,060.00	19,268.62
8	Gary ORR	SCO	72	70	67	71	280	-8	17,500.00	13,455.74
9	Martin WIEGELE	AUT	73	71	68	69	281	-7	15,680.00	12,056.34
10	Peter GUSTAFSSON	SWE	68	73	73	68	282	-6	12,180.00	9,365.20
	Sébastien DELAGRANGE	FRA	71	75	67	69	282	-6	12,180.00	9,365.20
	Ben EVANS	ENG	74	72	70	66	282	-6	12,180.00	9,365.20
	Peter LAWRIE	IRL	75	69	69	69	282	-6	12,180.00	9,365.20
	Matthew MILLAR	AUS	75	70	68	69	282	-6	12,180.00	9,365.20
15	Raphaël EYRAUD	FRA	70	71	74	68	283	-5	8,827.78	6,787.67
	Bradley DREDGE	WAL	75	69	69	69	283	-5	8,827.78	6,787.67
	Gareth PADDISON	NZL	70	75	69	69	283	-5	8,827.78	6,787.67
	Adilson DA SILVA	BRA	71	68	70	74	283	-5	8,827.78	6,787.67
	Miles TUNNICLIFF	ENG	71	69	71	72	283	-5	8,827.78	6,787.67
	Markus BRIER	AUT	71	74	71	67	283	-5	8,827.78	6,787.67
	Sion E BEBB	WAL	71	74	68	70	283	-5	8,827.78	6,787.67
	Pablo LARRAZABAL	ESP	73	70	71	69	283	-5	8,827.78	6,787.67
	Benn BARHAM	ENG	74	72	68	69	283	-5	8,827.78	6,787.67
24	Michael LORENZO-VERA	FRA	68	71	69	76	284	-4	7,280.00	5,597.59
	Peter WHITEFORD	SCO	70	75	71	68	284	-4	7,280.00	5,597.59
	Santiago LUNA	ESP	73	74	68	69	284	-4	7,280.00	5,597.59
27	Grégory BOURDY	FRA	68	76	71	70	285	-3	6,650.00	5,113.18
	Mattias ELIASSON	SWE	70	72	70	73	285	-3	6,650.00	5,113.18
	Alexander NOREN	SWE	71	73	70	71	285	-3	6,650.00	5,113.18
	Pedro FIGUEIREDO (AM)	POR	74	72	69	70	285	-3		
31	Joakim BÄCKSTRÖM	SWE	72	70	72	72	286	-2	6,020.00	4,628.78
	Hugo SANTOS	POR	72	71	71	72	286	-2	6,020.00	4,628.78
	Andrew COLTART	SCO	74	71	72	69	286	-2	6,020.00	4,628.78
34	Andrew OLDCORN	SCO	71	71	69	76	287	-1	5,337.50	4,104.00
	François DELAMONTAGNE	FRA	72	72	70	73	287	-1	5,337.50	4,104.00
	George MURRAY	SCO	73	74	68	72	287	-1	5,337.50	4,104.00
	Paul WARING	ENG	75	73	70	69	287	-1	5,337.50	4,104.00
38	Gary LOCKERBIE	ENG	71	74	69	74	288	0	4,760.00	3,659.96
	Jesus Maria ARRUTI	ESP	72	74	72	70	288	0	4,760.00	3,659.96
	Wade ORMSBY	AUS	73	73	73	69	288	0	4,760.00	3,659.96
	José-Filipe LIMA	POR	74	71	73	70	288	0	4,760.00	3,659.96
42	Nicolas VANHOOTEGEM	BEL	70	76	67	76	289	1	3,850.00	2,960.26
	Pedro LINHART	ESP	71	73	74	71	289	1	3,850.00	2,960.26
	Tom WHITEHOUSE	ENG	72	76	73	68	289	1	3,850.00	2,960.26
	Edoardo MOLINARI	ITA	72	76	70	71	289	1	3,850.00	2,960.26
	Marcus HIGLEY	ENG	74	72	74	69	289	1	3,850.00	2,960.26
	Ariel CANETE	ARG	74	73	70	72	289	1	3,850.00	2,960.26
	Christian NILSSON	SWE	76	70	70	73	289	1	3,850.00	2,960.26
	Iain PYMAN	ENG	76	72	69	72	289	1	3,850.00	2,960.26
	Steven JEPPESEN	SWE	79	68	70	72	289	1	3,850.00	2,960.26
51	Ben MASON	ENG	73	74	73	70	290	2	2,940.00	2,260.56
	Steve ALKER	NZL	76	70	75	69	290	2	2,940.00	2,260.56
	Robert COLES	ENG	76	70	70	74	290	2	2,940.00	2,260.56
	Henrik NYSTRÖM	SWE	76	71	72	71	290	2	2,940.00	2,260.56
55	Ulrich VAN DEN BERG	RSA	72	75	70	74	291	3	2,380.00	1,829.98
	Gabriel CANIZARES	ESP	73	72	72	74	291	3	2,380.00	1,829.98
	Andrew MCARTHUR	SCO	75	72	72	72	291	3	2,380.00	1,829.98
	Ian GARBUTT	ENG	75	73	71	72	291	3	2,380.00	1,829.98
59	Juan ABBATE	ARG	74	70	75	73	292	4	2,100.00	1,614.69
60	Manuel QUIROS	ESP	71	77	74	71	293	5	1,890.00	1,453.22
	Alan MCLEAN	SCO	72	72	73	76	293	5	1,890.00	1,453.22
	Tim DYKES	WAL	72	74	74	73	293	5	1,890.00	1,453.22
	Simon WAKEFIELD	ENG	74	73	71	75	293	5	1,890.00	1,453.22
	Nuno CAMPINO	POR	75	70	71	77	293	5	1,890.00	1,453.22
65	Notah BEGAY III	USA	71	74	73	76	294	6	1,610.00	1,237.93
	Lee SLATTERY	ENG	74	73	72	75	294	6	1,610.00	1,237.93
	Philip GOLDING	ENG	75	73	73	73	294	6	1,610.00	1,237.93
68	Liam BOND	WAL	72	71	76	76	295	7	1,470.00	1,130.28
69	Jamie MCLEARY	SCO	72	74	70	80	296	8	1,400.00	1,076.46
70	Ricardo SANTOS	POR	73	75	77	72	297	9	1,330.00	1,022.64
71	Matthew KING	ENG	69	76	79	77	301	13	1,290.00	991.88

Total Prize Fund

€700,000   £538,229

MEMBER

Alastair Forsyth's win meant a first Scottish triumph in the Madeira Islands Open BPI - Portugal. It also extended the number of consecutive winning years on The European Tour for Scottish players to five, dating back to the 2004 season.

Consummate
Composure

		271	-17
1 Geoff OGILVY			
2 Jim FURYK		272	-16
Retief GOOSEN		272	-16
Vijay SINGH		272	-16
5 Tiger WOODS		273	-15
6 Nick O'HERN		275	-13
Graeme STORM		275	-13
Steve STRICKER		275	-13
9 Zach JOHNSON		276	-12
Adam SCOTT		276	-12

Geoff Ogilvy is one of the world's foremost amblers. There is much to be said for studying the walks of the great golfers. Mickelson rolls, Woods strolls, Vijay shambles and Ernie rambles. But the world's best never hurry. It took Ogilvy five days to win the World Golf Championships - CA Championship, a tournament he led virtually from start to finish, and it looked like a walk in the park.

Nick O'Hern

Adam Scott

The Australian has a slightly more tippy-toed walk than many of his peers as if there are springs pushing him out of the ground, but it is all done in super slow motion. He looks like a man moving in a 100 degree heat. But when it came to closing out another big tournament, the 30 year old from Adelaide showed once again that he is ultra cool.

There was a remarkable coincidence between this win at the Doral Golf Resort and Spa and his victory in the US Open Championship two years previously, in that both were defined by a chip-in. In New York State in 2006 his wonder shot came on the penultimate hole; in Florida the momentum of his challenge was maintained by a pitch in for par on the 13th.

Tiger Woods himself admits you need a few strokes of good fortune to win a golf tournament – the trick is to take advantage of them, and

Ogilvy certainly did that. At both Winged Foot and Doral, his play in the pressure cooker of the final hole was consummate in its composure.

The drive at the 18th on both courses is renowned for its difficulty, but each time Ogilvy split the fairway. Indeed, so accurate was he with the latter stroke that his ball finished on the fairway's centre line defined by the change of mowing direction.

It was Ogilvy's second victory in a WGC event and he became only the third multiple winner in the series after Darren Clarke and Woods. The Australian also prevented the World Number One from winning his eighth tournament in a row.

Ironically, it had not looked that way on Friday afternoon. On the final green of his second round Woods faced a vicious, downhill, breaking putt. Six feet out from the hole he raised an arm;

CHAMPIONSHIP

as the ball dived below ground he raised the other arm along with his putter.

It looked like a victory celebration and there was not a soul around the green who would have adjudged it premature. After all, Woods had won this title for the previous three years and he was on a hot streak.

But a funny thing happened at the start of the third round; he three putted the first two greens, missing from five and three feet respectively. That just never happens. A few holes later play was suspended, because of lightning in the area. Even the elements, it appeared, were in shock.

As Woods continued to struggle, Jim Furyk, Retief Goosen and Vijay Singh caught and passed him to take a share of second place, one shot behind Ogilvy. The crowd, raised on a diet of Tiger triumphs, did not look too happy, but in truth there were not enough of them to make a fuss.

A week of weather delays meant an inevitable extra day was required to finish the 72 holes and while the South Floridians had turned out in good numbers to catch the stilted weekend action, by the time it came to Easter Monday, many of those lucky enough not to be at work had other family commitments to attend to.

None of which remotely bothered England's Graeme Storm – an affable lad from the north of the country who had celebrated his 30th birthday the week before crossing the Atlantic.

After turning professional in 2000, his early years on Tour were hard, so much so that he had to work in a cake factory in his native Hartlepool to make ends meet. Ironically, perhaps one of his former shop floor colleagues might have made a better start to the tournament as the former Amateur Champion found himself in the water on his first hole before pulling his tee shot at the second and missing the green. His caddie looked like a man who was considering seeking cheaper accommodation.

However, from the end of that first nine to the resumption of play on the Monday, Storm played as well as anyone. His superb third round 63 helped him tie for sixth place, the only European-born player to finish in the top ten.

In a week where the weather dominated the headlines almost as much as Geoff Ogilvy, perhaps a man called Storm was bound to succeed.

Mark Reason
Sunday Telegraph

Retief Goosen

Geoff Ogilvy (left), receives the trophy from Don Friedman, Executive Vice President & Chief Marketing Officer, CA

Zach Johnson

Vijay Singh

Doral Golf Resort and Spa

Final Results

Pos	Name		Rd1	Rd2	Rd3	Rd4	Total		€	£
1	Geoff OGILVY	AUS	65	67	68	71	271	-17	865,160.10	665,221.21
2	Jim FURYK	USA	69	71	64	68	272	-16	339,655.45	261,160.92
	Retief GOOSEN	RSA	71	69	64	68	272	-16	339,655.45	261,160.92
	Vijay SINGH	FIJ	73	68	63	68	272	-16	339,655.45	261,160.92
5	Tiger WOODS	USA	67	66	72	68	273	-15	182,644.91	140,435.59
6	Nick O'HERN	AUS	67	75	67	66	275	-13	127,103.77	97,730.03
	Steve STRICKER	USA	71	68	73	63	275	-13	127,103.77	97,730.03
	Graeme STORM	ENG	71	70	63	71	275	-13	127,103.77	97,730.03
9	Adam SCOTT	AUS	67	68	69	72	276	-12	94,526.75	72,681.58
	Zach JOHNSON	USA	69	72	67	68	276	-12	94,526.75	72,681.58
11	Søren KJELDSEN	DEN	69	71	71	66	277	-11	80,107.42	61,594.56
12	Anders HANSEN	DEN	67	71	67	73	278	-10	68,037.90	52,314.31
	K J CHOI	KOR	70	70	67	71	278	-10	68,037.90	52,314.31
	Tim CLARK	RSA	71	69	66	72	278	-10	68,037.90	52,314.31
15	Grégory HAVRET	FRA	68	74	68	69	279	-9	55,562.50	42,721.98
	Sergio GARCIA	ESP	69	73	69	68	279	-9	55,562.50	42,721.98
	Aaron BADDELEY	AUS	69	74	70	66	279	-9	55,562.50	42,721.98
	Justin ROSE	ENG	70	71	70	68	279	-9	55,562.50	42,721.98
	Stephen AMES	CAN	73	68	68	70	279	-9	55,562.50	42,721.98
20	Stewart CINK	USA	66	74	71	69	280	-8	48,064.45	36,956.73
	Phil MICKELSON	USA	67	74	70	69	280	-8	48,064.45	36,956.73
	Luke DONALD	ENG	68	72	70	70	280	-8	48,064.45	36,956.73
	Robert ALLENBY	AUS	69	75	66	70	280	-8	48,064.45	36,956.73
	Mike WEIR	CAN	73	69	67	71	280	-8	48,064.45	36,956.73
	John ROLLINS	USA	74	71	67	68	280	-8	48,064.45	36,956.73
26	Miguel Angel JIMÉNEZ	ESP	65	74	71	71	281	-7	42,617.15	32,768.30
	Jeev Milkha SINGH	IND	68	70	70	73	281	-7	42,617.15	32,768.30
	Toru TANIGUCHI	JPN	68	73	72	68	281	-7	42,617.15	32,768.30
	Camilo VILLEGAS	COL	71	72	68	70	281	-7	42,617.15	32,768.30
30	Robert KARLSSON	SWE	68	70	70	74	282	-6	40,053.71	30,797.28
	Mark CALCAVECCHIA	USA	68	71	71	72	282	-6	40,053.71	30,797.28
	Andres ROMERO	ARG	68	72	73	69	282	-6	40,053.71	30,797.28
	Boo WEEKLEY	USA	72	73	69	68	282	-6	40,053.71	30,797.28
34	Ross FISHER	ENG	68	73	70	72	283	-5	36,849.41	28,333.50
	Ryuji IMADA	JPN	68	73	73	69	283	-5	36,849.41	28,333.50
	Justin LEONARD	USA	69	74	70	70	283	-5	36,849.41	28,333.50
	Lee WESTWOOD	ENG	71	72	72	68	283	-5	36,849.41	28,333.50
	Daniel CHOPRA	SWE	72	70	69	72	283	-5	36,849.41	28,333.50
	Stuart APPLEBY	AUS	73	71	68	71	283	-5	36,849.41	28,333.50
40	J B HOLMES	USA	69	72	75	68	284	-4	33,645.11	25,869.71
	Trevor IMMELMAN	RSA	70	74	70	70	284	-4	33,645.11	25,869.71
	Scott VERPLANK	USA	71	70	74	69	284	-4	33,645.11	25,869.71
	Brendan JONES	AUS	76	75	66	67	284	-4	33,645.11	25,869.71
44	Woody AUSTIN	USA	70	70	74	71	285	-3	31,322.00	24,083.47
	Richard STERNE	RSA	71	77	67	70	285	-3	31,322.00	24,083.47
	Niclas FASTH	SWE	72	69	70	74	285	-3	31,322.00	24,083.47
	Hunter MAHAN	USA	72	72	71	70	285	-3	31,322.00	24,083.47
48	Graeme MCDOWELL	NIR	72	71	70	73	286	-2	30,120.39	23,159.55
	Brandt SNEDEKER	USA	74	70	72	70	286	-2	30,120.39	23,159.55
	Andrew MCLARDY	RSA	74	74	70	68	286	-2	30,120.39	23,159.55
51	Charles HOWELL III	USA	69	76	72	70	287	-1	28,678.46	22,050.85
	Nick DOUGHERTY	ENG	70	73	71	73	287	-1	28,678.46	22,050.85
	Arron OBERHOLSER	USA	72	70	72	73	287	-1	28,678.46	22,050.85
	Paul CASEY	ENG	72	75	67	73	287	-1	28,678.46	22,050.85
	Richard GREEN	AUS	74	72	71	70	287	-1	28,678.46	22,050.85
	S S P CHOWRASIA	IND	74	73	68	72	287	-1	28,678.46	22,050.85
57	Martin KAYMER	GER	74	73	73	68	288	0	27,076.31	20,818.96
	Ian POULTER	ENG	71	72	72	73	288	0	27,076.31	20,818.96
	Henrik STENSON	SWE	72	72	76	68	288	0	27,076.31	20,818.96
	D J TRAHAN	USA	74	73	75	66	288	0	27,076.31	20,818.96
61	Chapchai NIRAT	THA	70	70	74	77	291	3	25,794.59	19,833.45
	Brett WETTERICH	USA	70	74	76	71	291	3	25,794.59	19,833.45
	Peter HANSON	SWE	71	74	73	73	291	3	25,794.59	19,833.45
	Paul SHEEHAN	AUS	72	73	72	74	291	3	25,794.59	19,833.45
65	Anton HAIG	RSA	72	80	73	67	292	4	24,673.08	18,971.12
	Jonathan BYRD	USA	74	74	72	72	292	4	24,673.08	18,971.12
	Colin MONTGOMERIE	SCO	75	74	70	73	292	4	24,673.08	18,971.12
68	Louis OOSTHUIZEN	RSA	74	72	70	77	293	5	24,112.33	18,539.96
	Wen-chong LIANG	CHN	74	74	71	74	293	5	24,112.33	18,539.96
70	Rory SABBATINI	RSA	72	74	69	79	294	6	23,711.80	18,231.99
	James KINGSTON	RSA	74	75	68	77	294	6	23,711.80	18,231.99
	Søren HANSEN	DEN	77	77	68	72	294	6	23,711.80	18,231.99
73	Craig PARRY	AUS	73	75	72	75	295	7	23,311.26	17,924.02
	Shingo KATAYAMA	JPN	75	76	72	72	295	7	23,311.26	17,924.02
75	Ernie ELS	RSA	74	75	73	74	296	8	23,070.94	17,739.23
76	Mark BROWN	NZL	73	74	76	74	297	9	22,910.72	17,616.04
77	Heath SLOCUM	USA	74	72	78	74	298	10	22,750.51	17,492.85
78	Angel CABRERA	ARG	75	74	68	RETD			22,590.29	17,369.66
	Sean O'HAIR	USA	73	75	RETD				22,430.08	17,246.48

Total Prize Fund
€5,126,875 £3,942,050

Hole	Par	Yards	Metres
1	5	529	484
2	4	376	344
3	4	438	401
4	3	236	216
5	4	394	360
6	4	442	404
7	4	428	391
8	5	560	512
9	3	169	155
OUT	**36**	**3572**	**3267**
10	5	551	504
11	4	402	368
12	5	603	551
13	3	245	224
14	4	460	421
15	3	175	160
16	4	372	340
17	4	419	383
18	4	467	427
IN	**36**	**3694**	**3378**
TOTAL	**72**	**7266**	**6645**

After his latest World Golf Championship triumph, Geoff Ogilvy became only the third player, following Darren Clarke and Tiger Woods, to win multiple WGC events. Ogilvy won his first at the 2006 WGC – Accenture Match Play.

SUNDAY
MARCH 23, 2008

GROUNDS

SUNDAY
MARCH 23, 2008

Wheel of Fortune

LEADER BOARD

AT START	HOLE	1	2	3	4	5	6	7	8	9	10	11	12	13	14	15	16	17	18	TOTAL
	PAR	5	4	4	3	5	4	4	3	4	5	4	4	3	4	4	5	3	4	288
11	LEVET	12	13	13	14	14	14	15	13	13	14	14	13	14	14	15	16	16	★	272
11	FISHER	12	13	13	14	15	16	16	16	17	17	17	16	15	16	17	17	16		272
12	WESTWOOD	13	14	14	15	16	16	15	14	14	14	14	14	14	13	13				275
11	LYNN	11	11	11	12	12	13	12	13	12	10	10	11	11	10	9	10	9	9	279
10	HEDBLOM	11	11	11	10	10	10	10	10	10	10	9	8	8	8	9	9	7		281
9	JONZON	9	10	11	12	12	12	12	13	12	11	11	11	11	10	10				278
9	SJOLAND	9	10	11	10	10	10	10	10	10	11	10	11	11	12	13	13	12		276
1	QUIROS	2	2	3	3	4	5	5	6	7	7	8	8	9	8	8	8			280
	NOREN	9	10	11	10	10	11	12	12	12	12	12	10	10	11	12	12			276
4	DINWIDDIE	4	5	6	7	7	7	7	8	9	8	8	8	9	10	10				278

1	Thomas LEVET		272	-16
2	Oliver FISHER		272	-16
3	Lee WESTWOOD		275	-13
4	Alexander NOREN		276	-12
	Patrik SJÖLAND		276	-12
6	Robert DINWIDDIE		278	-10
	Michael JONZON		278	-10
8	Markus BRIER		279	-9
	David LYNN		279	-9
10	Manuel QUIROS		280	-8
	Alvaro VELASCO		280	-8

When the winner of the MAPFRE Open de Andalucia by Valle Romano fell flat on his back on the 18th green after a cliffhanger of a final round went to extra holes, it was no surprise that spectators rushed forward with fluids.

Alexander Noren

David Lynn

Oliver Fisher

The man on the ground was 39 year old Thomas Levet, whose two year battle against vertigo had threatened to end his career. Thankfully, though, the men who dashed from behind the ropes clutching open bottles were not paramedics but fellow French professionals, and the liquid with which they drenched their inert compatriot was champagne, not water.

Levet's comedy collapse was self-inflicted – prompted by a mixture of physical exhaustion, mental relief, sheer delight and a modicum of disbelief that his agony was finally over and one of golf's great comebacks was complete.

The word modicum is used because, frankly, Monsieur Levet does not do negativity. He never doubted he could and would return to the winner's circle, but he did confess his first Tour victory for four years had come quicker than he had dared hope.

The Parisian with the piercing blue eyes and perpetual smile admitted: "When you look at how it was for me in 2006, just standing up was a victory. Making cuts, trying to keep my card and winning were low priorities when you've been through what I've been through."

The slim Frenchman – who endeared himself to golf fans the world over when he lifted the towering Ernie Els high in the air after the South African had beaten him in a play-off for The 2002 Open Championship at Muirfield – had to fight all the way at Aloha Golf Club to eventually get the better of defending champion Lee Westwood and young Englishman Oliver Fisher, born just a few months after Levet turned professional in 1988.

The teenager looked like claiming his first European Tour International Schedule triumph until he bogeyed the 72nd and Levet, after a superb 25 foot putt for birdie on the 17th, deftly got up and down from a bunker short of the green at the last to tie on 16 under par 272.

Twenty years experience helped him claim the €166,660 (£129,849) winner's cheque with another par four at the same 18th in the play-off. Levet, as ever, was both gracious in victory and effusive in his praise of the younger man.

"It was tough on Oliver today, I must admit," he said. "But I think if he keeps on improving the way he has done, he will be at the level of Tiger Woods. He is that good."

Another young man to catch the eye over the week was English amateur Danny Willett, at that time top of The R&A World Amateur Golf Ranking, who, playing in his first professional tournament, carded a 66 in the first round to share second place before finishing in a share of 19th place overall.

But the tournament centred on Levet, a man with the purest of golfing pedigrees. Having represented his country in the Eisenhower Trophy as an amateur, he became the first Frenchman to win on home soil since the inception of The European Tour when he claimed the 1998 Cannes Open, before adding the 2001 British Masters and the 2004 Barclays Scottish Open titles to his collection, the latter in the same year he was one of the European heroes in the record nine point winning margin in The Ryder Cup at Oakland Hills County Club.

The future looked rosy but suddenly, out of the blue, came that first shattering attack of vertigo, an ailment of the inner ear often caused by a virus, which leaves victims suffering intense bouts of dizziness and nausea that can last for hours.

"I felt as though I was in a washing machine," he recalled. "I got out of the car and I didn't know my name. I couldn't even walk straight. There were days when I could only stand up for ten minutes then I'd have to lie down for three hours. Imagine a hamster spinning on its wheel; except I'm not the hamster, I'm the wheel."

With typical resilience and determination, however, Levet refused to succumb to the illness, undergoing months of medical treatment, then toiling to rebuild his fitness, his golf game, his confidence and finally, his competitive edge.

Ironically, given what happened in this year's tournament, he made his European Tour comeback at Aloha Golf Club in the 2007 Open de Andalucia, where an encouraging tie for 34th place gave him the impetus to finish 79th on the Order of Merit.

There must be something in the Andalucian air which encourages comebacks for the 2008 tournament also saw the return to competitive action of José Maria Olazábal – out for over seven months with the recurrence of a rheumatism problem – who thrilled the home spectators by playing all four rounds.

But the last word, fittingly, should go to Levet. "I've nothing to worry about any more," he said. "The illness was mental as well as physical but at last, I'm cured."

Welcome back Thomas.

Gordon Richardson

Thomas Levet (right), is presented with the trophy by Ana Gómez, Viceminister of Tourism, Trade and Sport from Junta de Andalucía

Peter Gustafsson

Robert Dinwiddie

Left to right: David Spencer, Chief Executive – Golf, Leisurecorp; Gonzalo Fernandez-Castaño from tournament promoters GFC Golf and Business; George O'Grady, Chief Executive of The European Tour; and Thomas Björn, Chairman of The European Tour Tournament Committee, herald the new European Tour Physio Unit sponsored by Leisurecorp

Hole	Par	Yards	Metres
1	5	596	545
2	4	362	331
3	4	344	315
4	3	226	207
5	5	511	467
6	4	410	375
7	4	349	319
8	3	195	178
9	4	343	314
OUT	**36**	**3336**	**3051**
10	5	561	513
11	4	386	353
12	4	412	377
13	3	214	196
14	4	369	337
15	4	399	365
16	5	526	481
17	3	230	210
18	4	448	410
IN	**36**	**3545**	**3242**
TOTAL	**72**	**6881**	**6293**

Michael Jonzon

The play-off between Thomas Levet and Oliver Fisher saw extra holes used for the fourth consecutive week to decide a tournament on The European Tour, thus creating a Tour record.

Aloha Golf Club

Final Results

Pos	Name		Rd1	Rd2	Rd3	Rd4	Total		€	£
1	Thomas LEVET	FRA	69	68	68	67	272	-16	166,660.00	129,849.08
2	Oliver FISHER	ENG	70	68	67	67	272	-16	111,110.00	86,568.65
3	Lee WESTWOOD	ENG	65	73	66	71	275	-13	62,600.00	48,773.27
4	Alexander NOREN	SWE	69	70	68	69	276	-12	46,200.00	35,995.61
	Patrik SJÖLAND	SWE	70	69	68	69	276	-12	46,200.00	35,995.61
6	Michael JONZON	SWE	69	69	69	71	278	-10	32,500.00	25,321.58
	Robert DINWIDDIE	ENG	72	65	75	66	278	-10	32,500.00	25,321.58
8	David LYNN	ENG	70	67	68	74	279	-9	23,700.00	18,465.28
	Markus BRIER	AUT	71	72	66	70	279	-9	23,700.00	18,465.28
10	Manuel QUIROS	ESP	72	72	71	65	280	-8	19,200.00	14,959.21
	Alvaro VELASCO	ESP	73	69	70	68	280	-8	19,200.00	14,959.21
12	Matthew MILLAR	AUS	67	69	72	73	281	-7	15,825.00	12,329.66
	Peter HEDBLOM	SWE	69	67	70	75	281	-7	15,825.00	12,329.66
	Marcel SIEM	GER	70	69	71	71	281	-7	15,825.00	12,329.66
	Anders HANSEN	DEN	71	72	70	68	281	-7	15,825.00	12,329.66
16	Maarten LAFEBER	NED	68	70	76	68	282	-6	13,500.00	10,518.20
	Emanuele CANONICA	ITA	70	73	72	67	282	-6	13,500.00	10,518.20
	Ariel CANETE	ARG	70	73	72	67	282	-6	13,500.00	10,518.20
19	Danny WILLETT (AM)	ENG	66	75	72	70	283	-5		
	Pelle EDBERG	SWE	70	68	69	76	283	-5	11,660.00	9,084.61
	Peter LAWRIE	IRL	72	72	70	69	283	-5	11,660.00	9,084.61
	Ricardo GONZALEZ	ARG	72	72	70	69	283	-5	11,660.00	9,084.61
	Joost LUITEN	NED	74	65	72	72	283	-5	11,660.00	9,084.61
	Miguel Angel JIMÉNEZ	ESP	74	67	69	73	283	-5	11,660.00	9,084.61
25	Christian CÉVAËR	FRA	68	71	74	71	284	-4	9,800.00	7,635.43
	Bradley DREDGE	WAL	70	68	71	75	284	-4	9,800.00	7,635.43
	Pablo MARTIN	ESP	70	70	74	70	284	-4	9,800.00	7,635.43
	Alastair FORSYTH	SCO	70	70	70	74	284	-4	9,800.00	7,635.43
	Simon DYSON	ENG	71	68	74	71	284	-4	9,800.00	7,635.43
	David FROST	RSA	72	70	68	74	284	-4	9,800.00	7,635.43
	Peter GUSTAFSSON	SWE	73	71	71	69	284	-4	9,800.00	7,635.43
32	Damien MCGRANE	IRL	68	72	71	74	285	-3	7,785.71	6,066.05
	Jarmo SANDELIN	SWE	70	74	68	73	285	-3	7,785.71	6,066.05
	Eduardo DE LA RIVA	ESP	71	71	71	72	285	-3	7,785.71	6,066.05
	Anthony WALL	ENG	72	71	74	68	285	-3	7,785.71	6,066.05
	Stephen GALLACHER	SCO	74	68	74	69	285	-3	7,785.71	6,066.05
	Pablo LARRAZABAL	ESP	74	69	70	72	285	-3	7,785.71	6,066.05
	Paul LAWRIE	SCO	78	66	73	68	285	-3	7,785.71	6,066.05
39	Rory MCILROY	NIR	68	73	71	74	286	-2	6,300.00	4,908.49
	Richard BLAND	ENG	70	71	72	73	286	-2	6,300.00	4,908.49
	Johan EDFORS	SWE	71	71	70	74	286	-2	6,300.00	4,908.49
	Gareth PADDISON	NZL	71	73	73	69	286	-2	6,300.00	4,908.49
	Martin KAYMER	GER	71	73	71	71	286	-2	6,300.00	4,908.49
	Mikael LUNDBERG	SWE	72	70	74	70	286	-2	6,300.00	4,908.49
	Robert-Jan DERKSEN	NED	73	69	72	72	286	-2	6,300.00	4,908.49
46	David GRIFFITHS	ENG	71	71	69	76	287	-1	5,300.00	4,129.37
	Lee SLATTERY	ENG	72	68	72	75	287	-1	5,300.00	4,129.37
	Garry HOUSTON	WAL	75	69	75	68	287	-1	5,300.00	4,129.37
49	Jan-Are LARSEN	NOR	66	72	76	74	288	0	4,500.00	3,506.07
	Henrik NYSTRÖM	SWE	69	72	74	73	288	0	4,500.00	3,506.07
	Grégory BOURDY	FRA	69	74	72	73	288	0	4,500.00	3,506.07
	John BICKERTON	ENG	72	71	73	72	288	0	4,500.00	3,506.07
	Peter WHITEFORD	SCO	73	69	75	71	288	0	4,500.00	3,506.07
54	Jamie DONALDSON	WAL	70	70	75	74	289	1	3,342.86	2,604.51
	Martin ERLANDSSON	SWE	71	71	69	78	289	1	3,342.86	2,604.51
	Peter HANSON	SWE	72	71	72	74	289	1	3,342.86	2,604.51
	Phillip ARCHER	ENG	72	72	72	73	289	1	3,342.86	2,604.51
	Sion E BEBB	WAL	73	69	76	71	289	1	3,342.86	2,604.51
	Per-Ulrik JOHANSSON	SWE	73	71	74	71	289	1	3,342.86	2,604.51
	Francesco MOLINARI	ITA	74	68	75	72	289	1	3,342.86	2,604.51
61	Gary ORR	SCO	71	72	76	71	290	2	2,700.00	2,103.64
	José Maria OLAZÁBAL	ESP	71	72	71	76	290	2	2,700.00	2,103.64
	Pedro LINHART	ESP	73	69	72	76	290	2	2,700.00	2,103.64
64	Gonzalo FDEZ-CASTAÑO	ESP	74	69	74	74	291	3	2,500.00	1,947.81
65	Carl SUNESON	ESP	69	70	76	77	292	4	2,350.00	1,830.95
	Florian PRAEGANT	AUT	69	73	72	78	292	4	2,350.00	1,830.95
67	Sébastien DELAGRANGE	FRA	74	70	80	70	294	6	2,200.00	1,714.08
68	Carlos RODILES	ESP	74	70	69	83	296	8	2,100.00	1,636.16
69	Birgir HAFTHORSSON	ISL	73	71	76	77	297	9	2,000.00	1,558.25

Total Prize Fund

€996,270 £776,219

Extra Time
Special

HOLE	1	2	3	4	5	6	7	8	9	10	11	12	13	14	15	16	17	18	TOTAL
PAR	4	4	3	4	4	4	5	5	3	4	4	3	5	3	3	5	4	4	284
17 BOURDY	17	16	15	15	15	14	14	14	15	16	16	17	17	18	18	18	★	266
13 FORSYTH	12	12	12	12	12	11	12	13	14	15	16	16	16	16	18	18	★	266
11 HOWELL	11	11	11	11	12	13	14	14	15	16	16	17	18	18	★	266
12 TUNNICLIFF	12	13	14	14	14	15	16	16	16	16	16	17		267
11 FDEZCASTANO	11	12	12	12	12	12	13	14	14	15	16	16	16	16		268
9 MCGINLEY	9		11	11	10	10	9	9	9		11	13	13		271
8 KHAN	8	8	8	8	9	9	10	11	10	10		11	12	12		272
SCHWARTZEL															271
8 MARTIN	10	10	10	10	11	12	13	13	12	11	12	11	13	12	11		273
1 MCGRANE	10	11	12	11	12	12	12	12	13	14	15		269

			TOTAL	
1	**Grégory BOURDY**		266	-18
2	Alastair FORSYTH		266	-18
	David HOWELL		266	-18
4	Miles TUNNICLIFF		267	-17
5	Gonzalo FERNANDEZ-CASTAÑO		268	-16
6	Damien McGRANE		269	-15
7	Paul McGINLEY		271	-13
	Charl SCHWARTZEL		271	-13
9	Peter BAKER		272	-12
	Johan EDFORS		272	-12
	Simon KHAN		272	-12
	José Manuel LARA		272	-12
	Andrew McLARDY		272	-12
	Steve WEBSTER		272	-12

For Grégory Bourdy one bottle of champagne was not enough, so he hurriedly sent his caddie off to buy another. Then the celebrations could really begin.

David Howell

Charl Schwartzel

However, this was not Oitavos Dunes and the Estoril Open de Portugal, but seven days earlier at Aloha Golf Club; the bubbly ready to be sprayed over Thomas Levet the second he beat Oliver Fisher in a play-off for the MAPFRE Open de Andalucia by Valle Romano.

The previous October Bourdy had received the traditional dousing himself from his compatriots on capturing the Mallorca Classic, his maiden European Tour International Schedule title, so he knew exactly what to expect when he overcame Scotland's Alastair Forsyth and David Howell of England in a play-off in Estoril for his second victory.

The 25 year old from Bordeaux was the first French victor in a tournament first contested in 1953 although, curiously, he was the second in a row to walk away with the winner's cheque. Twelve months earlier Raphaël Jacquelin had slipped it into his wallet when the only man to beat him was Spaniard Pablo Martin, who became the first amateur to win on The European Tour, hence rendering him ineligible for the first prize.

Being an avid movie fan, Bourdy would have appreciated the fact that European Tour staff had already likened his latest success to the 1993 film Groundhog Day, where Bill Murray plays Phil Connors, an egocentric Pittsburgh television weatherman who finds himself repeating the same day over and over again.

The reason for the comparison was the fact that, for the fifth week in succession on the 2008 schedule, extra holes were needed to determine the champion, following

similar excitement in Andalucia, the Madeira Islands Open BPI – Portugal, the Ballantine's Championship and the Maybank Malaysian Open.

It set a new record for The European Tour whose previous consecutive play-off run record had come in 1986 when, in the last three weeks of August, the Benson and Hedges International Open, the Scottish Open and the German Open all travelled past the 72nd hole.

At the beginning of the week, it appeared it might be defending champion Martin who would line up alongside Bourdy in any potential extra-curricular showdown after both men began with eight under par 63s. The young Spaniard, however, slipped back to finish in a share of 15th place as Bourdy's polished golf saw him press on.

When he signed for a 68 on Saturday afternoon his advantage had swelled to four and when his closest challenger Alastair Forsyth – who only two weeks before had made up a five stroke deficit to triumph in Madeira – began the final round with a bogey, Bourdy's lead was five.

However, by the time the final group reached the seventh tee, everything had changed. Bourdy had gone into reverse with bogeys at the second, third and sixth while England's Miles Tunnicliff birdied the same holes and added another at the seventh for good measure to take the lead momentarily.

It was to be the first of a dizzying 16 changes at the top of the leader board as the tournament built to its climax. Six players were out in front at one point or another but as the denouement arrived, attention focused on only three.

Bourdy was one after he fought back from his outward 39 with four birdies in a 70; David Howell was another as he produced a 64 - his lowest round for more than two years - to set the target of 18 under par 266; and third was Forsyth, who reignited his hopes with a 15 foot birdie putt on the 17th before repeating the feat from double that distance on the last for a 66.

The quiet and unassuming Scot had a chance for a second win in three weeks; Howell the opportunity for a glorious return to centre stage; while Bourdy's eyes were on a second win for himself and a second for France in successive weeks.

At the second time of asking on the 18th, Forsyth's drive into a bush put him out of the reckoning. On the third extra hole – the demanding 475 yard 17th – Howell pulled his second wide of the green and failed to get up and down leaving Bourdy's regulation four good enough for victory.

Echoing Colin Montgomerie's early progression on The European Tour, in the fact he has yet to take a backward step on the Order of Merit in his five years as a professional, one suspects there is a lot more to come from Monsieur Bourdy in the future.

Mark Garrod
Press Association

Grégory Bourdy (left), receives the trophy from Manuel Agrellos, President of the Portuguese Golf Federation

Søren Kjeldsen

Gonzalo Fernandez-Castaño

Alastair Forsyth

Hole	Par	Yards	Metres
1	4	416	380
2	4	340	311
3	3	201	184
4	4	354	324
5	4	475	434
6	4	436	399
7	5	501	458
8	5	582	532
9	3	156	143
OUT	36	3461	3165
10	4	444	406
11	4	348	318
12	3	234	214
13	5	531	486
14	3	167	153
15	3	186	170
16	5	573	524
17	4	475	434
18	4	474	433
IN	35	3432	3138
TOTAL	71	6893	6303

Grégory Bourdy's triumph created European Tour history for, following Thomas Levet's win the previous week, it meant French golfers had won consecutive European Tour events for the first time. It also stretched the record for consecutive weeks featuring a play-off to five.

Oitavos Dunes

Final Results

Pos	Name		Rd1	Rd2	Rd3	Rd4	Total		€	£
1	Grégory BOURDY	FRA	63	65	68	70	266	-18	208,330.00	165,060.93
2	Alastair FORSYTH	SCO	65	69	66	66	266	-18	108,565.00	86,016.61
	David HOWELL	ENG	67	68	67	64	266	-18	108,565.00	86,016.61
4	Miles TUNNICLIFF	ENG	69	69	63	66	267	-17	62,500.00	49,519.07
5	Gonzalo FDEZ-CASTAÑO	ESP	64	66	72	66	268	-16	53,000.00	41,992.17
6	Damien MCGRANE	IRL	67	69	67	66	269	-15	43,750.00	34,663.35
7	Charl SCHWARTZEL	RSA	65	70	66	70	271	-13	34,375.00	27,235.49
	Paul MCGINLEY	IRL	69	68	67	67	271	-13	34,375.00	27,235.49
9	José Manuel LARA	ESP	64	70	70	68	272	-12	22,791.67	18,057.95
	Simon KHAN	ENG	65	67	72	68	272	-12	22,791.67	18,057.95
	Andrew MCLARDY	RSA	66	68	72	66	272	-12	22,791.67	18,057.95
	Steve WEBSTER	ENG	67	66	70	69	272	-12	22,791.67	18,057.95
	Peter BAKER	ENG	67	69	69	67	272	-12	22,791.67	18,057.95
	Johan EDFORS	SWE	68	68	69	67	272	-12	22,791.67	18,057.95
15	Pablo MARTIN	ESP	63	71	69	70	273	-11	16,900.00	13,389.96
	Oliver FISHER	ENG	68	65	74	66	273	-11	16,900.00	13,389.96
	Søren KJELDSEN	DEN	69	65	68	71	273	-11	16,900.00	13,389.96
	Rory MCILROY	NIR	69	67	66	71	273	-11	16,900.00	13,389.96
	David DRYSDALE	SCO	71	67	66	69	273	-11	16,900.00	13,389.96
20	Lee SLATTERY	ENG	66	68	68	72	274	-10	14,343.75	11,364.63
	Felipe AGUILAR	CHI	68	68	71	67	274	-10	14,343.75	11,364.63
	Mads VIBE-HASTRUP	DEN	69	71	67	67	274	-10	14,343.75	11,364.63
	Ulrich VAN DEN BERG	RSA	69	71	69	65	274	-10	14,343.75	11,364.63
24	Thomas LEVET	FRA	67	64	72	72	275	-9	12,437.50	9,854.30
	David DIXON	ENG	68	68	70	69	275	-9	12,437.50	9,854.30
	Gareth PADDISON	NZL	68	68	68	71	275	-9	12,437.50	9,854.30
	Darren CLARKE	NIR	68	70	69	68	275	-9	12,437.50	9,854.30
	Jan-Are LARSEN	NOR	68	72	66	69	275	-9	12,437.50	9,854.30
	Martin ERLANDSSON	SWE	69	66	71	69	275	-9	12,437.50	9,854.30
30	James KAMTE	RSA	65	72	69	70	276	-8	10,053.57	7,965.50
	Mikko ILONEN	FIN	68	70	66	72	276	-8	10,053.57	7,965.50
	Pelle EDBERG	SWE	69	68	72	67	276	-8	10,053.57	7,965.50
	Sam LITTLE	ENG	69	68	68	71	276	-8	10,053.57	7,965.50
	Jean-François REMESY	FRA	70	63	74	69	276	-8	10,053.57	7,965.50
	Stephen GALLACHER	SCO	71	63	74	68	276	-8	10,053.57	7,965.50
	Brian DAVIS	ENG	71	68	69	68	276	-8	10,053.57	7,965.50
37	Michael JONZON	SWE	64	70	71	72	277	-7	8,125.00	6,437.48
	François DELAMONTAGNE	FRA	65	75	71	66	277	-7	8,125.00	6,437.48
	Zane SCOTLAND	ENG	69	65	75	68	277	-7	8,125.00	6,437.48
	Anthony WALL	ENG	69	70	67	71	277	-7	8,125.00	6,437.48
	Patrik SJÖLAND	SWE	70	70	68	69	277	-7	8,125.00	6,437.48
	Marc WARREN	SCO	71	69	69	68	277	-7	8,125.00	6,437.48
	Fredrik ANDERSSON HED	SWE	72	68	70	67	277	-7	8,125.00	6,437.48
44	Simon DYSON	ENG	67	66	70	75	278	-6	6,625.00	5,249.02
	Marius THORP	NOR	67	73	71	67	278	-6	6,625.00	5,249.02
	Ricardo GONZALEZ	ARG	69	70	68	71	278	-6	6,625.00	5,249.02
	Robert-Jan DERKSEN	NED	70	69	66	73	278	-6	6,625.00	5,249.02
	David PARK	WAL	72	67	68	71	278	-6	6,625.00	5,249.02
49	Ben EVANS	ENG	67	71	72	69	279	-5	5,750.00	4,555.75
	Jean-Baptiste GONNET	FRA	71	68	70	70	279	-5	5,750.00	4,555.75
51	Fabrizio ZANOTTI	PAR	68	70	72	70	280	-4	4,750.00	3,763.45
	Sam WALKER	ENG	69	68	76	67	280	-4	4,750.00	3,763.45
	Jarmo SANDELIN	SWE	70	68	74	68	280	-4	4,750.00	3,763.45
	Robert DINWIDDIE	ENG	70	70	71	69	280	-4	4,750.00	3,763.45
	John BICKERTON	ENG	71	68	70	71	280	-4	4,750.00	3,763.45
	Steven JEPPESEN	SWE	71	68	69	72	280	-4	4,750.00	3,763.45
57	Barry LANE	ENG	67	71	76	67	281	-3	3,750.00	2,971.14
	Jamie DONALDSON	WAL	70	67	73	71	281	-3	3,750.00	2,971.14
	Ross McGOWAN	ENG	70	70	68	73	281	-3	3,750.00	2,971.14
60	Santiago LUNA	ESP	66	71	75	70	282	-2	3,187.50	2,525.47
	Stuart MANLEY	WAL	67	68	76	71	282	-2	3,187.50	2,525.47
	Nuno CAMPINO	POR	67	69	73	73	282	-2	3,187.50	2,525.47
	Matthew MILLAR	AUS	68	69	74	71	282	-2	3,187.50	2,525.47
	Simon WAKEFIELD	ENG	68	71	71	72	282	-2	3,187.50	2,525.47
	Birgir HAFTHORSSON	ISL	69	70	66	77	282	-2	3,187.50	2,525.47
	Matt HAINES (AM)	ENG	72	68	73	69	282	-2		
67	Benoit TEILLERIA	FRA	70	70	68	75	283	-1	2,750.00	2,178.84
68	Marcel SIEM	GER	71	66	74	73	284	0	2,562.50	2,030.28
	Sven STRÜVER	GER	74	66	69	75	284	0	2,562.50	2,030.28
70	Emanuele CANONICA	ITA	70	70	76	70	286	2	2,375.00	1,881.72
71	Steven O'HARA	SCO	70	70	77	70	287	3	2,012.33	1,594.38
	Paolo TERRENI	ITA	71	67	73	76	287	3	2,012.33	1,594.38
	Pedro FIGUEIREDO (AM)	POR	72	66	78	71	287	3		
	Peter WHITEFORD	SCO	74	64	75	74	287	3	2,012.33	1,594.38
75	Peter GUSTAFSSON	SWE	68	71	74	75	288	4	1,867.50	1,479.63
	Ian GARBUTT	ENG	71	69	75	73	288	4	1,867.50	1,479.63
77	Henrik NYSTRÖM	SWE	71	65	80	74	290	6	1,863.00	1,476.06

Total Prize Fund

€1,259,345 £997,785

Indomitable Resolve

1	**Trevor IMMELMAN**		**280**	**-8**
2	Tiger WOODS		283	-5
3	Stewart CINK		284	-4
	Brandt SNEDEKER		284	-4
5	Steve FLESCH		286	-2
	Padraig HARRINGTON		286	-2
	Phil MICKELSON		286	-2
8	Miguel Angel JIMÉNEZ		287	-1
	Robert KARLSSON		287	-1
	Andres ROMERO		287	-1

There has not yet been an international winner of the Masters Tournament who did not have a special story to tell, of sacrifices made and fortitude shown on the road to being tailored for the green jacket. Trevor Immelman's story stands up there with the best of them.

Whatever shortcomings were responsible for the curious fact that, going into the week, no player under the age of 30 owned a Major Championship, the 28 year old South African emphatically answered them, all.

A too cushy life these days? Not Immelman who could barely walk last Christmas, owing to an operation to remove a benign tumour, yet he stood tall at Augusta National less than four months later.

Flakiness under pressure? Statistics show that the hardest Major to lead from the front is the Masters. No player had led or jointly led all four days since Seve Ballesteros slashed and burned his way round in 1980. Yet, at a time when the golf course has arguably never been tougher, Immelman emulated the Spaniard's feat, fulfilling the promise he showed while developing his craft on The European Tour where he garnered three victories in 16 months between January 2003 and May 2004.

Sometimes, Major victories owe more to luck than judgement. Not this one. In fact, few Champions have deserved their prize more. Immelman was not only the most accurate driver all week, hitting 48 out of 56 fairways, he also finished tied second in greens in regulation and tied fourth in total number of putts, with 112. He only had two three putts all week, just five

bogeys, and that is why he went one better than Ernie Els and Retief Goosen and became the first South African to win the Masters since Gary Player claimed his third green jacket in 1978.

What is additionally impressive about Immelman is that he never thinks he knows it all. It does not matter how many people tell him he has the sweetest swing on Tour, he always has another question. Two weeks before the Masters he went to Augusta with Ian Poulter and Justin Rose. When he saw Rose's coach Nick Bradley making notes, Immelman would make polite enquiries as to their nature.

Masters Champions may be tall, short, fat, thin, big hitters or arch-scramblers but the one thing they all have is indomitable resolve, and Immelman hinted at this 12 months previously, when he battled the debilitating effects of an intestinal parasite to walk up Magnolia Drive to play. So bad was it, he would eventually lose 22lbs off his already lean frame but it still did not cause him to quit the first Major of the 2007 season, where he somehow made the cut and finished tied 55th.

Immelman did miss the weekend action at the Shell Houston Open the week before this Masters but he did not turn up at Augusta sporting a bad attitude. On the first day, he played so well he found himself tied for pole

Andres Romero

Below left *Ian Poulter*

Mike Weir

Justin Rose

Robert Karlsson

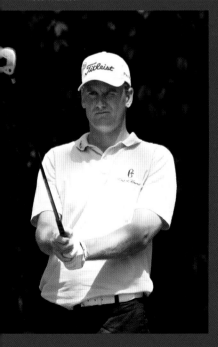

position with his great friend Rose, after both went round in 68. The third member of their gang, Poulter, did not do too badly either, registering Augusta's first hole in one in three years at the 16th in a round of 70.

The following day Rose got a bad break in being last out, when rounds were slow and the winds capricious. Immelman, by contrast, was out in the morning calm and made the field pay, taking advantage of his good fortune with a second 68.

Could anyone catch him? There was just one moment in the third round when it all threatened to unravel. A pitch to the par five 15th that was a fraction underclubbed came tumbling back towards the water protecting the front of the green.

American television commentator David Feherty has diligently patrolled that hole for 15 years while commentating for CBS and had never seen a ball stop on the hill. 'His only hope is a small depression which might hold it up,' remarked the Ulsterman prophetically, for that was indeed where it came to rest. On such small things can the fate of Masters' Champions be decided.

Once more Immelman took full advantage, going on to play arguably the best shot of this year's tournament at the 18th to set up a tap-in birdie for a two shot lead over his playing partner, the personable American, Brandt Snedeker.

What of Tiger Woods, the man who had dominated the build-up to the tournament? He had chances on the last day to apply some pressure. Six off the pace with a round to go, he would have pulled within two had a five foot birdie putt at the 13th been converted. It summed up the World Number One's week when it missed. He was a fraction off in all departments, and particularly with that fabled putter, requiring eight more putts for the week than the Champion, and hence finishing runner-up.

On the eve of the final round, Gary Player, a long-time friend of the Immelman family, had left a voice message on his telephone which said: 'Believe in yourself when adversity strikes.' If you had to sum up this Masters Tournament in one sentence, let it be that one.

Derek Lawrenson
Daily Mail

It's time to fly.

Over the course of 18 holes, you can see how far you've come, and how far the game can still take you.

United is proud to support The European Tour.

UNITED

A STAR ALLIANCE MEMBER

www.unitedairlines.co.uk

Gary Player and Miguel Angel Jiménez

Augusta National

Final Results

Pos	Name		Rd1	Rd2	Rd3	Rd4	Total		€	£
1	Trevor IMMELMAN	RSA	68	68	69	75	280	-8	857,957.64	676,793.54
2	Tiger WOODS	USA	72	71	68	72	283	-5	514,774.58	406,076.12
3	Brandt SNEDEKER	USA	69	68	70	77	284	-4	276,453.02	218,077.92
	Stewart CINK	USA	72	69	71	72	284	-4	276,453.02	218,077.92
5	Phil MICKELSON	USA	71	68	75	72	286	-2	173,974.74	137,238.69
	Steve FLESCH	USA	72	67	69	78	286	-2	173,974.74	137,238.69
	Padraig HARRINGTON	IRL	74	71	69	72	286	-2	173,974.74	137,238.69
8	Robert KARLSSON	SWE	70	73	71	73	287	-1	138,226.51	109,038.96
	Andres ROMERO	ARG	72	72	70	73	287	-1	138,226.51	109,038.96
	Miguel Angel JIMÉNEZ	ESP	77	70	72	68	287	-1	138,226.51	109,038.96
11	Lee WESTWOOD	ENG	69	73	73	73	288	0	109,627.92	86,479.17
	Paul CASEY	ENG	71	69	69	79	288	0	109,627.92	86,479.17
	Nick WATNEY	USA	75	70	72	71	288	0	109,627.92	86,479.17
14	Sean O'HAIR	USA	72	71	71	75	289	1	85,795.76	67,679.35
	Vijay SINGH	FIJ	72	71	72	74	289	1	85,795.76	67,679.35
	Stuart APPLEBY	AUS	76	70	72	71	289	1	85,795.76	67,679.35
17	Retief GOOSEN	RSA	71	71	72	76	290	2	71,496.47	56,399.46
	Mike WEIR	CAN	73	68	75	74	290	2	71,496.47	56,399.46
	Henrik STENSON	SWE	74	72	72	72	290	2	71,496.47	56,399.46
20	Brian BATEMAN	USA	69	76	72	74	291	3	53,574.69	42,262.00
	Zach JOHNSON	USA	70	76	68	77	291	3	53,574.69	42,262.00
	Boo WEEKLEY	USA	72	74	68	77	291	3	53,574.69	42,262.00
	Justin LEONARD	USA	72	74	72	73	291	3	53,574.69	42,262.00
	Bubba WATSON	USA	74	71	73	73	291	3	53,574.69	42,262.00
25	Ian POULTER	ENG	70	69	75	78	292	4	34,854.69	27,494.86
	Stephen AMES	CAN	70	70	77	75	292	4	34,854.69	27,494.86
	Arron OBERHOLSER	USA	71	70	74	77	292	4	34,854.69	27,494.86
	Jeev Milkha SINGH	IND	71	74	72	75	292	4	34,854.69	27,494.86
	J B HOLMES	USA	73	70	73	76	292	4	34,854.69	27,494.86
	Angel CABRERA	ARG	73	72	73	74	292	4	34,854.69	27,494.86
	Richard STERNE	RSA	73	72	73	74	292	4	34,854.69	27,494.86
	Adam SCOTT	AUS	75	71	70	76	292	4	34,854.69	27,494.86
33	Jim FURYK	USA	70	73	73	77	293	5	26,930.34	21,243.80
	Heath SLOCUM	USA	71	76	77	69	293	5	26,930.34	21,243.80
	Nick DOUGHERTY	ENG	74	69	74	76	293	5	26,930.34	21,243.80
36	Justin ROSE	ENG	68	78	73	76	295	7	23,434.95	18,486.49
	Johnson WAGNER	USA	72	74	74	75	295	7	23,434.95	18,486.49
	Todd HAMILTON	USA	74	73	75	73	295	7	23,434.95	18,486.49
39	Niclas FASTH	SWE	75	70	76	75	296	8	20,972.30	16,543.84
	Geoff OGILVY	AUS	75	71	76	74	296	8	20,972.30	16,543.84
41	K J CHOI	KOR	72	75	78	73	298	10	19,542.37	15,415.85
42	Robert ALLENBY	AUS	72	74	72	81	299	11	18,112.44	14,287.86
	David TOMS	USA	73	74	72	80	299	11	18,112.44	14,287.86
44	Ian WOOSNAM	WAL	75	71	76	78	300	12	16,682.51	13,159.87
45	Sandy LYLE	SCO	72	75	78	77	302	14	15,729.22	12,407.88

Hole	Par	Yards	Metres
1	4	455	416
2	5	575	526
3	4	350	320
4	3	240	219
5	4	455	416
6	3	180	165
7	4	450	411
8	5	570	521
9	4	460	421
OUT	**36**	**3735**	**3415**
10	4	495	453
11	4	505	462
12	3	155	142
13	5	510	466
14	4	440	402
15	5	530	485
16	3	170	155
17	4	440	402
18	4	465	425
IN	**36**	**3710**	**3392**
TOTAL	**72**	**7445**	**6807**

Total Prize Fund

€4,783,274 £3,773,250

i Trevor Immelman's win at Augusta National meant he became the fifth South African golfer to win a Major Championship. He followed Gary Player (nine), Bobby Locke (five), Ernie Els (three) and Retief Goosen (two).

Olympian
Achievement

	Player			
1	**Damien McGRANE**		278	-10
2	Simon GRIFFITHS		287	-1
	Michael LORENZO-VERA		287	-1
	Oliver WILSON		287	-1
5	Markus BRIER		288	0
	Mark BROWN		288	0
	Graeme McDOWELL		288	0
8	Jason KNUTZON		289	1
	Wen-chong LIANG		289	1
	Seung-yul NOH		289	1
	Peter WHITEFORD		289	1

O ne World, One Dream. The motto for the Olympics in Beijing could easily have been taken from the philosophy of The European Tour which, over the years, has embraced the Olympic ideal in golfing terms by fostering the sport, widening its appeal and attracting new participants.

Mikko Ilonen

Michael Lorenzo-Vera

The Volvo China Open has certainly done that too, from its inception in 1995 through to becoming part of The European Tour International Schedule a decade later. The Chinese might claim to have invented a form of golf centuries ago, but for a country of 1.3 billion people, their players' impact on the world has been, up to now, rarer than the birth of a panda in captivity.

Yet Zhang Lian-wei carried the torch and found European Tour success in the 2003 Singapore Masters. Liang Wen-chong took up the baton, won the same tournament in 2007, and played at the Beijing CBD International Golf Club on the back of his debut in the Masters Tournament in April. While the Chinese were not able to celebrate a winner in their national open this year, a new record number – five – made the cut. Plus, the appeal and knowledge of the game is growing simultaneously.

In truth Liang – despite a creditable share of eighth place overall – did not make much impression on the leaderboard over the four days. Europeans have dominated the Roll of Honour down the years, and the scoreboards around the Beijing course once again showed French, English and Irish ascendency.

Michael Lorenzo-Vera, an exuberant young Frenchman who topped the Challenge Tour Rankings last season, led for the first two days before eventually settling for his best European Tour finish to date, sharing second with Englishmen Simon Griffiths and Oliver Wilson. Yet the trio were a long, long way adrift of the winner.

Damien McGrane had chased his dream of glory around the world to the extent that this was his 169th European Tour event in 17 years as a professional. However, the travelling is not a chore. The Irishman loves experiencing new cultures, so much so that when a recent winter trip to the Antarctic was rescheduled after his intended carrier flirted with an iceberg, he had two weeks in Santiago in Chile instead.

The 37 year old reckoned it reinvigorated him for the season ahead, one in which he did battle with Tiger Woods in Dubai, and led for a spell in the Indian Masters in New Delhi. It all proved part of the path to his first victory - although exotic China more resembled his home haunt of County Meath come the final day.

The rain was relentless, hard and heavy. The wind, too, was cold, awkward and gusting. Only one player, England's John Bickerton, made par and proved to be the only man to better McGrane's exceptional closing 73 which gave him a ten under par total of 278 and an astonishing nine shot winning margin.

ROLEX

Paul Lawrie

Wilson, like Lorenzo-Vera, carded a closing 79 and admitted: "It was like the worst of the Open Championship weather out there."

McGrane, who had celebrated his birthday the previous weekend, took time to reflect on his career once the final putt had dropped. "I'm in it for the long haul," he said. "I knew I'd have to do it the hard way and the long way. This week I gave myself an opportunity and I snatched it. I made sure nobody could get near it."

The Irishman may not be of athletic build and stature and to see him at the airport complete with a heavy coat and backpack, you would not immediately identify a sportsman; but his victory was nevertheless an Olympian achievement – the durability of Haile Gebrselassie combined with the dominance of Bob Beaman and the accuracy of Malcolm Cooper – and all done with humility and modesty.

Beijing has been transformed since the Volvo China Open first visited. The National 'Bird's Nest' Stadium, which will host the Olympic opening and closing ceremonies as well as the athletics events, is an architectural marvel, the swimming complex is on a par, and thousands of trees have brightened the landscape and are helping improve the atmosphere.

Slowly, but surely, China is opening up to the world, one of the main intentions when the Olympics were awarded to its nation's capital. Golf has played a significant part in this progress too. Prior to the tournament, debate centred on whether golf should be an Olympic sport - it certainly ticks all the boxes for a gold medal performance.

Nick Dye
European Tour Radio

Left to right: Gerry Keaney, SVP of Volvo Car Corporation, Damien McGrane and Klas Magnusson, SVP Communications of Volvo Construction Equipment

Liang Wen-chong

Simon Griffiths

Beijing CBD International Golf Club

Final Results

Pos	Name		Rd1	Rd2	Rd3	Rd4	Total		€	£
1	Damien MCGRANE	IRL	68	69	68	73	278	-10	232,121.24	186,055.70
2	Michael LORENZO-VERA	FRA	67	69	72	79	287	-1	103,857.15	83,246.22
	Simon GRIFFITHS	ENG	68	72	73	74	287	-1	103,857.15	83,246.22
	Oliver WILSON	ENG	72	66	70	79	287	-1	103,857.15	83,246.22
5	Markus BRIER	AUT	71	69	72	76	288	0	49,860.55	39,965.49
	Mark BROWN	NZL	71	71	69	77	288	0	49,860.55	39,965.49
	Graeme MCDOWELL	NIR	73	72	68	75	288	0	49,860.55	39,965.49
8	Jason KNUTZON	USA	68	72	72	77	289	1	29,874.55	23,945.80
	Seung-yul NOH	KOR	71	71	74	73	289	1	29,874.55	23,945.80
	Wen-chong LIANG	CHN	73	68	73	75	289	1	29,874.55	23,945.80
	Peter WHITEFORD	SCO	73	72	71	73	289	1	29,874.55	23,945.80
12	Richard FINCH	ENG	68	69	76	77	290	2	23,189.33	18,587.30
	John BICKERTON	ENG	70	76	72	72	290	2	23,189.33	18,587.30
14	Joost LUITEN	NED	68	73	74	76	291	3	20,055.64	16,075.51
	Scott STRANGE	AUS	73	71	66	81	291	3	20,055.64	16,075.51
	Wen-teh LU	TPE	73	71	71	76	291	3	20,055.64	16,075.51
	David BRANSDON	AUS	73	72	68	78	291	3	20,055.64	16,075.51
18	Adam GROOM	AUS	73	70	72	77	292	4	17,618.32	14,121.88
	Christian CÉVAËR	FRA	73	74	72	73	292	4	17,618.32	14,121.88
20	Miles TUNNICLIFF	ENG	70	74	74	75	293	5	15,981.84	12,810.17
	Paul LAWRIE	SCO	71	75	72	75	293	5	15,981.84	12,810.17
	Daniel VANCSIK	ARG	73	74	69	77	293	5	15,981.84	12,810.17
	Louis OOSTHUIZEN	RSA	74	72	72	75	293	5	15,981.84	12,810.17
24	Simon YATES	SCO	72	72	75	75	294	6	14,275.72	11,442.63
	Stuart MANLEY	WAL	72	74	74	74	294	6	14,275.72	11,442.63
	Marcus BOTH	AUS	73	73	73	75	294	6	14,275.72	11,442.63
	Mikko ILONEN	FIN	75	71	70	78	294	6	14,275.72	11,442.63
28	Zane SCOTLAND	ENG	68	72	74	81	295	7	11,268.64	9,032.32
	Chao LI	CHN	68	74	76	77	295	7	11,268.64	9,032.32
	Fabrizio ZANOTTI	PAR	71	71	70	83	295	7	11,268.64	9,032.32
	Rhys DAVIES	WAL	71	74	71	79	295	7	11,268.64	9,032.32
	Jean-François LUCQUIN	FRA	72	72	72	79	295	7	11,268.64	9,032.32
	David HOWELL	ENG	72	73	71	79	295	7	11,268.64	9,032.32
	Ross BAIN	SCO	73	73	76	73	295	7	11,268.64	9,032.32
	Scott BARR	AUS	73	74	74	74	295	7	11,268.64	9,032.32
	Phillip PRICE	WAL	74	71	74	76	295	7	11,268.64	9,032.32
	Sam LITTLE	ENG	74	73	71	77	295	7	11,268.64	9,032.32
	Gaurav GHEI	IND	76	69	75	75	295	7	11,268.64	9,032.32
39	Sam WALKER	ENG	71	71	73	81	296	8	9,052.89	7,256.30
	Antonio LASCUNA	PHI	72	71	72	81	296	8	9,052.89	7,256.30
	Carlos RODILES	ESP	72	74	72	78	296	8	9,052.89	7,256.30
42	Airil RIZMAN	MAS	69	72	72	84	297	9	8,356.52	6,698.13
	Wei-chih LU	TPE	75	73	72	77	297	9	8,356.52	6,698.13
44	Gaganjeet BHULLAR	IND	69	75	73	81	298	10	7,381.59	5,916.68
	Marcus FRASER	AUS	76	71	73	78	298	10	7,381.59	5,916.68
	Francesco MOLINARI	ITA	75	72	73	78	298	10	7,381.59	5,916.68
	Marcel SIEM	GER	76	71	73	78	298	10	7,381.59	5,916.68
	David FROST	RSA	76	72	74	76	298	10	7,381.59	5,916.68
49	Robert-Jan DERKSEN	NED	70	71	75	83	299	11	6,128.11	4,911.96
	Todd VERNON	USA	71	72	74	82	299	11	6,128.11	4,911.96
	Mardan MAMAT	SIN	72	74	74	79	299	11	6,128.11	4,911.96
	Jean-Baptiste GONNET	FRA	72	74	72	81	299	11	6,128.11	4,911.96
53	Gavin FLINT	AUS	73	74	76	77	300	12	5,153.19	4,130.51
	Paul BROADHURST	ENG	76	72	73	79	300	12	5,153.19	4,130.51
	Barry LANE	ENG	78	70	71	81	300	12	5,153.19	4,130.51
56	Ross FISHER	ENG	74	72	74	81	301	13	4,363.96	3,497.91
	Søren KJELDSEN	DEN	75	72	76	78	301	13	4,363.96	3,497.91
	Keng-chi LIN	TPE	75	73	77	76	301	13	4,363.96	3,497.91
59	Simon WAKEFIELD	ENG	72	71	78	81	302	14	3,969.35	3,181.61
	Sung LEE	KOR	73	75	73	81	302	14	3,969.35	3,181.61
61	Kang-chun WU	CHN	70	73	80	80	303	15	3,690.79	2,958.34
	Prom MEESAWAT	THA	71	76	74	82	303	15	3,690.79	2,958.34
63	Frankie MINOZA	PHI	73	72	77	82	304	16	3,412.24	2,735.07
	S S P CHOWRASIA	IND	74	73	76	81	304	16	3,412.24	2,735.07
65	Rafa ECHENIQUE	ARG	69	76	82	82	309	21	3,133.69	2,511.80
	Mu HU (Am)	CHN	74	74	77	84	309	21		
	Raphaël JACQUELIN	FRA	75	71	79	84	309	21	3,133.69	2,511.80
68	Wei-huang WU	CHN	73	75	77	86	311	23	2,924.78	2,344.34
69	Julio ZAPATA	ARG	70	78	80	84	312	24	2,785.51	2,232.71

Total Prize Fund

€1,387,562 £1,112,193

Hole	Par	Yards	Metres
1	4	474	433
2	4	442	404
3	3	199	182
4	4	419	383
5	4	377	345
6	3	181	165
7	4	441	403
8	4	432	395
9	5	570	521
OUT	**35**	**3535**	**3231**
10	5	557	509
11	4	355	325
12	3	199	182
13	5	588	538
14	4	470	430
15	4	413	378
16	3	164	150
17	4	476	435
18	5	564	516
IN	**37**	**3786**	**3463**
TOTAL	**72**	**7321**	**6694**

One of the telling factors in Damien McGrane's victory in the Volvo China Open was his ability on the greens. The Irishman only used his putter 96 times during the four rounds. This is only two outside The European Tour record for fewest putts in a tournament, held by Jeev Milkha Singh in the 2001 Dubai Desert Classic with 94. Russell Claydon also took 96 in the 2000 Italian Open.

BMW Golfsport

bmw-golfsport.com
bmw.co.uk

The Ultimate
Driving Machine

BMW Asian Open

Momentous
Milestone

1	**Darren CLARKE**		**280**	**-8**
2	Robert-Jan DERKSEN		281	-7
3	Robert DINWIDDIE		283	-5
	Wen-tang LIN		283	-5
	Francesco MOLINARI		283	-5
6	Henrik STENSON		284	-4
7	John BICKERTON		285	-3
	Martin KAYMER		285	-3
9	Scott HEND		286	-2
	Peter LAWRIE		286	-2

F rom Malaysia to Korea, India to Indonesia and Singapore to Hong Kong, The European Tour International Schedule has travelled far and wide in an exciting journey that has captivated golfing destinations across the Far East.

Robert Dinwiddie

Therefore, it was a truly momentous milestone when the Tour arrived in China for the 2008 BMW Asian Open, a tournament which heralded its 50th co-sanctioned tournament with the Asian Tour since the concept was first formalised in 1999.

Shanghai, located on the banks of the Yangtze River Delta, offered the ideal backdrop for the landmark occasion as the largest city in the Middle Kingdom is regarded as the citadel of China's modern economy.

With Asia's Tiger economies in full roar, international companies, including BMW, have pursued The European Tour's lead and headed full speed to golf's Promised Land.

Through each passing season, The European Tour has broken new ground. From the inaugural joint-sanctioned tournament, the Malaysian Open in 1999, the International Schedule now journeys to exciting and exotic locations such as Jakarta, Jeju Island, Kuala Lumpur and New Delhi.

Northern Irishman Darren Clarke is a firm believer in the saying that you have to travel the world's airways in search of success on the world's fairways, which was why it was surprising to the crowds who turned up at the Tomson Shanghai Pudong Golf Club to find he had never set foot in China previously, having won three times in neighbouring Japan.

But the moment the 39 year old arrived for the BMW Asian Open, he took an instant shine to the golf course and went on to produce a memorable victory which culminated in an audacious 40 foot birdie putt on the 72nd hole to see off the brave challenge of Dutchman Robert-Jan Derksen by a solitary stroke.

The triumph ended Clarke's five year title drought on The European Tour but, more

poignantly, it delivered a first success anywhere in the world since the passing of his wife Heather in 2006.

Understandably, the man who has been part of four memorable European Ryder Cup triumphs, had wondered if there was light at the end of the tunnel following his life's tribulations and it was no surprise his form dipped to the extent that, for a spell, he dropped out of the top 200 in the Official World Golf Ranking.

A heroic performance in The 2006 Ryder Cup at The K Club served only as a temporary respite as, in 2007, he struggled to find the focus or the game which had made him such a fierce competitor and a winner worldwide.

However, playing alongside boyhood idol Greg Norman in the opening two rounds in Shanghai was the perfect fillip for Clarke as he showed signs of life once more in his golf. With each passing day, he gained a good measure of the tight Tomson course, improving each day too with rounds of 71-69-67 to lead by a shot into the final round.

Derksen was Clarke's main challenger in what unfolded into a compelling Sunday shoot-out, but it was the old battling Clarke who prevailed. The Ulsterman led by two with four holes

remaining but lapses in concentration saw him card bogeys on both the 16th and 17th holes which allowed the Dutchman to draw level.

Then, like a bolt from the blue, Clarke holed an improbable birdie putt on the final green, before screaming in delight, looking up to the heavens and hugging caddie Phil 'Wobbly' Morbey after the ball disappeared into the cup.

Clarke revealed he had let his mind wander as the finishing line appeared in view. "I started thinking about Heather and the boys and in this game, unless you keep your concentration for the whole way, you make mistakes. But on the last green, I gathered myself and told myself to hit a solid putt. It was tracking six foot out and, I suppose, sometimes they're meant to go in.

"This is very special and this win is for my boys Tyrone and Conor. They would have enjoyed that putt more than I did. Sometimes things are meant to happen, sometimes not. I guess today was my day."

Chuah Choo Chiang
Asian Tour

Robert-Jan Derksen

Henrik Stenson

Darren Clarke (right), receives the trophy from Karl-Heinz Schmid, President, BMW China Automotive Trading Ltd

Hole	Par	Yards	Metres
1	4	404	369
2	5	550	503
3	3	235	215
4	4	490	448
5	4	414	379
6	4	440	402
7	4	388	355
8	3	182	166
9	5	590	539
OUT	**36**	**3693**	**3376**
10	4	386	353
11	4	371	339
12	3	228	208
13	5	568	519
14	3	216	198
15	5	570	521
16	4	461	422
17	4	356	326
18	4	477	436
IN	**36**	**3633**	**3322**
TOTAL	**72**	**7326**	**6698**

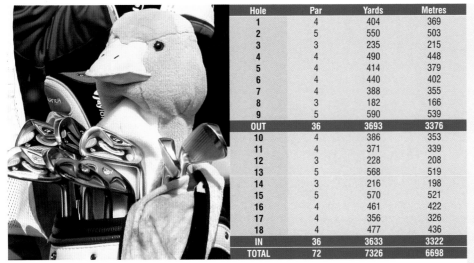

Paul Broadhurst

Miles Tunnicliff

The 2008 BMW Asian Open marked the 50th event co-sanctioned between The European and Asian Tours. The first of them was the 1999 Benson and Hedges Malaysian Open, won by American Gerry Norquist. The 50 tournaments have produced a total of 42 different winners, of which 29 were European-based players. Miguel Angel Jimenez currently has the distinction of winning the most co-sanctioned with four. The 42 winners have come from a total of 20 different countries.

Tomson Shanghai Pudong Golf Club

Final Results

Pos	Name		Rd1	Rd2	Rd3	Rd4	Total		€	£
1	Darren CLARKE	NIR	71	69	67	73	280	-8	243,507.19	192,001.00
2	Robert-Jan DERKSEN	NED	70	69	69	73	281	-7	162,336.01	127,999.00
3	Robert DINWIDDIE	ENG	70	73	66	74	283	-5	75,487.89	59,520.83
	Wen-tang LIN	TPE	71	71	69	72	283	-5	75,487.89	59,520.83
	Francesco MOLINARI	ITA	71	75	68	69	283	-5	75,487.89	59,520.83
6	Henrik STENSON	SWE	68	76	72	68	284	-4	51,136.95	40,320.56
7	John BICKERTON	ENG	71	75	69	70	285	-3	40,179.04	31,680.44
	Martin KAYMER	GER	72	72	74	67	285	-3	40,179.04	31,680.44
9	Scott HEND	AUS	69	74	71	72	286	-2	30,974.38	24,422.74
	Peter LAWRIE	IRL	72	74	70	70	286	-2	30,974.38	24,422.74
11	Oliver WILSON	ENG	68	74	74	71	287	-1	25,178.86	19,853.08
	Paul BROADHURST	ENG	71	73	71	72	287	-1	25,178.86	19,853.08
	Retief GOOSEN	RSA	72	70	72	73	287	-1	25,178.86	19,853.08
14	Wen-chong LIANG	CHN	71	71	73	73	288	0	21,039.20	16,589.03
	Greg NORMAN	AUS	71	73	73	71	288	0	21,039.20	16,589.03
	Scott STRANGE	AUS	71	75	70	72	288	0	21,039.20	16,589.03
	Joost LUITEN	NED	71	75	70	72	288	0	21,039.20	16,589.03
18	Miles TUNNICLIFF	ENG	71	70	73	75	289	1	17,591.11	13,870.27
	Iain STEEL	MAS	71	74	71	73	289	1	17,591.11	13,870.27
	Simon WAKEFIELD	ENG	73	72	75	69	289	1	17,591.11	13,870.27
	Søren KJELDSEN	DEN	74	73	69	73	289	1	17,591.11	13,870.27
	Michael LORENZO-VERA	FRA	75	69	69	76	289	1	17,591.11	13,870.27
23	Peter O'MALLEY	AUS	67	74	72	77	290	2	15,414.14	12,153.77
	Jeev Milkha SINGH	IND	68	76	70	76	290	2	15,414.14	12,153.77
	Jean-François LUCQUIN	FRA	74	70	74	72	290	2	15,414.14	12,153.77
	Digvijay SINGH	IND	74	72	67	77	290	2	15,414.14	12,153.77
27	Chris RODGERS	ENG	71	73	71	76	291	3	12,784.24	10,080.14
	Sam LITTLE	ENG	71	76	70	74	291	3	12,784.24	10,080.14
	Young NAM	KOR	72	73	72	74	291	3	12,784.24	10,080.14
	David FROST	RSA	72	75	72	72	291	3	12,784.24	10,080.14
	Rory MCILROY	NIR	73	73	69	76	291	3	12,784.24	10,080.14
	Mardan MAMAT	SIN	73	74	71	73	291	3	12,784.24	10,080.14
	Paul LAWRIE	SCO	75	72	71	73	291	3	12,784.24	10,080.14
	Jean-Baptiste GONNET	FRA	75	72	73	71	291	3	12,784.24	10,080.14
35	Marcus FRASER	AUS	70	73	73	76	292	4	10,227.39	8,064.11
	José-Filipe LIMA	POR	70	74	72	76	292	4	10,227.39	8,064.11
	Ross McGOWAN	ENG	71	74	75	72	292	4	10,227.39	8,064.11
	Michael CAMPBELL	NZL	71	76	70	75	292	4	10,227.39	8,064.11
	Mu HU (Am)	CHN	73	69	71	79	292	4		
	David GLEESON	AUS	73	73	68	78	292	4	10,227.39	8,064.11
	Mark BROWN	NZL	75	67	73	77	292	4	10,227.39	8,064.11
42	Ross FISHER	ENG	72	73	74	74	293	5	8,766.33	6,912.10
	Marcus BOTH	AUS	73	74	72	74	293	5	8,766.33	6,912.10
	Raphaël JACQUELIN	FRA	73	74	74	72	293	5	8,766.33	6,912.10
	Simon YATES	SCO	74	73	71	75	293	5	8,766.33	6,912.10
46	Lian-wei ZHANG	CHN	70	69	76	79	294	6	7,013.07	5,529.68
	Hendrik BUHRMANN	RSA	71	75	71	77	294	6	7,013.07	5,529.68
	Shiv KAPUR	IND	71	75	74	74	294	6	7,013.07	5,529.68
	Peter HEDBLOM	SWE	72	73	78	71	294	6	7,013.07	5,529.68
	Mikael LUNDBERG	SWE	73	71	75	75	294	6	7,013.07	5,529.68
	Phillip PRICE	WAL	73	73	78	70	294	6	7,013.07	5,529.68
	Barry LANE	ENG	74	71	73	76	294	6	7,013.07	5,529.68
	Wei-chih LU	TPE	75	71	70	78	294	6	7,013.07	5,529.68
54	Gary MURPHY	IRL	74	73	73	75	295	7	5,698.12	4,492.86
55	S S P CHOWRASIA	IND	72	73	72	79	296	8	5,259.80	4,147.26
	Adam BLYTH	AUS	74	70	73	79	296	8	5,259.80	4,147.26
57	Carl SUNESON	ESP	71	75	75	78	297	9	4,675.38	3,686.45
	Scott BARR	AUS	72	74	76	75	297	9	4,675.38	3,686.45
59	Mikko ILONEN	FIN	68	76	77	77	298	10	4,310.11	3,398.45
	Keith HORNE	RSA	77	70	75	76	298	10	4,310.11	3,398.45
61	Chao LI	CHN	71	72	75	81	299	11	4,090.96	3,225.64
62	Richard LEE	NZL	70	75	74	81	300	12	3,725.69	2,937.64
	Richard FINCH	ENG	72	75	78	75	300	12	3,725.69	2,937.64
	Mong-nan HSU	TPE	73	74	77	76	300	12	3,725.69	2,937.64
	Wook-soon KANG	KOR	74	72	79	75	300	12	3,725.69	2,937.64
66	Julio ZAPATA	ARG	73	72	76	84	305	17	3,360.43	2,649.64

Total Prize Fund

€1,446,407 £1,140,465

137

Day of Destiny

			TOTAL
1	Peter LAWRIE	273	-15
2	Ignacio GARRIDO	273	-15
3	Søren HANSEN	274	-14
4	Alfredo GARCIA-HEREDIA	275	-13
	Miguel Angel JIMÉNEZ	275	-13
	David LYNN	275	-13
7	Richard FINCH	276	-12
8	Martin ERLANDSSON	277	-11
	Peter HANSON	277	-11
10	Robert-Jan DERKSEN	278	-10
	Niclas FASTH	278	-10
	Andrew McLARDY	278	-10
	Alexander NOREN	278	-10
	Danny WILLETT (AM)	278	-10

By early May, The European Tour had gone decidedly green. Not that the Wentworth staff were not already ecologically sound, one hastens to add. This green is in reference to Ireland – both the north and south of the country.

Ignacio Garrido

Søren Hansen

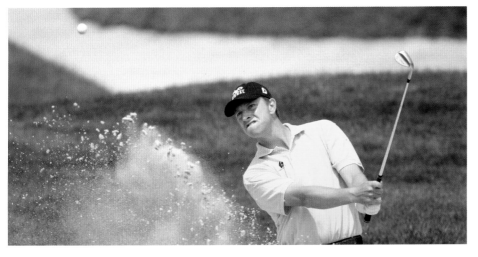

The reason for Emerald Isle elation? Simple. An unprecedented run had just seen three successive Irish winners on The European Tour International Schedule for the first time in history, culminating in a long-awaited maiden victory for Peter Lawrie.

In his sixth full year on Tour, the 34 year old Dubliner was beginning to wonder if such an occurrence would ever happen when he arrived in the beautiful city of Seville. However, by the time he left the Real Club de Golf de Sevilla, following an exhilarating and spectacular see-saw finalé, he knew for certain it had.

As the dust settled on a wonderful week, the record books showed Lawrie had come out on top from a play-off with host country favourite Ignacio Garrido, enabling him to follow in the footsteps of his roommate and compatriot Damien McGrane, who won the Volvo China Open two weeks earlier, and Ulsterman Darren Clarke who had claimed the BMW Asian Open the previous Sunday.

Furthermore, later on that day, capping a truly amazing Sunday for Ireland, another Ulsterman, Michael Hoey, claimed the Banque Populaire Moroccan Classic 2008 title on the European Challenge Tour.

Although naturally quiet and unassuming, Lawrie was used to making history having been the first Irish player since the inception of the award in 1960 to be named The Sir Henry Cotton Rookie of the Year – that accolade coming in 2003.

It was a bittersweet honour, for the joy of a first triumph in that rookie year, ironically in the very same Open de España played that season in Tenerife at the Golf Costa Adeje, was taken from him when he, and Swede Peter Hedblom, lost in a play-off to England's Kenneth Ferrie.

The former Irish Amateur champion carried the hurt of losing with him and although chances came and went over the next five seasons, he was unable to shrug the monkey from his back.

On a searing final afternoon in Spain, it hardly looked as though this would be his day of destiny either. He began the final round five strokes behind Garrido, who had powered into pole position with the help of a magnificent course record second round 63.

Garrido had replaced Sweden's Martin Erlandsson on top of the leaderboard at the halfway stage and, having taken a three shot lead into the final day over Andalucía's favourite son, Miguel Angel Jiménez, he stood on the verge of providing his own piece of history for the annals of The European Tour.

Martin Erlandsson

David Lynn

Peter Lawrie (right), receives the trophy from Emma Villacieros, President Real Federación Española de Golf

Already there as one of only three father and son combinations to have won on The European Tour – Craig/Kevin Stadler and José Maria/Alejandro Cañizares being the other two – the Garridos were trying to elevate that to a new level.

For no father and son combination had ever won the same event on The European Tour and should Ignacio have gone on to pick up the €333,330 (£262,758) first prize, he would have emulated father Antonio who won the 1972 Open de España – the first official European Tour event – just 19 days after Ignacio was born.

Understandably, come Saturday night, Lawrie was far from the thoughts of most. It was the prospect of a final day 'Duel in the Sun' between Garrido and Jiménez, which held the attention of media and Spanish golfing fans alike.

However, with Garrido teetering at the top and Jiménez's challenge disappearing with a triple bogey seven at the tenth, Lawrie imposed himself, picking up four birdies in the last six holes to set a 15 under par target of 273 that looked unlikely to be bettered.

The Irishman watched on television and, although he knew it unwise, he could not stop himself going over a winner's speech in his head, especially as Garrido faced a 35 foot birdie putt on the final green to force a play-off. Surely he couldn't, could he? He did, amidst tumultuous acclaim from the grandstands.

Lesser men might have wilted but, incredibly, Lawrie repeated the feat ten minutes later on the same green to extend the play-off, the normally calm and unruffled Irishman turning into a whirling dervish as he celebrated the ball dropping below ground.

If Garrido was taken aback by that, it was nothing compared to his disappointment moments later when, a seemingly perfect approach on his return to the 18th green for the second extra hole, grabbed the grain on the putting surface and spun back into the water.

The Seville public, superb all week in both number and nature, greeted the new champion warmly while Lawrie smiled as he got to use his winner's speech after all.

Norman Dabell

Alfredo García-Heredia

Real Club de Golf de Sevilla

Final Results

Pos	Name		Rd1	Rd2	Rd3	Rd4	Total		€	£
1	Peter LAWRIE	IRL	68	70	68	67	273	-15	333,330.00	262,758.36
2	Ignacio GARRIDO	ESP	66	63	72	72	273	-15	222,220.00	175,172.24
3	Søren HANSEN	DEN	68	70	67	69	274	-14	125,200.00	98,693.03
4	Alfredo GARCIA-HEREDIA	ESP	69	69	69	68	275	-13	84,933.33	66,951.50
	David LYNN	ENG	70	66	73	66	275	-13	84,933.33	66,951.50
	Miguel Angel JIMÉNEZ	ESP	70	67	67	71	275	-13	84,933.33	66,951.50
7	Richard FINCH	ENG	72	69	67	68	276	-12	60,000.00	47,296.98
8	Martin ERLANDSSON	SWE	65	68	73	71	277	-11	47,400.00	37,364.61
	Peter HANSON	SWE	74	67	69	67	277	-11	47,400.00	37,364.61
10	Robert-Jan DERKSEN	NED	71	68	69	70	278	-10	35,850.00	28,259.94
	Andrew MCLARDY	RSA	72	65	69	72	278	-10	35,850.00	28,259.94
	Niclas FASTH	SWE	72	69	71	66	278	-10	35,850.00	28,259.94
	Danny WILLETT (AM)	ENG	73	70	64	71	278	-10		
	Alexander NOREN	SWE	74	64	70	70	278	-10	35,850.00	28,259.94
15	Marco RUIZ	PAR	70	66	69	74	279	-9	29,400.00	23,175.52
	Hennie OTTO	RSA	72	66	71	70	279	-9	29,400.00	23,175.52
	Pablo MARTIN	ESP	72	70	67	70	279	-9	29,400.00	23,175.52
18	Iain PYMAN	ENG	71	68	71	70	280	-8	25,400.00	20,022.39
	Michael JONZON	SWE	72	68	69	71	280	-8	25,400.00	20,022.39
	Gareth PADDISON	NZL	73	69	67	71	280	-8	25,400.00	20,022.39
	Eduardo DE LA RIVA	ESP	74	65	71	70	280	-8	25,400.00	20,022.39
22	Carlos RODILES	ESP	68	68	70	75	281	-7	20,500.00	16,159.80
	Steven O'HARA	SCO	68	70	75	68	281	-7	20,500.00	16,159.80
	Peter FOWLER	AUS	68	66	70	75	281	-7	20,500.00	16,159.80
	Mark FOSTER	ENG	70	67	68	76	281	-7	20,500.00	16,159.80
	Alejandro CAÑIZARES	ESP	70	69	71	71	281	-7	20,500.00	16,159.80
	Ricardo GONZALEZ	ARG	70	71	72	68	281	-7	20,500.00	16,159.80
	Fabrizio ZANOTTI	PAR	71	69	68	73	281	-7	20,500.00	16,159.80
	Edoardo MOLINARI	ITA	71	71	70	69	281	-7	20,500.00	16,159.80
	Darren CLARKE	NIR	72	69	67	73	281	-7	20,500.00	16,159.80
	Gary LOCKERBIE	ENG	72	71	70	68	281	-7	20,500.00	16,159.80
32	Henrik NYSTRÖM	SWE	68	69	71	74	282	-6	16,040.00	12,644.06
	Manuel QUIROS	ESP	69	70	70	73	282	-6	16,040.00	12,644.06
	José Manuel LARA	ESP	71	66	70	75	282	-6	16,040.00	12,644.06
	Felipe AGUILAR	CHI	72	71	70	69	282	-6	16,040.00	12,644.06
	Liam BOND	WAL	76	65	71	70	282	-6	16,040.00	12,644.06
37	Peter WHITEFORD	SCO	68	72	72	71	283	-5	12,800.00	10,090.02
	Fredrik ANDERSSON HED	SWE	70	69	70	74	283	-5	12,800.00	10,090.02
	Pedro LINHART	ESP	70	70	73	70	283	-5	12,800.00	10,090.02
	Anthony WALL	ENG	71	66	73	73	283	-5	12,800.00	10,090.02
	Gary ORR	SCO	71	68	75	69	283	-5	12,800.00	10,090.02
	Julio ZAPATA	ARG	72	71	68	72	283	-5	12,800.00	10,090.02
	Alvaro QUIROS	ESP	73	70	71	69	283	-5	12,800.00	10,090.02
	Simon WAKEFIELD	ENG	73	70	71	69	283	-5	12,800.00	10,090.02
	Per-Ulrik JOHANSSON	SWE	74	67	70	72	283	-5	12,800.00	10,090.02
	Paul MCGINLEY	IRL	74	68	70	71	283	-5	12,800.00	10,090.02
47	Gary CLARK	ENG	67	74	70	73	284	-4	10,000.00	7,882.83
	Francis VALERA	ESP	71	68	72	73	284	-4	10,000.00	7,882.83
	Mads VIBE-HASTRUP	DEN	71	71	72	70	284	-4	10,000.00	7,882.83
	Thomas AIKEN	RSA	72	70	69	73	284	-4	10,000.00	7,882.83
51	Miles TUNNICLIFF	ENG	72	68	70	75	285	-3	9,000.00	7,094.55
52	François DELAMONTAGNE	FRA	69	71	73	73	286	-2	8,400.00	6,621.58
	Garry HOUSTON	WAL	75	68	74	69	286	-2	8,400.00	6,621.58
54	Robert ROCK	ENG	69	71	73	74	287	-1	7,200.00	5,675.64
	Matthew MILLAR	AUS	70	72	76	69	287	-1	7,200.00	5,675.64
	Grégory HAVRET	FRA	71	71	73	72	287	-1	7,200.00	5,675.64
	Magnus A CARLSSON	SWE	73	68	74	72	287	-1	7,200.00	5,675.64
58	Stephen GALLACHER	SCO	70	69	77	72	288	0	5,600.00	4,414.38
	Jean-François LUCQUIN	FRA	70	71	70	77	288	0	5,600.00	4,414.38
	Florian PRAEGANT	AUT	70	72	75	71	288	0	5,600.00	4,414.38
	Ian GARBUTT	ENG	71	70	75	72	288	0	5,600.00	4,414.38
	Alan MCLEAN	SCO	72	71	72	73	288	0	5,600.00	4,414.38
	Jan-Are LARSEN	NOR	73	70	77	68	288	0	5,600.00	4,414.38
	Santiago LUNA	ESP	74	69	72	73	288	0	5,600.00	4,414.38
65	Peter BAKER	ENG	69	74	73	73	289	1	4,700.00	3,704.93
	Sion E BEBB	WAL	75	67	74	73	289	1	4,700.00	3,704.93
67	Pelle EDBERG	SWE	73	70	71	76	290	2	4,300.00	3,389.62
	Carl SUNESON	ESP	76	67	75	72	290	2	4,300.00	3,389.62
69	Klas ERIKSSON	SWE	71	68	76	76	291	3	4,000.00	3,153.13
70	Colin MONTGOMERIE	SCO	70	73	74	75	292	4	3,725.00	2,936.35
	Gary BOYD	ENG	75	68	72	77	292	4	3,725.00	2,936.35
72	Jamie DONALDSON	WAL	72	70	78	73	293	5	2,998.50	2,363.67
	Rafael CABRERA BELLO	ESP	70	74	76	73	293	5	2,998.50	2,363.67
74	Jordi GARCIA	ESP	66	76	77	76	295	7	2,994.00	2,360.12
75	José Manuel CARRILES	ESP	70	72	76	78	296	8	2,991.00	2,357.75

Total Prize Fund
€2,011,982 £1,586,011

Hole	Par	Yards	Metres
1	4	398	364
2	4	451	413
3	3	168	154
4	4	436	399
5	5	514	470
6	4	451	413
7	3	231	211
8	4	379	347
9	5	545	499
OUT	**36**	**3573**	**3270**
10	4	422	386
11	3	198	181
12	4	379	347
13	5	517	473
14	4	428	392
15	4	437	400
16	5	522	478
17	3	226	207
18	4	432	395
IN	**36**	**3561**	**3259**
TOTAL	**72**	**7134**	**6529**

Peter Lawrie's victory beats his previous best European Tour performance of tied second in the 2003 Open de España, when he lost a play-off to Kenneth Ferrie. He now joins Eddie Polland (1976, 80), Eamonn Darcy (1983) and Padraig Harrington (1996) as Irish winners of the Open de España.

One Step at a Time

1	**Hennie OTTO**		263	-25
2	Oliver WILSON		264	-24
3	Robert KARLSSON		265	-23
4	Phillip ARCHER		267	-21
	Marcel SIEM		267	-21
6	Ross McGOWAN		268	-20
7	Grégory HAVRET		270	-18
	Christian NILSSON		270	-18
	Alvaro VELASCO		270	-18
10	Nick DOUGHERTY		271	-17
	Marco SOFFIETTI		271	-17

Sometimes it was an uncomfortable ride, but in a week of unbroken sunshine on the outskirts of the most fashionable of Italian cities, Hennie Otto at last found solace in golfing fulfilment.

Oliver Wilson

Ross McGowan

Seven weeks earlier the 31 year old South African had lost in a play-off to Scotland's Alastair Forsyth in the Madeira Islands Open BPI – Portugal, and before that he was a victim not only of spasmodic back trouble - which eventually required surgery – but also a simmering anger which, at times, boiled over.

After failing to make the cut in the 2001 Nashua Masters at the appropriately named Wild Coast Sun Country Club, Otto tossed his clubs into the nearby Umtamvuna River after firstly dismantling them in the golf course car park. "I felt much better after that," he admitted. "I wanted to change my clubs anyway."

On another occasion, once again playing on the Sunshine Tour, he was fined for bringing the game into disrepute after he was heard swearing live on television. "My anger may have held me back in my early career," conceded the stocky Springbok, a rugby fly-half at club level in his teens. "But I didn't let it linger."

Certainly that is the case today, for the Hennie Otto of 2008 has undoubtedly mellowed. For a start he is happily married to Liezel with a two year old son, Hendrik, and, with his maturing and contentment off the course, has come another level of golfing ability on it.

Gaining a two year exemption on The European Tour International Schedule was a huge bonus for a player whose main goal upon arrival at the superbly conditioned Castello di Tolcinasco Golf and Country Club was to secure the top ten finish that would have seen him qualify for The Irish Open the following week.

However, come the end of the week, a player with much of the natural ability of his fellow countrymen, Ernie Els and Retief Goosen, was on his way, the road cleared of impediments.

With his Tour status secured until the end of the 2010 season, Otto abandoned the flight to Shannon and, instead, headed home to Johannesburg to celebrate quietly, and, more importantly, see Leizel and Hendrik before flying back to London for the BMW PGA Championship at Wentworth Club.

"I've come close to winning a few times on The European Tour, so maybe it was high time it happened," he said before leaving Milan. "My schedule has just changed after today. I can now plan two or three years ahead. It's a huge weight off my shoulders.

"Everybody knows I am not the best at relaxing, but I do try my best and I believe I am getting better at it. I also have to thank my caddie for keeping me together. If it wasn't for him I might not have won. He told me to concentrate on the here and now, and not look too far ahead."

Crisis time, possibly even one of the key moments in his entire career, arrived when he bogeyed the 12th hole in the final round. Four shots ahead overnight, he was suddenly level with England's Oliver Wilson, who had started out six shots adrift that afternoon. Otto had been five clear of the field after 54 holes in Madeira - was this to be another eleventh hour failure when so close to the breakthrough he craved?

However, having been through a similar situation at Santo da Serra, he was better prepared mentally to deal with it this time. Also, importantly, he was in tune with his putter on, arguably, the best greens on Tour up to that point in the season.

Showing immense resolve, he immediately holed from 20 feet for a birdie three at the 13th. Crucially, he was in front once more, and although Wilson returned the round of the day, a closing eight under par 64, he never again regained parity.

There was one more defining moment for Otto. On the 18th his drive finished up in a spot in the semi rough which required him to place one foot in a bunker to execute his second shot. "It wasn't a bad lie," he said, modestly, later. But it was awkward enough to have had an effect, especially in the circumstances.

However, now completely in control of any nerves he might have had, he struck the shot so purely that the ball landed a mere eight feet from the flag. He missed the putt, but it mattered not. He was the Methorios Capital Italian Open champion, the first South African to take the title since Dale Hayes at Pevero 30 years earlier.

Jock MacVicar
Scottish Daily Express

Hennie Otto (right), receives the trophy from Franco Chimenti, President of the Italian Golf Federation

Left *Alvaro Velasco*

Grégory Havret

Marcel Siem

Hole	Par	Yards	Metres
1	5	526	481
2	4	462	423
3	4	469	429
4	4	425	389
5	3	210	192
6	4	492	450
7	4	473	433
8	3	224	205
9	5	513	469
OUT	36	3794	3471
10	4	342	313
11	4	411	376
12	5	566	518
13	4	433	396
14	3	167	153
15	5	554	507
16	3	206	188
17	4	387	354
18	4	423	387
IN	36	3489	3192
TOTAL	72	7283	6663

The Castello di Tolcinasco Golf and Country Club maintained its tradition for wonderful scoring. Hennie Otto's winning score of 25 under par 263 set the record for the lowest in the tournament's history in relation to par, beating the 23 under par total of 265 carded by Francesco Molinari in 2006. In the five years the Arnold Palmer-designed course has staged the Methorios Capital Italian Open, the average winning score in relation to par is 20 under.

FOTOGRAFO

Castello di Tolcinasco Golf and Country Club

Final Results

Pos	Name		Rd1	Rd2	Rd3	Rd4	Total		€	£
1	Hennie OTTO	RSA	65	66	63	69	263	-25	283,330.00	221,303.15
2	Oliver WILSON	ENG	66	69	65	64	264	-24	188,880.00	147,530.23
3	Robert KARLSSON	SWE	68	61	69	67	265	-23	106,420.00	83,122.44
4	Phillip ARCHER	ENG	70	64	65	68	267	-21	78,540.00	61,345.96
	Marcel SIEM	GER	70	66	65	66	267	-21	78,540.00	61,345.96
6	Ross McGOWAN	ENG	64	71	64	69	268	-20	59,500.00	46,474.21
7	Christian NILSSON	SWE	67	67	64	72	270	-18	43,860.00	34,258.13
	Alvaro VELASCO	ESP	70	64	64	72	270	-18	43,860.00	34,258.13
	Grégory HAVRET	FRA	70	67	63	70	270	-18	43,860.00	34,258.13
10	Nick DOUGHERTY	ENG	71	66	67	67	271	-17	32,640.00	25,494.42
	Marco SOFFIETTI	ITA	72	66	63	70	271	-17	32,640.00	25,494.42
12	Mark FOSTER	ENG	65	66	72	70	273	-15	26,316.00	20,554.88
	Estanislao GOYA	ARG	66	67	68	72	273	-15	26,316.00	20,554.88
	Fabrizio ZANOTTI	PAR	66	72	66	69	273	-15	26,316.00	20,554.88
	Paul BROADHURST	ENG	69	67	67	70	273	-15	26,316.00	20,554.88
	Jarmo SANDELIN	SWE	71	66	67	69	273	-15	26,316.00	20,554.88
17	Per-Ulrik JOHANSSON	SWE	66	73	66	69	274	-14	20,881.67	16,310.23
	Marcus FRASER	AUS	67	67	69	71	274	-14	20,881.67	16,310.23
	Edoardo MOLINARI	ITA	67	69	69	69	274	-14	20,881.67	16,310.23
	Anders HANSEN	DEN	68	65	68	73	274	-14	20,881.67	16,310.23
	Shiv KAPUR	IND	70	65	70	69	274	-14	20,881.67	16,310.23
	Paul WARING	ENG	70	67	67	70	274	-14	20,881.67	16,310.23
23	Steve WEBSTER	ENG	66	69	71	69	275	-13	17,170.00	13,411.13
	John DALY	USA	67	73	68	67	275	-13	17,170.00	13,411.13
	Maarten LAFEBER	NED	68	66	69	72	275	-13	17,170.00	13,411.13
	Henrik NYSTRÖM	SWE	68	70	69	68	275	-13	17,170.00	13,411.13
	Scott BARR	AUS	70	69	65	71	275	-13	17,170.00	13,411.13
	David PARK	WAL	70	70	67	68	275	-13	17,170.00	13,411.13
	Santiago LUNA	ESP	71	68	68	68	275	-13	17,170.00	13,411.13
30	Grégory BOURDY	FRA	66	73	69	68	276	-12	13,472.50	10,523.09
	Matthew MILLAR	AUS	68	70	69	69	276	-12	13,472.50	10,523.09
	Ignacio GARRIDO	ESP	68	70	67	71	276	-12	13,472.50	10,523.09
	Bradley DREDGE	WAL	69	65	70	72	276	-12	13,472.50	10,523.09
	Miles TUNNICLIFF	ENG	69	68	68	71	276	-12	13,472.50	10,523.09
	Peter BAKER	ENG	69	71	68	68	276	-12	13,472.50	10,523.09
	David FROST	RSA	71	68	65	72	276	-12	13,472.50	10,523.09
	Lee SLATTERY	ENG	71	68	66	71	276	-12	13,472.50	10,523.09
38	Marco RUIZ	PAR	64	70	70	73	277	-11	11,050.00	8,630.92
	Søren KJELDSEN	DEN	66	71	71	69	277	-11	11,050.00	8,630.92
	Alexandre ROCHA	BRA	69	68	66	74	277	-11	11,050.00	8,630.92
	Michael JONZON	SWE	69	70	72	66	277	-11	11,050.00	8,630.92
	Thomas LEVET	FRA	69	70	67	71	277	-11	11,050.00	8,630.92
43	Alexander NOREN	SWE	66	71	70	71	278	-10	8,840.00	6,904.74
	David LYNN	ENG	68	67	73	70	278	-10	8,840.00	6,904.74
	Doug McGUIGAN	RSA	68	68	70	72	278	-10	8,840.00	6,904.74
	Ben MASON	ENG	68	68	69	73	278	-10	8,840.00	6,904.74
	Emanuele CANONICA	ITA	68	70	68	72	278	-10	8,840.00	6,904.74
	José Manuel LARA	ESP	69	70	70	69	278	-10	8,840.00	6,904.74
	Stephen DODD	WAL	72	68	71	67	278	-10	8,840.00	6,904.74
	Mark PILKINGTON	WAL	74	64	71	69	278	-10	8,840.00	6,904.74
51	Rafael CABRERA BELLO	ESP	67	71	69	73	280	-8	6,141.25	4,796.80
	Charl SCHWARTZEL	RSA	67	73	72	68	280	-8	6,141.25	4,796.80
	Richard BLAND	ENG	68	71	72	69	280	-8	6,141.25	4,796.80
	Sam LITTLE	ENG	69	66	74	71	280	-8	6,141.25	4,796.80
	Alessandro TADINI	ITA	71	67	71	71	280	-8	6,141.25	4,796.80
	Gary CLARK	ENG	71	69	71	69	280	-8	6,141.25	4,796.80
	Robert ROCK	ENG	71	69	74	66	280	-8	6,141.25	4,796.80
	Martin WIEGELE	AUT	71	69	72	68	280	-8	6,141.25	4,796.80
59	Gareth PADDISON	NZL	67	72	74	68	281	-7	4,675.00	3,651.54
	James KAMTE	RSA	69	70	72	70	281	-7	4,675.00	3,651.54
	Federico COLOMBO (AM)	ITA	69	70	67	75	281	-7		
	Ulrich VAN DEN BERG	RSA	70	68	71	72	281	-7	4,675.00	3,651.54
	Lorenzo GAGLI	ITA	71	66	73	71	281	-7	4,675.00	3,651.54
64	Jean-François REMESY	FRA	67	72	70	73	282	-6	4,250.00	3,319.59
65	Marc WARREN	SCO	65	70	72	76	283	-5	3,740.00	2,921.24
	Gary ORR	SCO	69	69	73	72	283	-5	3,740.00	2,921.24
	Pedro LINHART	ESP	70	70	71	72	283	-5	3,740.00	2,921.24
	Christian CÉVAËR	FRA	71	69	70	73	283	-5	3,740.00	2,921.24
	Alastair FORSYTH	SCO	74	67	71	71	283	-5	3,740.00	2,921.24
70	José-Filipe LIMA	POR	67	70	70	80	287	-1	3,230.00	2,522.89
71	Raphaël JACQUELIN	FRA	67	71	72	78	288	0	3,110.00	2,429.16
72	Ian GARBUTT	ENG	67	66	73	77	290	2	2,550.00	1,991.75
73	Jan-Are LARSEN	NOR	69	70	82	70	291	3	2,547.00	1,989.41
74	Nunzio LOMBARDI (AM)	ITA	68	71	76	77	292	4		
75	Renaud GUILLARD	FRA	72	67	75	81	295	7	2,544.00	1,987.07
76	Claudio VIGANO (AM)	ITA	75	65	78	78	296	8		

Total Prize Fund
€1,707,641 £1,333,802

River Dance

1	Richard FINCH		278	-10
2	Felipe AGUILAR		280	-8
3	Robert KARLSSON		281	-7
	Maarten LAFEBER		281	-7
	Gary MURPHY		281	-7
	Lee WESTWOOD		281	-7
7	Rory McILROY		282	-6
8	Bradley DREDGE		283	-5
	Alvaro QUIROS		283	-5
10	Martin KAYMER		284	-4
	James KINGSTON		284	-4
	Anthony WALL		284	-4

The River Maigue might be merely a tributary of the lordly Shannon, but when it comes to golf and fishing, it holds a very special place in the hearts and minds of advocates of both pastimes.

What is more, when it is the week of The Irish Open at the Adare Manor Hotel and Golf Resort, the certainty is that an otherwise harmless looking and pleasant stretch of Limerick water will grab the headlines and play a key role in identifying the eventual champion.

Bradley Dredge's ball succumbed to the river's darker side during the play-off against Padraig Harrington which determined the outcome of The 2007 Irish Open, but Richard Finch could hardly have imagined what lay in store for him in the final round twelve months on.

Finch stood on the tee at the 18th enjoying a three stroke advantage over Chilean Felipe Aguilar. He was confident in his ability to complete his second victory of The 2008 European Tour International Schedule while, at the same time, all too well aware that the prize would not be safely within his grasp until he had completed the treacherous but spectacular 548 yard par five, where the Maigue has to be traversed at some stage, either with the second or third shot.

Not for nothing had the renowned course designer Robert Trent Jones Snr claimed it as the "finest finishing hole in all of golf."

Conscious there was no requirement for risk taking, Finch opted to lay up with his second

only to see the ball cross the line of the hazard but come to rest on the slope of the river bank. "I considered chipping it out sideways but when I got down to the ball, I thought, 'Well, it looks fine and I've got room to swing and a stance' so I never gave falling into the river a thought," he explained.

"As I hit the ball, I knew straight away I had made decent contact - that was the only thing I was really bothered about. I don't know if it was from the momentum of hitting the shot or whether I slipped, but the next thing I knew I was falling down the bank!

"I kept trying to follow the ball and looked up and saw it on the green, but by then I was up to my waist in water! However, knowing the ball was on the green was the main thing."

There have been, and will be, greater golf shots but few that will be as well remembered and, quite correctly, it was voted The European Tour Shot of the Month for May. With the aid of watching officials and photographers, the sodden Finch struggled back up the bank, towelled himself down as best he could and beamed broadly before accepting the thunderous applause of the gallery.

The Englishman knew only too well he would be the subject of constant jokes and pranks from the locker room for years to come, let alone the

Alvaro Quiros

Alastair Forsyth

***Left** Martin Kaymer*

Steven O'Hara

Richard Finch (centre), with Judy and Tom Kane, owners of Adare Manor Hotel & Golf Resort

Bradley Dredge

Rory McIlroy

fact his own unique river dance would likely end up as a clip on YouTube let alone as part of the 'What Happened Next?' section of the BBC quiz programme, 'A Question of Sport'.

However, with a cheque for €416, 660 (£330,297) to add to his bank account and a move to fifth place on The European Tour Order of Merit to savour, he had little cause to worry.

For a man who did not confirm his playing privileges for The 2008 European Tour until a brave showing in the 2007 season's penultimate event, the Mallorca Classic, saw him finish in a tie for seventh, the win, following on from his breakthrough success in the Michael Hill New Zealand Open in December, was massive.

He had yet to compete in a Major Championship but all that was about to change and the future could hardly be brighter for a man with a ready smile and a happy disposition to life to go along with it.

Meanwhile, second placed Aguilar confirmed the favourable impression he had created when winning the Enjoy Jakarta Astro Indonesia Open in February by finishing only two shots behind the eventual champion.

The huge Irish crowds longed for another winning performance from defending champion Padraig Harrington but, with that not forthcoming, Kilkenny man Gary Murphy gave them something to cheer by flirting with the lead on the final day before settling for a share of third place alongside Sweden's Robert Karlsson, Dutchman Maarten Lafeber and Lee Westwood of England.

Nevertheless, there was no question that the talk in the local hostelries that evening, was of a 30 year old Englishman and a shot that will be replayed around the world for years to come.

Charlie Mulqueen
Irish Examiner

Always on target to make a splash!

Delivering high quality bespoke printed material for
The European Tour over 14 years

Design & Print Solutions

01252 643668
07747025569 (mobile)
mbaldwin@printhouseltd.co.uk

T C COMMUNICATIONS LTD

ADVERTISING • MARKETING • PR • NEW MEDIA

01344 622280
timl@tc-comms.co.uk
www.tc-comms.co.uk

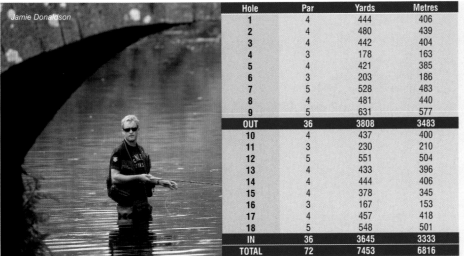

Jamie Donaldson

Hole	Par	Yards	Metres
1	4	444	406
2	4	480	439
3	4	442	404
4	3	178	163
5	4	421	385
6	3	203	186
7	5	528	483
8	4	481	440
9	5	631	577
OUT	36	3808	3483
10	4	437	400
11	3	230	210
12	5	551	504
13	4	433	396
14	4	444	406
15	4	378	345
16	3	167	153
17	4	457	418
18	5	548	501
IN	36	3645	3333
TOTAL	72	7453	6816

Adare Manor Hotel and Golf Resort

Final Results

Pos	Name		Rd1	Rd2	Rd3	Rd4	Total		€	£
1	Richard FINCH	ENG	71	72	65	70	278	-10	416,660.00	330,297.19
2	Felipe AGUILAR	CHI	71	72	67	70	280	-8	277,770.00	220,195.49
3	Robert KARLSSON	SWE	71	70	69	71	281	-7	118,750.00	94,136.21
	Maarten LAFEBER	NED	71	71	72	67	281	-7	118,750.00	94,136.21
	Gary MURPHY	IRL	74	70	68	69	281	-7	118,750.00	94,136.21
	Lee WESTWOOD	ENG	75	70	64	72	281	-7	118,750.00	94,136.21
7	Rory MCILROY	NIR	70	72	70	70	282	-6	75,000.00	59,454.45
8	Bradley DREDGE	WAL	68	73	66	76	283	-5	59,250.00	46,969.01
	Alvaro QUIROS	ESP	72	72	68	71	283	-5	59,250.00	46,969.01
10	Anthony WALL	ENG	72	70	70	72	284	-4	46,333.33	36,729.64
	James KINGSTON	RSA	75	68	69	72	284	-4	46,333.33	36,729.64
	Martin KAYMER	GER	77	68	70	69	284	-4	46,333.33	36,729.64
13	Johan EDFORS	SWE	68	73	73	71	285	-3	38,416.67	30,453.89
	Alvaro VELASCO	ESP	69	72	72	72	285	-3	38,416.67	30,453.89
	David FROST	RSA	74	70	66	75	285	-3	38,416.67	30,453.89
16	Lee S JAMES	ENG	69	73	70	74	286	-2	31,875.00	25,268.14
	Pablo LARRAZABAL	ESP	70	70	73	73	286	-2	31,875.00	25,268.14
	Darren CLARKE	NIR	72	69	72	73	286	-2	31,875.00	25,268.14
	Paul MCGINLEY	IRL	73	69	73	71	286	-2	31,875.00	25,268.14
	Jarmo SANDELIN	SWE	76	66	71	73	286	-2	31,875.00	25,268.14
	Mikko ILONEN	FIN	77	66	68	75	286	-2	31,875.00	25,268.14
22	Peter LAWRIE	IRL	71	75	72	69	287	-1	27,875.00	22,097.24
	Oliver FISHER	ENG	72	75	69	71	287	-1	27,875.00	22,097.24
24	Peter O'MALLEY	AUS	70	73	71	74	288	0	24,500.00	19,421.79
	Stephen GALLACHER	SCO	73	71	68	76	288	0	24,500.00	19,421.79
	Paul BROADHURST	ENG	73	74	68	73	288	0	24,500.00	19,421.79
	Ross FISHER	ENG	74	68	69	77	288	0	24,500.00	19,421.79
	Steven O'HARA	SCO	74	68	72	74	288	0	24,500.00	19,421.79
	Peter HEDBLOM	SWE	77	69	71	71	288	0	24,500.00	19,421.79
	Grégory HAVRET	FRA	77	70	65	76	288	0	24,500.00	19,421.79
31	Michael LORENZO-VERA	FRA	68	70	75	76	289	1	20,375.00	16,151.79
	Stuart MANLEY	WAL	71	72	76	70	289	1	20,375.00	16,151.79
	Padraig HARRINGTON	IRL	72	71	70	76	289	1	20,375.00	16,151.79
	Martin ERLANDSSON	SWE	73	73	70	73	289	1	20,375.00	16,151.79
35	Søren KJELDSEN	DEN	70	77	74	69	290	2	17,750.00	14,070.89
	Scott STRANGE	AUS	71	74	74	71	290	2	17,750.00	14,070.89
	John BICKERTON	ENG	72	70	77	71	290	2	17,750.00	14,070.89
	Oliver WILSON	ENG	74	73	71	72	290	2	17,750.00	14,070.89
	Thomas AIKEN	RSA	75	69	73	73	290	2	17,750.00	14,070.89
40	Richard GREEN	AUS	66	74	75	76	291	3	15,250.00	12,089.07
	Jeev Milkha SINGH	IND	66	76	75	74	291	3	15,250.00	12,089.07
	Edoardo MOLINARI	ITA	70	73	72	76	291	3	15,250.00	12,089.07
	Gary ORR	SCO	71	73	73	74	291	3	15,250.00	12,089.07
	Simon KHAN	ENG	71	74	75	71	291	3	15,250.00	12,089.07
45	Peter BAKER	ENG	72	69	76	75	292	4	13,250.00	10,503.62
	Alejandro CAÑIZARES	ESP	72	72	73	75	292	4	13,250.00	10,503.62
	Julio ZAPATA	ARG	72	73	72	75	292	4	13,250.00	10,503.62
48	Ulrich VAN DEN BERG	RSA	71	75	75	72	293	5	11,250.00	8,918.17
	François DELAMONTAGNE	FRA	73	72	72	76	293	5	11,250.00	8,918.17
	Jean VAN DE VELDE	FRA	74	70	72	77	293	5	11,250.00	8,918.17
	Steven JEPPESEN	SWE	74	72	73	74	293	5	11,250.00	8,918.17
	Colin MONTGOMERIE	SCO	75	69	73	76	293	5	11,250.00	8,918.17
53	Louis OOSTHUIZEN	RSA	72	73	72	77	294	6	9,750.00	7,729.08
54	Marcel SIEM	GER	68	71	75	81	295	7	9,000.00	7,134.53
	Barry LANE	ENG	73	72	73	77	295	7	9,000.00	7,134.53
56	Alastair FORSYTH	SCO	71	72	75	78	296	8	8,000.00	6,341.81
	Stephen DODD	WAL	74	71	75	76	296	8	8,000.00	6,341.81
58	José Manuel LARA	ESP	71	74	75	77	297	9	7,375.00	5,846.35
	Peter HANSON	SWE	74	73	75	75	297	9	7,375.00	5,846.35
60	Emanuele CANONICA	ITA	72	74	77	75	298	10	6,750.00	5,350.90
	Mikael LUNDBERG	SWE	73	74	76	75	298	10	6,750.00	5,350.90
	Ross McGOWAN	ENG	72	71	75	78	298	10	6,750.00	5,350.90
63	Pedro LINHART	ESP	71	76	74	78	299	11	6,125.00	4,855.45
	David DRYSDALE	SCO	74	72	79	74	299	11	6,125.00	4,855.45
65	Matthew MILLAR	AUS	73	73	79	76	301	13	5,750.00	4,558.17
66	Paul WARING	ENG	76	70	75	81	302	14	5,500.00	4,359.99
67	Luis CLAVERIE	ESP	73	73	73	85	304	16	5,250.00	4,161.81
68	Benoit TEILLERIA	FRA	75	72	77	82	306	18	5,000.00	3,963.63

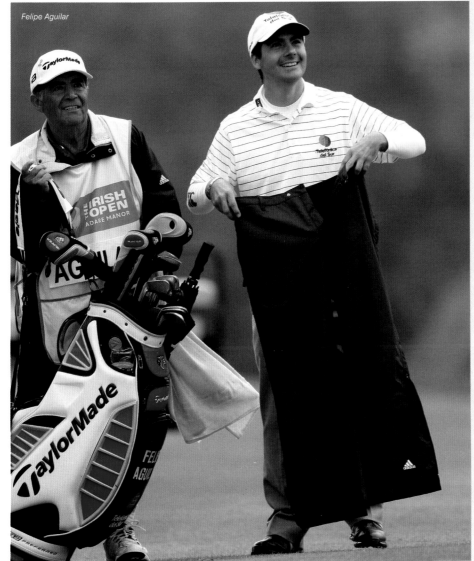

Felipe Aguilar

Richard Finch claimed his second European Tour International Schedule title in his 100th European Tour event. The Englishman played 89 tournaments without success until his breakthrough victory came in his 90th - the 2008 Michael Hill New Zealand Open. He then only had to wait a further ten tournaments for his second triumph.

Total Prize Fund

€2,490, 680 £1,974,426

BMW Golfsport

bmw-golfsport.com
bmw.co.uk

BMW
The Ultimate
Driving Machine

BMW PGA Championship

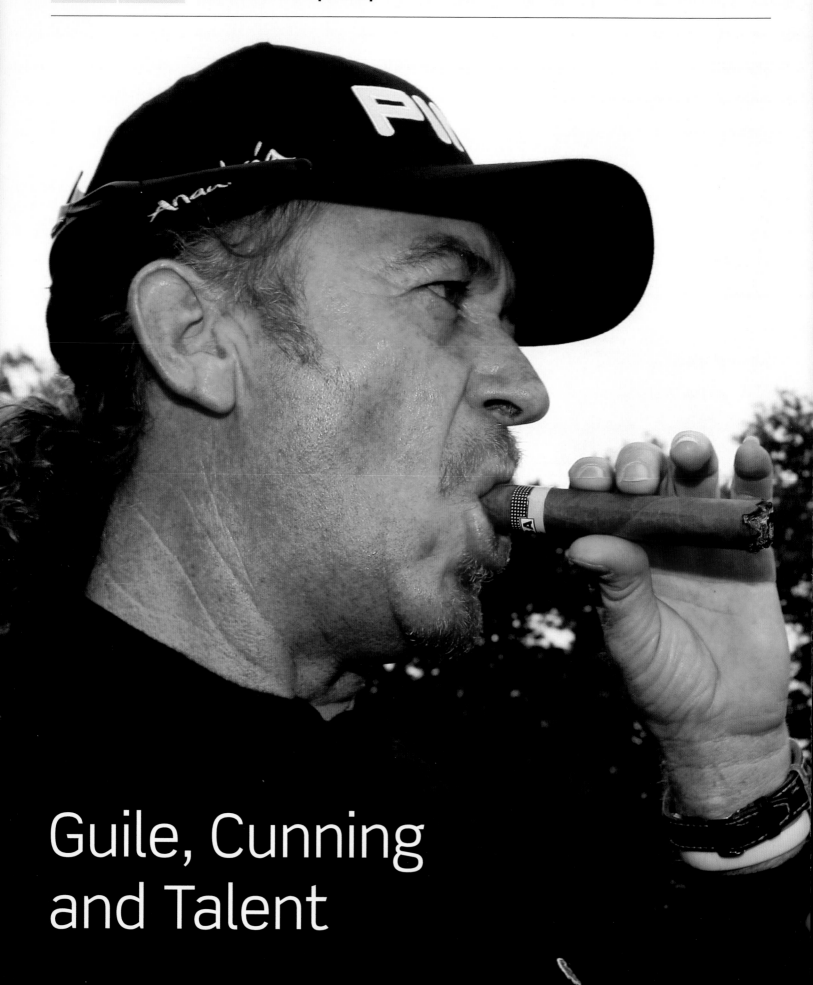

Guile, Cunning
and Talent

1	**Miguel Angel JIMÉNEZ**	**277**	**-11**
2	Oliver WILSON	277	-11
3	Luke DONALD	279	-9
	Robert KARLSSON	279	-9
5	Jyoti RANDHAWA	280	-8
6	Retief GOOSEN	281	-7
	Richard GREEN	281	-7
	Alexander NOREN	281	-7
	Andres ROMERO	281	-7
10	Alejandro CAÑIZARES	282	-6
	Paul CASEY	282	-6
	Simon KHAN	282	-6
	Søren KJELDSEN	282	-6
	Paul McGINLEY	282	-6
	Steve WEBSTER	282	-6

BMW Golfsport

bmw-golfsport.com
bmw.co.uk

The Ultimate
Driving Machine

BMW PGA Championship

I t was, as ever, vibrant, glamorous and exciting. You never knew what was going to happen next; who was going to do what; which delight was suddenly going to be set before you.

The above, of course, refers to the flagship event of The European Tour International Schedule – the BMW PGA Championship – a jewel in an ever-expanding golfing crown. However, it could equally apply to the event which traditionally heralds the week; namely the annual European Tour Dinner at Wentworth Club.

Staged in the club ballroom – not many clubs can say that – the Black Tie affair was as glittering as usual, a near-perfect celebration of, and by, a Tour that continues to set new and relevant benchmarks.

The fun, of course, continued when it came to the actual tournament 48 hours later. There was much golf to admire and much general gaiety to enjoy during a week that, each year, seems to manage to provide ever better staging than 12 months previously.

From the glorious 18th green hospitality unit, to the packed grandstands and the thronging fairways, visitors to this Surrey hinterland were treated to a week full of intrigue, achievement, disappointment and, ultimately, joy. Most of this last quality belonged to Miguel Angel Jiménez who, at 44 years and 141 days, crowned an already stellar career with his most significant victory.

It was a win that took guile, cunning and talent during four days when the wind at times whipped capriciously across the thousands of treetops that embroider the West Course. No accident either, that the biggest prize ultimately went to a Spaniard who has always seemed to treat the twin imposters of success and failure with equanimity.

There would have been genuine pleasure if young Englishman Oliver Wilson had prevailed

Robert Dinwiddie completes a course record 63 during the second round

Oliver Wilson

Paul McGinley and Robert Karlsson

Right *Paul Broadhurst, is presented with an engraved ice bucket by Keith Waters, Director of International Policy for The European Tour, to celebrate reaching the milestone of 500 European Tour events*

Luke Donald

in the sudden-death play-off that came after Jiménez did not get up and down at the 72nd hole, but there was a sliver more satisfaction at witnessing the wily old Spanish fox see off his final challenger with a birdie four at the second extra hole, the 18th.

For those of us who pay rapt attention to the playing of this grand old game, Saturday's third round offered much to savour. This was when the wind offered itself in truly playful mood, teasing the players with sudden gusts so that carefully prepared yardage charts were as much use as a banana in a sword fight.

Ireland's eternal battler, Paul McGinley, went into the day with a four stroke lead after an opening 36 holes sprinkled with stardust, but ended it five shots adrift of Robert Karlsson, the tall, elegant Swede having explored the very tips of his considerable game. With more wind and rain apparent for the final round, it was clear from the outset that Karlsson's own lead was fragile, and so it proved. When he uncharacteristically three putted the final hole to miss out on the play-off, we were left with Jiménez and Wilson.

155

BMW Golfsport

bmw-golfsport.com
bmw.co.uk

The Ultimate
Driving Machine

BMW PGA Championship

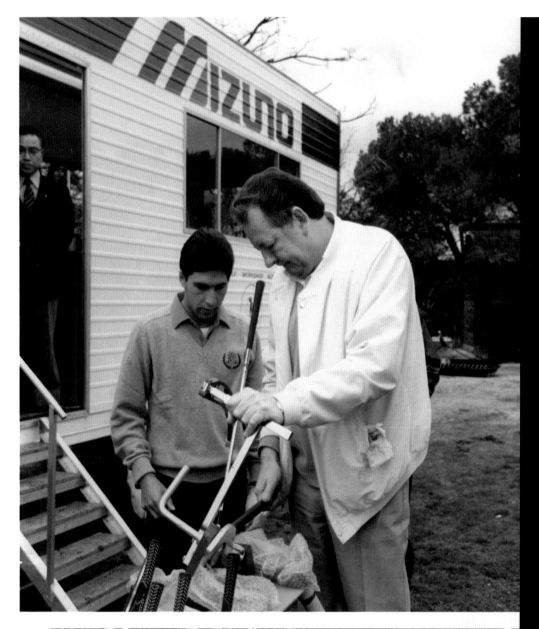

Barry Willett, who died in July aged 70, was at the forefront of bringing to reality the vision of Neil Coles, Chairman of the PGA European Tour Board of Directors, namely to provide the burgeoning European Tour with a mobile workshop that would herald a new level of professionalism on the circuit.

The duo forged a lifetime friendship after meeting at the St George's Hill Golf Club in Surrey where Willett first pitched up as a caddie in 1950. However the lure of turning Coles' dream into reality took him away from the club after 35 years to spend much of his life in a mobile workshop on the edge of practice grounds at European Tour events throughout Britain and the continent.

The project started in 1984 when Willett set up a temporary workshop at The Open Championship at St Andrews. The success of the facility that week persuaded Coles to urge Willett to plan a mobile workshop to follow the players on The European Tour and to help bridge the gap in standards between the European and the United States Tours. After Japanese club manufacturers Mizuno embraced the concept, Willett marshalled the service.

The Mizuno Official European Tour Workshop quickly became a fixture as did Willett at the helm of a popular team to whom many of the game's leading players such as Seve Ballesteros, Nick Faldo and a young José Maria Olazábal (pictured left with Barry) sought guidance on a variety of club matters.

Barry Willett, who retired in 1998 following the PGA Championship at Wentworth Club, and who courageously battled illness for several years, leaves his wife, Barbara, and their daughter, Kim.

Neil Coles summed up the feelings of the golfing world when he said: "Barry was a very special person, loved by all professional golfers who met him and he was a master of his craft with the unique gift of understanding what the professional wanted out of his clubs. He will be impossible to replace."

The legacy of the work begun by Barry Willett a quarter of a century ago can be seen now in the state-of-the-art European Tour Official Workshop available to all players on the range at European Tour International Schedule tournaments.

Jyoti Randhawa

Above and Below *Tented Village*

Thongchai Jaidee

The evening before, the Spaniard was asked if, despite his many other victories over the years, he might feel uncommonly nervous going into the last round given the stature of this particular tournament.

"No, why should I?" he countered in his deep, Marbella accent. "It is no different to any other time in this position. It is a golf tournament and so I must try to play well and hope I am lucky on the day. What else can I do? I will prepare as usual. I will have breakfast and then I will have a big espresso and a big cigar."

This philosophy might well fly in the face of more considered modern strategies – that invariably include a visit to the gym and the imbibing of several recommended health drinks – but it resonates for many of us. Here, clearly, is a man who takes these things seriously but not too seriously. This, it seems, is exactly the right approach, and though the intake of a small bucket of heavy duty coffee and the smoking of a cigar large enough to require stowing in the hold may be a couple of steps too far for most, it does offer its own peculiar attraction.

The BMW M5 Touring. Crafted at BMW M.

Official fuel economy figures for the M5 Touring: Extra-Urban 26.9 mpg (10.5 l/100km). Urban 13.0 m

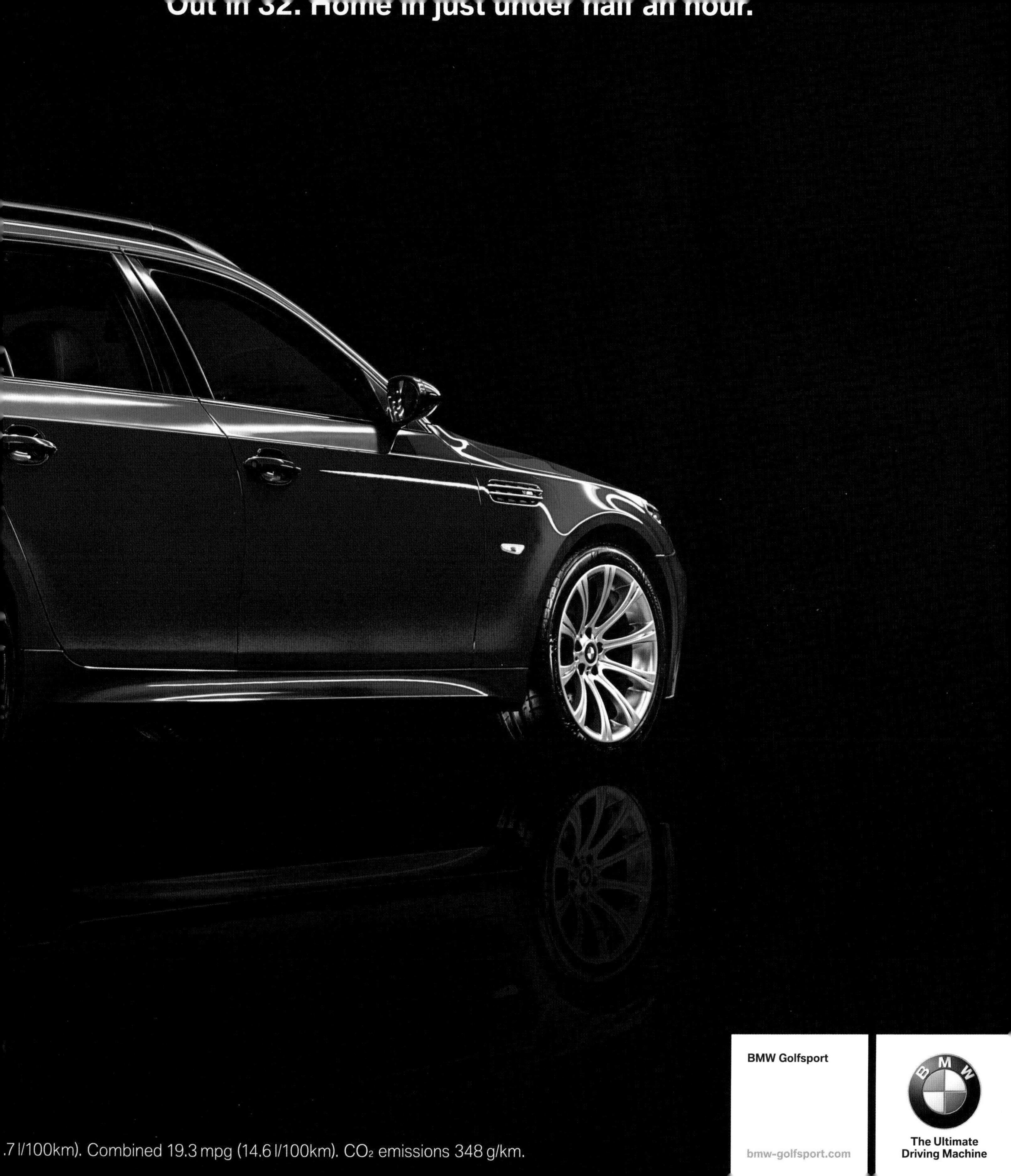

Out in 32. Home in just under half an hour.
.7 l/100km). Combined 19.3 mpg (14.6 l/100km). CO_2 emissions 348 g/km.
BMW Golfsport
bmw-golfsport.com
BMW
The Ultimate
Driving Machine

FONDÉ ✦ EN 1743

MOËT & CHANDON

The point is that, for Miguel, it works. When he found a dodgy lie in the rough beside the final green and failed to even make the three yards to the putting surface, it was a moment which might have snapped the resolve of some. Not him. His next chip was exquisite in the circumstances, the ball snaking its gentle way to stop a few inches from the hole.

When, 20 minutes later, he returned to the same green against his young English opponent, his fairway wood approach this time found the green – underlining his claim to be the best player of this particular shot in Europe – and his two putt birdie was enough to clinch victory. Suddenly the barrel-chest, that starts out impressively enough, expanded a few inches more.

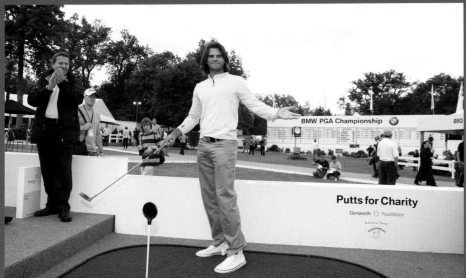

For Wilson second place was a disappointment but one that he embraced well. There have been several such runner-up spots for him over the last couple of years but if that means anything at all, it means that he is good enough to win, and he surely will soon. Certainly he accepted his fate with the very best of grace. "It is a good field, a great tournament and a great course," he said. "Second here is a good result. If every event were like this it would be amazing."

Bill Elliott
The Observer

Top Ian Robertson (left), Member of the Board, Sales and Marketing BMW Group, and George O'Grady, Chief Executive of The European Tour, celebrate the announcement of BMW as Official Partner and Official Car to The 2010 Ryder Cup

Above Johan Edfors' one putt on the specially constructed putting green in the Tented Village, helped Genworth Financial's 'Putts for Charity' initiative raise £15,975 over the week

Right Left to right: George O'Grady, Justin Rose, winner of the 2007 Harry Vardon Trophy; and Neil Coles, Chairman of The PGA European Tour Board of Directors, at The European Tour Annual Dinner at Wentworth Club

Below Martin Kaymer with the 2007 Sir Henry Cotton Rookie of the Year Award

BMW Golfsport

bmw-golfsport.com
bmw.co.uk

The Ultimate
Driving Machine

BMW PGA Championship

Mick Hucknall and his band Simply Red played a special charity 'Concert on the Course' on the eve of the Championship

Wentworth Club
(West Course)

Final Results

Pos	Name		Rd1	Rd2	Rd3	Rd4	Total		€	£
1	Miguel Angel JIMÉNEZ	ESP	70	67	72	68	277	-11	750,000.00	597,205.08
2	Oliver WILSON	ENG	70	66	73	68	277	-11	500,000.00	398,136.72
3	Robert KARLSSON	SWE	66	69	70	74	279	-9	253,350.00	201,735.88
	Luke DONALD	ENG	72	69	73	65	279	-9	253,350.00	201,735.88
5	Jyoti RANDHAWA	IND	73	68	69	70	280	-8	190,800.00	151,928.97
6	Richard GREEN	AUS	70	69	73	69	281	-7	126,450.00	100,688.78
	Andres ROMERO	ARG	72	69	73	67	281	-7	126,450.00	100,688.78
	Alexander NOREN	SWE	75	68	71	67	281	-7	126,450.00	100,688.78
	Retief GOOSEN	RSA	76	69	70	66	281	-7	126,450.00	100,688.78
10	Paul MCGINLEY	IRL	65	66	79	72	282	-6	76,275.00	60,735.76
	Søren KJELDSEN	DEN	71	65	76	70	282	-6	76,275.00	60,735.76
	Paul CASEY	ENG	71	68	73	70	282	-6	76,275.00	60,735.76
	Steve WEBSTER	ENG	71	70	72	69	282	-6	76,275.00	60,735.76
	Simon KHAN	ENG	71	71	71	69	282	-6	76,275.00	60,735.76
	Alejandro CAÑIZARES	ESP	72	66	74	70	282	-6	76,275.00	60,735.76
16	Daniel VANCSIK	ARG	68	70	72	73	283	-5	57,375.00	45,686.19
	Gary ORR	SCO	70	68	73	72	283	-5	57,375.00	45,686.19
	Felipe AGUILAR	CHI	71	67	74	71	283	-5	57,375.00	45,686.19
	Martin KAYMER	GER	71	70	71	71	283	-5	57,375.00	45,686.19
	Oliver FISHER	ENG	71	73	69	70	283	-5	57,375.00	45,686.19
	Peter HANSON	SWE	72	71	70	70	283	-5	57,375.00	45,686.19
22	Charl SCHWARTZEL	RSA	68	71	73	72	284	-4	49,500.00	39,415.54
	Marc WARREN	SCO	69	70	75	70	284	-4	49,500.00	39,415.54
	Paul LAWRIE	SCO	72	73	70	69	284	-4	49,500.00	39,415.54
25	Robert-Jan DERKSEN	NED	70	70	76	69	285	-3	44,100.00	35,115.66
	Carlos RODILES	ESP	72	71	70	72	285	-3	44,100.00	35,115.66
	James KINGSTON	RSA	72	71	71	71	285	-3	44,100.00	35,115.66
	Simon DYSON	ENG	75	67	73	70	285	-3	44,100.00	35,115.66
	Jean-Baptiste GONNET	FRA	75	69	73	68	285	-3	44,100.00	35,115.66
30	Miles TUNNICLIFF	ENG	70	65	77	74	286	-2	38,025.00	30,278.30
	Thongchai JAIDEE	THA	72	69	74	71	286	-2	38,025.00	30,278.30
	Alastair FORSYTH	SCO	72	70	72	72	286	-2	38,025.00	30,278.30
	Sam LITTLE	ENG	74	68	73	71	286	-2	38,025.00	30,278.30
34	Marcus FRASER	AUS	67	69	76	75	287	-1	33,300.00	26,515.91
	Rafa ECHENIQUE	ARG	70	73	68	76	287	-1	33,300.00	26,515.91
	Peter LAWRIE	IRL	73	72	70	72	287	-1	33,300.00	26,515.91
	Søren HANSEN	DEN	76	66	73	72	287	-1	33,300.00	26,515.91
38	Grégory HAVRET	FRA	70	74	73	71	288	0	30,600.00	24,365.97
	Grégory BOURDY	FRA	72	71	71	74	288	0	30,600.00	24,365.97
40	Louis OOSTHUIZEN	RSA	67	76	74	72	289	1	27,000.00	21,499.38
	Simon WAKEFIELD	ENG	68	71	77	73	289	1	27,000.00	21,499.38
	Hennie OTTO	RSA	71	69	75	74	289	1	27,000.00	21,499.38
	Damien MCGRANE	IRL	72	66	77	74	289	1	27,000.00	21,499.38
	Henrik STENSON	SWE	74	70	74	71	289	1	27,000.00	21,499.38
	Anders HANSEN	DEN	75	69	77	68	289	1	27,000.00	21,499.38
46	Garry HOUSTON	WAL	68	74	75	73	290	2	21,150.00	16,841.18
	Alvaro VELASCO	ESP	69	76	71	74	290	2	21,150.00	16,841.18
	Peter O'MALLEY	AUS	71	72	74	73	290	2	21,150.00	16,841.18
	Henrik NYSTRÖM	SWE	72	72	70	76	290	2	21,150.00	16,841.18
	Ricardo GONZALEZ	ARG	73	70	74	73	290	2	21,150.00	16,841.18
	Angel CABRERA	ARG	73	72	72	73	290	2	21,150.00	16,841.18
	Sam WALKER	ENG	75	68	72	75	290	2	21,150.00	16,841.18
53	Nick DOUGHERTY	ENG	70	73	76	72	291	3	16,200.00	12,899.63
	Paul BROADHURST	ENG	72	71	74	74	291	3	16,200.00	12,899.63
	Jamie DONALDSON	WAL	72	72	74	73	291	3	16,200.00	12,899.63
	Ariel CANETE	ARG	74	71	71	75	291	3	16,200.00	12,899.63
57	Graeme MCDOWELL	NIR	70	73	75	74	292	4	13,950.00	11,108.01
58	Michael LORENZO-VERA	FRA	69	76	75	73	293	5	12,825.00	10,212.21
	Johan EDFORS	SWE	71	74	73	75	293	5	12,825.00	10,212.21
	Mark FOSTER	ENG	72	70	73	78	293	5	12,825.00	10,212.21
	Thomas LEVET	FRA	74	71	73	75	293	5	12,825.00	10,212.21
62	Anton HAIG	RSA	70	75	75	74	294	6	11,700.00	9,316.40
63	David HOWELL	ENG	70	71	77	79	297	9	11,025.00	8,778.91
	Ignacio GARRIDO	ESP	73	68	74	82	297	9	11,025.00	8,778.91
65	Magnus A CARLSSON	SWE	70	72	79	77	298	10	10,125.00	8,062.27
	Marcel SIEM	GER	71	73	78	76	298	10	10,125.00	8,062.27
67	Robert DINWIDDIE	ENG	78	63	79	79	299	11	9,450.00	7,524.78
68	Matthew MORRIS	ENG	71	74	76	79	300	12	8,775.00	6,987.30
	Ross FISHER	ENG	72	73	80	75	300	12	8,775.00	6,987.30
70	Ross McGOWAN	ENG	73	72	74	83	302	14	8,200.00	6,529.44

Hole	Par	Yards	Metres
1	4	473	433
2	3	154	141
3	4	465	425
4	5	552	505
5	3	212	194
6	4	418	382
7	4	396	362
8	4	401	367
9	4	449	411
OUT	**35**	**3520**	**3220**
10	3	184	168
11	4	416	380
12	5	531	486
13	4	470	430
14	3	179	164
15	4	489	447
16	4	383	350
17	5	610	558
18	5	538	492
IN	**37**	**3800**	**3475**
TOTAL	**72**	**7320**	**6695**

Left to right: Special Olympic Athletes Siarna Peate, Daniel Moore and Kemlyn Shard visited the BMW PGA Championship and were given a putting lesson by Wentworth Club attached professional Seve Benson

Miguel Angel Jiménez became the first golfer to win all three BMW events on The European Tour. His win in the BMW PGA Championship went alongside his victories in the 2004 BMW Asian Open and the 2004 BMW International Open. He also became only the second player in European Tour history to win a tournament with a hole-in-one in the final round. The first player to achieve the feat was Thongchai Jaidee in the 2004 Malaysian Open.

Total Prize Fund
€4,500,000 £3,583,230

1	**Scott STRANGE**		262	-22
2	Robert KARLSSON		266	-18
3	Raphaël JACQUELIN		270	-14
4	Benn BARHAM		271	-13
	Darren CLARKE		271	-13
	Nick DOUGHERTY		271	-13
	Rafa ECHENIQUE		271	-13
	Francesco MOLINARI		271	-13
9	Gonzalo FERNANDEZ-CASTAÑO		272	-12
10	Robert DINWIDDIE		273	-11
	Ross FISHER		273	-11
	Ross McGOWAN		273	-11
	Jeev Milkha SINGH		273	-11
	Alvaro VELASCO		273	-11

Poignant Victory

With Open Champion Padraig Harrington making his debut amongst a high-quality field, it was generally felt it would take something strange to stop one of Europe's many prospective Ryder Cup charges in action from lifting The Celtic Manor Wales Open trophy. In the end, that was exactly what happened.

To be precise, not something strange, but someone Strange. Australian Scott Strange produced some truly sensational golf over The Twenty Ten Course – named to commemorate the year The Celtic Manor Resort's newest 18 holes will host The Ryder Cup – to triumph.

Rounds of 63-66-69-64 propelled the 31 year old from Perth to his maiden European Tour victory on 22 under par 262; Strange's nerveless golf seeing him lead from wire-to-wire, ending four shots clear of his nearest challenger Robert Karlsson and out of sight of the rest of the field.

Every breakthrough victory is emotional but this one was even more so for the Australian who, during the week, alluded to the fact of how his exploits were helping him deal with difficult personal circumstances, and how they would "put a smile on the face of someone very special back home."

He declined to divulge exactly what those circumstances were at the time, but it later transpired he had been referring to his sister who was suffering from cancer. Thankfully, she was able to watch his victory on television and he was able to fly home to share the recollections of his moment of triumph with her the day before she sadly passed away.

Given the circumstances, it was a remarkable achievement for Strange to keep focused on the task in hand over the four days but he did just that. His opening 63 would have been recognised as a course record but for the preferred lies in operation. Nevertheless, it saw him climb to the top of the pile, a position he did not relinquish.

Having spent the week looking down on the rest of the field, it was little wonder the Australian suffered a touch of vertigo. He complained of

Benn Barham

Ross Fisher

Robert Dinwiddie

Thomas Levet

Scott Strange (left), receives the trophy from Sir Terry Matthews, Chairman of The Celtic Manor Resort

feeling dizzy during his third round, but was clearly back on an even keel on the final day as four birdies in the opening six holes confirmed he was in no mood to relinquish his grip on the event.

With players allowed to lift, clean and place throughout the week and several of the tees pushed forward due to the course being so wet, it was difficult to gauge precisely what sort of test The Twenty Ten Course would offer at The Ryder Cup in 2010.

However, the general consensus was that it should provide the ideal setting for some pulsating drama. The original Wentwood Hills course has undergone a dramatic makeover, supervised by Ross McMurray from European Golf Design. He has created nine new holes and reshaped plenty more, making full use of the River Usk winding through the property.

It got the thumbs-up from experienced Ryder Cup campaigners such as Darren Clarke, Colin Montgomerie and Harrington, as well as from Karlsson, who has enjoyed a rewarding love affair with the Welsh venue in the past.

The Swede set European Tour records for the lowest 36 and 54 holes totals - 124 and 189 respectively - before coasting to victory over the neighbouring Roman Road course in 2006.

Going into the final round four shots adrift of Strange, he threw down the gauntlet with six successive birdies around the turn, but could scarcely believe his eyes when the final tally told him his closing 64 had left him exactly where he had begun.

Bemused, Karlsson admitted: "I thought I was off to a good start, but I caught a leaderboard out of the corner of my eye on the eighth hole and I was five behind! I was thinking, 'What's happening here?' I thought maybe I could sneak up on him. Some chance."

Clarke, who finished in a share of fourth place with Benn Barham, Nick Dougherty, Rafa Echenique and Francesco Molinari, offered his own assessment of Strange's stunning performance. "I'm just glad Australians don't play in The Ryder Cup, so we won't have to face him in 2010," said the Ulsterman.

Smiling through the slightest glistening of tears after the presentation ceremony, Strange confided that winning golf tournaments cannot take away the pain at such times - but it does help. There cannot have been a more poignant victory in the whole of 2008.

David Facey
The Sun

167

6, 7, 5, 6, 7, 7, 9, 7, 5, 6, 6, 7, 8, 6, 7, 6, 8, 5, but happy.

We all get those days.
Where you seriously consider
packing it all in and taking up
darts or something.
But even a bad round here
has its positives.
Stunning championship courses.
Very reasonable green fees.
No pretentious nonsense.
A good walk through our
beautiful countryside.
And best of all, in Wales
tomorrow's always another day.

**Wales: Host Nation for
The 2010 Ryder Cup**

golfasitshouldbe.com

Wales
Cymru

Francesco Molinari

Rafa Echenique

Howard Clark and Ken Brown

The Celtic Manor Resort
(The Twenty Ten Course)

Final Results

Pos	Name		Rd1	Rd2	Rd3	Rd4	Total		€	£
1	Scott STRANGE	AUS	63	66	69	64	262	-22	376,671.02	300,000.00
2	Robert KARLSSON	SWE	67	67	68	64	266	-18	251,114.01	200,000.00
3	Raphaël JACQUELIN	FRA	66	68	68	68	270	-14	141,477.63	112,680.00
4	Rafa ECHENIQUE	ARG	67	67	69	68	271	-13	82,445.75	65,664.00
	Nick DOUGHERTY	ENG	67	69	67	68	271	-13	82,445.75	65,664.00
	Benn BARHAM	ENG	69	64	70	68	271	-13	82,445.75	65,664.00
	Darren CLARKE	NIR	70	68	67	66	271	-13	82,445.75	65,664.00
	Francesco MOLINARI	ITA	72	66	69	64	271	-13	82,445.75	65,664.00
9	Gonzalo FDEZ-CASTAÑO	ESP	67	68	70	67	272	-12	50,624.58	40,320.00
10	Jeev Milkha SINGH	IND	65	68	69	71	273	-11	39,324.45	31,320.00
	Alvaro VELASCO	ESP	65	68	68	72	273	-11	39,324.45	31,320.00
	Ross McGOWAN	ENG	66	68	69	70	273	-11	39,324.45	31,320.00
	Ross FISHER	ENG	67	70	67	69	273	-11	39,324.45	31,320.00
	Robert DINWIDDIE	ENG	68	65	70	70	273	-11	39,324.45	31,320.00
15	Hennie OTTO	RSA	67	68	71	68	274	-10	29,983.01	23,880.00
	Pablo LARRAZABAL	ESP	69	67	67	71	274	-10	29,983.01	23,880.00
	Thomas LEVET	FRA	69	69	65	71	274	-10	29,983.01	23,880.00
	Mikko ILONEN	FIN	69	70	66	69	274	-10	29,983.01	23,880.00
	Marcel SIEM	GER	71	69	68	66	274	-10	29,983.01	23,880.00
	Jamie DONALDSON	WAL	72	66	67	69	274	-10	29,983.01	23,880.00
21	Magnus A CARLSSON	SWE	66	73	71	65	275	-9	24,182.28	19,260.00
	Sam LITTLE	ENG	68	70	67	70	275	-9	24,182.28	19,260.00
	Gary ORR	SCO	70	67	72	66	275	-9	24,182.28	19,260.00
	Grégory BOURDY	FRA	70	67	69	69	275	-9	24,182.28	19,260.00
	Michael LORENZO-VERA	FRA	70	70	68	67	275	-9	24,182.28	19,260.00
	Martin KAYMER	GER	71	66	68	70	275	-9	24,182.28	19,260.00
	Thomas BJÖRN	DEN	71	68	70	66	275	-9	24,182.28	19,260.00
28	Charl SCHWARTZEL	RSA	69	68	72	67	276	-8	20,792.24	16,560.00
	Mark FOSTER	ENG	69	71	68	68	276	-8	20,792.24	16,560.00
	Fredrik ANDERSSON HED	SWE	71	67	71	67	276	-8	20,792.24	16,560.00
31	Edoardo MOLINARI	ITA	64	70	72	71	277	-7	18,419.21	14,670.00
	Per-Ulrik JOHANSSON	SWE	69	70	67	71	277	-7	18,419.21	14,670.00
	Maarten LAFEBER	NED	71	68	71	67	277	-7	18,419.21	14,670.00
	Garry HOUSTON	WAL	71	68	68	70	277	-7	18,419.21	14,670.00
35	Søren HANSEN	DEN	68	68	69	73	278	-6	16,272.19	12,960.00
	Julio ZAPATA	ARG	69	69	72	68	278	-6	16,272.19	12,960.00
	Simon WAKEFIELD	ENG	71	66	72	69	278	-6	16,272.19	12,960.00
	David HOWELL	ENG	75	66	68	69	278	-6	16,272.19	12,960.00
39	Paul WARING	ENG	66	72	69	72	279	-5	13,560.16	10,800.00
	Rory MCILROY	NIR	68	71	68	72	279	-5	13,560.16	10,800.00
	Mikael LUNDBERG	SWE	69	69	71	70	279	-5	13,560.16	10,800.00
	Johan EDFORS	SWE	69	70	69	71	279	-5	13,560.16	10,800.00
	Christian CÉVAËR	FRA	69	70	69	71	279	-5	13,560.16	10,800.00
	Graeme MCDOWELL	NIR	69	72	68	70	279	-5	13,560.16	10,800.00
	Thongchai JAIDEE	THA	69	70	69	71	279	-5	13,560.16	10,800.00
	Barry LANE	ENG	71	69	66	70	279	-5	13,560.16	10,800.00
47	Ricardo GONZALEZ	ARG	66	70	77	67	280	-4	11,074.13	8,820.00
	Peter WHITEFORD	SCO	68	67	72	73	280	-4	11,074.13	8,820.00
	David LYNN	ENG	72	68	71	69	280	-4	11,074.13	8,820.00
50	Phillip PRICE	WAL	68	71	70	72	281	-3	8,588.10	6,840.00
	David FROST	RSA	69	71	70	71	281	-3	8,588.10	6,840.00
	Kyron SULLIVAN	WAL	70	68	72	71	281	-3	8,588.10	6,840.00
	Luis CLAVERIE	ESP	70	71	69	71	281	-3	8,588.10	6,840.00
	Ariel CANETE	ARG	72	69	70	70	281	-3	8,588.10	6,840.00
	Tom WHITEHOUSE	ENG	73	68	69	71	281	-3	8,588.10	6,840.00
	Gareth PADDISON	NZL	73	68	71	69	281	-3	8,588.10	6,840.00
	Emanuele CANONICA	ITA	73	68	73	67	281	-3	8,588.10	6,840.00
58	Colin MONTGOMERIE	SCO	69	68	73	72	282	-2	6,554.08	5,220.00
	Stephen GALLACHER	SCO	69	69	71	73	282	-2	6,554.08	5,220.00
	Chapchai NIRAT	THA	71	68	73	70	282	-2	6,554.08	5,220.00
61	José Manuel LARA	ESP	69	70	74	70	283	-1	5,537.06	4,410.00
	Peter O'MALLEY	AUS	69	72	71	71	283	-1	5,537.06	4,410.00
	Lee SLATTERY	ENG	70	71	70	72	283	-1	5,537.06	4,410.00
	Danny WILLETT	ENG	70	71	69	73	283	-1	5,537.06	4,410.00
	Søren KJELDSEN	DEN	72	68	72	71	283	-1	5,537.06	4,410.00
	Jean-François LUCQUIN	FRA	74	66	73	70	283	-1	5,537.06	4,410.00
67	Niclas FASTH	SWE	70	71	73	72	286	2	4,633.05	3,690.00
	Carlos RODILES	ESP	71	68	75	72	286	2	4,633.05	3,690.00
69	Peter BAKER	ENG	70	70	75	72	287	3	4,294.05	3,420.00
70	Alastair FORSYTH	SCO	67	73	72	76	288	4	3,754.13	2,989.98
	Rafael CABRERA BELLO	ESP	71	69	73	75	288	4	3,754.13	2,989.98
72	Jarmo SANDELIN	SWE	70	71	75	75	291	7	3,387.00	2,697.58
73	François DELAMONTAGNE	FRA	70	70	77	76	293	9	3,384.00	2,695.19

Hole	Par	Yards	Metres
1	4	465	425
2	5	610	558
3	3	189	173
4	4	461	422
5	4	433	396
6	4	452	413
7	3	213	195
8	4	439	401
9	5	580	530
OUT	**36**	**3842**	**3513**
10	3	210	192
11	5	562	514
12	4	458	419
13	3	189	173
14	4	413	378
15	4	377	345
16	4	477	436
17	3	211	193
18	5	613	561
IN	**35**	**3510**	**3211**
TOTAL	**71**	**7352**	**6724**

Scott Strange's emphatic wire-to-wire victory in The Celtic Manor Wales Open took its place in the tournament's record books for the lowest winning total in relation to par. His 72 hole total of 22 under par beat the previous mark of 21 under par by both Simon Khan and Paul Casey in 2004; Khan going on to win the title in a play-off.

Total Prize Fund
€2,270,187 £1,808,092

Race to the Title

1	**Jeev Milkha SINGH**		198	-15
2	Simon WAKEFIELD		199	-14
3	Pelle EDBERG		201	-12
	Martin ERLANDSSON		201	-12
	Peter FOWLER		201	-12
	Michael JONZON		201	-12
	Iain PYMAN		201	-12
8	François DELAMONTAGNE		202	-11
	Søren HANSEN		202	-11
	Sam LITTLE		202	-11
	Graeme McDOWELL		202	-11
	Robert ROCK		202	-11

I n his excellent book 'In Search of the North', the writer and broadcaster Stuart Maconie bemoans the homogenisation of British society and in particular its high streets, with every town or city centre seeming to possess a Starbucks on one corner and a McDonalds on the other.

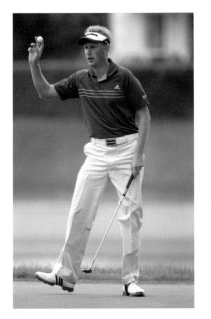

Simon Wakefield

Markus Brier

His views on golf are lacking from an otherwise at times expansive diatribe, but it is safe to assume he would have been heartened by Jeev Milkha Singh's triumph in the Bank Austria GolfOpen presented by Telekom Austria.

For, in a world of conformity, where one good idea simply leads to a rash of cheap copies, Singh stands out from the crowd as a truly unique individual. How so? Let us count the ways.

For a start, no other player in the 156 strong field at the magnificent Fontana Golf Club in Vienna has a former Olympic sprinter for a father, especially one who revelled in the nickname of 'The Flying Sikh.'

No other player staying in a town playing host to the Italian football team, and in a country acting as joint host to Euro 2008, could have displayed such cheery indifference to the prospect of 22 overpaid prima donnas kicking a ball around.

No other player watched a Bollywood film when the first day's play was washed out mid-morning. For the record, and for anyone interested in nipping down to their local branch of Blockbuster, 'Race' is an action-packed thriller with a tagline of 'The only thing more deadly than passion is betrayal.'

No other player has been awarded the Padma Shri for their contribution to golf, one of the highest honours a civilian can receive in India and the equivalent of a knighthood.

No other player contests around 40 tournaments a year and is planning to cut down to "just" 35 or 36, nor does any player swing the club in quite the same way, nor, with all due respect, would they probably want to.

Finally, no other player in the field has won a European Tour event with a final round containing 18 straight pars since The 2008 European Ryder Cup Captain Nick Faldo did just that on his way to capturing The Open Championship at Muirfield in 1987.

Different he may be, but even the 36 year old 2006 Volvo Masters champion could not separate himself entirely from the field in the opening round, delayed 24 hours by the torrential rain which had swept over Austria over the previous two and a half days, and which required the assistance of the local fire brigade to clear flooded bunkers and fairways.

Remarkably the course shrugged off the deluge and when play did get underway, the universally

Emanuele Canonica

praised greens yielded a barrage of first round birdies which saw 81 players under par and Singh share the lead with five others including local favourite Martin Wiegele, who was looking to emulate fellow countryman Markus Brier's victory in the tournament in 2006.

Despite Singh's best efforts, escaping the clutches of Euro 2008 proved impossible with Wiegele admitting he would be happy to miss his side's opening fixture against Croatia on Sunday evening, as it would mean he would likely be involved in the prize giving ceremony, while Emanuele Canonica - one off the lead after an opening 65 - was cheered on by Italian manager Roberto Donadoni and former Chelsea star Gianfranco Zola.

But it was Singh who put the boot in the rest of the field with a second round 63, culminating in an eagle three on the ninth - his 18th - to open up a four shot lead over England's Simon Wakefield going into the third and final round.

Ireland's Gary Murphy – another of the men who shared the first round lead –described the 54 hole event as "a sprint" so who better than

the son of a legendary runner to claim victory? However, although the finishing line was in sight, the chasing pack had not yet hung the gold medal around Singh's neck.

Peter Fowler and Graeme McDowell – who edged out Singh in a play-off for the Ballantine's Championship in Korea in March – cut the Indian's advantage in half before slipping back, while Wakefield birdied three of the last four holes to get to within a shot of the leader. Suddenly Singh's two foot putt for par on the 18th looked far from a formality.

However, the ball dropped below ground leaving Singh to quip: "I think the golfing gods were looking out for me today. They didn't want a play-off with the possibility of further bad weather forecast. I feel very fortunate to win with 18 pars. It is tough to win shooting even par and Simon put up a great fight."

Phil Casey
Press Association

Darren Clarke

Jeev Milkha Singh (right), is presented with the trophy by Robert Zadrazil, COO of Bank Austria

Pelle Edberg

Hole	Par	Yards	Metres
1	4	412	377
2	4	491	449
3	4	374	342
4	3	195	178
5	4	412	377
6	4	420	384
7	3	206	188
8	4	465	425
9	5	528	483
OUT	35	3503	3203
10	4	452	413
11	3	158	145
12	4	396	362
13	4	423	387
14	4	458	419
15	5	547	500
16	4	401	367
17	3	183	167
18	5	545	498
IN	36	3563	3258
TOTAL	71	7066	6461

In winning the BankAustria GolfOpen presented by Telekom Austria, Jeev Milkha Singh dropped only one shot in the entire 72 holes. He is the first player to achieve such a feat since Tiger Woods at the 2002 World Golf Championships – CA Championship.

Fontana Golf Club

Final Results

Pos	Name		Rd1	Rd2	Rd3	Rd4	Total		€	£
1	Jeev Milkha SINGH	IND	64	63	71		198	-15	216,660.00	170,324.83
2	Simon WAKEFIELD	ENG	66	65	68		199	-14	144,440.00	113,549.89
3	Pelle EDBERG	SWE	64	72	65		201	-12	57,200.00	44,967.14
	Peter FOWLER	AUS	65	67	69		201	-12	57,200.00	44,967.14
	Martin ERLANDSSON	SWE	67	69	65		201	-12	57,200.00	44,967.14
	Iain PYMAN	ENG	69	67	65		201	-12	57,200.00	44,967.14
	Michael JONZON	SWE	70	64	67		201	-12	57,200.00	44,967.14
8	Graeme MCDOWELL	NIR	67	67	68		202	-11	26,780.00	21,052.80
	Søren HANSEN	DEN	68	65	69		202	-11	26,780.00	21,052.80
	Sam LITTLE	ENG	68	67	67		202	-11	26,780.00	21,052.80
	Robert ROCK	ENG	68	69	65		202	-11	26,780.00	21,052.80
	François DELAMONTAGNE	FRA	69	68	65		202	-11	26,780.00	21,052.80
13	Steven JEPPESEN	SWE	67	71	65		203	-10	18,763.33	14,750.58
	Francesco MOLINARI	ITA	68	67	68		203	-10	18,763.33	14,750.58
	Paul WARING	ENG	68	68	67		203	-10	18,763.33	14,750.58
	Mark BROWN	NZL	69	63	71		203	-10	18,763.33	14,750.58
	Kyron SULLIVAN	WAL	71	67	65		203	-10	18,763.33	14,750.58
	Thongchai JAIDEE	THA	71	68	64		203	-10	18,763.33	14,750.58
19	Emanuele CANONICA	ITA	65	69	70		204	-9	14,950.00	11,752.78
	Richard BLAND	ENG	66	67	71		204	-9	14,950.00	11,752.78
	Stephen GALLACHER	SCO	67	70	67		204	-9	14,950.00	11,752.78
	Graeme STORM	ENG	69	69	66		204	-9	14,950.00	11,752.78
	James MORRISON	ENG	70	67	67		204	-9	14,950.00	11,752.78
	Darren CLARKE	NIR	70	69	65		204	-9	14,950.00	11,752.78
25	Christian NILSSON	SWE	64	71	70		205	-8	11,765.00	9,248.92
	Alessandro TADINI	ITA	67	70	68		205	-8	11,765.00	9,248.92
	Steven O'HARA	SCO	67	70	68		205	-8	11,765.00	9,248.92
	Garry HOUSTON	WAL	68	67	70		205	-8	11,765.00	9,248.92
	Markus BRIER	AUT	68	70	67		205	-8	11,765.00	9,248.92
	Lee SLATTERY	ENG	69	70	66		205	-8	11,765.00	9,248.92
	Julio ZAPATA	ARG	70	65	70		205	-8	11,765.00	9,248.92
	Andrew MARSHALL	ENG	70	69	66		205	-8	11,765.00	9,248.92
	David HIGGINS	IRL	71	66	68		205	-8	11,765.00	9,248.92
	Sion E BEBB	WAL	74	63	68		205	-8	11,765.00	9,248.92
35	Fabrizio ZANOTTI	PAR	67	68	71		206	-7	9,490.00	7,460.46
	Anthony WALL	ENG	67	71	68		206	-7	9,490.00	7,460.46
	Juan ABBATE	ARG	70	65	71		206	-7	9,490.00	7,460.46
38	Gary MURPHY	IRL	64	69	74		207	-6	8,190.00	6,438.48
	Chris GANE	ENG	68	68	71		207	-6	8,190.00	6,438.48
	Pablo LARRAZABAL	ESP	68	68	71		207	-6	8,190.00	6,438.48
	Paul LAWRIE	SCO	68	69	70		207	-6	8,190.00	6,438.48
	Adilson DA SILVA	BRA	69	68	70		207	-6	8,190.00	6,438.48
	Edoardo MOLINARI	ITA	69	69	69		207	-6	8,190.00	6,438.48
	Jan-Are LARSEN	NOR	71	66	70		207	-6	8,190.00	6,438.48
45	Adam GEE	ENG	66	71	71		208	-5	6,760.00	5,314.30
	Kariem BARAKA	GER	69	68	71		208	-5	6,760.00	5,314.30
	Andrew TAMPION	AUS	70	69	69		208	-5	6,760.00	5,314.30
	Jean-François LUCQUIN	FRA	70	70	68		208	-5	6,760.00	5,314.30
49	Martin WIEGELE	AUT	64	71	74		209	-4	4,845.45	3,809.20
	Scott BARR	AUS	64	73	72		209	-4	4,845.45	3,809.20
	Thomas AIKEN	RSA	66	71	72		209	-4	4,845.45	3,809.20
	Ian GARBUTT	ENG	66	71	72		209	-4	4,845.45	3,809.20
	Maarten LAFEBER	NED	67	70	72		209	-4	4,845.45	3,809.20
	Terry PILKADARIS	AUS	67	72	70		209	-4	4,845.45	3,809.20
	Joakim BÄCKSTRÖM	SWE	68	71	70		209	-4	4,845.45	3,809.20
	Scott STRANGE	AUS	69	67	73		209	-4	4,845.45	3,809.20
	Peter BAKER	ENG	70	68	71		209	-4	4,845.45	3,809.20
	Andrew COLTART	SCO	71	65	73		209	-4	4,845.45	3,809.20
	Santiago LUNA	ESP	72	68	69		209	-4	4,845.45	3,809.20
60	Louis OOSTHUIZEN	RSA	73	64	73		210	-3	3,640.00	2,861.55
61	Liam BOND	WAL	66	70	75		211	-2	3,315.00	2,606.05
	Stuart MANLEY	WAL	69	71	71		211	-2	3,315.00	2,606.05
	Sven STRÜVER	GER	70	65	76		211	-2	3,315.00	2,606.05
	Zane SCOTLAND	ENG	70	70	71		211	-2	3,315.00	2,606.05
65	Tim DYKES	WAL	67	73	72		212	-1	2,925.00	2,299.46
	Alejandro CAÑIZARES	ESP	70	68	74		212	-1	2,925.00	2,299.46
67	Craig LEE	SCO	71	69	73		213	0	2,665.00	2,095.06
	Steve ALKER	NZL	76	64	73		213	0	2,665.00	2,095.06
69	Robert MCGUIRK	ENG	74	66	75		215	2	2,470.00	1,941.76
70	Toni KARJALAINEN	FIN	70	70	78		218	5	2,380.00	1,871.01

Total Prize Fund
€1,300,000 £1,021,980

Two Hundred
Not Out

HOLE	PLAYER	PAR
18	DIXON*	-5
17	NILSSON	-4

1	David DIXON		279	-5
2	Christian NILSSON		280	-4
3	Steven O'HARA		281	-3
4	Seve BENSON		282	-2
	Richard BLAND		282	-2
	François DELAMONTAGNE		282	-2
7	Robert COLES		283	-1
	David DRYSDALE		283	-1
	Roope KAKKO		283	-1
10	Mikko KORHONEN		284	0
	John E MORGAN		284	0

A s the irrepressible Tiger Woods was preparing to take his haul of Major Championships to 14 at Torrey Pines, England's David Dixon was marking his own entry in golf's record books with his maiden European Tour triumph in the 12th edition of the SAINT-OMER OPEN presented by Neuflize OBC.

François Delamontagne

Steven O'Hara

Some 17 years after Sweden's Per-Ulrik Johansson set the ball rolling with his win in the 1991 Renault Belgian Open; Dixon's two putt for par on the final hole at the Aa Saint Omer Golf Club took the number of European Tour victories by former Challenge Tour players to 200.

Having shot to the top of the leaderboard with a final day 66, Dixon retired to the relative comfort of the Players' Lounge balcony, from where he was able to watch overnight leader Christian Nilsson's valiant birdie attempt from short of the 18th green – which would have taken the tournament to a play-off – drift past the hole.

Overcome with emotion, the unassuming Dixon was momentarily lost for words, before gathering his composure. "I'm still trying to make sense of it all," he admitted. "It's everyone's dream to win a European Tour event – what an awesome feeling."

Thus, the relatively unheralded 31 year old added his name to those of the 96 other students who had honed their techniques on the European Challenge Tour before graduating with first class honours – an esteemed list which includes the reigning European Tour Number One, Justin Rose; Major Championship winners Michael Campbell and Trevor Immelman; and prolific European Tour champions Thomas Björn, Niclas Fasth, Ian Poulter and Henrik Stenson.

Much like his compatriot Rose before him, Dixon first shot to prominence when winning the Silver Medal as the leading amateur in The Open Championship at Royal Lytham & St Annes in 2001, only to subsequently struggle in his formative years as a professional.

With hindsight, the man from Somerset reflected that his immediate conversion to the paid ranks may have been a touch premature. "I probably wasn't ready to turn professional in 2001," he said. "I had just played The Open as an amateur, and got a bit carried away with everything. Maybe I was taken by surprise, as it's been a slow process since then.

"It's such a big step up from amateur golf, playing against the stars on The European Tour. They're a different breed – all mentally strong, as well as great golfers. But I'm not worried about what's happened in the past – all I can control is the future. It's been tough to get my first win on the board, but now I have, I hope for many more."

That Dixon's maiden victory came at the fiendishly difficult Aa Saint Omer Golf Club made his feat all the more impressive. The rolling Aa Valley countryside might appear welcoming enough, but the course itself – despite only

measuring 6,845 yards in length – can be a brute, to put it mildly. It is the proverbial wolf in sheep's clothing.

Perhaps England's Marcus Higley – who experienced both sides with an opening 69 and a closing 77 – summed it up best, when he said: "It's not a long course, so everyone thinks they can rip it apart – but they never do."

As if the task facing the players was not sufficiently testing, heavy downpours on the opening morning made for treacherous conditions for most of the day. That perhaps explained why just two players – England's John E Morgan and Nilsson – were under par at the halfway stage.

Nilsson cited Sweden's victory over defending champions Greece in the group stages of Euro 2008 as the motivation for his stunning second day 64, whilst Morgan was merely grateful to be relieved of nappy-changing duties for a few days, having recently become a father.

He said: "I've been scouring the internet for deals on cots, so that takes my focus

away from golf – which is a good thing at times. When I wake up in the morning and my daughter smiles at me, nothing else matters. It's the best feeling in the world."

A sizeable cheque for finishing in a share of tenth place helped him stock up on supplies of baby food and nappies, whilst fellow Challenge Tour Member Roope Kakko had his own incentive for chasing a hefty slice of the €604,470 on offer.

The Finn, who eventually finished in a tie for seventh place, was keen to reclaim bragging rights from his girlfriend and caddie Minea Blomqvist, a four time winner on the Ladies European Tour. "I think she's won more money than me recently," he said. "But after a good week here, it's my turn to buy the drinks!"

However, it was Dixon who walked away with the champagne and the biggest cheque of his career for €100,000 (£79,872) – but most importantly of all, with his place in the record books assured.

Paul Symes

Left to right: Championship Director Jean-Jaques Durand, David Dixon, and Gerard Botteri, CEO of Neuflize OBC

Jan-Are Larsen

Christian Nilsson

Neuflize OBC
ABN AMRO

Aa Saint Omer Golf Club

Final Results

Pos	Name		Rd1	Rd2	Rd3	Rd4	Total		€	£
1	David DIXON	ENG	77	67	69	66	279	-5	100,000.00	79,872.84
2	Christian NILSSON	SWE	75	64	70	71	280	-4	66,660.00	53,243.24
3	Steven O'HARA	SCO	74	69	70	68	281	-3	37,560.00	30,000.24
4	Seve BENSON	ENG	71	72	72	67	282	-2	25,480.00	20,351.60
	François DELAMONTAGNE	FRA	72	72	67	71	282	-2	25,480.00	20,351.60
	Richard BLAND	ENG	78	69	67	68	282	-2	25,480.00	20,351.60
7	Roope KAKKO	FIN	68	74	72	69	283	-1	15,480.00	12,364.32
	Robert COLES	ENG	74	71	66	72	283	-1	15,480.00	12,364.32
	David DRYSDALE	SCO	78	66	72	67	283	-1	15,480.00	12,364.32
10	John E MORGAN	ENG	69	72	73	70	284	0	11,520.00	9,201.35
	Mikko KORHONEN	FIN	69	73	73	69	284	0	11,520.00	9,201.35
12	Jan-Are LARSEN	NOR	70	73	72	70	285	1	9,990.00	7,979.30
	Marco RUIZ	PAR	74	68	75	68	285	1	9,990.00	7,979.30
14	Alessandro TADINI	ITA	73	72	72	69	286	2	9,000.00	7,188.56
	Nicolas VANHOOTEGEM	BEL	74	69	69	74	286	2	9,000.00	7,188.56
16	Cesar MONASTERIO	ARG	71	73	70	73	287	3	7,935.00	6,337.91
	Gareth PADDISON	NZL	71	75	69	72	287	3	7,935.00	6,337.91
	Michael HOEY	NIR	73	72	72	70	287	3	7,935.00	6,337.91
	Robert ROCK	ENG	75	70	71	71	287	3	7,935.00	6,337.91
20	Eric RAMSAY	SCO	70	73	74	71	288	4	7,080.00	5,655.00
	Matthew CORT	ENG	75	70	76	67	288	4	7,080.00	5,655.00
22	David GRIFFITHS	ENG	72	73	74	70	289	5	6,330.00	5,055.95
	Benoit TEILLERIA	FRA	73	73	72	71	289	5	6,330.00	5,055.95
	Chris GANE	ENG	74	71	73	71	289	5	6,330.00	5,055.95
	Iain PYMAN	ENG	74	72	71	72	289	5	6,330.00	5,055.95
	Benjamin MIARKA	GER	75	72	70	72	289	5	6,330.00	5,055.95
	Gustavo ROJAS	ARG	76	71	72	70	289	5	6,330.00	5,055.95
28	Marco SOFFIETTI	ITA	72	70	75	73	290	6	5,160.00	4,121.44
	Terry PILKADARIS	AUS	73	70	75	72	290	6	5,160.00	4,121.44
	Richard TREIS	GER	73	71	70	76	290	6	5,160.00	4,121.44
	Sébastien DELAGRANGE	FRA	75	72	68	75	290	6	5,160.00	4,121.44
	Richard MCEVOY	ENG	76	70	73	71	290	6	5,160.00	4,121.44
	Juan ABBATE	ARG	76	71	70	73	290	6	5,160.00	4,121.44
	Wil BESSELING	NED	78	68	70	74	290	6	5,160.00	4,121.44
35	Ben MASON	ENG	71	74	72	74	291	7	4,200.00	3,354.66
	Liam BOND	WAL	73	69	70	79	291	7	4,200.00	3,354.66
	Scott BARR	AUS	73	71	72	75	291	7	4,200.00	3,354.66
	Andrew COLTART	SCO	73	73	75	70	291	7	4,200.00	3,354.66
	Mark F HAASTRUP	DEN	74	69	75	73	291	7	4,200.00	3,354.66
	Edward RUSH	ENG	74	72	73	72	291	7	4,200.00	3,354.66
41	Marcus HIGLEY	ENG	69	75	71	77	292	8	3,540.00	2,827.50
	Steven JEPPESEN	SWE	70	76	71	75	292	8	3,540.00	2,827.50
	Lawrence DODD	ENG	71	74	74	73	292	8	3,540.00	2,827.50
	Christophe BRAZILLIER	FRA	72	71	80	69	292	8	3,540.00	2,827.50
	Steve ALKER	NZL	74	72	72	74	292	8	3,540.00	2,827.50
46	Gareth MAYBIN	NIR	70	72	77	74	293	9	2,880.00	2,300.34
	Alvaro SALTO	ESP	71	74	74	74	293	9	2,880.00	2,300.34
	David BRANSDON	AUS	72	73	75	73	293	9	2,880.00	2,300.34
	Klas ERIKSSON	SWE	73	72	76	72	293	9	2,880.00	2,300.34
	Anthony SNOBECK	FRA	75	69	75	74	293	9	2,880.00	2,300.34
	Andreas HÖGBERG	SWE	75	72	74	72	293	9	2,880.00	2,300.34
52	Anders Schmidt HANSEN	DEN	73	74	73	74	294	10	2,280.00	1,821.10
	Ian GARBUTT	ENG	74	71	72	77	294	10	2,280.00	1,821.10
	Colm MORIARTY	IRL	75	72	74	73	294	10	2,280.00	1,821.10
	Tim DYKES	WAL	77	69	78	70	294	10	2,280.00	1,821.10
56	Julien QUESNE	FRA	71	75	71	78	295	11	1,686.67	1,347.19
	Rikard KARLBERG	SWE	72	75	76	72	295	11	1,686.67	1,347.19
	Sion E BEBB	WAL	73	70	73	79	295	11	1,686.67	1,347.19
	Fredrik WIDMARK	SWE	74	71	76	74	295	11	1,686.67	1,347.19
	Julien XANTHOPOULOS	FRA	75	70	75	75	295	11	1,686.67	1,347.19
	Jeppe HULDAHL	DEN	76	68	73	78	295	11	1,686.67	1,347.19
	Olivier DAVID	FRA	76	69	75	75	295	11	1,686.67	1,347.19
	Jordi GARCIA	ESP	76	70	78	71	295	11	1,686.67	1,347.19
	Thomas AIKEN	RSA	77	70	73	75	295	11	1,686.67	1,347.19
65	Thomas FEYRSINGER	AUT	71	74	75	77	297	13	1,260.00	1,006.40
	Kyron SULLIVAN	WAL	72	73	73	79	297	13	1,260.00	1,006.40
	Matthew KING	ENG	73	74	75	75	297	13	1,260.00	1,006.40
	Toni KARJALAINEN	FIN	73	74	73	77	297	13	1,260.00	1,006.40
	Rodolfo GONZALEZ	ARG	75	71	74	77	297	13	1,260.00	1,006.40
70	David HIGGINS	IRL	74	73	76	75	298	14	947.75	756.99
	Alexandre ROCHA	BRA	75	67	78	78	298	14	947.75	756.99
	James MORRISON	ENG	75	72	74	77	298	14	947.75	756.99
	Alessio BRUSCHI	ITA	76	71	75	76	298	14	947.75	756.99
74	Joakim BÄCKSTRÖM	SWE	75	71	74	79	299	15	891.00	711.67
75	François CALMELS	FRA	81	66	76	78	301	17	888.00	709.27

Total Prize Fund

€604,470 £482,807

Hole	Par	Yards	Metres
1	4	396	362
2	3	216	198
3	4	435	398
4	3	170	155
5	4	325	297
6	4	379	347
7	5	575	526
8	4	389	356
9	5	500	457
OUT	**36**	**3385**	**3096**
10	4	422	386
11	3	198	181
12	4	347	317
13	4	439	401
14	5	531	486
15	4	476	435
16	4	417	381
17	3	191	175
18	4	439	401
IN	**35**	**3460**	**3163**
TOTAL	**71**	**6845**	**6259**

David Dixon had the honour of making the SAINT-OMER OPEN presented by Neuflize OBC the 200th European Tour victory by a former European Challenge Tour player. In addition, Dixon's first round of 77 was the second highest first round score by a winner in European Tour history. Only George Burns (1975 Kerrygold International) and Thomas Björn (2006 Irish Open), both with 78, have shot higher on day one and still won.

Defying the Barrier

178

1	**Tiger WOODS**		**283**	**-1**
2	Rocco MEDIATE		283	-1
3	Lee WESTWOOD		284	0
4	Robert KARLSSON		286	2
	D J TRAHAN		286	2
6	Miguel Angel JIMÉNEZ		287	3
	John MERRICK		287	3
	Carl PETTERSSON		287	3
9	Eric AXLEY		288	4
	Geoff OGILVY		288	4
	Heath SLOCUM		288	4
	Brandt SNEDEKER		288	4
	Camilo VILLEGAS		288	4

When the trophy had been presented, the cheering had died and the crowd had dispersed, it was still 48 hours after the Monday play-off before the full story of the 108th US Open Championship emerged. Tiger Woods, the champion for a third time, faced surgery on the anterior cruciate ligament of his left knee and would be out of action for the remainder of the year if not longer.

Only then could we fully appreciate the astonishing achievement of the previous weekend. Looking back on his limping, his stifled shouts of pain and general discomfort almost from the outset, it seemed inconceivable that he could have lasted 91 holes, culminating in a play-off triumph over Rocco Mediate. But he did.

It brought to mind the much-loved golfing tale of 1936 when the great Bobby Jones made a sentimental trip back to the Old Course at St Andrews. It is said that, while observing a performance of breathtaking quality, his youthful caddie was moved to whisper reverentially: "Aye, you're a wonder sir. A bloomin' wonder." What Woods produced at Torrey Pines Golf Club was truly wonderful to behold, too.

While most observers believed he was recovering from the keyhole surgery to remove fragments of cartilage from the knee he had undergone two days after the Masters Tournament, it transpired that the underlying problem was ligament damage sustained the previous July, while running at his home in Orlando after returning from The Open at Carnoustie. Added to that, there was the small matter of a double fracture of the left tibia, sustained during overzealous rehabilitation.

However, despite all this, there proved to be plenty of life in the wounded Tiger, as he displayed in a stunning, inward nine of 30 on the Friday afternoon.

By that stage, European hopes were buoyant. Miguel Angel Jiménez set the ball rolling in that second round with a best of championship 66; Lee Westwood joined him on one under par 141 to be only two strokes behind the leader, Stuart Appleby; while Robert Karlsson was a shot closer after superb opening rounds of 70-70.

As usual, there were optimistic souls predicting a winning score of five or six under par, but old heads knew differently. Even on a relatively generous course set-up, the screw was tightened over the weekend. As David Fay, Executive Director of the United States Golf Association, acknowledged: "It's in our DNA to be the toughest golf championship."

Yet it seemed neither a damaged knee nor the machinations of the USGA could curb Woods on a course dear to his heart. He proceeded to generate huge excitement among a record attendance of 53,000 by completing a faltering third round with an eagle three on the 13th, a chip in birdie on the 17th, and a further eagle three on the long 18th, where a 40 foot downhill putt miraculously found the target.

Carl Pettersson

Tiger Woods (right), and Jim Vernon, President of the USGA

Left *Lee Westwood*

Miguel Angel Jiménez

Robert Karlsson

Rocco Mediate

So it was that he entered Sunday as a most improbable leader, given his physical condition, with Westwood, his final-round partner, only a stroke behind and carrying the hopes of Europe on his shoulders. Optimistically, Westwood supporters recalled the Deutsche Bank – SAP Open TPC of Europe in 2000, where the Englishman gave Woods a two stroke lead in similar circumstances and proceeded to take the trophy, beating the World Number One into third place.

That remained the most precious of the 18th hole flags Westwood had accumulated from his tournament victories. Would the 18th at Torrey Pines be added to his collection, so bridging a gap back to Tony Jacklin as Europe's last winner, at Hazeltine in 1970?

In the penultimate Sunday pairing, 45 year old Rocco Mediate became an admirably stubborn challenger. Solid driving and sound putting met the demands of this particular test and his closing level par 71 set the clubhouse target on one under par 283. While he waited in the Recorder's Hut, Westwood and Woods needed birdies on the last to join him in a play-off.

Both were in trouble off the tee on the 573 yard 18th, but whereas Woods pitched his third shot out of the rough to 12 feet, Westwood's wedge from the fairway finished a treacherous 18 feet above the target. After the Englishman missed to end his challenge, Woods holed, as you sensed he would.

In Monday's 18 hole play-off, Woods again birdied the closing hole to draw level. Defying the pain barrier, he went on to claim the title and his 14th Major Championship, with a par four at the first sudden-death hole – the 461 yard seventh – where Mediate was bunkered.

Two days later, George O'Grady, Chief Executive of The European Tour, said: "Everyone in sport will be shocked and saddened by the news (of Woods' absence from golf for the rest of the year). We at The European Tour wish him a swift and full recovery and look forward to making him welcome when he is fit to return to the fairways of the world."

It was a wish shared by everybody who had thrilled to what was arguably, the most exciting US Open Championship in living memory.

Dermot Gilleece
Sunday Independent

Torrey Pines Golf Club
(South Course)

Final Results

Pos	Name		Rd1	Rd2	Rd3	Rd4	Total		€	£
1	Tiger WOODS	USA	72	68	70	73	283	-1	858,180.50	685,453.16
2	Rocco MEDIATE	USA	69	71	72	71	283	-1	514,908.30	411,271.90
3	Lee WESTWOOD	ENG	70	71	70	73	284	0	312,755.94	249,807.06
4	Robert KARLSSON	SWE	70	70	75	71	286	2	195,349.22	156,030.97
	D J TRAHAN	USA	72	69	73	72	286	2	195,349.22	156,030.97
6	Carl PETTERSSON	SWE	71	71	77	68	287	3	140,287.72	112,051.79
	John MERRICK	USA	73	72	71	71	287	3	140,287.72	112,051.79
	Miguel Angel JIMÉNEZ	ESP	75	66	74	72	287	3	140,287.72	112,051.79
9	Geoff OGILVY	AUS	69	73	72	74	288	4	102,199.13	81,629.35
	Eric AXLEY	USA	69	79	71	69	288	4	102,199.13	81,629.35
	Camilo VILLEGAS	COL	73	71	71	73	288	4	102,199.13	81,629.35
	Heath SLOCUM	USA	75	74	74	65	288	4	102,199.13	81,629.35
	Brandt SNEDEKER	USA	76	73	68	71	288	4	102,199.13	81,629.35
14	Ernie ELS	RSA	70	72	74	73	289	5	77,655.16	62,025.39
	Stewart CINK	USA	72	73	77	67	289	5	77,655.16	62,025.39
	Rodney PAMPLING	AUS	74	70	75	70	289	5	77,655.16	62,025.39
	Retief GOOSEN	RSA	76	69	77	67	289	5	77,655.16	62,025.39
18	Robert ALLENBY	AUS	70	72	73	75	290	6	55,451.17	44,290.43
	Phil MICKELSON	USA	71	75	76	68	290	6	55,451.17	44,290.43
	Hunter MAHAN	USA	72	74	69	75	290	6	55,451.17	44,290.43
	Mike WEIR	CAN	73	74	69	74	290	6	55,451.17	44,290.43
	Brandt JOBE	USA	73	75	69	73	290	6	55,451.17	44,290.43
	Ryuji IMADA	JPN	74	75	70	71	290	6	55,451.17	44,290.43
	Sergio GARCIA	ESP	76	70	70	74	290	6	55,451.17	44,290.43
	Chad CAMPBELL	USA	77	72	71	70	290	6	55,451.17	44,290.43
26	Adam SCOTT	AUS	73	73	75	70	291	7	38,937.24	31,100.28
	Boo WEEKLEY	USA	73	76	70	72	291	7	38,937.24	31,100.28
	Anthony KIM	USA	74	75	70	72	291	7	38,937.24	31,100.28
29	Patrick SHEEHAN	USA	71	74	74	73	292	8	30,819.49	24,616.40
	Scott VERPLANK	USA	72	72	74	74	292	8	30,819.49	24,616.40
	Steve STRICKER	USA	73	76	71	72	292	8	30,819.49	24,616.40
	Aaron BADDELEY	AUS	74	73	71	74	292	8	30,819.49	24,616.40
	Michael THOMPSON (AM)	USA	74	73	73	72	292	8		
	Bart BRYANT	USA	75	70	78	69	292	8	30,819.49	24,616.40
	Jeff QUINNEY	USA	79	70	70	73	292	8	30,819.49	24,616.40
36	Stuart APPLEBY	AUS	69	76	79	75	293	9	22,699.83	18,131.00
	Andres ROMERO	ARG	71	73	77	72	293	9	22,699.83	18,131.00
	Joe OGILVIE	USA	71	76	73	73	293	9	22,699.83	18,131.00
	Oliver WILSON	ENG	72	71	74	76	293	9	22,699.83	18,131.00
	Jon MILLS	USA	72	75	75	71	293	9	22,699.83	18,131.00
	Robert DINWIDDIE	ENG	73	71	75	74	293	9	22,699.83	18,131.00
	Daniel CHOPRA	SWE	73	75	75	70	293	9	22,699.83	18,131.00
	Jim FURYK	USA	74	71	73	75	293	9	22,699.83	18,131.00
	Todd HAMILTON	USA	74	74	73	72	293	9	22,699.83	18,131.00
	Justin LEONARD	USA	75	72	75	71	293	9	22,699.83	18,131.00
	Pat PEREZ	USA	75	73	75	70	293	9	22,699.83	18,131.00
	Padraig HARRINGTON	IRL	78	67	77	71	293	9	22,699.83	18,131.00
48	Tim CLARK	RSA	73	72	74	75	294	10	15,247.01	12,178.22
	Matt KUCHAR	USA	73	73	76	72	294	10	15,247.01	12,178.22
	Dustin JOHNSON	USA	74	72	75	73	294	10	15,247.01	12,178.22
	John ROLLINS	USA	75	68	79	72	294	10	15,247.01	12,178.22
	Jarrod LYLE	AUS	75	74	74	71	294	10	15,247.01	12,178.22
53	Kevin STREELMAN	USA	68	77	78	72	295	11	12,873.34	10,282.31
	Davis LOVE III	USA	72	69	76	78	295	11	12,873.34	10,282.31
	Martin KAYMER	GER	75	70	73	77	295	11	12,873.34	10,282.31
	Ben CRANE	USA	75	72	77	71	295	11	12,873.34	10,282.31
	Søren HANSEN	DEN	78	70	76	71	295	11	12,873.34	10,282.31
58	Rory SABBATINI	RSA	73	72	75	76	296	12	11,864.50	9,476.52
	Stephen AMES	CAN	74	74	77	71	296	12	11,864.50	9,476.52
60	Rickie FOWLER (AM)	USA	70	79	76	72	297	13		
	Brett QUIGLEY	USA	73	72	77	75	297	13	11,245.98	8,982.48
	Nick WATNEY	USA	73	75	77	72	297	13	11,245.98	8,982.48
	David TOMS	USA	76	72	72	77	297	13	11,245.98	8,982.48
	Alastair FORSYTH	SCO	76	73	74	74	297	13	11,245.98	8,982.48
65	Vijay SINGH	FIJ	71	78	76	73	298	14	10,497.77	8,384.87
	John MALLINGER	USA	75	75	78	72	298	14	10,497.77	8,384.87
	Trevor IMMELMAN	RSA	75	73	72	78	298	14	10,497.77	8,384.87
	Paul CASEY	ENG	79	70	76	73	298	14	10,497.77	8,384.87
69	Derek FATHAUER (AM)	USA	73	73	78	75	299	15		
	D A POINTS	USA	74	71	77	77	299	15	10,029.91	8,011.17
71	Woody AUSTIN	USA	72	72	77	79	300	16	9,655.48	7,712.11
	Andrew DRESSER	USA	76	73	79	72	300	16	9,655.48	7,712.11
	Andy SVOBODA	USA	77	71	74	78	300	16	9,655.48	7,712.11
74	Justin HICKS	USA	68	80	75	78	301	17	9,094.17	7,263.77
	Ian LEGGATT	CAN	72	76	76	77	301	17	9,094.17	7,263.77
	Jesper PARNEVIK	SWE	77	72	77	75	301	17	9,094.17	7,263.77
77	Ross McGOWAN	ENG	76	72	78	77	303	19	8,720.39	6,965.22
78	Rich BEEM	USA	74	74	80	76	304	20	8,439.41	6,740.80
	Chris KIRK	USA	75	74	78	77	304	20	8,439.41	6,740.80
80	Luke DONALD	ENG	71	71	77	RETD			1,271.38	1,015.49

Hole	Par	Yards	Metres
1	4	448	410
2	4	389	356
3	3	195	178
4	4	488	446
5	4	453	414
6	4	515	471
7	4	461	422
8	3	177	162
9	5	612	560
OUT	**35**	**3738**	**3419**
10	4	414	379
11	3	221	202
12	4	504	461
13	5	614	561
14	4	435	398
15	4	478	437
16	3	225	206
17	4	441	403
18	5	573	524
IN	**36**	**3905**	**3571**
TOTAL	**71**	**7643**	**6990**

Camilo Villegas

In winning his third US Open Championship and the 14th Major Championship of his career, Tiger Woods celebrated his 500th career week as Number One on the Official World Golf Ranking, a position he first attained on June 15, 1997. History was also made by Robert Karlsson (tied fourth) and Carl Pettersson (tied sixth), as this marked the first time two Swedish players had finished in the top ten of the same US Open.

Total Prize Fund
€4,766,396 £3,807,055

BMW Golfsport

bmw-golfsport.com
bmw.co.uk

The Ultimate
Driving Machine

BMW International Open

BMW
International Open
Winner's Cup

1989 David Feherty.
      N. Ireland
1990 Paul Azinger.
      U.S.A.
1991 Sandy Lyle.
      Scotland
1992 Paul Azinger.
      U.S.A.
1993 Peter Fowler.
      Australia
1994 Marc McNulty.
      Zimbabwe
1995 Frank Nobilo.
      New Zealand
1996 Marc Farry.
      France
1997 Robert Karlsson.
      Sweden
1998 Russel Claydon.
      England
1999 Colin Montgomerie.
      Scotland

Symbolic Torch

1	**Martin KAYMER**		273	-15
2	Anders HANSEN		273	-15
3	John BICKERTON		275	-13
	Paul CASEY		275	-13
	Mark FOSTER		275	-13
6	François DELAMONTAGNE		277	-11
	Robert-Jan DERKSEN		277	-11
	Martin ERLANDSSON		277	-11
	Thomas LEVET		277	-11
	Charl SCHWARTZEL		277	-11
	Henrik STENSON		277	-11

BMW International Open

It was, without doubt, an anniversary to remember for all of Germany. In winning the 20th edition of the BMW International Open, Martin Kaymer not only took over the symbolic torch of German golf from Bernhard Langer, he also confirmed his status as one of the European game's brightest young stars, a fact first recognised by his capture of The Sir Henry Cotton Rookie of the Year award in 2007.

Taking a six stroke lead into the final round at Golfclub München Eichenried – in a tournament which had never enjoyed a home victory – the 23 year old eventually followed up his earlier season success in the Abu Dhabi Golf Championship with another triumph, even though he made the huge numbers of spectators wait anxiously for their desired outcome.

Always in control over the first three rounds, he had impressed everyone at the Munich venue – staging the tournament for the 12th successive year – in particular with his breathtaking nine under par second round 63 which gave him a five stroke lead at the halfway stage.

Langer, paired with him for the first two days, was one of many transfixed by the undoubted class of his young compatriot: "It gave me a chance to watch him under tournament conditions and I was very impressed," said the winning 2004 European Ryder Cup Captain. "He

drove the ball fantastically well and hit some solid iron shots. He's long, he's straight and he made a lot of putts."

Unquestionably talented, Kaymer also showed he possessed a thoughtful head on young shoulders when, despite finishing 11 shots better than Langer at the halfway stage, he still made time after the round to seek out the doyen of German golf on the range to ask advice on how he could yet further improve.

The two time Masters Tournament Champion was delighted to pass on the benefit of his experience, none more so than in the realm of how best to handle the fervent expectations of a home crowd and succeed; something Langer achieved ten times in European Tour competition in the 20 years from 1981 to 2001.

Playing with a big lead and the hopes of an entire nation on your shoulders is never easy but

Mark Foster

John Bickerton

Anders Hansen

Retief Goosen

George O'Grady (left), Chief Executive of The European Tour, paid tribute to BMW during the prize-giving ceremony when he presented Ian Robertson, Member of the Board of Management, Sales and Marketing BMW Group, with a silver salver to mark the 20th anniversary

Kaymer's achievement – and perhaps the reason the final round became a battle rather than the procession many people believed it would be – was all the more laudable considering the difficult personal circumstances he faced at home.

He revealed later he had nearly withdrawn from the event because he wanted to be at the bedside of his gravely ill mother, a decision she overturned. "She wanted me to play, so I played," he said. It proved the right decision for his mother was able to watch her son record his greatest triumph to date before her suffering ended three weeks later.

A portent for the final day arrived for Kaymer on the first green where he three putted for a bogey five before a triple bogey eight on the 11th – where two balls found their way into the lake short of the green – gave the pursuing pack hope that their chase would not be in vain.

Main beneficiary was Denmark's Anders Hansen – looking to add the BMW International Open title to the two BMW PGA Championships titles at Wentworth Club already on his golfing CV – whose excellent final round 67 for a 15 under par total of 273 set the clubhouse target, one clear of the English trio of John Bickerton, Paul Casey and Mark Foster.

When he arrived on the 18th tee, Kaymer needed a birdie four at the 568 yard hole to force a play-off with Hansen and he achieved the task with aplomb, almost holing his 40 foot eagle putt for an outright victory.

Returning to the 18th moments later, Hansen – who himself nearly did not compete after having undergone knee surgery only four weeks previously – found two bunkers whereas Kaymer found the green in two thanks to a monstrous drive and a six iron to the heart of the putting surface.

Three putts for a bogey six ended the Dane's hopes of the title as Kaymer two putted for a winning birdie four. Understandably, the emotion of the occasion got to him as he hugged friends and family at greenside before bravely going on television to announce: "That was for you, mum."

Langer, to date the only German to play in The Ryder Cup, had no doubts. "He is a winner and he has proved that," he said. "Judging by this week, I don't think there are any limits for him if he keeps that up."

Petra Himmel
Süddeutsche Zeitung

HOW DO YOU MARK YOUR TITLEIST?

Paul Casey

Hole	Par	Yards	Metres
1	4	432	395
2	3	208	190
3	4	447	409
4	4	349	319
5	4	331	303
6	5	481	440
7	4	441	403
8	3	197	180
9	5	557	509
OUT	36	3443	3148
10	4	472	431
11	5	555	508
12	3	153	140
13	4	372	340
14	4	490	448
15	4	396	362
16	4	319	292
17	3	189	173
18	5	568	519
IN	36	3514	3213
TOTAL	72	6957	6361

Golfclub München Eichenried

Final Results

Pos	Name		Rd1	Rd2	Rd3	Rd4	Total		€	£
1	Martin KAYMER	GER	68	63	67	75	273	-15	333,330.00	262,752.15
2	Anders HANSEN	DEN	69	70	67	67	273	-15	222,220.00	175,168.10
3	Mark FOSTER	ENG	67	72	68	68	275	-13	103,333.33	81,453.98
	Paul CASEY	ENG	70	68	67	70	275	-13	103,333.33	81,453.98
	John BICKERTON	ENG	70	70	68	67	275	-13	103,333.33	81,453.98
6	Henrik STENSON	SWE	69	68	72	68	277	-11	50,266.67	39,623.42
	Thomas LEVET	FRA	69	69	67	72	277	-11	50,266.67	39,623.42
	Charl SCHWARTZEL	RSA	69	69	66	73	277	-11	50,266.67	39,623.42
	François DELAMONTAGNE	FRA	70	66	70	71	277	-11	50,266.67	39,623.42
	Martin ERLANDSSON	SWE	70	70	71	66	277	-11	50,266.67	39,623.42
	Robert-Jan DERKSEN	NED	74	69	69	65	277	-11	50,266.67	39,623.42
12	Ross FISHER	ENG	70	68	67	73	278	-10	34,400.00	27,116.29
13	Søren KJELDSEN	DEN	68	73	68	70	279	-9	30,733.33	24,225.99
	Andrew MCLARDY	RSA	68	75	73	63	279	-9	30,733.33	24,225.99
	Retief GOOSEN	RSA	69	69	69	72	279	-9	30,733.33	24,225.99
16	Mardan MAMAT	SIN	66	71	74	69	280	-8	24,700.00	19,470.13
	David LYNN	ENG	67	73	66	74	280	-8	24,700.00	19,470.13
	Graeme STORM	ENG	68	69	70	73	280	-8	24,700.00	19,470.13
	Alexander NOREN	SWE	68	73	72	67	280	-8	24,700.00	19,470.13
	Tino SCHUSTER	GER	69	68	69	74	280	-8	24,700.00	19,470.13
	Iain PYMAN	ENG	69	74	64	73	280	-8	24,700.00	19,470.13
	Colin MONTGOMERIE	SCO	70	71	68	71	280	-8	24,700.00	19,470.13
	Alex CEJKA	GER	74	67	71	68	280	-8	24,700.00	19,470.13
24	Peter O'MALLEY	AUS	66	75	68	72	281	-7	19,900.00	15,686.46
	Benn BARHAM	ENG	68	68	69	76	281	-7	19,900.00	15,686.46
	Gary MURPHY	IRL	71	70	68	72	281	-7	19,900.00	15,686.46
	Joel SJOHOLM	SWE	71	71	65	74	281	-7	19,900.00	15,686.46
	Alastair FORSYTH	SCO	74	68	71	68	281	-7	19,900.00	15,686.46
	David FROST	RSA	74	69	68	70	281	-7	19,900.00	15,686.46
30	Peter HEDBLOM	SWE	69	72	71	70	282	-6	16,600.00	13,085.19
	Stephan GROSS JR (AM)	GER	71	68	71	72	282	-6		
	Mikael LUNDBERG	SWE	72	68	74	68	282	-6	16,600.00	13,085.19
	Peter HANSON	SWE	72	70	69	71	282	-6	16,600.00	13,085.19
	Ariel CANETE	ARG	73	65	70	74	282	-6	16,600.00	13,085.19
	Simon KHAN	ENG	75	65	71	71	282	-6	16,600.00	13,085.19
36	Oliver FISHER	ENG	71	70	71	71	283	-5	15,000.00	11,823.96
37	Daniel VANCSIK	ARG	67	74	69	74	284	-4	14,200.00	11,193.35
	Barry LANE	ENG	70	70	72	72	284	-4	14,200.00	11,193.35
	Bernhard LANGER	GER	70	72	71	71	284	-4	14,200.00	11,193.35
40	Rafa ECHENIQUE	ARG	66	73	71	75	285	-3	13,000.00	10,247.44
	Grégory BOURDY	FRA	70	72	70	73	285	-3	13,000.00	10,247.44
	Shiv KAPUR	IND	71	72	71	71	285	-3	13,000.00	10,247.44
43	Jean-Baptiste GONNET	FRA	67	72	75	72	286	-2	11,400.00	8,986.21
	David HOWELL	ENG	69	69	71	77	286	-2	11,400.00	8,986.21
	Jyoti RANDHAWA	IND	71	69	75	71	286	-2	11,400.00	8,986.21
	Francesco MOLINARI	ITA	71	72	72	71	286	-2	11,400.00	8,986.21
	Peter LAWRIE	IRL	73	68	71	74	286	-2	11,400.00	8,986.21
48	Pelle EDBERG	SWE	70	68	73	76	287	-1	9,600.00	7,567.34
	Maarten LAFEBER	NED	70	68	75	74	287	-1	9,600.00	7,567.34
	Gareth PADDISON	NZL	70	70	74	73	287	-1	9,600.00	7,567.34
	Thomas BJÖRN	DEN	71	67	76	73	287	-1	9,600.00	7,567.34
52	Peter FOWLER	AUS	71	70	74	73	288	0	8,400.00	6,621.42
	Markus BRIER	AUT	71	70	74	73	288	0	8,400.00	6,621.42
54	Carl SUNESON	ESP	69	73	75	73	290	2	7,800.00	6,148.46
55	Richard FINCH	ENG	69	68	73	81	291	3	6,800.00	5,360.20
	Jarmo SANDELIN	SWE	71	69	79	72	291	3	6,800.00	5,360.20
	Bradley DREDGE	WAL	73	65	72	81	291	3	6,800.00	5,360.20
	Florian PRAEGANT	AUT	74	67	79	71	291	3	6,800.00	5,360.20
59	Niclas FASTH	SWE	70	72	81	69	292	4	5,900.00	4,650.76
	Jean-François LUCQUIN	FRA	73	70	75	74	292	4	5,900.00	4,650.76
61	Anton HAIG	RSA	66	73	79	76	294	6	5,400.00	4,256.63
	Pablo LARRAZABAL	ESP	69	69	74	82	294	6	5,400.00	4,256.63
	Pedro LINHART	ESP	70	73	73	78	294	6	5,400.00	4,256.63
64	Mark BROWN	NZL	72	71	80	73	296	8	5,000.00	3,941.32
65	Hennie OTTO	RSA	73	68	77	80	298	10	4,800.00	3,783.67
66	Tom WHITEHOUSE	ENG	72	71	79	77	299	11	4,600.00	3,626.02

Total Prize Fund

€1,979,950 £1,560,723

Martin Kaymer's victory in the BMW International Open saw him become only the second German golfer to win a European Tour event on home soil, following in the footsteps of Bernhard Langer. Having won the Abu Dhabi Golf Championship in January, Kaymer also became the third German golfer after Alex Cejka and Langer to record multiple European Tour victories in the same season.

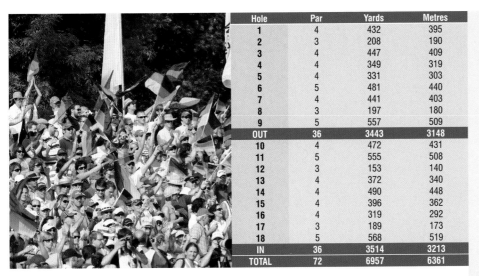

Spanish Double

1	**Pablo LARRAZABAL**		**269**	**-15**
2	Colin MONTGOMERIE		273	-11
3	Søren HANSEN		274	-10
4	Richard GREEN		276	-8
5	Markus BRIER		277	-7
	Lee WESTWOOD		277	-7
7	John BICKERTON		279	-5
	Oliver FISHER		279	-5
	Søren KJELDSEN		279	-5
	Paul McGINLEY		279	-5
	Hennie OTTO		279	-5
	Charl SCHWARTZEL		279	-5

Just about the time Barcelona midfielder Andrés Iniesta was starting to feel nervous about the upcoming Euro 2008 final between his nation, Spain, and Germany, his old school friend Pablo Larrazabal was climbing out of the lake fronting the 18th green at Le Golf National into which he had been flung by joyous compatriots.

They were celebrating not only a superb maiden European Tour triumph by an up and coming talent, but also the diverse range of champions this historic and prestigious tournament has produced over its illustrious 102 year history.

Eighteen winners of Major Championships are etched on the Roll of Honour, starting with Frenchman Arnaud Massy in 1906 through to José Maria Olazábal in 2001, with European Tour greats such as Seve Ballesteros, Nick Faldo, Retief Goosen, Bernhard Langer, Sandy Lyle and Greg Norman scattered in between for good measure.

Also on the Champions' Board are stalwarts of The European Tour such as Englishmen Malcolm Mackenzie and Philip Golding whose unstinting support over decades was rewarded with their respective maiden Tour victories in 2002 and 2003 respectively; and their fellow countryman John Bickerton who followed up his triumph in the Abama Open de Canarias in 2005 with success at Le Golf National in 2006.

In 2007, the silverware became the preserve of the Tour's younger brigade when the then 29 year old Englishman Graeme Storm won his first European Tour event and the youthful theme was carried on by the 25 year old Larrazabal who became the Open de France ALSTOM champion on only his 17th outing since emerging from the previous year's Qualifying School.

The prankster who juggled the letters at the top of the media centre leaderboard going into the final round to form the word 'Olazabal' must have known a thing or two as Larrazabal, three ahead after 54 holes, produced a swashbuckling performance the great 'Chema' would have been proud of to hold off the challenge of, among others, two former European Number Ones in the shape of Colin Montgomerie and Lee Westwood.

Having come through the qualifying tournament at nearby Chantilly – and therefore becoming the first player to do that and go on to win the tournament – Larrazabal used his putter a mere

Colin Montgomerie

Oliver Fisher

Søren Hansen

Richard Green

Left to right: George O'Grady, Chief Executive of The European Tour; Georges Barbaret, President of the French Golf Federation; Pablo Larrazabal; Patrice Clerc, President of ASO and Patrick Kron, Président Alstom

21 times in an opening round of 65 that set the tone for the week. He was never overhauled.

A field that – aside from Montgomerie and Westwood – also included Robert Karlsson, who had finished fourth, one place behind the Englishman in the US Open Championship two weeks previously; Miguel Angel Jiménez, tied sixth at Torrey Pines; and no fewer than 96 Tour winners, was left gasping in his wake.

After celebrating Spain's European Championship semi-final win over Russia, Larrazabal was up at 5.30am the following day to tee off first at 7.30am and shoot 70 on day two. It was, he revealed later, no big deal, for he regularly rose at that hour after his father put him to work for seven months on the family fish farm near Santander to learn and appreciate how hard ordinary people have to work for a living.

He had previous knowledge of the golf course having caddied in the 2003 tournament for older brother Alejandro, winner of the 2002 Amateur Championship. He caddied for him in the Masters Tournament and The Open Championship in 2003 as well – a useful experience as his knowledge of how to plot one's way around a golf course

proved an integral part of his success for which he picked up the princely sum of €666,660 (£527,800) and an exemption on The European Tour until the end of the 2010 season.

Golf is in the blood for Larrazabal. Dad, mum, and brother, as well as he himself, all represented their country in the amateur game. Fittingly, they were all greenside to share his moment of glory.

He admitted:" I came to try and make some money for my Order of Merit position but played probably the greatest golf of my life at the weekend. Having Monty, one of the best European players ever, and Westwood, who I saw nearly win the US Open, challenging me and shooting lower than both of them gave me great pride."

It began a truly magnificent weekend for Spain for, with glass of champagne in hand, Larrazabal was able to sit in front of the television later that evening and cheer on his old school chum Iniesta as he helped Spain to victory in Euro 2008.

Gordon Richardson

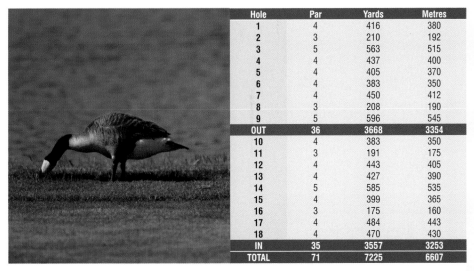

Hole	Par	Yards	Metres
1	4	416	380
2	3	210	192
3	5	563	515
4	4	437	400
5	4	405	370
6	4	383	350
7	4	450	412
8	3	208	190
9	5	596	545
OUT	**36**	**3668**	**3354**
10	4	383	350
11	3	191	175
12	4	443	405
13	4	427	390
14	5	585	535
15	4	399	365
16	3	175	160
17	4	484	443
18	4	470	430
IN	**35**	**3557**	**3253**
TOTAL	**71**	**7225**	**6607**

Ian Poulter

Le Golf National
(Albatross Course)
Final Results

Pos	Name		Rd1	Rd2	Rd3	Rd4	Total		€	£
1	Pablo LARRAZABAL	ESP	65	70	67	67	269	-15	666,660.00	527,800.87
2	Colin MONTGOMERIE	SCO	69	68	68	68	273	-11	444,440.00	351,867.25
3	Søren HANSEN	DEN	69	69	67	69	274	-10	250,400.00	198,243.99
4	Richard GREEN	AUS	73	71	65	67	276	-8	200,000.00	158,341.84
5	Lee WESTWOOD	ENG	69	68	69	71	277	-7	154,800.00	122,556.59
	Markus BRIER	AUT	70	71	66	70	277	-7	154,800.00	122,556.59
7	Oliver FISHER	ENG	66	73	69	71	279	-5	88,666.67	70,198.22
	Hennie OTTO	RSA	70	69	75	65	279	-5	88,666.67	70,198.22
	Paul MCGINLEY	IRL	71	73	70	65	279	-5	88,666.67	70,198.22
	John BICKERTON	ENG	72	69	68	70	279	-5	88,666.67	70,198.22
	Søren KJELDSEN	DEN	72	71	66	70	279	-5	88,666.67	70,198.22
	Charl SCHWARTZEL	RSA	73	70	66	70	279	-5	88,666.67	70,198.22
13	Angel CABRERA	ARG	67	70	74	69	280	-4	55,500.00	43,939.86
	Ignacio GARRIDO	ESP	68	69	73	70	280	-4	55,500.00	43,939.86
	Francesco MOLINARI	ITA	68	75	69	68	280	-4	55,500.00	43,939.86
	Rafa ECHENIQUE	ARG	69	71	69	71	280	-4	55,500.00	43,939.86
	Graeme MCDOWELL	NIR	69	73	67	71	280	-4	55,500.00	43,939.86
	Peter O'MALLEY	AUS	71	72	67	70	280	-4	55,500.00	43,939.86
	Robert KARLSSON	SWE	72	71	68	69	280	-4	55,500.00	43,939.86
	Danny WILLETT	ENG	74	70	67	69	280	-4	55,500.00	43,939.86
21	Graeme STORM	ENG	68	70	72	71	281	-3	44,000.00	34,835.21
	Miles TUNNICLIFF	ENG	68	71	71	71	281	-3	44,000.00	34,835.21
	Jamie DONALDSON	WAL	68	73	72	68	281	-3	44,000.00	34,835.21
	Jeev Milkha SINGH	IND	68	74	70	69	281	-3	44,000.00	34,835.21
	Shiv KAPUR	IND	75	63	76	67	281	-3	44,000.00	34,835.21
26	Peter LAWRIE	IRL	66	71	74	71	282	-2	38,600.00	30,559.98
	Martin ERLANDSSON	SWE	68	73	71	70	282	-2	38,600.00	30,559.98
	David LYNN	ENG	70	65	71	76	282	-2	38,600.00	30,559.98
	Louis OOSTHUIZEN	RSA	70	73	67	72	282	-2	38,600.00	30,559.98
30	Paul BROADHURST	ENG	69	69	72	73	283	-1	32,666.67	25,862.50
	David FROST	RSA	69	74	70	70	283	-1	32,666.67	25,862.50
	Alejandro CAÑIZARES	ESP	71	69	70	73	283	-1	32,666.67	25,862.50
	Ian POULTER	ENG	72	72	71	68	283	-1	32,666.67	25,862.50
	Thomas LEVET	FRA	75	69	69	70	283	-1	32,666.67	25,862.50
	Scott BARR	AUS	75	69	68	71	283	-1	32,666.67	25,862.50
36	Michael JONZON	SWE	68	72	73	71	284	0	28,400.00	22,484.54
	Thongchai JAIDEE	THA	70	73	72	69	284	0	28,400.00	22,484.54
	Carl SUNESON	ESP	72	67	76	69	284	0	28,400.00	22,484.54
39	Simon DYSON	ENG	70	70	72	73	285	1	26,000.00	20,584.44
	Grégory BOURDY	FRA	70	72	71	72	285	1	26,000.00	20,584.44
	Jarmo SANDELIN	SWE	74	70	73	68	285	1	26,000.00	20,584.44
42	Tom WHITEHOUSE	ENG	71	70	69	76	286	2	23,600.00	18,684.34
	Peter HANSON	SWE	71	73	74	68	286	2	23,600.00	18,684.34
	Maarten LAFEBER	NED	73	67	73	73	286	2	23,600.00	18,684.34
45	José Manuel LARA	ESP	68	73	72	74	287	3	21,200.00	16,784.24
	Martin WIEGELE	AUT	68	76	69	74	287	3	21,200.00	16,784.24
	Steve WEBSTER	ENG	73	68	69	77	287	3	21,200.00	16,784.24
48	Barry LANE	ENG	68	76	71	73	288	4	18,000.00	14,250.77
	Phillip ARCHER	ENG	69	74	74	71	288	4	18,000.00	14,250.77
	Mikael LUNDBERG	SWE	71	71	75	71	288	4	18,000.00	14,250.77
	Paul LAWRIE	SCO	73	71	70	74	288	4	18,000.00	14,250.77
	Gonzalo FDEZ-CASTAÑO	ESP	74	69	77	68	288	4	18,000.00	14,250.77
53	Nick DOUGHERTY	ENG	71	71	74	73	289	5	13,371.43	10,586.28
	Mikko ILONEN	FIN	71	71	74	73	289	5	13,371.43	10,586.28
	Jean VAN DE VELDE	FRA	71	72	70	76	289	5	13,371.43	10,586.28
	Raphaël JACQUELIN	FRA	71	73	70	75	289	5	13,371.43	10,586.28
	Rick KULACZ	AUS	72	71	70	76	289	5	13,371.43	10,586.28
	Ricardo GONZALEZ	ARG	72	72	70	75	289	5	13,371.43	10,586.28
	Grégory HAVRET	FRA	73	70	70	76	289	5	13,371.43	10,586.28
60	Andrew MCLARDY	RSA	72	71	72	75	290	6	11,000.00	8,708.80
	Felipe AGUILAR	CHI	74	69	74	73	290	6	11,000.00	8,708.80
62	Andrew COLTART	SCO	68	76	73	74	291	7	10,400.00	8,233.78
63	Daniel VANCSIK	ARG	69	75	75	73	292	8	10,000.00	7,917.09
64	Alvaro QUIROS	ESP	70	74	70	79	293	9	9,400.00	7,442.07
	Ross FISHER	ENG	73	71	73	76	293	9	9,400.00	7,442.07
66	Jyoti RANDHAWA	IND	70	74	81	69	294	10	8,600.00	6,808.70
	Miguel Angel JIMÉNEZ	ESP	72	71	75	76	294	10	8,600.00	6,808.70
68	Sébastien DELAGRANGE	FRA	72	72	77	75	296	12	8,000.00	6,333.67

As well as being the first qualifier to win Continental Europe's oldest National Open, Spain's Pablo Larrazabal was also the first player since Vincent Tshabalala in 1976 to win the tournament on his first appearance.

Total Prize Fund
€3,985,100 £3,155,040

Brave New World

OPEAN OPEN

1	**Ross FISHER**		**268**	**-20**
2	Sergio GARCIA		275	-13
3	Graeme McDOWELL		276	-12
4	David FROST		277	-11
5	Søren HANSEN		281	-7
6	Peter HANSON		282	-6
	Robert KARLSSON		282	-6
8	Markus BRIER		283	-5
	Stephen GALLACHER		283	-5
10	Sion E BEBB		284	-4
	Jamie DONALDSON		284	-4
	Rory McILROY		284	-4
	Jeev Milkha SINGH		284	-4

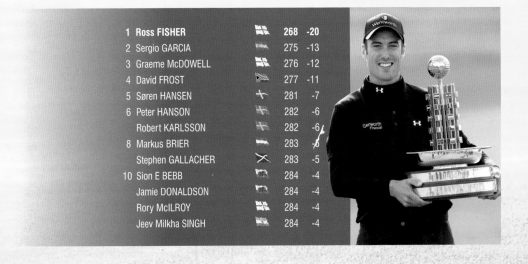

U nmistakeably here was the brave new world of The European Tour International Schedule. A new identity. A new venue. A new star. The same old unpredictable British summer weather at times, of course, but you cannot have everything. So it was that Ross Fisher survived early morning wind and rain on the final day to shine like the late afternoon sunshine and win The European Open, one of the Tour's most prestigious titles, at The London Golf Club by a mighty seven strokes from Spain's Sergio Garcia.

Fisher is tall and slim, yet athletic and strong. He is the very model of a modern professional golfer, a product of the Wentworth Club academy but hardly of the old school. He hits drives for miles, holes yards and yards of putts and does everything in between with commendable panache.

In the worst of the weather in Sunday's final round he only dropped one stroke and completed a wire-to-wire victory on the Jack Nicklaus-designed Heritage Course. The 27 year old Englishman had let leads slip before and had learned some harsh lessons. His second European Tour title, following his maiden victory in the 2007 KLM Open, proved the education was paying off.

It is not just the players that have to move on. In professional sport there is no area that can afford to stand still. So The European Open saw the unveiling of the new branding and logo, based on The Harry Vardon Trophy, that would come in to coincide with the start of the 2009 season and The Race to Dubai. The week also saw the start of the implementation of the Anti-Doping Policy, something championed by The European Tour and supported by all the other major golfing bodies.

But most notably there was a new course, The London Golf Club, where former European Ryder Cup Captain Sam Torrance had twice won Senior Masters titles. At a little over four months notice, a marvellous new set-up was put together at a venue high on the Kent Downs just outside the south eastern corner of the M25 motorway. The question remained however; would anyone turn up – either players or spectators? There was no problem on either count.

Colin Montgomerie, the defending champion, was first in with his entry. The reigning Open Champion, Padraig Harrington, and Garcia, winner of The Players' Championship on the US PGA Tour, were among other big name players to tee up.

Sergio Garcia

David Frost

Markus Brier

*Ross Fisher (left), receives the trophy from
Sir Henry Cooper*

*Peter Fowler (left), receives an engraved ice bucket
from Scott Kelly, European Tour Group Marketing
Director, to celebrate his 500th European Tour event*

As for spectators, almost 60,000 descended on the venue over the course of the four tournament days. With plenty of room around the course and excellent viewing positions, it worked brilliantly, even when 23,856 turned up on the first day thanks to a free-ticket offer. What an atmosphere from the off.

Fisher thrived on it. He opened with a course record of nine under par 63, one better than the previous mark set by Seve Ballesteros when he opened the course with Tony Jacklin and Nicklaus himself in 1994. All of which was slightly ironic given the fact that Fisher, after a long run of tournaments and successfully qualifying for The Open Championship over 36 holes at Sunningdale on the Monday, had almost withdrawn.

On Tuesday, his wife's birthday, he took her to Wimbledon. On Wednesday he was still tired and settled for a spot of practice. The next day he took on the course blind. His caddie, Adam Marrow, had walked it twice and talked him through. Fisher followed his directions precisely. "I felt comfortable straight away," he said. "It really suits my eye. I can hit my driver on all but a couple of the par fours."

At the ninth hole, his last of the day, Fisher collected his sixth successive birdie after driving just short of the green at the 448 yard hole. "That's just sick," joked a marshal on the tee. He repeated the feat on Saturday.

Montgomerie was moved to comment that Fisher's power was "Nadal-like". In fact it is Garcia who is a friend of the Spanish tennis star. But while Nadal went on to dethrone Roger Federer at Wimbledon later on the Sunday evening, earlier in the day Garcia could not bring further joy to Spain's already excellent sporting summer, despite a superb closing 66 which featured only 21 putts.

With such high quality greens the scoring was always going to be low and Fisher, who holed from 50 feet for an eagle at the fifth and pitched in from the greenside bunker at the 18th to provide a grandstand finish, won at 20 under par 268.

The finishing shot came as a direct result of work on his short game with Mark Roe, whose assistance the young Englishman praised once the dust had settled. "It might have looked easy but it was far from it and I've worked hard for it," Fisher said of his victory. "I so wanted to get my second win and for it to come against such strong opposition is special."

There will be the odd tweak to the course but with its rolling fairways, high rough, deep bunkers and exposed setting, there was a wonderful links-like feel. Both the winner and the course seem to have a bright future on The European Tour.

Andy Farrell
Independent on Sunday

IMPROVED PERFORMANCE

baselayer ionx

- **CCC BaseLayer IonX** is revolutionary in apparel technology as it delivers ionic energy to the body through a negatively charged electromagnetic field.

- **CCC BaseLayer IonX** improves performance. Ionisation improves the flow of oxygen-enriched blood to bring more energy to the muscles, which increases your average power output, improving speed and strength.

- **CCC BaseLayer IonX** accelerates recovery. The improvement in blood flow efficiently flushes out residual waste products, such as lactic acid, which is left in the muscles after high intensity activity. Recovery is accelerated, therefore training or competition can begin again sooner.

Canterbury IonX is the official supplier of BaseLayer to Michael Campbell, Jim Furyk, the European Tour Physio Unit, English Golf Union, and used by many of the European Tour's leading Professionals.

Available on line at **www.CanterburyNZ.com**

canterbury

EUROPEAN TOUR OFFICIAL SUPPLIER ENGLISH GOLF UNION

Left to right: European Tour 2007 Number One, Justin Rose, with three former Harry Vardon Trophy winners; Retief Goosen, Padraig Harrington and Colin Montgomerie, helped unveil the new European Tour branding and logo, based on the Harry Vardon Trophy, ahead of the 2009 season and The Race to Dubai

Hole	Par	Yards	Metres
1	4	398	364
2	4	412	377
3	3	194	177
4	4	384	351
5	5	541	495
6	4	454	415
7	3	187	171
8	5	563	515
9	4	448	410
OUT	36	3581	3275
10	4	426	390
11	3	208	190
12	5	531	486
13	4	338	309
14	4	443	405
15	5	548	501
16	4	486	444
17	3	225	206
18	4	471	431
IN	36	3676	3362
TOTAL	72	7257	6637

Ross Fisher's wire-to-wire victory was the fifth in the history of the tournament. He followed Isao Aoki (1983), Andrew Murray (1989), Gordon Brand Jnr (1993) and Phillip Price (2003).

The London Golf Club
(Heritage Course)

Final Results

Pos	Name		Rd1	Rd2	Rd3	Rd4	Total		€	£
1	Ross FISHER	ENG	63	68	69	68	268	-20	506,392.00	400,000.00
2	Sergio GARCIA	ESP	71	64	74	66	275	-13	337,586.23	266,660.00
3	Graeme MCDOWELL	NIR	65	67	71	73	276	-12	190,200.84	150,240.00
4	David FROST	RSA	65	72	69	71	277	-11	151,917.60	120,000.00
5	Søren HANSEN	DEN	69	67	72	73	281	-7	128,826.13	101,760.00
6	Peter HANSON	SWE	68	71	71	72	282	-6	98,746.44	78,000.00
	Robert KARLSSON	SWE	74	66	73	69	282	-6	98,746.44	78,000.00
8	Stephen GALLACHER	SCO	70	68	71	74	283	-5	72,008.94	56,880.00
	Markus BRIER	AUT	71	71	71	70	283	-5	72,008.94	56,880.00
10	Rory MCILROY	NIR	67	71	72	74	284	-4	54,462.46	43,020.00
	Jeev Milkha SINGH	IND	68	72	69	75	284	-4	54,462.46	43,020.00
	Jamie DONALDSON	WAL	73	70	73	68	284	-4	54,462.46	43,020.00
	Sion E BEBB	WAL	74	67	71	72	284	-4	54,462.46	43,020.00
14	Michael JONZON	SWE	69	68	71	77	285	-3	44,663.77	35,280.00
	Mikko ILONEN	FIN	69	73	73	70	285	-3	44,663.77	35,280.00
	Maarten LAFEBER	NED	71	71	70	73	285	-3	44,663.77	35,280.00
17	Paul MCGINLEY	IRL	69	68	71	78	286	-2	36,764.06	29,040.00
	Anthony WALL	ENG	70	70	75	71	286	-2	36,764.06	29,040.00
	David HOWELL	ENG	71	72	73	70	286	-2	36,764.06	29,040.00
	Padraig HARRINGTON	IRL	72	70	69	75	286	-2	36,764.06	29,040.00
	Thomas LEVET	FRA	72	70	72	72	286	-2	36,764.06	29,040.00
	Ignacio GARRIDO	ESP	72	71	67	76	286	-2	36,764.06	29,040.00
	Simon DYSON	ENG	73	69	76	68	286	-2	36,764.06	29,040.00
24	Colin MONTGOMERIE	SCO	70	67	73	77	287	-1	31,598.86	24,960.00
	Oliver FISHER	ENG	72	70	74	71	287	-1	31,598.86	24,960.00
	Gary ORR	SCO	73	67	72	75	287	-1	31,598.86	24,960.00
27	Robert ROCK	ENG	68	71	73	76	288	0	27,497.09	21,720.00
	James KINGSTON	RSA	69	69	74	76	288	0	27,497.09	21,720.00
	Rafa ECHENIQUE	ARG	70	69	74	75	288	0	27,497.09	21,720.00
	Jean-Baptiste GONNET	FRA	71	70	72	75	288	0	27,497.09	21,720.00
	Mark BROWN	NZL	75	68	72	73	288	0	27,497.09	21,720.00
	Robert COLES	ENG	76	66	72	74	288	0	27,497.09	21,720.00
33	David LYNN	ENG	68	72	77	72	289	1	22,848.41	18,048.00
	Pelle EDBERG	SWE	71	72	74	72	289	1	22,848.41	18,048.00
	Grégory HAVRET	FRA	73	68	73	75	289	1	22,848.41	18,048.00
	Andrew OLDCORN	SCO	73	70	73	73	289	1	22,848.41	18,048.00
	Jean VAN DE VELDE	FRA	75	67	70	77	289	1	22,848.41	18,048.00
38	Justin ROSE	ENG	69	73	77	71	290	2	19,749.29	15,600.00
	Jean-François LUCQUIN	FRA	69	73	73	75	290	2	19,749.29	15,600.00
	Carl SUNESON	ESP	72	69	72	77	290	2	19,749.29	15,600.00
	Steve WEBSTER	ENG	73	70	71	76	290	2	19,749.29	15,600.00
	Alvaro VELASCO	ESP	73	70	73	74	290	2	19,749.29	15,600.00
43	Francesco MOLINARI	ITA	70	73	73	75	291	3	16,710.94	13,200.00
	Fredrik ANDERSSON HED	SWE	72	69	74	76	291	3	16,710.94	13,200.00
	Gary MURPHY	IRL	72	71	73	75	291	3	16,710.94	13,200.00
	Chapchai NIRAT	THA	74	69	72	76	291	3	16,710.94	13,200.00
	Patrik SJÖLAND	SWE	76	66	73	76	291	3	16,710.94	13,200.00
48	José Manuel LARA	ESP	68	75	76	73	292	4	13,672.58	10,800.00
	Ian POULTER	ENG	70	67	77	78	292	4	13,672.58	10,800.00
	Stuart MANLEY	WAL	70	70	76	76	292	4	13,672.58	10,800.00
	Simon KHAN	ENG	70	72	77	73	292	4	13,672.58	10,800.00
	David GRIFFITHS	ENG	71	72	75	74	292	4	13,672.58	10,800.00
53	Peter HEDBLOM	SWE	68	73	79	73	293	5	10,381.04	8,200.00
	Benn BARHAM	ENG	70	72	74	77	293	5	10,381.04	8,200.00
	François DELAMONTAGNE	FRA	73	69	72	79	293	5	10,381.04	8,200.00
	Grégory BOURDY	FRA	73	70	77	73	293	5	10,381.04	8,200.00
	Bradley DREDGE	WAL	75	66	75	77	293	5	10,381.04	8,200.00
	Graeme STORM	ENG	75	68	73	77	293	5	10,381.04	8,200.00
59	Gonzalo FDEZ-CASTAÑO	ESP	68	75	73	78	294	6	8,507.39	6,720.00
	Martin WIEGELE	AUT	71	68	72	83	294	6	8,507.39	6,720.00
	Hennie OTTO	RSA	72	70	78	74	294	6	8,507.39	6,720.00
62	Santiago LUNA	ESP	70	71	74	80	295	7	7,595.88	6,000.00
	Garry HOUSTON	WAL	72	75	74	74	295	7	7,595.88	6,000.00
	Michael LORENZO-VERA	FRA	74	66	80	75	295	7	7,595.88	6,000.00
65	Paul LAWRIE	SCO	73	68	79	77	297	9	6,836.29	5,400.00
	Richard GREEN	AUS	73	69	72	83	297	9	6,836.29	5,400.00
67	Raphaël JACQUELIN	FRA	71	71	77	79	298	10	6,228.62	4,920.00
	Paul BROADHURST	ENG	72	71	76	79	298	10	6,228.62	4,920.00
69	Emanuele CANONICA	ITA	72	70	77	80	299	11	5,772.87	4,560.00
70	Thomas BJÖRN	DEN	72	70	76	W/D				

Total Prize Fund
€3,032,807 £2,395,620

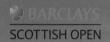

On Course
Navigation

1	**Graeme McDOWELL**		**271**	**-13**
2	James KINGSTON		273	-11
3	Richard GREEN		274	-10
	Miguel Angel JIMÉNEZ		274	-10
5	Simon KHAN		275	-9
6	Robert DINWIDDIE		276	-8
	Stephen GALLACHER		276	-8
	Francesco MOLINARI		276	-8
9	Ernie ELS		277	-7
	Paul LAWRIE		277	-7
	Alvaro QUIROS		277	-7
	Jeev Milkha SINGH		277	-7
	Oliver WILSON		277	-7

Anyone who stood by the first fairway at Slaley Hall on Thursday June 20, 2002, and subsequently ducked for cover as Graeme McDowell launched his professional career in The Great North Open with an inauspicious hook out of bounds, would have been surprised, perhaps, but nevertheless mightily impressed to learn that, six years later, the key attributes of the Ulsterman's success in the professional ranks are the accuracy of his work off the tee and the knack of finding fairways in regulation.

When he stepped up to collect the first prize of €631,044 (£500,000) in The Barclays Scottish Open – the most rewarding cheque of his career to date – the victory was thanks to timely ball striking allied to shrewd iron play.

Loch Lomond is a second shot golf course and the 28 year old from Portrush was a model of composure when he found the fairway of the home hole on Sunday before threatening the pin on the 18th green with a glorious approach. McDowell located more greens in regulation than any other player on the Bonnie Banks over the four days and it was this precision which proved the key to his success.

After taking time to digest why he had produced the best performance of his career to date, the Irishman – who recently employed a new coach in Clive Tucker to help with matters inside the ropes as well as a new management team to take care of all matters away from the golf course – pinpointed significant alterations in his technique.

"I've been moving the ball a little more left to right in the air than I have done in the past," he surmised. "That means my irons are coming in a little softer onto the greens, which has a lot to do with why the ball has gone closer to the hole. That's probably the most important change I've made. My iron play has been great this year, and at Loch Lomond it was especially good."

The journey McDowell has undertaken from that nervy first tee pull in Northumberland to the expert command of line and length he demonstrated in Scotland has been impressively navigated, though not without a few detours along the way.

In spite of beginning life in the paid ranks as someone who appeared he might struggle to cope with the burden of being such a feted amateur – he was America's top collegiate golfer during his time at the University of Alabama – McDowell did not take long to confirm why he had been such a valued part of the victorious Great Britain and Ireland Walker Cup side in Georgia in 2001, a team which also included European Tour winners of the calibre of Luke Donald, Nick Dougherty and Marc Warren.

He won the Volvo Scandinavian Masters in only his fourth appearance on Tour the following season and triumphed again in 2004 in the

Ernie Els

Jeev Milkha Singh

Graeme McDowell (left), receives the trophy from Bob Diamond, President, Barclays PLC

Stephen Gallacher

Sweden's Pelle Edberg with the BMW X6 he won for holing in one at the 17th hole during the first round of The Barclays Scottish Open

BARCLAYS | SCOTTISH OPEN

Simon Khan

Telecom Italia Open, playing well enough in bursts that year to claim a career-high sixth place finish on the Order of Merit.

However, like a flare from a rocket, McDowell's flashes of brilliances burned out all too quickly and his early professional career was notable for its inconsistency. "I was jumping into the unknown," he recalled. "As I stand here six years on, I realise how much I've learned. How much your game has to adapt and how important it is to structure your life and pace yourself properly."

He was referring, of course, to the 2006 season where he attempted to play a full schedule on each side of the Atlantic. The challenge of playing both The European Tour and the US PGA Tour at the same time is demanding, even for seasoned champions; McDowell found the task simply overwhelming and quickly abandoned the idea.

He regrouped in 2007 and in March of this year he rediscovered the joy of winning, coming out on top of a remarkable final day duel with Jeev

Milkha Singh to take the title in the inaugural Ballantine's Championship – The European Tour's first foray into Korea.

Having gone into the final round at the Pinx Golf Club level with Singh before matching the Indian's closing 66 and winning at the third play-off hole, McDowell now possessed the experience and mental fortitude to cope with exactly the same situation at Loch Lomond.

Tied with Simon Khan going into the closing 18 holes, McDowell grew strong as the round unfolded, his supremely controlled 68 more than evidence of that. "I've had a pretty up-and-down career, but I feel I've kept learning about myself and how to play this game," he reflected. "Hopefully I've turned the corner now and can keep moving up in the world."

Mike Aitken
The Scotsman

The Tee Location

The Caddie's Advice

The Wind Direction

The Wind Speed

The Humidity

The Temperature

The Morning Dew

The Type Of Grass On The Fairway

The Grass Length

The Lie Of The Ball

The Lie Of The Land

The Dogleg Left

The Right-Hand Bunker

The Left-Hand Bunker

The Towering Trees

The Semi Rough

The Water Hazard

The Amount Of Rainfall Last Week

The Green Location

The Green Firmness

The Green Elevation

The Pin Position

The Nap Of The Green

The Make Of Ball

The Amount Of Spin

The Tee Height

The Backswing

The Yardage To The Exact Millimetre

SUCCESS IS GAINED BY PAYING ATTENTION TO THE SMALLEST DETAIL.
THAT'S WHY WE MAKE IT OUR PRIORITY.

Earn Success Every Day

Scotland's Alastair Forsyth and a group of local school children give their backing to the Scottish Golf Union's national junior programme, Clubgolf, which celebrated its fifth birthday during the week at Loch Lomond

Loch Lomond Golf Club

Final Results

Pos	Name		Rd1	Rd2	Rd3	Rd4	Total		€	£
1	Graeme MCDOWELL	NIR	67	70	66	68	271	-13	631,044.98	500,000.00
2	James KINGSTON	RSA	70	70	67	66	273	-11	420,692.45	333,300.00
3	Richard GREEN	AUS	67	68	70	69	274	-10	213,167.00	168,900.00
	Miguel Angel JIMÉNEZ	ESP	68	69	68	69	274	-10	213,167.00	168,900.00
5	Simon KHAN	ENG	69	66	68	72	275	-9	160,537.84	127,200.00
6	Robert DINWIDDIE	ENG	68	68	71	69	276	-8	113,588.10	90,000.00
	Francesco MOLINARI	ITA	69	68	72	67	276	-8	113,588.10	90,000.00
	Stephen GALLACHER	SCO	72	68	72	64	276	-8	113,588.10	90,000.00
9	Paul LAWRIE	SCO	68	67	72	70	277	-7	71,257.60	56,460.00
	Jeev Milkha SINGH	IND	68	68	69	72	277	-7	71,257.60	56,460.00
	Alvaro QUIROS	ESP	69	70	74	64	277	-7	71,257.60	56,460.00
	Oliver WILSON	ENG	71	66	71	69	277	-7	71,257.60	56,460.00
	Ernie ELS	RSA	72	66	70	69	277	-7	71,257.60	56,460.00
14	Patrik SJÖLAND	SWE	67	71	71	69	278	-6	53,386.41	42,300.00
	Oliver FISHER	ENG	68	69	70	71	278	-6	53,386.41	42,300.00
	Christian CÉVAËR	FRA	70	67	70	71	278	-6	53,386.41	42,300.00
	Peter HEDBLOM	SWE	70	68	72	68	278	-6	53,386.41	42,300.00
	Andrew MCLARDY	RSA	70	70	69	69	278	-6	53,386.41	42,300.00
19	Lee WESTWOOD	ENG	67	69	70	73	279	-5	43,542.10	34,500.00
	Damien MCGRANE	IRL	68	66	76	69	279	-5	43,542.10	34,500.00
	Gary MURPHY	IRL	68	70	72	69	279	-5	43,542.10	34,500.00
	Fredrik ANDERSSON HED	SWE	70	67	69	73	279	-5	43,542.10	34,500.00
	Rory MCILROY	NIR	70	69	68	72	279	-5	43,542.10	34,500.00
	Anthony WALL	ENG	70	70	69	70	279	-5	43,542.10	34,500.00
25	Thongchai JAIDEE	THA	64	71	71	74	280	-4	35,401.62	28,050.00
	John BICKERTON	ENG	66	71	72	71	280	-4	35,401.62	28,050.00
	Ross FISHER	ENG	68	69	68	75	280	-4	35,401.62	28,050.00
	David LYNN	ENG	69	67	70	74	280	-4	35,401.62	28,050.00
	Ian POULTER	ENG	69	69	68	74	280	-4	35,401.62	28,050.00
	Grégory HAVRET	FRA	69	70	72	69	280	-4	35,401.62	28,050.00
	Jean-François LUCQUIN	FRA	72	65	71	72	280	-4	35,401.62	28,050.00
	Adam SCOTT	AUS	72	66	68	74	280	-4	35,401.62	28,050.00
33	Henrik STENSON	SWE	67	69	72	73	281	-3	28,472.75	22,560.00
	Martin ERLANDSSON	SWE	67	70	77	67	281	-3	28,472.75	22,560.00
	Pelle EDBERG	SWE	68	70	74	69	281	-3	28,472.75	22,560.00
	Simon WAKEFIELD	ENG	71	68	72	70	281	-3	28,472.75	22,560.00
	Hennie OTTO	RSA	71	69	71	70	281	-3	28,472.75	22,560.00
38	Alexander NOREN	SWE	64	73	71	74	282	-2	24,232.13	19,200.00
	Angel CABRERA	ARG	65	68	78	71	282	-2	24,232.13	19,200.00
	David HOWELL	ENG	69	70	70	73	282	-2	24,232.13	19,200.00
	Phil MICKELSON	USA	71	67	71	73	282	-2	24,232.13	19,200.00
	Søren KJELDSEN	DEN	73	66	74	69	282	-2	24,232.13	19,200.00
	Mark BROWN	NZL	73	66	71	72	282	-2	24,232.13	19,200.00
44	Thomas BJÖRN	DEN	67	68	75	73	283	-1	20,067.23	15,900.00
	Johan EDFORS	SWE	67	71	76	69	283	-1	20,067.23	15,900.00
	Mark FOSTER	ENG	68	70	73	72	283	-1	20,067.23	15,900.00
	Mardan MAMAT	SIN	69	70	73	71	283	-1	20,067.23	15,900.00
	Alejandro CAÑIZARES	ESP	73	67	71	72	283	-1	20,067.23	15,900.00
49	Maarten LAFEBER	NED	67	70	76	71	284	0	17,416.84	13,800.00
	Andres ROMERO	ARG	68	71	75	70	284	0	17,416.84	13,800.00
51	Garry HOUSTON	WAL	66	71	74	74	285	1	14,009.20	11,100.00
	Ross McGOWAN	ENG	69	70	74	72	285	1	14,009.20	11,100.00
	Grégory BOURDY	FRA	70	68	72	75	285	1	14,009.20	11,100.00
	Paul MCGINLEY	IRL	70	70	72	73	285	1	14,009.20	11,100.00
	Andrew OLDCORN	SCO	71	69	72	73	285	1	14,009.20	11,100.00
	Matthew MILLAR	AUS	72	64	77	72	285	1	14,009.20	11,100.00
	Alastair FORSYTH	SCO	73	67	72	73	285	1	14,009.20	11,100.00
58	David DIXON	ENG	68	70	75	74	287	3	10,980.18	8,700.00
	Tom WHITEHOUSE	ENG	68	71	75	73	287	3	10,980.18	8,700.00
	Peter LAWRIE	IRL	71	68	77	71	287	3	10,980.18	8,700.00
61	David DRYSDALE	SCO	68	71	74	75	288	4	10,033.62	7,950.00
	Scott STRANGE	AUS	70	68	77	73	288	4	10,033.62	7,950.00
63	Carlos RODILES	ESP	69	70	75	75	289	5	9,276.36	7,350.00
	Iain PYMAN	ENG	69	71	76	73	289	5	9,276.36	7,350.00
65	Jean-François REMESY	FRA	70	68	75	79	292	8	8,708.42	6,900.00

Hole	Par	Yards	Metres
1	4	425	389
2	4	455	416
3	5	518	473
4	4	385	352
5	3	190	174
6	5	625	572
7	4	440	402
8	3	160	146
9	4	340	311
OUT	**36**	**3538**	**3235**
10	4	455	416
11	3	235	215
12	4	415	379
13	5	560	512
14	4	371	339
15	4	415	379
16	4	490	448
17	3	215	197
18	4	455	414
IN	**35**	**3611**	**3299**
TOTAL	**71**	**7149**	**6534**

i James Kingston was within two shots of making history in The Barclays Scottish Open. His opening rounds of 70-70 left him right on the cut mark before stunning weekend rounds of 67-66 saw him finish in second place behind Graeme McDowell. It was the best performance of the season from the cut line and he became only the 14th player in European Tour history to finish second in this way. No player has ever won a European Tour event from the cut mark.

Total Prize Fund

€3,748,319 £2,969,930

Focus and Preparation

1	**Padraig HARRINGTON**		283	3
2	Ian POULTER		287	7
3	Greg NORMAN		289	9
	Henrik STENSON		289	9
5	Jim FURYK		290	10
	Chris WOOD (AM)		290	10
7	Robert ALLENBY		292	12
	Stephen AMES		292	12
	Paul CASEY		292	12
	Ben CURTIS		292	12
	Ernie ELS		292	12
	David HOWELL		292	12
	Robert KARLSSON		292	12
	Anthony KIM		292	12
	Steve STRICKER		292	12

The Irish, it has to be said, do not need much of an excuse to enjoy themselves. Therefore, one can only imagine the strain on the supplies of Guinness across the entire Emerald Isle in the third week of July as the nation's favourite golfing son came up with the goods once again.

While, at times, such raucous revelry might seem out of proportion, on this occasion it was more than justified; indeed Padraig Harrington's successful defence of The Open Championship – the first European golfer to achieve the feat since Scotland's James Braid in 1905-06 – was worthy of extended and frenzied celebration and not just from those bedecked in green.

In truth, everyone with an appreciation of this grand old game joined together and rejoiced in an Open Championship that was filled with lots of the right stuff, most of it blowing in off the Irish Sea.

Old mariners would probably suggest that the wind which howled over and across Royal Birkdale during the days of play amounted to

no more than a mild zephyr. Golfers, however, are not able to raise a spinnaker and run before the wind; their job is to battle it, to caress it, stand up to it and, ultimately, use it to their advantage.

This, inevitably, takes courage and a massive amount of self-belief on top of a decent slice of luck, but, ultimately, it also demands immense talent. Throw in imagination and thirst for a real challenge and you have the identikit group photograph of the men who were to contend this great Championship.

Jim Furyk, Greg Norman, Ian Poulter, Henrik Stenson and Harrington, not to mention the amateur Chris Wood – who brought memories flooding back of Justin Rose's performance

Paul Casey

Ian Poulter

Ben Curtis

Greg Norman takes 'time out' with Camilo Villegas (left) and Rocco Mediate (right) during his exciting challenge for The 137th Open Championship

over these great links a decade ago – were the players who excelled, the men who occupied the top six places at the end of the week, and those who kept their wits about them while most of the rest were being blown hither and thither.

Conditions were hard, indeed the four days amounted to perhaps the most sustained period of buffeting many people had witnessed at an Open Championship, but they also presented a glorious opportunity because, in such conditions, anything was possible and almost anyone could win.

Except the World Number One, of course, who was forced to gnaw on his own frustrations back home in Florida while resting the knee that prevented him from competing.

How much did we miss Tiger Woods in Southport? Given the stature of the great man, naturally his absence was felt, but not anywhere near as much as some of us had feared. Mostly, this was down to the unexpected re-emergence of the original World Number One, the man known as The Great White Shark: Greg Norman.

For a decade from the mid 1980s, the Australian bestrode the golfing world like a latter-day Colossus.

He did everything during this period except win enough Major Championships. Two Open titles does not properly reflect his dominance

Turnberry, Scotland

homecomingscotland2009.com

In July 2009 The Open Championship returns to Scotland, The Home of Golf and to the mighty Turnberry, universally renowned as one of golf's greatest challenges. So what better way to celebrate Scotland's year of Homecoming than to experience the drama and excitement that only The Open in The Home of Golf can deliver.

With over 550 courses to choose from across Scotland you're never far from a course that's perfect for you. From hidden gems to legendary links you'll always find somewhere you want to play at a time that suits. So why not visit Scotland in 2009 and join the celebrations in The Home of Golf. We'll see you on the tee!

For further information visit **homecomingscotland2009.com**

England's Chris Wood with the Silver Medal he won as the leading amateur

although it may more accurately sum up his instinct which was always to go for it and try to throttle the living daylights out of any given situation. This made for many spectacular wins but it also led to some equally spectacular losses. Those critics who reflect for a few seconds on a man's life before reaching a superficial conclusion often took the easy option over Norman's record and suggested a lack of nerve was to blame.

Although this theory may have some resonance when applied to one final approach shot to the last green at Augusta National during the 1987 Masters Tournament, it is ludicrous for anyone to try and pin it to Norman's curriculum vitae as some sort of general note. While Harrington's successful defence ensures he will be the man most recalled by future fans, those of us who watched this Open unfold will know that the week was made equally compelling by Norman's outrageous and unexpected assault on the Claret Jug at 53 years of age.

Supported by his new bride, the former tennis champion Chris Evert, Norman's lifelong obsession with physical fitness very nearly paid off. Eventually it proved too much and his final round slip from leader to a tie for third with Stenson reflected no loss of nerve but instead the mental tiredness common with someone who has not found himself in that position for several years. Still, it had been a grand effort.

Norman carried a two shot lead into the final round but when his first three holes slid by in a flurry of dropped shots, it was game on for the chasing pack. It was now that Harrington's focus and preparation began to pay off.

Poulter, in the sixth last group of the day, played one of the rounds of his career, carding a 69 to set a decent clubhouse target of seven over par 287. In the last group alongside Norman, Harrington remained calm. He needed to because he seemed to be coming apart during the middle section of his round; shots frittered

here and there, opportunities missed. However, he rectified matters in style over the closing stretch.

Crucial birdies came at the 13th and 15th before he sealed the deal with a stunning eagle three at the 17th after his five wood second shot, from 249 yards, came to rest within a few feet of the hole. It was a wonderful shot and one which came wrapped in the tiny bit of luck any man needs on a links such as Royal Birkdale, his ball flipping away from the greenside bunker before sweeping up the putting surface and accepting the invitation to trundle down close to the pin.

It was a blow worthy of loud acclaim and it got it from the galleries who had swarmed merrily over the dunes all week. It was also a blow that afforded the defending champion a four shot lead as he played the last.

It meant that following the jittery, often despairing moments he had to endure before victory in Scotland twelve months earlier, he was now able to unzip that familiar lop-sided grin before striding jauntily up the final fairway, his cap in hand as he accepted the tumultuous applause which rolled down from the packed grandstands.

"I was overcome with all sorts of emotions at Carnoustie," he admitted later. "But this time I was able to enjoy that walk. This was harder work but it was also more satisfying. Not many have successfully defended The Open and I'm very proud to be a member of that club."

Happy, too, to be able to take the Claret Jug back home to Dublin. Last July he had promised son Patrick that he could fill it with ladybirds. This time it is more likely to be cornflakes because, after much consideration, the Harrington family have decided the best place for the old trophy is slap-bang in the middle of the breakfast table.

Gazing upon your undeniable place in history; there can be no better way to start each day.

Bill Elliott
The Observer

Robert Allenby

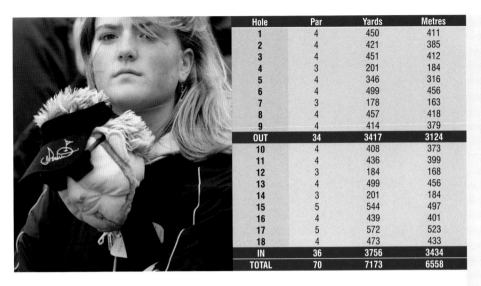

Hole	Par	Yards	Metres
1	4	450	411
2	4	421	385
3	4	451	412
4	3	201	184
5	4	346	316
6	4	499	456
7	3	178	163
8	4	457	418
9	4	414	379
OUT	**34**	**3417**	**3124**
10	4	408	373
11	4	436	399
12	3	184	168
13	4	499	456
14	3	201	184
15	5	544	497
16	4	439	401
17	5	572	523
18	4	473	433
IN	**36**	**3756**	**3434**
TOTAL	**70**	**7173**	**6558**

Royal Birkdale Golf Club

Final Results

Pos	Name		Rd1	Rd2	Rd3	Rd4	Total		€	£
1	Padraig HARRINGTON	IRL	74	68	72	69	283	3	938,565.00	750,000.00
2	Ian POULTER	ENG	72	71	75	69	287	7	563,139.00	450,000.00
3	Greg NORMAN	AUS	70	70	72	77	289	9	319,112.10	255,000.00
	Henrik STENSON	SWE	76	72	70	71	289	9	319,112.10	255,000.00
5	Jim FURYK	USA	71	71	77	71	290	10	225,255.60	180,000.00
	Chris WOOD (AM)	ENG	75	70	73	72	290	10		
7	Robert ALLENBY	AUS	69	73	76	74	292	12	121,318.22	96,944.45
	Anthony KIM	USA	72	74	71	75	292	12	121,318.22	96,944.45
	Stephen AMES	CAN	73	70	78	71	292	12	121,318.22	96,944.45
	Robert KARLSSON	SWE	75	73	75	69	292	12	121,318.22	96,944.45
	David HOWELL	ENG	76	71	78	67	292	12	121,318.22	96,944.45
	Steve STRICKER	USA	77	71	71	73	292	12	121,318.22	96,944.45
	Ben CURTIS	USA	78	69	70	75	292	12	121,318.22	96,944.45
	Paul CASEY	ENG	78	71	73	70	292	12	121,318.22	96,944.45
	Ernie ELS	RSA	80	69	74	69	292	12	121,318.22	96,944.45
16	Adam SCOTT	AUS	70	74	77	72	293	13	66,533.83	53,166.67
	K J CHOI	KOR	72	67	75	79	293	13	66,533.83	53,166.67
	Justin LEONARD	USA	77	70	73	73	293	13	66,533.83	53,166.67
19	Rocco MEDIATE	USA	69	73	76	76	294	14	47,267.18	37,770.83
	Graeme MCDOWELL	NIR	69	73	80	72	294	14	47,267.18	37,770.83
	Fredrik JACOBSON	SWE	71	72	79	72	294	14	47,267.18	37,770.83
	Simon WAKEFIELD	ENG	71	74	70	79	294	14	47,267.18	37,770.83
	Grégory HAVRET	FRA	71	75	77	71	294	14	47,267.18	37,770.83
	Alexander NOREN	SWE	72	70	75	77	294	14	47,267.18	37,770.83
	Jean VAN DE VELDE	FRA	73	71	80	70	294	14	47,267.18	37,770.83
	Paul WARING	ENG	73	74	76	71	294	14	47,267.18	37,770.83
	Trevor IMMELMAN	RSA	74	74	73	73	294	14	47,267.18	37,770.83
	Davis LOVE III	USA	75	74	70	75	294	14	47,267.18	37,770.83
	Thomas SHERREARD (AM)	ENG	77	69	76	72	294	14		
	Anders HANSEN	DEN	78	68	74	74	294	14	47,267.18	37,770.83
	Phil MICKELSON	USA	79	68	76	71	294	14	47,267.18	37,770.83
32	Retief GOOSEN	RSA	71	75	73	76	295	15	31,330.19	25,035.71
	Heath SLOCUM	USA	73	76	74	72	295	15	31,330.19	25,035.71
	Tom LEHMAN	USA	74	73	73	75	295	15	31,330.19	25,035.71
	Todd HAMILTON	USA	74	74	72	75	295	15	31,330.19	25,035.71
	Nick O'HERN	AUS	74	75	74	72	295	15	31,330.19	25,035.71
	Richard GREEN	AUS	76	72	76	71	295	15	31,330.19	25,035.71
	Andres ROMERO	ARG	77	72	74	72	295	15	31,330.19	25,035.71
39	Bart BRYANT	USA	70	78	74	74	296	16	20,830.93	16,645.83
	Mike WEIR	CAN	71	76	74	75	296	16	20,830.93	16,645.83
	Ross FISHER	ENG	72	74	71	79	296	16	20,830.93	16,645.83
	David DUVAL	USA	73	69	83	71	296	16	20,830.93	16,645.83
	Jay WILLIAMSON	USA	73	72	77	74	296	16	20,830.93	16,645.83
	Grégory BOURDY	FRA	74	74	75	73	296	16	20,830.93	16,645.83
	Thomas AIKEN	RSA	75	71	82	68	296	16	20,830.93	16,645.83
	Camilo VILLEGAS	COL	76	65	79	76	296	16	20,830.93	16,645.83
	Graeme STORM	ENG	76	70	72	78	296	16	20,830.93	16,645.83
	Woody AUSTIN	USA	76	72	74	74	296	16	20,830.93	16,645.83
	Simon KHAN	ENG	77	72	71	76	296	16	20,830.93	16,645.83
	Ariel CANETE	ARG	78	71	76	71	296	16	20,830.93	16,645.83
51	Anthony WALL	ENG	71	73	81	72	297	17	14,748.88	11,785.71
	Stuart APPLEBY	AUS	72	71	79	75	297	17	14,748.88	11,785.71
	Sergio GARCIA	ESP	72	73	74	78	297	17	14,748.88	11,785.71
	Zach JOHNSON	USA	73	72	76	76	297	17	14,748.88	11,785.71
	David FROST	RSA	75	73	73	76	297	17	14,748.88	11,785.71
	Michael CAMPBELL	NZL	75	74	74	74	297	17	14,748.88	11,785.71
	Douglas LABELLE	USA	78	70	74	75	297	17	14,748.88	11,785.71
58	Peter HANSON	SWE	71	72	78	77	298	18	13,327.62	10,650.00
	Kevin STADLER	USA	72	75	78	73	298	18	13,327.62	10,650.00
	Colin MONTGOMERIE	SCO	73	75	74	76	298	18	13,327.62	10,650.00
	Tom GILLIS	USA	74	72	79	73	298	18	13,327.62	10,650.00
	Richard FINCH	ENG	75	73	78	72	298	18	13,327.62	10,650.00
	Scott VERPLANK	USA	77	67	78	76	298	18	13,327.62	10,650.00
64	Søren HANSEN	DEN	75	69	77	78	299	19	12,764.48	10,200.00
	Jonathan LOMAS	ENG	75	73	76	75	299	19	12,764.48	10,200.00
	Wen-chong LIANG	CHN	77	71	77	74	299	19	12,764.48	10,200.00
67	David HORSEY	ENG	74	70	79	77	300	20	12,389.06	9,900.00
	Jean-Baptiste GONNET	FRA	75	72	73	80	300	20	12,389.06	9,900.00
	Lee WESTWOOD	ENG	75	74	78	73	300	20	12,389.06	9,900.00
70	Jeff OVERTON	USA	72	75	75	79	301	21	11,700.78	9,350.00
	John ROLLINS	USA	73	75	77	76	301	21	11,700.78	9,350.00
	José-Filipe LIMA	POR	73	75	77	76	301	21	11,700.78	9,350.00
	Justin ROSE	ENG	74	72	82	73	301	21	11,700.78	9,350.00
	Brendan JONES	AUS	74	73	83	71	301	21	11,700.78	9,350.00
	Martin WIEGELE	AUT	74	74	78	74	301	21	11,700.78	9,350.00
	Pablo LARRAZABAL	ESP	75	74	73	79	301	21	11,700.78	9,350.00
	Craig PARRY	AUS	77	70	77	77	301	21	11,700.78	9,350.00
78	Nick DOUGHERTY	ENG	75	71	79	77	302	22	11,075.07	8,850.00
	Lucas GLOVER	USA	78	71	77	76	302	22	11,075.07	8,850.00
80	Martin KAYMER	GER	75	72	79	77	303	23	10,887.35	8,700.00
81	Phillip ARCHER	ENG	75	74	78	77	304	24	10,762.21	8,600.00
82	Sean O'HAIR	USA	75	73	80	78	306	26	10,637.07	8,500.00
83	Chih-Bing LAM	SIN	72	75	83	81	311	31	10,511.93	8,400.00

Total Prize Fund

€5,335,867 £4,263,850

Dennis Watson, Captain, Royal Birkdale Golf Club, presents Padraig Harrington with the Claret Jug, with David Harrison (left), Captain, The Royal and Ancient Golf Club and Michael Halsall (right), Chairman of the Championship Committee – Royal Birkdale Golf Club

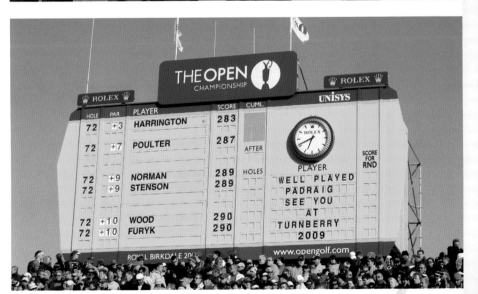

By making a successful defence of his Open Championship title, Padraig Harrington is the first European to win back-to-back since James Braid achieved the feat in 1906. The Irishman also became the 26th different golfer to record multiple triumphs in The Open Championship.

Meridien Man

1	Mikael LUNDBERG		267	-21
2	José Manuel LARA		269	-19
3	Benn BARHAM		270	-18
4	Jan-Are LARSEN		271	-17
5	David DRYSDALE		272	-16
6	Darren FICHARDT		273	-15
	Jamie MOUL		273	-15
	Lloyd SALTMAN		273	-15
9	Soren JUUL		274	-14
	Sam LITTLE		274	-14
	Robert ROCK		274	-14

T he cameras of the assembled Russian paparazzi clicked, flashed and whirred into overdrive as Mikael Lundberg made his way into the Media Centre cradling the Inteco Russian Open Golf Championship trophy.

José Manuel Lara

Benn Barham

The Swede had just secured victory at Le Meridien Moscow Country Club and, having been presented with the beautifully hand crafted award along with a not inconsiderable cheque for €210,237 (£166,790), took his place in the interview room to dissect a wonderful performance.

In position, centre stage, it was only a matter of seconds before the first question was pitched: "Do you think they should rename this place the Mikael Lundberg Country Club?"

A huge grin creased the face of the 34 year old from Helsingborg and, while the gentlemen of Russia's fourth estate certainly saw the funny side of the playfully mischievous question too, Lundberg's interrogator was making a serious point.

For here was a man who has dominated the Inteco Russian Open Golf Championship like no other, winning the tournament twice and finishing third in the space of four years.

It seems there are two certainties that are bound to occur every time The European Tour touches down in Russia: firstly, there is the guarantee of a unique experience – for example, not many top professional tournaments have a Friday night 'cut' party – and secondly, you can bet your bottom dollar that Mikael Lundberg will be in the mix come Sunday afternoon.

Time and time again the Swede has arrived at Le Meridien Moscow Country Club lacking confidence and form, yet time and time again he has stood on the first tee of the beautiful Robert Trent Jones Jnr layout and instantly become Lord of all he surveys. This year was no exception.

Having missed six cuts out of 16 appearances on The 2008 European Tour International Schedule, and with his best being a share of 13th place in the Enjoy Jakarta Astro Indonesia Open in February, Lundberg arrived in Moscow in late July hoping to rediscover the form that had seen him win the trophy for the first time in 2005 and then defend the title gallantly with a tied third place finish in 2006.

On his way at 2.30pm on Thursday afternoon, he instantly let the good memories and positive vibes overwhelm him before cracking his drive down the middle of the fairway. Business as usual: he was off and running once more, en route to an opening score of five under par 67 that would leave him just two shots off the early pace.

That he pushed on from there came as no surprise to any student of the record books. Lundberg was, once more, relentless in Russia, moving into a share of the lead after a stunning second round of eight under par 64, which was followed by a third round 68 for a 17 under par total of 199 and a one stroke lead over a bunched chasing pack.

"I don't know why I love this place so much, but every time I come here I feel like I can't do anything wrong," he admitted on the eve of the final round. "I just see all the shots. I know exactly where to put the ball and, more often than not, it goes exactly where I want it to."

Apart from one nervy moment on Sunday, where he found the trees from the 15th tee, his ball continued to behave itself, helping him to a second weekend round of 68 for a 21 under par aggregate of 267 and a two stroke victory over José Manuel Lara of Spain, with England's Benn Barham taking third place a further shot behind.

And so, having collected the trophy and prize money, as well as the enthusiastic plaudits of the crowd, Lundberg made his way to face the media and 'that' first question.

"It would be nice," came the reply. "But, in all honesty, I wouldn't change anything about this place. Let's keep everything how it is....after all, this is my tournament!"

Michael Gibbons

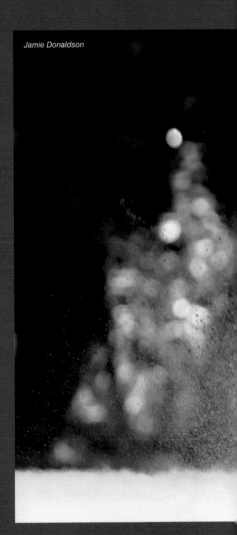
Jamie Donaldson

Mikael Lundberg (right), receives the trophy from Gennady Gennadievitch Terebkov, Head of PR of INTECO

Jamie Moul

Hole	Par	Yards	Metres
1	4	331	303
2	5	525	480
3	4	475	434
4	3	177	162
5	5	576	527
6	4	413	378
7	4	418	382
8	3	197	180
9	4	421	385
OUT	**36**	**3533**	**3231**
10	4	436	399
11	3	175	160
12	4	406	371
13	4	427	390
14	4	399	365
15	5	561	513
16	3	193	177
17	5	548	501
18	4	476	435
IN	**36**	**3621**	**3311**
TOTAL	**72**	**7154**	**6542**

i Mikael Lundberg claimed his second European Tour International Schedule title in the Inteco Russian Open Golf Championship 2008. The Swede won his first European title in the same event in 2005 and became the tenth player in European Tour history to win the same event for their first two victories.

Le Meridien Moscow Country Club

Final Results

Pos	Name		Rd1	Rd2	Rd3	Rd4	Total		€	£
1	Mikael LUNDBERG	SWE	67	64	68	68	267	-21	210,237.23	166,790.09
2	José Manuel LARA	ESP	67	68	70	64	269	-19	140,158.16	111,193.39
3	Benn BARHAM	ENG	69	68	65	68	270	-18	78,965.90	62,646.98
4	Jan-Are LARSEN	NOR	68	65	72	66	271	-17	63,071.80	50,037.53
5	David DRYSDALE	SCO	68	71	69	64	272	-16	53,484.89	42,431.82
6	Darren FICHARDT	RSA	66	71	66	70	273	-15	37,843.08	30,022.52
	Jamie MOUL	ENG	68	68	64	73	273	-15	37,843.08	30,022.52
	Lloyd SALTMAN	SCO	69	70	66	68	273	-15	37,843.08	30,022.52
9	Robert ROCK	ENG	68	64	71	71	274	-14	25,565.10	20,281.88
	Soren JUUL	DEN	69	68	69	68	274	-14	25,565.10	20,281.88
	Sam LITTLE	ENG	70	69	70	65	274	-14	25,565.10	20,281.88
12	Michiel BOTHMA	RSA	68	68	66	73	275	-13	19,527.03	15,491.62
	Gareth PADDISON	NZL	68	71	69	67	275	-13	19,527.03	15,491.62
	Robert-Jan DERKSEN	NED	68	73	68	66	275	-13	19,527.03	15,491.62
	Danny WILLETT	ENG	69	66	69	71	275	-13	19,527.03	15,491.62
	Alessandro TADINI	ITA	70	68	68	69	275	-13	19,527.03	15,491.62
17	Carl SUNESON	ESP	67	68	71	70	276	-12	15,494.64	12,292.55
	Paul WARING	ENG	69	72	69	66	276	-12	15,494.64	12,292.55
	Lee SLATTERY	ENG	70	67	68	71	276	-12	15,494.64	12,292.55
	Jamie DONALDSON	WAL	70	68	72	66	276	-12	15,494.64	12,292.55
	Craig LEE	SCO	71	67	69	69	276	-12	15,494.64	12,292.55
	Jean-François LUCQUIN	FRA	73	64	71	68	276	-12	15,494.64	12,292.55
23	Shiv KAPUR	IND	67	70	69	71	277	-11	13,118.93	10,407.81
	Per-Ulrik JOHANSSON	SWE	69	68	71	69	277	-11	13,118.93	10,407.81
	Marcel SIEM	GER	69	71	69	68	277	-11	13,118.93	10,407.81
	Stephen GALLACHER	SCO	69	72	66	70	277	-11	13,118.93	10,407.81
	Markus BRIER	AUT	71	69	70	67	277	-11	13,118.93	10,407.81
28	Fredrik ANDERSSON HED	SWE	68	69	72	69	278	-10	11,794.43	9,357.02
	Patrik SJÖLAND	SWE	71	67	70	70	278	-10	11,794.43	9,357.02
30	Jarmo SANDELIN	SWE	67	64	72	76	279	-9	9,713.06	7,705.78
	François DELAMONTAGNE	FRA	67	67	74	71	279	-9	9,713.06	7,705.78
	Luis CLAVERIE	ESP	67	68	73	71	279	-9	9,713.06	7,705.78
	Andrew MARSHALL	ENG	67	69	72	71	279	-9	9,713.06	7,705.78
	Garry HOUSTON	WAL	67	71	71	70	279	-9	9,713.06	7,705.78
	Robert DINWIDDIE	ENG	70	67	72	70	279	-9	9,713.06	7,705.78
	Henrik NYSTRÖM	SWE	70	70	69	70	279	-9	9,713.06	7,705.78
	James KAMTE	RSA	71	69	68	71	279	-9	9,713.06	7,705.78
	Tom WHITEHOUSE	ENG	72	70	71	66	279	-9	9,713.06	7,705.78
	David HIGGINS	IRL	72	70	68	69	279	-9	9,713.06	7,705.78
40	Ignacio SANCHEZ-PALENCIA	ESP	68	66	73	73	280	-8	7,947.05	6,304.73
	Mark FOSTER	ENG	71	68	69	72	280	-8	7,947.05	6,304.73
	Christian NILSSON	SWE	72	67	70	71	280	-8	7,947.05	6,304.73
43	David CARTER	ENG	65	73	76	67	281	-7	6,685.61	5,303.98
	Richard BLAND	ENG	69	69	71	72	281	-7	6,685.61	5,303.98
	Adilson DA SILVA	BRA	69	73	68	71	281	-7	6,685.61	5,303.98
	Philip GOLDING	ENG	70	72	70	69	281	-7	6,685.61	5,303.98
	Rafa ECHENIQUE	ARG	72	69	68	72	281	-7	6,685.61	5,303.98
	Steve ALKER	NZL	73	67	71	70	281	-7	6,685.61	5,303.98
	Rob HARRIS	ENG	73	69	70	69	281	-7	6,685.61	5,303.98
	Steven UZZELL (AM)	ENG	74	68	68	71	281	-7		
51	Ben MASON	ENG	68	69	72	73	282	-6	5,424.17	4,303.23
	Guido VAN DER VALK	NED	70	72	65	75	282	-6	5,424.17	4,303.23
	Mads VIBE-HASTRUP	DEN	74	68	69	71	282	-6	5,424.17	4,303.23
54	Joakim BÄCKSTRÖM	SWE	65	73	76	69	283	-5	4,415.03	3,502.63
	Kyron SULLIVAN	WAL	71	71	70	71	283	-5	4,415.03	3,502.63
	Steven O'HARA	SCO	71	71	71	70	283	-5	4,415.03	3,502.63
	Stuart MANLEY	WAL	72	68	72	71	283	-5	4,415.03	3,502.63
	Maarten LAFEBER	NED	72	70	67	74	283	-5	4,415.03	3,502.63
59	Juan ABBATE	ARG	68	71	75	70	284	-4	3,595.09	2,852.14
	Peter WHITEFORD	SCO	68	74	72	70	284	-4	3,595.09	2,852.14
	Magnus A CARLSSON	SWE	70	70	70	74	284	-4	3,595.09	2,852.14
	Gary ORR	SCO	71	67	75	71	284	-4	3,595.09	2,852.14
63	Christopher HANELL	SWE	71	71	71	72	285	-3	3,279.73	2,601.95
64	Gary MURPHY	IRL	69	72	73	72	286	-2	3,090.52	2,451.84
	Sébastien DELAGRANGE	FRA	71	71	69	75	286	-2	3,090.52	2,451.84
66	Johan SKÖLD	SWE	68	72	73	74	287	-1	2,838.23	2,251.69
	André BOSSERT	SUI	70	68	76	73	287	-1	2,838.23	2,251.69
68	Roope KAKKO	FIN	65	73	72	78	288	0	2,649.02	2,101.58
69	Phil WORTHINGTON	ENG	70	71	72	76	289	1	2,522.87	2,001.50
70	Peter BAKER	ENG	71	71	72	77	291	3	2,396.73	1,901.43
71	Fredrik HENGE	SWE	71	71	79	292	4	2,027.71	1,608.67
	Gareth DAVIES	ENG	68	74	77	73	292	4	2,027.71	1,608.67
	Gonzalo FDEZ-CASTAÑO	ESP	74	68	75	75	292	4	2,027.71	1,608.67

Total Prize Fund

€1,265,217 £1,003,750

Constant Threat

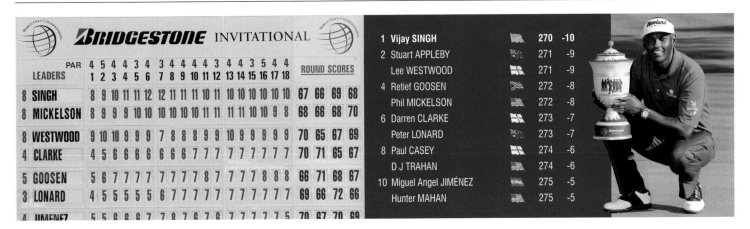

BRIDGESTONE INVITATIONAL

LEADERS	PAR	4	5	4	4	3	3	4	4	4	3	4	4	3	5	4	4	ROUND SCORES			
		1	2	3	4	5	6	7	8	9	10	11	12	13	14	15	16	17	18		
8 SINGH		8	9	10	11	11	12	12	11	11	11	10	11	10	10	10	10	10	10	67	66	69	68
8 MICKELSON		8	9	9	9	10	10	10	10	10	10	11	11	11	11	10	10	9	8	68	66	68	70
8 WESTWOOD		9	10	10	9	9	9	7	8	8	9	9	10	9	9	9	9	9	9	70	65	67	69
4 CLARKE		4	5	6	6	6	6	6	6	7	7	7	7	7	7	7	7	7	7	70	71	65	67
5 GOOSEN		5	6	7	7	7	7	7	7	7	7	8	7	7	7	7	8	8	8	66	71	68	67
3 LONARD		4	5	5	5	5	5	6	7	7	7	7	7	7	7	7	7	7	7	69	66	72	66
4 JIMENEZ		5	5	6	6	6	7	8	7	6	7	8	7	7	7	7	5			70	67	70	69

1	Vijay SINGH		270	-10
2	Stuart APPLEBY		271	-9
	Lee WESTWOOD		271	-9
4	Retief GOOSEN		272	-8
	Phil MICKELSON		272	-8
6	Darren CLARKE		273	-7
	Peter LONARD		273	-7
8	Paul CASEY		274	-6
	D J TRAHAN		274	-6
10	Miguel Angel JIMÉNEZ		275	-5
	Hunter MAHAN		275	-5

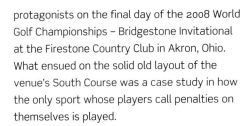

For all the rapid change professional golf has undergone in the last decade – huge prize fund increases, a 12 month season, longer courses, continuing distance gains and better conditioned athletes – it still remains the most civilised sport on the planet.

Retief Goosen

Paul Casey

Almost without exception, the game's players and fans are better behaved than their counterparts in every other sport and all aim to keep it that way. This is a good thing. Covering golf should not include checking the following morning's court rota, and it rarely does.

No one is suggesting, mind you, that we order 156 halos to be distributed to touring professionals on the first tee by officials of the various Tours and governing bodies. Some of the lads, after all, have been known to drop the odd salty-language bomb now and again. Plus, there is the occasional disagreement out there among golfers, including a couple of highly ranked players who are essentially the same height but rarely see eye-to-eye.

As it happens, these two stars – Phil Mickelson and Vijay Singh – were two of the three protagonists on the final day of the 2008 World Golf Championships – Bridgestone Invitational at the Firestone Country Club in Akron, Ohio. What ensued on the solid old layout of the venue's South Course was a case study in how the only sport whose players call penalties on themselves is played.

Competition, conflict and resolution all are part of golf's compelling intrigue. Because 45 year old Singh and Mickelson, seven years his junior, have a history – having had a heated argument over the length of Mickelson's golf spikes in the sanctuary of the Champions' Locker Room at Augusta National a few years back – Sunday at the WGC-Bridgestone Invitational had that little extra dramatic tension.

Truth be told, the duo have settled most of their differences. Indeed they are actually both silent investors in a swing aid currently being marketed on The Golf Channel in the United States. Once inside the ropes, however, they are the golfing version of Chelsea versus Manchester United. When paired on Saturday in Akron, their first tee greeting was as warm as a defense attorney and prosecutor before a day in court; a handshake, a cursory nod, a thin smile and let's get it on.

That they did, battling to a draw with each man finishing at eight under par 202. The only thing that kept them from closing the deal in the same pairing on Sunday was Lee Westwood, who finished on the same total with a sparkling 67, thereby making it into the final group with Singh to provide both subplot and buffer between the two old adversaries.

The large galleries that swarmed across the South Course for the final day were courteous,

knowledgeable, deferential and loud, really loud. They screamed for Mickelson, yelled for Singh and cheered for Westwood. All this despite the absence of Tiger Woods, the defending champion and winner of the past three WGC - Bridgestone Invitational titles. The World Number One was at home in Orlando having just commenced some light stationary bike work as he embarked on the long road to recovery from knee surgery. He may have even sneaked a peek at the television to watch two of his main rivals have a go at one another.

Had he done so he would have seen Singh on song, winning for the first time in 17 months by shooting 68, a score helped by holing crucial putts down the stretch. He would have also seen Mickelson – who stood on the 15th tee with a one stroke lead – bogey three of the final four holes only to proclaim he had "played great." To be fair to the left hander, he had, until driving into trouble at both the 17th and 18th holes.

In fact, it was Singh who played well, if not great. His swing changes are complete, and while watching the return of his syrupy

tempo and flowing action was a treat for the appreciative galleries, it must have caused consternation among some fellow competitors who had written him off.

Instead, back from the dead, Singh stood on the 18th green with a four and a half footer to win. The stroke may not have been totally authoritative, but it was effective. Down went the ball, ending a year-long battle with his putting during which he switched back and forth between a conventional length putter to a belly putter and back again. The European Tour Honorary Member's 32nd victory on the US PGA Tour gave him the most of anyone in history whose passport was not issued by the United States.

It also helped put the word 'world' into the final World Golf Championship of the year and served notice that, for all the sport's changes, Singh remains a constant threat.

Larry Dorman
New York Times

Vijay Singh (left), is congratulated by Richard Hills, European Ryder Cup Director

Ian Poulter

Lee Westwood

Miguel Angel Jiménez

Hole	Par	Yards	Metres
1	4	399	365
2	5	526	481
3	4	442	404
4	4	471	431
5	3	200	183
6	4	469	429
7	3	219	200
8	4	482	441
9	4	494	452
OUT	35	3702	3386
10	4	410	375
11	4	418	382
12	3	180	165
13	4	471	431
14	4	467	427
15	3	221	202
16	5	667	610
17	4	400	366
18	4	464	424
IN	35	3698	3382
TOTAL	70	7400	6768

Vijay Singh made history by becoming the oldest winner of a WGC event, aged 45 and 163 days. The Fijian beat the previous record of David Toms, who was 38 and 54 days when he claimed the 2005 WGC – Accenture Match Play. Singh also became the oldest winner on The European Tour International Schedule since Mark O'Meara at the 2004 Dubai Desert Classic, who was 47 and 54 days. The oldest winner in Tour history still remains Ireland's Des Smyth who was 48 and 34 days when he captured the 2001 Madeira Island Open.

Firestone Country Club
(South Course)
Final Results

Pos	Name		Rd1	Rd2	Rd3	Rd4	Total		€	£
1	Vijay SINGH	FIJ	67	66	69	68	270	-10	860,584.24	679,074.43
2	Lee WESTWOOD	ENG	70	65	67	69	271	-9	404,793.33	319,416.50
	Stuart APPLEBY	AUS	70	66	67	68	271	-9	404,793.33	319,416.50
4	Retief GOOSEN	RSA	66	71	68	67	272	-8	197,615.64	155,935.61
	Phil MICKELSON	USA	68	66	68	70	272	-8	197,615.64	155,935.61
6	Peter LONARD	AUS	69	66	72	66	273	-7	140,243.36	110,663.98
	Darren CLARKE	NIR	70	71	65	67	273	-7	140,243.36	110,663.98
8	D J TRAHAN	USA	69	67	70	68	274	-6	103,588.84	81,740.44
	Paul CASEY	ENG	70	71	68	65	274	-6	103,588.84	81,740.44
10	Miguel Angel JIMÉNEZ	ESP	70	66	70	69	275	-5	84,783.48	66,901.41
	Hunter MAHAN	USA	71	66	70	68	275	-5	84,783.48	66,901.41
12	Sean O'HAIR	USA	68	67	73	68	276	-4	70,759.15	55,835.01
	Chris DIMARCO	USA	68	70	68	70	276	-4	70,759.15	55,835.01
14	Daniel CHOPRA	SWE	67	74	66	70	277	-3	60,878.37	48,038.23
	Chad CAMPBELL	USA	68	71	68	70	277	-3	60,878.37	48,038.23
16	Zach JOHNSON	USA	67	68	72	71	278	-2	52,670.94	41,561.87
	Ian POULTER	ENG	70	68	69	71	278	-2	52,670.94	41,561.87
	K J CHOI	KOR	73	67	70	68	278	-2	52,670.94	41,561.87
	Henrik STENSON	SWE	73	70	68	67	278	-2	52,670.94	41,561.87
20	Tim CLARK	RSA	67	71	71	70	279	-1	45,260.36	35,714.28
	Justin LEONARD	USA	68	70	70	71	279	-1	45,260.36	35,714.28
	Padraig HARRINGTON	IRL	69	75	68	67	279	-1	45,260.36	35,714.28
	Robert KARLSSON	SWE	71	67	71	70	279	-1	45,260.36	35,714.28
	Scott VERPLANK	USA	71	70	70	68	279	-1	45,260.36	35,714.28
	Robert ALLENBY	AUS	71	70	70	68	279	-1	45,260.36	35,714.28
	Steve LOWERY	USA	75	67	70	67	279	-1	45,260.36	35,714.28
27	Jim FURYK	USA	68	69	71	72	280	0	38,248.19	30,181.09
	Charles HOWELL III	USA	68	70	72	70	280	0	38,248.19	30,181.09
	Rory SABBATINI	RSA	69	67	70	74	280	0	38,248.19	30,181.09
	Ernie ELS	RSA	69	74	69	68	280	0	38,248.19	30,181.09
	Paul MCGINLEY	IRL	70	67	72	71	280	0	38,248.19	30,181.09
	Nick O'HERN	AUS	70	68	71	71	280	0	38,248.19	30,181.09
	Oliver WILSON	ENG	71	69	72	68	280	0	38,248.19	30,181.09
	Justin ROSE	ENG	71	70	68	71	280	0	38,248.19	30,181.09
	Vaughn TAYLOR	USA	72	67	69	72	280	0	38,248.19	30,181.09
36	J B HOLMES	USA	69	68	72	72	281	1	33,148.43	26,156.94
	Sergio GARCIA	ESP	69	72	68	72	281	1	33,148.43	26,156.94
	Brendan JONES	AUS	69	73	69	70	281	1	33,148.43	26,156.94
	Richard FINCH	ENG	69	75	70	67	281	1	33,148.43	26,156.94
	Anthony KIM	USA	71	72	70	68	281	1	33,148.43	26,156.94
	Angel CABRERA	ARG	72	73	68	68	281	1	33,148.43	26,156.94
	Trevor IMMELMAN	RSA	75	64	68	74	281	1	33,148.43	26,156.94
43	Stewart CINK	USA	68	68	74	72	282	2	29,706.09	23,440.64
	Steve STRICKER	USA	68	69	75	70	282	2	29,706.09	23,440.64
	Brandt SNEDEKER	USA	68	76	69	69	282	2	29,706.09	23,440.64
	Richard GREEN	AUS	72	73	70	67	282	2	29,706.09	23,440.64
	Aaron BADDELEY	AUS	79	69	66	68	282	2	29,706.09	23,440.64
48	Stephen AMES	CAN	69	71	71	72	283	3	28,208.04	22,258.55
	Steve FLESCH	USA	70	70	73	70	283	3	28,208.04	22,258.55
	David TOMS	USA	72	72	70	69	283	3	28,208.04	22,258.55
	Hidemasa HOSHINO	JPN	75	73	65	70	283	3	28,208.04	22,258.55
52	Rocco MEDIATE	USA	68	73	71	72	284	4	26,933.10	21,252.51
	Chez REAVIE	USA	68	74	70	72	284	4	26,933.10	21,252.51
	Woody AUSTIN	USA	71	70	72	71	284	4	26,933.10	21,252.51
	Niclas FASTH	SWE	71	71	72	70	284	4	26,933.10	21,252.51
56	Rodney PAMPLING	AUS	69	71	75	70	285	5	25,498.79	20,120.72
	Ross FISHER	ENG	69	73	70	73	285	5	25,498.79	20,120.72
	Adam SCOTT	AUS	69	76	72	68	285	5	25,498.79	20,120.72
	Graeme MCDOWELL	NIR	70	71	73	71	285	5	25,498.79	20,120.72
	Fredrik JACOBSON	SWE	71	71	70	73	285	5	25,498.79	20,120.72
61	Steve WEBSTER	ENG	68	72	72	74	286	6	24,383.22	19,240.44
	Nick DOUGHERTY	ENG	72	76	69	69	286	6	24,383.22	19,240.44
63	Scott STRANGE	AUS	68	74	73	72	287	7	23,586.38	18,611.67
	Lucas GLOVER	USA	70	75	72	70	287	7	23,586.38	18,611.67
	Andres ROMERO	ARG	73	71	73	70	287	7	23,586.38	18,611.67
66	Boo WEEKLEY	USA	72	73	71	72	288	8	22,789.55	17,982.90
	Kenny PERRY	USA	74	69	73	72	288	8	22,789.55	17,982.90
68	Prayad MARKSAENG	THA	67	73	73	76	289	9	21,992.71	17,354.12
	Geoff OGILVY	AUS	71	67	79	72	289	9	21,992.71	17,354.12
	Martin KAYMER	GER	72	79	68	70	289	9	21,992.71	17,354.12
71	Johnson WAGNER	USA	70	74	75	71	290	10	21,195.87	16,725.35
	Brett RUMFORD	AUS	75	70	76	69	290	10	21,195.87	16,725.35
73	J J HENRY	USA	69	73	73	77	292	12	20,717.77	16,348.09
	David HOWELL	ENG	70	75	70	77	292	12	20,717.77	16,348.09
	Søren HANSEN	DEN	75	73	70	74	292	12	20,717.77	16,348.09
76	Pablo LARRAZABAL	ESP	72	75	71	76	294	14	20,399.03	16,096.58
77	Colin MONTGOMERIE	SCO	72	71	76	76	295	15	20,239.67	15,970.82
78	James KINGSTON	RSA	73	72	71	80	296	16	20,080.30	15,845.07
79	Craig PARRY	AUS	70	75	75	77	297	17	19,920.93	15,719.32
80	Mark BROWN	NZL	80	75	76	70	301	21	19,761.56	15,593.56

Total Prize Fund
€5,022,306 £3,963,028

The Eyes
Have It

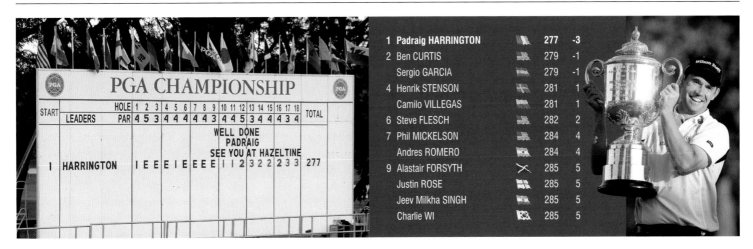

PGA CHAMPIONSHIP

START	HOLE	1	2	3	4	5	6	7	8	9	10	11	12	13	14	15	16	17	18	TOTAL
LEADERS	PAR	4	5	3	4	4	4	4	4	3	4	4	5	3	4	4	4	3	4	
								WELL DONE												
								PADRAIG												
								SEE YOU AT HAZELTINE												
I HARRINGTON		I	E	E	I	E	E	E	E	I	I	2	3	2	2	2	3	3		277

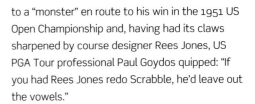

1	**Padraig HARRINGTON**		277	-3
2	Ben CURTIS		279	-1
	Sergio GARCIA		279	-1
4	Henrik STENSON		281	1
	Camilo VILLEGAS		281	1
6	Steve FLESCH		282	2
7	Phil MICKELSON		284	4
	Andres ROMERO		284	4
9	Alastair FORSYTH		285	5
	Justin ROSE		285	5
	Jeev Milkha SINGH		285	5
	Charlie WI		285	5

L ife is a journey, not a destination. So, when Padraig Harrington turned up at Oakland Hills Country Club in the township of Bloomfield in the northern suburbs of Detroit for the 90th US PGA Championship there was a sense, before a shot had been struck, that this was to be another step on a career path that, increasingly, was being measured by his achievements in the Major arena.

Alastair Forsyth

Sergio Garcia

Harrington does not do baggage but, if he had cared to rummage, the stockpile of reminders of past failings of European players in this particular Championship were not hard to uncover. No European player in generations – not since the Scot, Tommy Armour, at Fresh Meadows in 1930 – had won the imposing Wanamaker Trophy, and no European player in history had managed to win back-to-back Majors since Armour went on to win The Open Championship at Carnoustie the following year; a feat the Irishman was attempting to match having retained the Claret Jug at Royal Birkdale just three weeks previously.

What is more, the course had established a reputation that, if you listened to players in the locker room or on the range, had a right to be in a Stephen King novel. Ben Hogan had likened it

to a "monster" en route to his win in the 1951 US Open Championship and, having had its claws sharpened by course designer Rees Jones, US PGA Tour professional Paul Goydos quipped: "If you had Rees Jones redo Scrabble, he'd leave out the vowels."

Golf is not a board game however, it is tougher than that; but someone will always find an answer to the examination and there was a genuine gut feeling among the European players in Michigan that this was their time. After all, no fewer than eight of them retained fond memories of the course from The 2004 Ryder Cup where Europe had won by 18 ½ points to 9 ½, forging a record win on American soil in the process. Fittingly, as it transpired, Sergio Garcia and Harrington were among those who had played key roles that week. They would do so again.

Yet, Thursday's opening round – which saw European Tour Members Robert Karlsson of Sweden and India's Jeev Milkha Singh shoot two under par 68s to share the lead – was as much about survival as contending as the course bared its teeth, playing to an average of 74. 9 – almost five shots above its par.

By Friday evening, with big hitting American J B Holmes now the pacesetter, Harrington sounded like a beaten man. Fatigue had suddenly hit the Irishman and his army golf of the last few holes – spraying shots left, right, left, right – saw him sign for a 74 and a five over par total of 145.

When he returned to his rented house that evening, he stood six shots off the pace and felt exhausted. But anyone who has rejoiced in both his Open Championship successes knew

that throwing in the towel or raising the white flag were simply not options. He spent the time at base sleeping, recharging his batteries, and drinking fluids in order to rehydrate his body.

Then, thankfully, the weather gods contrived to provide additional assistance. On the Saturday, an ominous front closed in on Detroit and Harrington, who had completed nine holes of his third round – critically birdieing the short ninth – was allowed the rest of the day off as further play was impossible from mid-afternoon. Equally crucial, none of the leaders had managed to start their third rounds meaning they would have to play 36 holes on the Sunday.

By the time Harrington answered an alarm call at four on Sunday morning and completed his third round, he had invigorated both himself and his challenge. He was now a contender thanks to a back nine which featured four birdies on his way to a 66, which had moved him into a share of fourth place.

Leader Ben Curtis, J B Holmes and Henrik Stenson made up the final grouping of the day while Harrington teamed up once again with Garcia, the European duo having Korean Charlie Wi for company in the penultimate three ball.

What unfolded in the final round could not be scripted. Curtis' grip on affairs loosened around the turn and, like two gunslingers in the Wild West, Harrington and Garcia took aim at the flagsticks with unnerving precision; one in search of back-to-back Majors with the other attempting to claim his first. It was a nerve-wracking, rollercoaster ride that ultimately saw Harrington single putt the last three greens to finish with his second consecutive weekend 66 for 277 and a two stroke winning margin.

The following morning, dressed casually in tee shirt and shorts, Harrington sat on a poolside deck chair in his rented house with the Wanamaker Trophy and the Claret Jug on a table in front of him. The killer eyes that had possessed him down the final holes the previous afternoon had gone, replaced by ones that danced with sheer delight as, finally, his achievement started to sink in.

"You know," he said, referring to the obsessive desire for glory that accompanies him nowadays down the last nine holes in the final round of a Major Championship; "When I get those eyes, I do things."

Scary. Just like a Stephen King novel indeed; but with a much happier ending.

Philip Reid
The Irish Times

Andres Romero

Padraig Harrington (right), receives the trophy from Brian Whitcomb, President of the PGA of America

Henrik Stenson

Justin Rose

Hole	Par	Yards	Metres
1	4	435	398
2	5	529	484
3	3	198	181
4	4	446	408
5	4	490	448
6	4	387	354
7	4	449	411
8	4	491	449
9	3	257	235
OUT	35	3682	3368
10	4	462	422
11	4	423	387
12	5	593	542
13	3	191	175
14	4	501	458
15	4	401	367
16	4	406	371
17	3	238	218
18	4	498	455
IN	35	3713	3395
TOTAL	70	7395	6763

By winning consecutive Major Championships, Padraig Harrington became the first European golfer since Tommy Armour (1930 US PGA Championship and 1931 Open Championship) to win back-to-back Majors. He also became the 21st different player to win successive Major titles. His final 36 holes of 132 equalled the lowest by the winner in the history of the US PGA Championship, set by Steve Elkington (1995) and Davis Love III (1997).

Oakland Hills Country Club
(South Course)
Final Results

Pos	Name		Rd1	Rd2	Rd3	Rd4	Total		€	£
1	Padraig HARRINGTON	IRL	71	74	66	66	277	-3	867,219.26	683,786.65
2	Sergio GARCIA	ESP	69	73	69	68	279	-1	423,973.86	334,295.70
	Ben CURTIS	USA	73	67	68	71	279	-1	423,973.86	334,295.70
4	Henrik STENSON	SWE	71	70	68	72	281	1	211,986.93	167,147.85
	Camilo VILLEGAS	COL	74	72	67	68	281	1	211,986.93	167,147.85
6	Steve FLESCH	USA	73	70	70	69	282	2	173,443.85	136,757.33
7	Andres ROMERO	ARG	69	78	65	72	284	4	148,551.45	117,130.12
	Phil MICKELSON	USA	70	73	71	70	284	4	148,551.45	117,130.12
9	Jeev Milkha SINGH	IND	68	74	70	73	285	5	113,525.42	89,512.73
	Charlie WI	KOR	70	70	71	74	285	5	113,525.42	89,512.73
	Justin ROSE	ENG	73	67	74	71	285	5	113,525.42	89,512.73
	Alastair FORSYTH	SCO	73	72	70	70	285	5	113,525.42	89,512.73
13	Ken DUKE	USA	69	73	73	71	286	6	88,167.29	69,518.31
	Aaron BADDELEY	AUS	71	71	71	73	286	6	88,167.29	69,518.31
15	David TOMS	USA	72	69	72	74	287	7	68,773.70	54,226.81
	Paul CASEY	ENG	72	74	72	69	287	7	68,773.70	54,226.81
	Graeme MCDOWELL	NIR	74	72	68	73	287	7	68,773.70	54,226.81
	Prayad MARKSAENG	THA	76	70	68	73	287	7	68,773.70	54,226.81
	Stuart APPLEBY	AUS	76	70	69	72	287	7	68,773.70	54,226.81
20	Robert KARLSSON	SWE	68	77	71	72	288	8	50,684.15	39,963.53
	Angel CABRERA	ARG	70	72	72	74	288	8	50,684.15	39,963.53
	J Brian GAY	USA	70	74	72	72	288	8	50,684.15	39,963.53
	Boo WEEKLEY	USA	72	71	79	66	288	8	50,684.15	39,963.53
24	Brandt SNEDEKER	USA	71	71	74	73	289	9	36,615.92	28,870.99
	Nicholas THOMPSON	USA	71	72	73	73	289	9	36,615.92	28,870.99
	Retief GOOSEN	RSA	72	74	69	74	289	9	36,615.92	28,870.99
	Fredrik JACOBSON	SWE	75	71	70	73	289	9	36,615.92	28,870.99
	Mark BROWN	NZL	77	69	74	69	289	9	36,615.92	28,870.99
29	J B HOLMES	USA	71	68	70	81	290	10	30,545.39	24,084.49
	Jim FURYK	USA	71	77	70	72	290	10	30,545.39	24,084.49
31	Sean O'HAIR	USA	69	73	76	73	291	11	24,940.58	19,665.20
	Ernie ELS	RSA	71	75	70	75	291	11	24,940.58	19,665.20
	D J TRAHAN	USA	72	71	76	72	291	11	24,940.58	19,665.20
	Geoff OGILVY	AUS	73	74	74	70	291	11	24,940.58	19,665.20
	Paul GOYDOS	USA	74	69	73	75	291	11	24,940.58	19,665.20
	Ian POULTER	ENG	74	71	73	73	291	11	24,940.58	19,665.20
	Chris DIMARCO	USA	75	72	72	72	291	11	24,940.58	19,665.20
	Robert ALLENBY	AUS	76	72	72	71	291	11	24,940.58	19,665.20
39	Steve ELKINGTON	AUS	71	73	73	75	292	12	19,400.02	15,296.56
	Steve STRICKER	USA	71	75	77	69	292	12	19,400.02	15,296.56
	Rory SABBATINI	RSA	72	73	73	74	292	12	19,400.02	15,296.56
42	Briny BAIRD	USA	71	72	73	77	293	13	15,738.42	12,409.46
	Michael CAMPBELL	NZL	73	71	75	74	293	13	15,738.42	12,409.46
	Mike WEIR	CAN	73	75	71	74	293	13	15,738.42	12,409.46
	Tom LEHMAN	USA	74	70	75	74	293	13	15,738.42	12,409.46
	John SENDEN	AUS	76	72	72	73	293	13	15,738.42	12,409.46
47	Billy MAYFAIR	USA	69	78	75	72	294	14	11,607.89	9,152.61
	Michael ALLEN	USA	70	75	71	78	294	14	11,607.89	9,152.61
	Carl PETTERSSON	SWE	71	74	76	73	294	14	11,607.89	9,152.61
	Charles HOWELL III	USA	72	76	77	69	294	14	11,607.89	9,152.61
	Dean WILSON	USA	73	73	77	71	294	14	11,607.89	9,152.61
52	Peter HANSON	SWE	71	73	75	76	295	15	10,438.75	8,230.77
	John MERRICK	USA	73	75	70	77	295	15	10,438.75	8,230.77
	Charl SCHWARTZEL	RSA	77	70	73	75	295	15	10,438.75	8,230.77
55	Anthony KIM	USA	70	75	74	77	296	16	10,117.56	7,977.51
	James KINGSTON	RSA	72	76	74	74	296	16	10,117.56	7,977.51
	Tim CLARK	RSA	76	72	73	75	296	16	10,117.56	7,977.51
58	Pat PEREZ	USA	73	73	79	72	297	17	9,876.66	7,787.57
	Justin LEONARD	USA	74	71	72	80	297	17	9,876.66	7,787.57
60	John MALLINGER	USA	72	75	77	74	298	18	9,635.77	7,597.63
	Steve MARINO	USA	73	74	75	76	298	18	9,635.77	7,597.63
	Chez REAVIE	USA	78	70	78	72	298	18	9,635.77	7,597.63
63	Mark CALCAVECCHIA	USA	71	76	76	76	299	19	9,314.58	7,344.38
	Paul AZINGER	USA	72	76	76	75	299	19	9,314.58	7,344.38
	Niclas FASTH	SWE	73	73	75	78	299	19	9,314.58	7,344.38
	Corey PAVIN	USA	75	73	73	78	299	19	9,314.58	7,344.38
	Kevin SUTHERLAND	USA	76	71	77	75	299	19	9,314.58	7,344.38
68	Peter LONARD	AUS	74	74	74	78	300	20	9,089.74	7,167.10
	Hiroyuki FUJITA	JPN	77	70	76	77	300	20	9,089.74	7,167.10
70	Bubba WATSON	USA	75	73	77	76	301	21	8,993.38	7,091.12
71	Richard GREEN	AUS	71	77	79	76	303	23	8,929.15	7,040.47
72	Rocco MEDIATE	USA	73	74	72	85	304	24	8,864.91	6,989.82
73	Louis OOSTHUIZEN	RSA	76	72	81	77	306	26	8,800.67	6,939.17

Total Prize Fund
€4,767,714 £3,759,256

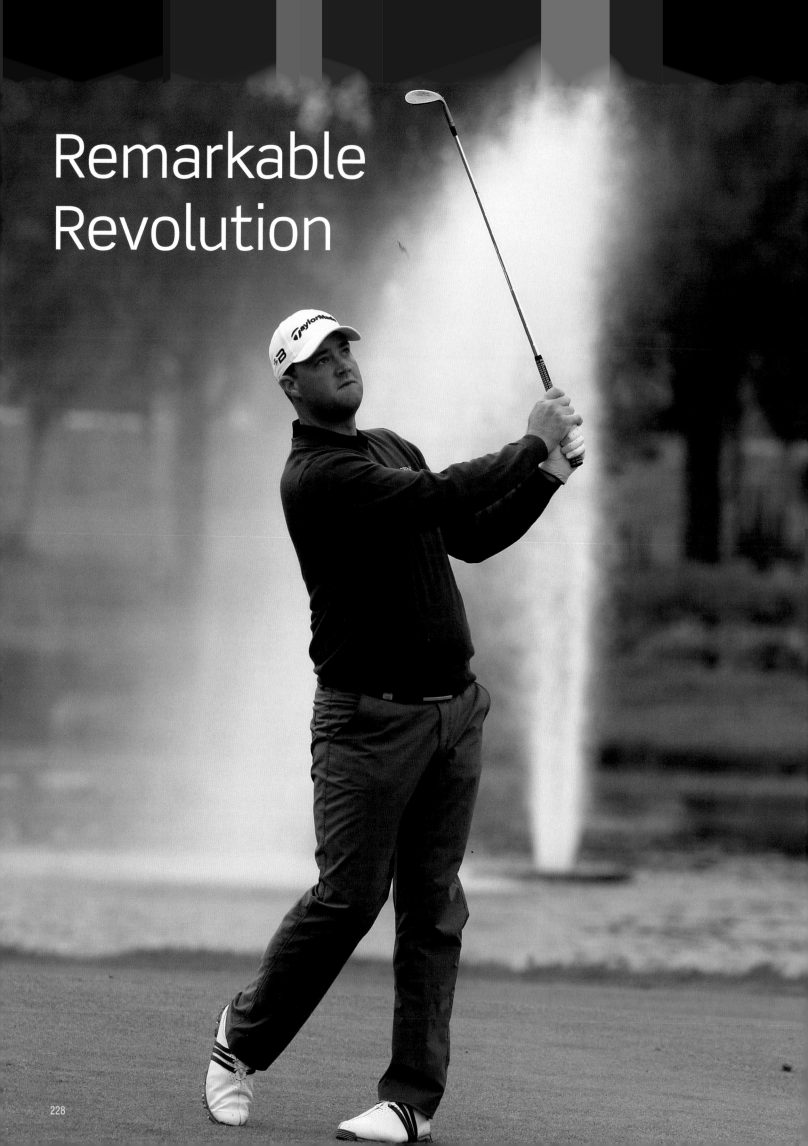

Remarkable
Revolution

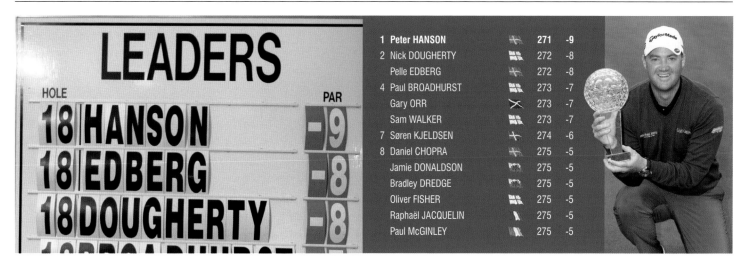

1	Peter HANSON		271	-9
2	Nick DOUGHERTY		272	-8
	Pelle EDBERG		272	-8
4	Paul BROADHURST		273	-7
	Gary ORR		273	-7
	Sam WALKER		273	-7
7	Søren KJELDSEN		274	-6
8	Daniel CHOPRA		275	-5
	Jamie DONALDSON		275	-5
	Bradley DREDGE		275	-5
	Oliver FISHER		275	-5
	Raphaël JACQUELIN		275	-5
	Paul McGINLEY		275	-5

When the stylish Peter Hanson won the SAS Masters at Arlandastad Golf – an unpretentious but thoroughly enjoyable and excellent test – the softly spoken Swede ended a ten year period during which no home player had triumphed in what is, in effect, the Swedish Open.

Nick Dougherty

Daniel Chopra

It is a surprising statistic because the professional golfing revolution in the country has been nothing short of remarkable. Since 1986 a total of 24 Swedish golfers have amassed no fewer than 76 victories on The European Tour International Schedule but only Joakim Haeggman and Jesper Parnevik (twice) – before Hanson – had won their national title.

While Hanson was battling to a well deserved victory through the wind and rain on a cold August afternoon, the man whose name is inexorably linked to golf in Sweden was quietly looking after his stall in the tented village. Sven Tumba is as popular in his country as Sir Henry Cooper is in Britain, and is widely acknowledged as the modern day founder of the incredible Swedish golfing success story.

Back in the early 1970's all-rounder Tumba, a former Olympic ice hockey star who played soccer for Sweden, and who was also fairly impressive on water skis, fell in love with golf – and wanted everyone to enjoy it with him. He was a convincing ambassador. He had a way about him. His enthusiasm rubbed off on everyone and when he started inviting Jack Nicklaus, Lee Trevino and other world stars to Sweden, the public knew he was serious.

He built his own golf course at Ullna, opened the first indoor range in a huge tent and made the country believe that Sweden had the potential to produce world golfing stars. An added bonus was the fact that, for a nation obsessed with fitness and conditioning, it was a healthy game to play too.

It took time but that was to be expected. However, Swedes are naturally methodical and patient – qualities ideally suited to the sport. The dawn of Swedish professional golf on the international stage began modestly enough when Ove Sellberg won the Epson Grand Prix at St Pierre in 1986, before Mats Lanner did the same a year later. From there, however, the bandwagon rolled on.

In 1993 Joakim Haeggman became the first Swedish golfer to play in The Ryder Cup and Niclas Fasth, Pierre Fulke, Per-Ulrik Johansson, Robert Karlsson, Jesper Parnevik, Jarmo Sandelin and Henrik Stenson soon followed suit. At the latest count Karlsson remains the most successful in individual competition having won seven European Tour titles – one more than Fasth, Forsbrand, Johansson and Stenson. Indeed, there has been at least one Swedish win on Tour now for 20 consecutive years.

Sweden, two and a half times the size of Great Britain, is fortunate, however, in its quest for growth in the respect that there is plenty of land on which to build new courses. In 1973 there were 123 across the country, today there are over 500 and the number of golfers has grown from 51,000 to 600,000.

It is now even possible to take a three year course in the sport at the Scandinavian School of Golf connected to the University of Halmstadt in the south west of the country where psychology, physiology, biomechanics and diet are among the subjects studied.

The athletic Swedes, descended from the ultra-competitive Vikings, still enjoy skiing, skating,

Søren Kjeldsen

rowing, swimming, sailing and ice-hockey in the winter but golf has become the summer game. As if to illustrate the point, just as Hanson, helped by some superb iron play, was tapping in the winning putt in the SAS Masters, Klas Eriksson was taking the Trophée du Golf Club de Genève on the European Challenge Tour and Lotta Wahlin was winning the S4C Wales Ladies Championship of Europe on the Ladies European Tour. Later that evening, continuing a remarkable day for the country, Carl Pettersson triumphed in the Wyndham Championship on the US PGA Tour.

But it was Hanson's victory which drew the biggest cheer from the thousands of spectators who traditionally make the SAS Masters one of the best attended tournaments of the year on The European Tour International Schedule.

Pushed all the way by fellow Swede Pelle Edberg and England's Nick Dougherty, Hanson held his nerve to take the title and the €266,660 (£209,056) first prize, finally claiming a second Tour title to go with his maiden victory in the 2005 Jazztel Open de España en Andalucia where he had again overcome a compatriot, that time Peter Gustafsson, in a play-off.

Consistency, in the shape of four top five finishes in 2007, had helped him to a career high finish of 20th on the Order of Merit, with the only thing missing being a second victory. Now that statistic had been put right.

Renton Laidlaw
The Golf Channel

Left to right: Claus Sonberg, Executive Vice President, Corporate Communications & Investor Relations, SAS, Peter Hanson and Erik Knudsen, Director of Sponsoring, SAS

Pelle Edberg

Gary Orr

Arlandastad Golf

Final Results

Pos	Name		Rd1	Rd2	Rd3	Rd4	Total		€	£
1	Peter HANSON	SWE	66	66	68	71	271	-9	266,660.00	209,056.56
2	Nick DOUGHERTY	ENG	66	66	70	70	272	-8	138,965.00	108,946.02
	Pelle EDBERG	SWE	69	67	66	70	272	-8	138,965.00	108,946.02
4	Paul BROADHURST	ENG	67	68	70	68	273	-7	67,946.67	53,268.94
	Gary ORR	SCO	67	68	67	71	273	-7	67,946.67	53,268.94
	Sam WALKER	ENG	72	68	64	69	273	-7	67,946.67	53,268.94
7	Søren KJELDSEN	DEN	69	65	68	72	274	-6	48,000.00	37,631.12
8	Jamie DONALDSON	WAL	68	68	71	68	275	-5	31,760.00	24,899.26
	Oliver FISHER	ENG	69	69	68	69	275	-5	31,760.00	24,899.26
	Paul MCGINLEY	IRL	69	70	67	69	275	-5	31,760.00	24,899.26
	Daniel CHOPRA	SWE	71	64	67	73	275	-5	31,760.00	24,899.26
	Bradley DREDGE	WAL	71	69	66	69	275	-5	31,760.00	24,899.26
	Raphaël JACQUELIN	FRA	73	68	65	69	275	-5	31,760.00	24,899.26
14	Martin KAYMER	GER	69	70	68	69	276	-4	23,040.00	18,062.94
	David LYNN	ENG	70	69	68	69	276	-4	23,040.00	18,062.94
	Ross McGOWAN	ENG	70	70	65	71	276	-4	23,040.00	18,062.94
	Jarmo SANDELIN	SWE	72	68	68	68	276	-4	23,040.00	18,062.94
18	Chris WOOD	ENG	70	67	68	72	277	-3	20,240.00	15,867.79
	Damien MCGRANE	IRL	71	69	68	69	277	-3	20,240.00	15,867.79
20	Ignacio GARRIDO	ESP	69	70	66	73	278	-2	17,866.67	14,007.14
	Graeme STORM	ENG	70	66	71	71	278	-2	17,866.67	14,007.14
	Niclas FASTH	SWE	70	68	70	70	278	-2	17,866.67	14,007.14
	Mikko ILONEN	FIN	70	70	69	69	278	-2	17,866.67	14,007.14
	Craig LEE	SCO	72	65	73	68	278	-2	17,866.67	14,007.14
	Christian CÉVAËR	FRA	72	67	69	70	278	-2	17,866.67	14,007.14
26	Peter BAKER	ENG	67	68	73	71	279	-1	15,440.00	12,104.68
	Robert DINWIDDIE	ENG	69	69	68	73	279	-1	15,440.00	12,104.68
	Carlos RODILES	ESP	71	70	69	69	279	-1	15,440.00	12,104.68
	Fabrizio ZANOTTI	PAR	74	67	65	73	279	-1	15,440.00	12,104.68
30	Patrik SJÖLAND	SWE	68	66	70	76	280	0	12,497.78	9,798.03
	Magnus A CARLSSON	SWE	68	70	69	73	280	0	12,497.78	9,798.03
	Marc WARREN	SCO	68	71	69	72	280	0	12,497.78	9,798.03
	Thomas AIKEN	RSA	69	69	70	72	280	0	12,497.78	9,798.03
	Maarten LAFEBER	NED	69	70	71	70	280	0	12,497.78	9,798.03
	Markus BRIER	AUT	70	70	70	70	280	0	12,497.78	9,798.03
	Michael JONZON	SWE	70	70	68	72	280	0	12,497.78	9,798.03
	Alexander NOREN	SWE	72	68	71	69	280	0	12,497.78	9,798.03
	Anthony WALL	ENG	72	69	70	69	280	0	12,497.78	9,798.03
39	Robert-Jan DERKSEN	NED	67	71	72	71	281	1	9,760.00	7,651.66
	Jean-Baptiste GONNET	FRA	69	69	70	73	281	1	9,760.00	7,651.66
	Andreas HÖGBERG	SWE	70	67	68	76	281	1	9,760.00	7,651.66
	Henrik BJORNSTAD	NOR	70	68	72	71	281	1	9,760.00	7,651.66
	Barry LANE	ENG	71	69	69	72	281	1	9,760.00	7,651.66
	Lee S JAMES	ENG	72	68	67	74	281	1	9,760.00	7,651.66
	Fredrik ANDERSSON HED	SWE	74	66	70	71	281	1	9,760.00	7,651.66
46	Martin ERLANDSSON	SWE	67	74	72	69	282	2	7,360.00	5,770.11
	Jesper PARNEVIK	SWE	68	69	71	74	282	2	7,360.00	5,770.11
	Felipe AGUILAR	CHI	68	70	72	72	282	2	7,360.00	5,770.11
	Peter WHITEFORD	SCO	70	69	71	72	282	2	7,360.00	5,770.11
	Gary MURPHY	IRL	72	67	69	74	282	2	7,360.00	5,770.11
	Anders HANSEN	DEN	72	69	72	69	282	2	7,360.00	5,770.11
	Paul WARING	ENG	72	69	69	72	282	2	7,360.00	5,770.11
	Thomas LEVET	FRA	73	68	67	74	282	2	7,360.00	5,770.11
54	Martin WIEGELE	AUT	71	66	71	75	283	3	5,600.00	4,390.30
	Miles TUNNICLIFF	ENG	72	69	72	70	283	3	5,600.00	4,390.30
	Johan EDFORS	SWE	74	66	71	72	283	3	5,600.00	4,390.30
57	Carl SUNESON	ESP	70	71	71	72	284	4	4,720.00	3,700.39
	Alejandro CAÑIZARES	ESP	71	66	72	75	284	4	4,720.00	3,700.39
	Manuel QUIROS	ESP	71	66	73	74	284	4	4,720.00	3,700.39
	Phillip ARCHER	ENG	71	69	71	73	284	4	4,720.00	3,700.39
61	Peter HEDBLOM	SWE	69	71	69	76	285	5	4,000.00	3,135.93
	Matthew MILLAR	AUS	71	67	71	76	285	5	4,000.00	3,135.93
	Phillip PRICE	WAL	71	69	69	76	285	5	4,000.00	3,135.93
	Mattias ELIASSON	SWE	71	70	71	73	285	5	4,000.00	3,135.93
	Peter O'MALLEY	AUS	74	67	67	77	285	5	4,000.00	3,135.93
66	Anton HAIG	RSA	69	72	72	73	286	6	3,440.00	2,696.90
	Robert ROCK	ENG	72	69	78	67	286	6	3,440.00	2,696.90
	David PALM (AM)	SWE	79	62	73	72	286	6		
69	Pedro LINHART	ESP	66	74	72	75	287	7	3,120.00	2,446.02
	Simon WAKEFIELD	ENG	71	68	73	75	287	7	3,120.00	2,446.02
71	Johan BJERHAG	SWE	72	68	73	75	288	8	2,930.00	2,297.07
72	Gareth PADDISON	NZL	68	72	75	74	289	9	2,400.00	1,881.56

Total Prize Fund

€1,602,400 £1,256,252

Hole	Par	Yards	Metres
1	4	344	315
2	3	191	175
3	4	479	438
4	3	194	177
5	3	175	160
6	4	379	347
7	4	481	440
8	4	410	375
9	5	558	510
OUT	34	3211	2937
10	4	388	355
11	4	428	391
12	4	442	404
13	4	448	410
14	4	399	365
15	5	545	498
16	3	203	186
17	5	568	519
18	3	213	195
IN	36	3634	3323
TOTAL	70	6845	6260

Peter Hanson became the third different Swede to win the SAS Masters, following Jesper Parnevik (1995 and 1998) and Joakim Haeggman (1997). With fellow countryman, Pelle Edberg finshing in joint runners-up position, this marked the first time in the history of the SAS Masters that players from the host country had claimed places in the top two.

The Glorious Twelfth

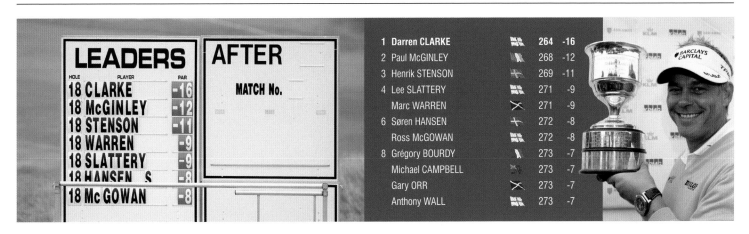

1	Darren CLARKE		264	-16
2	Paul McGINLEY		268	-12
3	Henrik STENSON		269	-11
4	Lee SLATTERY		271	-9
	Marc WARREN		271	-9
6	Søren HANSEN		272	-8
	Ross McGOWAN		272	-8
8	Grégory BOURDY		273	-7
	Michael CAMPBELL		273	-7
	Gary ORR		273	-7
	Anthony WALL		273	-7

Momentum, they say, is a vital component to success in golf and so it was proved once again by Darren Clarke during his victory in The KLM Open on the challenging Kennemer Golf and Country Club near the little seaside town of Zandvoort in The Netherlands.

Henrik Stenson

Paul McGinley

In April, the Ulsterman ended a seemingly never-ending wait of four years and eight months to record his 11th victory on The European Tour International Schedule in the BMW Asian Open. A mere four months later, however, he secured success number 12 just to the west of Amsterdam, playing what at times seemed almost carefree golf.

With the added bonus of having sons Tyrone and Conor in the gallery, Clarke, who had turned 40 a mere ten days previously, carded four rounds in the 60s to beat his good friend and fellow Irishman Paul McGinley by four shots with Sweden's Henrik Stenson a further shot behind in third.

It was an appropriate venue for Clarke to notch his glorious 12th success for his first, fifteen

years earlier, had come on another wonderful course in the Low Countries – the marvellous Royal Zoute, Belgium's gem in Knokke on the North Sea coast, where he beat the then World Number One Nick Faldo and Vijay Singh to win the 1993 Alfred Dunhill Open.

A lot has happened in the life of Darren Christopher Clarke since then. He has won all over the world, including beating Tiger Woods in the final of the 2000 World Golf Championships - Accenture Match Play, and represented Europe in five consecutive Ryder Cups. But now his attention was firmly focused on events in Zandvoort.

He opened with a 68 on the relatively short but challenging course, four shots behind one of the greats of Dutch golf, Rolf Muntz, who enjoyed a welcome, if albeit brief, return to form.

The 39 year old was Holland's first winner on The European Tour when he prevailed in the 2000 Qatar Masters, but after he lost his card at the culmination of the 2005 season, he had not had much chance to perform at the highest level. Trying to fight his way back to centre stage, he has played tournaments on the European Challenge Tour and the Canadian Tour, and qualified for The KLM Open by beating dozens of younger Dutchman in an 18 hole qualifying tournament.

In the end, he was the only Dutchman who made the cut, finishing in a tie for 34th place. "I don't give up. Never," he said afterwards, acknowledging he will need another trip to the Qualifying School Final Stage at the end of this season to try to regain his European Tour playing rights once again.

Simon Dyson

Ross McGowan

Clarke made his move on day two with an excellent 64, a round which contained only 26 putts and one which moved him into a share of the lead with Alexander Noren of Sweden and England's Robert Rock on eight under par 132.

Twenty four hours later, he was in sole possession of pole position having staked a strong claim for the €300,000 (£236,367) first prize with a solid 66 to lead by three shots. Four holes into the last round, however, his lead was gone as Stenson burst from the blocks with birdies at the first three holes, while he bogeyed the long second.

So was he frightened after the lacklustre start? "I'm forty years of age, six foot two and slightly overweight," he said afterwards. "I'm not frightened that easily. Plus, golf is a marathon, not a sprint."

With that in mind, and with the impetus of having his sons see their dad win in the flesh for the first time, Clarke got his game back on track pretty quickly. By the turn, he had reversed matters to lead by four which turned out to be the winning margin.

"It's great to win and it was great having Tyrone and Conor here to watch me do it," said the new KLM Open champion moments after receiving the gleaming silver trophy. "It hasn't been easy for us over the last couple of years. All I try to do is be a good dad for them."

Jan Kees van der Velden
Golfers Magazine and GOLFjournaal

Marc Warren

Darren Clarke (right), is presented with the trophy by Peter Hartman, CEO KLM

Lee Slattery

Hole	Par	Yards	Metres
1	4	434	397
2	5	570	521
3	3	148	135
4	4	399	365
5	4	419	383
6	4	363	332
7	5	562	514
8	3	222	203
9	4	418	382
OUT	36	3535	3232
10	4	447	409
11	3	158	144
12	5	525	480
13	4	374	342
14	4	384	351
15	3	163	149
16	4	473	432
17	3	170	155
18	4	397	363
IN	34	3091	2825
TOTAL	70	6626	6057

i Champion Darren Clarke's victory was his 19th professional success worldwide and has now seen him win in 11 different counties: Belgium, China, England, Germany, Ireland, Japan, Northern Ireland, South Africa, Spain, United States and now The Netherlands.

Kennemer Golf and Country Club

Final Results

Pos	Name		Rd1	Rd2	Rd3	Rd4	Total		€	£
1	Darren CLARKE	NIR	68	64	66	66	264	-16	300,000.00	236,367.50
2	Paul MCGINLEY	IRL	69	68	67	64	268	-12	200,000.00	157,578.34
3	Henrik STENSON	SWE	68	65	68	68	269	-11	112,680.00	88,779.63
4	Lee SLATTERY	ENG	70	69	67	65	271	-9	83,160.00	65,521.07
	Marc WARREN	SCO	72	64	67	68	271	-9	83,160.00	65,521.07
6	Søren HANSEN	DEN	65	69	70	68	272	-8	58,500.00	46,091.66
	Ross McGOWAN	ENG	69	64	72	67	272	-8	58,500.00	46,091.66
8	Anthony WALL	ENG	67	68	69	69	273	-7	38,610.00	30,420.50
	Michael CAMPBELL	NZL	68	66	69	70	273	-7	38,610.00	30,420.50
	Gary ORR	SCO	68	67	71	67	273	-7	38,610.00	30,420.50
	Grégory BOURDY	FRA	69	67	68	69	273	-7	38,610.00	30,420.50
12	John BICKERTON	ENG	65	71	66	72	274	-6	26,145.00	20,599.43
	Alexander NOREN	SWE	66	66	72	70	274	-6	26,145.00	20,599.43
	Anders HANSEN	DEN	69	66	70	69	274	-6	26,145.00	20,599.43
	Simon DYSON	ENG	70	64	70	70	274	-6	26,145.00	20,599.43
	David LYNN	ENG	70	66	71	67	274	-6	26,145.00	20,599.43
	Paul WARING	ENG	70	68	70	66	274	-6	26,145.00	20,599.43
	Peter BAKER	ENG	71	67	72	64	274	-6	26,145.00	20,599.43
	Patrik SJÖLAND	SWE	72	66	67	69	274	-6	26,145.00	20,599.43
20	Damien MCGRANE	IRL	67	69	69	70	275	-5	20,100.00	15,836.62
	Oliver WILSON	ENG	69	70	66	70	275	-5	20,100.00	15,836.62
	Thongchai JAIDEE	THA	70	69	71	65	275	-5	20,100.00	15,836.62
	Ross FISHER	ENG	70	70	69	66	275	-5	20,100.00	15,836.62
	Jamie DONALDSON	WAL	71	65	71	68	275	-5	20,100.00	15,836.62
	Fredrik ANDERSSON HED	SWE	71	67	68	69	275	-5	20,100.00	15,836.62
26	Raphaël JACQUELIN	FRA	67	72	73	64	276	-4	16,830.00	13,260.22
	Felipe AGUILAR	CHI	70	64	73	69	276	-4	16,830.00	13,260.22
	Peter FOWLER	AUS	71	67	69	69	276	-4	16,830.00	13,260.22
	Chapchai NIRAT	THA	71	69	66	70	276	-4	16,830.00	13,260.22
	Matthew MILLAR	AUS	71	69	69	67	276	-4	16,830.00	13,260.22
	David HOWELL	ENG	72	67	71	66	276	-4	16,830.00	13,260.22
32	Paul LAWRIE	SCO	71	66	70	70	277	-3	14,670.00	11,558.37
	Edoardo MOLINARI	ITA	72	68	69	68	277	-3	14,670.00	11,558.37
34	Rolf MUNTZ	NED	64	72	69	73	278	-2	12,960.00	10,211.08
	Justin ROSE	ENG	67	69	71	71	278	-2	12,960.00	10,211.08
	Jean-Baptiste GONNET	FRA	67	70	69	72	278	-2	12,960.00	10,211.08
	Alastair FORSYTH	SCO	68	71	70	69	278	-2	12,960.00	10,211.08
	Mathias GRÖNBERG	SWE	68	71	68	71	278	-2	12,960.00	10,211.08
	Jan-Are LARSEN	NOR	69	67	73	69	278	-2	12,960.00	10,211.08
40	Simon KHAN	ENG	67	70	72	70	279	-1	10,980.00	8,651.05
	Alvaro VELASCO	ESP	68	68	70	73	279	-1	10,980.00	8,651.05
	Mark FOSTER	ENG	68	71	69	71	279	-1	10,980.00	8,651.05
	Jean-François LUCQUIN	FRA	70	68	74	67	279	-1	10,980.00	8,651.05
	Sam WALKER	ENG	72	67	69	71	279	-1	10,980.00	8,651.05
45	Robert ROCK	ENG	68	64	80	68	280	0	9,180.00	7,232.85
	Graeme STORM	ENG	71	64	73	72	280	0	9,180.00	7,232.85
	Peter WHITEFORD	SCO	72	65	74	69	280	0	9,180.00	7,232.85
	Fabrizio ZANOTTI	PAR	72	66	71	71	280	0	9,180.00	7,232.85
	Alejandro CAÑIZARES	ESP	74	65	70	71	280	0	9,180.00	7,232.85
50	Phillip PRICE	WAL	67	73	70	71	281	1	7,380.00	5,814.64
	Carlos FRANCO	PAR	68	72	68	73	281	1	7,380.00	5,814.64
	Santiago LUNA	ESP	69	69	72	71	281	1	7,380.00	5,814.64
	Mikael LUNDBERG	SWE	71	69	73	68	281	1	7,380.00	5,814.64
	David FROST	RSA	72	68	72	69	281	1	7,380.00	5,814.64
55	José-Filipe LIMA	POR	68	70	69	75	282	2	6,120.00	4,821.90
	Martin KAYMER	GER	72	66	74	70	282	2	6,120.00	4,821.90
57	Iain PYMAN	ENG	69	71	72	71	283	3	5,580.00	4,396.44
58	Daniel VANCSIK	ARG	69	68	76	72	285	5	5,040.00	3,970.97
	Joakim BÄCKSTRÖM	SWE	69	70	73	73	285	5	5,040.00	3,970.97
	Sven STRÜVER	GER	71	69	72	73	285	5	5,040.00	3,970.97
	Peter O'MALLEY	AUS	71	69	70	75	285	5	5,040.00	3,970.97
	Danny WILLETT	ENG	74	66	74	71	285	5	5,040.00	3,970.97
63	Ignacio GARRIDO	ESP	70	69	76	71	286	6	4,410.00	3,474.60
	Magnus A CARLSSON	SWE	74	65	70	77	286	6	4,410.00	3,474.60
65	Martin WIEGELE	AUT	69	70	74	74	287	7	4,140.00	3,261.87
66	Jean VAN DE VELDE	FRA	70	70	76	72	288	8	3,960.00	3,120.05
67	Rafa ECHENIQUE	ARG	67	71	75	76	289	9	3,690.00	2,907.32
	Thomas LEVET	FRA	74	66	72	77	289	9	3,690.00	2,907.32

Total Prize Fund
€1,793,300 £1,412,926

1	**Grégory HAVRET**		**278**	**-14**
2	Graeme STORM		279	-13
3	Peter HANSON		281	-11
	David HOWELL		281	-11
5	Justin ROSE		282	-10
	Marcel SIEM		282	-10
7	Nick DOUGHERTY		284	-8
	Bradley DREDGE		284	-8
	Anthony WALL		284	-8
10	Michael CAMPBELL		285	-7
	Rafa ECHENIQUE		285	-7
	Ross FISHER		285	-7
	Mark FOSTER		285	-7
	Stephen GALLACHER		285	-7
	Søren HANSEN		285	-7
	Lee WESTWOOD		285	-7
	Oliver WILSON		285	-7

Double Scotch

L ike a set of Russian dolls, each revealing another within, the Johnnie Walker Championship at Gleneagles was blessed with layers of intrigue, all of them variations on a Ryder Cup theme. The ten automatic qualifiers for The European Team were signed and sealed, the two wild card picks announced, and a player with the potential to take on the United States in future years dramatically identified.

After The Ryder Cup's year long qualification process had reached its conclusion on the Sunday night, Søren Hansen, Justin Rose and Oliver Wilson had played their way into Nick Faldo's Team, joining the seven players already there; Paul Casey and Ian Poulter had been named as the Captain's selections; and Frenchman Grégory Havret's victory in the tournament had underlined his potential to represent Europe in years to come.

All in all, it was quite a week on the testing PGA Centenary Course, felt by many to be one of the longest and hardest walks of the season. In 2014, it will certainly present the most demanding of challenges when it stages The 40th Ryder Cup.

If Havret is in The European Team for that match, the first to be held in Scotland since 1973, the hope is that he will reproduce the form he seems to reserve for these parts. This was his third European Tour title, 13 months after a thrilling play-off defeat of Phil Mickelson in The Barclays Scottish Open at Loch Lomond. On each occasion, his fellow Frenchmen have rushed on to the final green to shower him with champagne.

Havret's putt of ten feet for par on the 18th hole, after splashing out of a greenside bunker, gave him a final round 70 for a 14 under par total of 278. He finished one stroke clear of England's Graeme Storm with Sweden's Peter Hanson, seeking his second European Tour title in three weeks, and another Englishman, David Howell, two strokes further back. The winner's cheque for €292,355 (£233,300) lifted the Frenchman to 29th on The European Tour Order of Merit and, perhaps more importantly, led him to believe that a place among Europe's elite was within his capabilities.

"The Ryder Cup is definitely a goal," he said. "I feel more and more like somebody who is able to play in that kind of tournament. I would like to play in The Ryder Cup at least once. I am 31, so there are still many to come. These victories help me to trust myself which is very important. I will trust myself to keep working and make it possible in two years time."

As Havret was targeting The Celtic Manor Resort in 2010, Rose was looking forward to Valhalla Golf Club in Kentucky the following month. The Englishman, who started the week in eighth position on the list of automatic qualifiers, remained there after posting a ten under par total of 282. It earned him a cheque for €67,885 (£54,180) which confirmed his Ryder Cup debut. "It's the highlight of my season so far," he admitted.

Grégory Havret (left), receives the trophy from Andrew Morgan, President Diageo Europe

Graeme Storm

David Howell

Michael Campbell

Paul Waring

Hansen, meanwhile, became only the second Dane to qualify for a Ryder Cup Team, following in the footsteps of the current Chairman of The European Tour's Tournament Committee, Thomas Björn. He all but secured his place with a third round 68, after which he turned his attention to the Johnnie Walker Championship title itself. In the circumstances, a final round 75 was not what he had hoped for, but victory was still his in the tournament within a tournament. "I am going away with a smile on my face because of The Ryder Cup," he said.

So, too, was Wilson who produced arguably the most courageous performance of the week in pursuit of his Ryder Cup dream. The young Englishman occupied the last automatic place when play began and held firm under pressure, most notably from his compatriot Nick Dougherty.

In danger of missing the cut on Friday, Wilson survived with an eagle three on the 12th, and a birdie four on the 16th, the catalyst for which was a superb driver from a tight fairway lie for his second shot. Having secured his berth in the weekend's action, he followed up with excellent rounds of 68-69; a tie for tenth place in the

tournament; and confirmation of his place on the charter to Louisville. "It's proved to people that I can do it when I really need to," he said.

With Casey and Poulter later added to the side, it was undoubtedly a good week for England, with five of its players taking their place in Nick Faldo's Team. It was also a good week for France, but most of all, it was another great week for Europe.

Hopefully, there will be another one to come in three weeks time.

Paul Forsyth
The Sunday Times

ROLEX.COM

OYSTER PERPETUAL DAY-DATE
IN PLATINUM

ROLEX

Marcel Siem

Hole	Par	Yards	Metres
1	4	426	390
2	5	516	472
3	4	431	394
4	3	239	219
5	4	461	422
6	3	201	184
7	4	468	428
8	4	419	383
9	5	618	565
OUT	**36**	**3779**	**3457**
10	3	208	190
11	4	350	320
12	5	503	460
13	4	481	440
14	4	320	293
15	4	463	423
16	5	543	497
17	3	194	177
18	5	533	487
IN	**37**	**3595**	**3287**
TOTAL	**73**	**7374**	**6744**

European Ryder Cup Captain Nick Faldo (left), with Vice Captain José Maria Olazábal, as The 2008 European Team is finalised

i Grégory Havret's victory in the Johnnie Walker Championship at Gleneagles was his third on The European Tour International Schedule and his second in Scotland following his success in The Barclays Scottish Open at Loch Lomond in 2007. His win was the first by a Frenchman in the tournament and he became the ninth different player to win in the event's ten year history.

The Gleneagles Hotel
(PGA Centenary Course)

Final Results

Pos	Name		Rd1	Rd2	Rd3	Rd4	Total		€	£
1	Grégory HAVRET	FRA	68	71	69	70	278	-14	292,355.49	233,330.00
2	Graeme STORM	ENG	74	69	68	68	279	-13	194,899.48	155,550.00
3	Peter HANSON	SWE	74	72	66	69	281	-11	98,759.09	78,820.00
	David HOWELL	ENG	75	67	68	71	281	-11	98,759.09	78,820.00
5	Justin ROSE	ENG	73	71	67	71	282	-10	67,885.91	54,180.00
	Marcel SIEM	GER	74	70	66	72	282	-10	67,885.91	54,180.00
7	Bradley DREDGE	WAL	71	70	70	73	284	-8	45,257.28	36,120.00
	Anthony WALL	ENG	71	73	65	75	284	-8	45,257.28	36,120.00
	Nick DOUGHERTY	ENG	73	72	69	70	284	-8	45,257.28	36,120.00
10	Søren HANSEN	DEN	71	71	68	75	285	-7	28,351.58	22,627.50
	Lee WESTWOOD	ENG	72	72	66	75	285	-7	28,351.58	22,627.50
	Ross FISHER	ENG	72	74	73	66	285	-7	28,351.58	22,627.50
	Michael CAMPBELL	NZL	73	69	71	72	285	-7	28,351.58	22,627.50
	Mark FOSTER	ENG	73	75	70	67	285	-7	28,351.58	22,627.50
	Stephen GALLACHER	SCO	75	72	65	73	285	-7	28,351.58	22,627.50
	Rafa ECHENIQUE	ARG	76	68	70	71	285	-7	28,351.58	22,627.50
	Oliver WILSON	ENG	76	72	68	69	285	-7	28,351.58	22,627.50
18	Simon DYSON	ENG	73	72	69	72	286	-6	22,628.64	18,060.00
19	Francesco MOLINARI	ITA	73	70	69	75	287	-5	19,897.16	15,880.00
	Paul WARING	ENG	73	71	69	74	287	-5	19,897.16	15,880.00
	Johan EDFORS	SWE	73	73	71	70	287	-5	19,897.16	15,880.00
	Pelle EDBERG	SWE	73	75	70	69	287	-5	19,897.16	15,880.00
	Ignacio GARRIDO	ESP	74	71	73	69	287	-5	19,897.16	15,880.00
	Paul MCGINLEY	IRL	76	69	70	72	287	-5	19,897.16	15,880.00
	Benn BARHAM	ENG	77	70	68	72	287	-5	19,897.16	15,880.00
26	Gareth PADDISON	NZL	72	73	71	72	288	-4	17,190.75	13,720.00
	Alvaro VELASCO	ESP	74	73	71	70	288	-4	17,190.75	13,720.00
	Louis OOSTHUIZEN	RSA	75	71	68	74	288	-4	17,190.75	13,720.00
29	Robert ROCK	ENG	70	70	76	73	289	-3	15,612.01	12,460.00
	Gary ORR	SCO	70	72	72	75	289	-3	15,612.01	12,460.00
	Anton HAIG	RSA	75	70	71	73	289	-3	15,612.01	12,460.00
32	Paul BROADHURST	ENG	70	74	72	74	290	-2	13,419.31	10,710.00
	Martin WIEGELE	AUT	71	74	70	75	290	-2	13,419.31	10,710.00
	Grégory BOURDY	FRA	71	77	74	68	290	-2	13,419.31	10,710.00
	Thongchai JAIDEE	THA	73	73	72	72	290	-2	13,419.31	10,710.00
	José Manuel LARA	ESP	75	70	75	70	290	-2	13,419.31	10,710.00
	Ricardo GONZALEZ	ARG	76	67	67	80	290	-2	13,419.31	10,710.00
38	Christian CÉVAËR	FRA	70	75	73	73	291	-1	11,226.61	8,960.00
	Benoit TEILLERIA	FRA	71	75	74	71	291	-1	11,226.61	8,960.00
	Peter WHITEFORD	SCO	73	68	75	75	291	-1	11,226.61	8,960.00
	Colin MONTGOMERIE	SCO	74	70	76	71	291	-1	11,226.61	8,960.00
	Luis CLAVERIE	ESP	75	72	70	74	291	-1	11,226.61	8,960.00
	Lee SLATTERY	ENG	77	71	70	73	291	-1	11,226.61	8,960.00
44	Lee S JAMES	ENG	72	74	73	73	292	0	9,297.04	7,420.00
	Darren CLARKE	NIR	72	73	73	74	292	0	9,297.04	7,420.00
	David LYNN	ENG	73	71	75	73	292	0	9,297.04	7,420.00
	Paul MCKECHNIE	SCO	75	73	75	69	292	0	9,297.04	7,420.00
	Peter O'MALLEY	AUS	78	69	72	73	292	0	9,297.04	7,420.00
49	Patrik SJÖLAND	SWE	72	74	73	74	293	1	7,893.71	6,300.00
	Gonzalo FDEZ-CASTAÑO	ESP	75	73	69	76	293	1	7,893.71	6,300.00
	Mark BROWN	NZL	78	70	69	76	293	1	7,893.71	6,300.00
52	Juan ABBATE	ARG	72	76	72	74	294	2	6,665.80	5,320.00
	Chris WOOD	ENG	75	69	75	75	294	2	6,665.80	5,320.00
	Jamie DONALDSON	WAL	75	71	76	72	294	2	6,665.80	5,320.00
	Gary MURPHY	IRL	75	73	71	75	294	2	6,665.80	5,320.00
56	Matthew MILLAR	AUS	74	74	73	74	295	3	5,496.36	4,386.67
	Marcus FRASER	AUS	75	70	71	79	295	3	5,496.36	4,386.67
	Peter FOWLER	AUS	75	73	73	74	295	3	5,496.36	4,386.67
59	François DELAMONTAGNE	FRA	75	70	74	77	296	4	4,823.93	3,850.00
	Peter BAKER	ENG	75	70	74	77	296	4	4,823.93	3,850.00
	Sam WALKER	ENG	76	72	72	76	296	4	4,823.93	3,850.00
	Michael JONZON	SWE	78	70	75	73	296	4	4,823.93	3,850.00
63	Jonathan LOMAS	ENG	72	74	73	79	298	6	4,122.27	3,290.00
	Emanuele CANONICA	ITA	75	72	73	78	298	6	4,122.27	3,290.00
	Alvaro QUIROS	ESP	74	74	75	75	298	6	4,122.27	3,290.00
	Robert DINWIDDIE	ENG	82	66	73	77	298	6	4,122.27	3,290.00
67	Steven MCEWAN (AM)	SCO	78	70	76	75	299	7		
68	Stephen GRAY	SCO	75	72	79	82	308	16	3,683.73	2,940.00
69	Robert ARNOTT	SCO	76	72	88	75	311	19	3,508.32	2,800.00
70	Daniel VANCSIK	ARG	77	71	67	DISQ				

Total Prize Fund
€1,747,617 £1,387,328

French
Connection

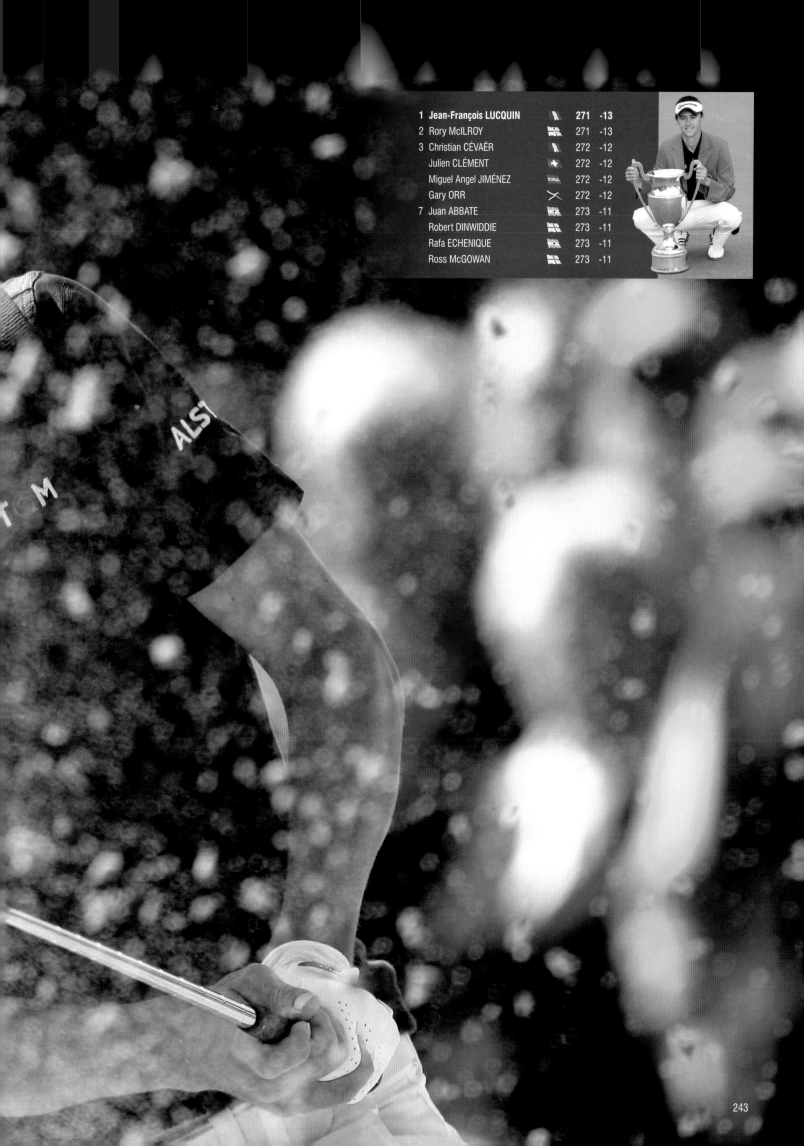

1	Jean-François LUCQUIN		271	-13
2	Rory McILROY		271	-13
3	Christian CÉVAËR		272	-12
	Julien CLÉMENT		272	-12
	Miguel Angel JIMÉNEZ		272	-12
	Gary ORR		272	-12
7	Juan ABBATE		273	-11
	Robert DINWIDDIE		273	-11
	Rafa ECHENIQUE		273	-11
	Ross McGOWAN		273	-11

The splendour of Crans Montana has been drawing visitors to the Swiss Alps for decades. Situated on a sun-drenched plateau some 1500 metres above the Rhone Valley and with a panoramic view of a chain of mountain peaks stretching from the Matterhorn to Mont Blanc, it is easy to understand why.

Similarly, the delights of Crans-sur-Sierre – the town's wonderful golf course – have attracted the cream of European Tour talent since the Tour itself was born in 1972.

Every year the spectators turn out in their thousands to rejoice in professional golf at its very best and to toast a truly eclectic mix of champions befitting such an international gathering. In the past 36 years, the tournament has seen winners emerge from Europe, North America, South America and Australasia and the Roll of Honour feature such iconic golfing names as Ballesteros, Faldo, Montgomerie, Olazábal and Woosnam.

The only thing missing from the record books, for the locals in the gallery at least, has been a home triumph. Indeed in the history of The European Tour there has only ever been one Swiss champion, namely André Bossert, who claimed the Cannes Open in 1995 at Royal Mougins.

They did not get one at Crans-sur-Sierre in 2008 either but they did unearth a new hero in the shape of 27 year old Julien Clement, a Challenge Tour Member from Berne, playing on a sponsor's invitation, who carded four excellent rounds under 70 for a 12 under par total of 272 and an eventual share of third place with Christian Cévaër, Miguel Angel Jiménez and Gary Orr.

The winner might not have been a local but, having made his home in the delightful Swiss town of Crassier, Jean-François Lucquin was nevertheless celebrated as one.

The 29 year old Frenchman claimed his maiden European Tour title in dramatic fashion after a play-off with one of the Tour's young lions, Rory McIlory.

Left to right: Jean-François Emery, representing Credit Suisse, Jean-François Lucquin, Gaston Barras, President of the Omega European Masters Committee, and Stephen Urquhart, President of Omega

Christian Cévaër

Rory McIlroy

The teenager from Northern Ireland had already written his name in record books when, at the end of the 2007 season, he became the youngest and quickest Affiliate Member to secure his European Tour card in just two events, after finishing tied 42nd in The Quinn Direct British Masters and third in the Alfred Dunhill Links Championship.

Now the 19 year old was aiming to become the youngest winner in the illustrious history of the Omega European Masters, surpassing the previous best set by three time winner Seve Ballesteros who was 20 and 99 days when he celebrated the first of his triumphs in 1977.

Requiring only a par four at the 72nd hole to achieve it, and with his ball in the middle of the fairway after a solid drive, most people would have wagered large amounts of money that he would succeed. However, an understandable rush of adrenalin saw him fly the green with his approach shot before pitching to six feet and missing the par putt which would have sealed the €333,330 (£268,010) first prize.

With the first play-off hole halved in par four, the duo returned to the 18th moments later, only for McIlroy's inexperience to resurface. Where more seasoned campaigners would have marked their ball and taken a moment to compose themselves before knocking in the two footer for par, the youngster opted to step straight up and putt; visibly wincing in agony as his ball touched the hole and stayed above ground.

Gary Orr

It left Luquin two putts from 12 feet for a par four and the title, the fact he needed only one of interest largely to the statisticians and, of course, to McIlroy who suddenly did not feel quite so bad about his bogey five.

It continued an impressive season for French golf and marked the second time in 2008 that French professionals had won in successive weeks; Luquin following Grégory Havret's victory in last week's Johnnie Walker Championship at Gleneagles, just as Grégory Bourdy's win in the Estoril Open de Portugal in April followed the previous week's success by Thomas Levet in the MAPFRE Open de Andalucia by Valle Romano.

As is now traditional after any French victory, Luquin's triumph was heralded with a shower of champagne supplied by his delighted watching compatriots Raphaël Jacquelin and Michael Lorenzo-Vera. While the champion might have

expected it, the spray of bubbles did come as a bit of a shock to his baby son Arthur, who was passing on his own congratulations to daddy from the arms of mum Iris at the time.

Although only four years old and perhaps a bit young to fully appreciate the delights of a Moet, Bollinger or Veuve Clicquot, you get the feeling if his father continues to play the way he did in the mountains of Switzerland over the rest of his career, Arthur may get very used to the taste of fine champagne in the future.

Scott Crockett

Alejandro Cañizares

Rafa Echenique

Hole	Par	Yards	Metres
1	5	543	494
2	4	440	400
3	3	192	175
4	4	506	460
5	4	341	310
6	4	326	296
7	4	330	303
8	3	176	160
9	5	632	575
OUT	**36**	**3486**	**3173**
10	4	407	370
11	3	206	187
12	4	412	375
13	3	200	182
14	5	598	544
15	5	519	472
16	3	236	215
17	4	388	353
18	4	405	368
IN	**35**	**3371**	**3066**
TOTAL	**71**	**6857**	**6239**

George O'Grady, Chief Executive of The European Tour was accorded Honorary Life Membership of Crans-Sur-Sierre Golf Club during the week of the Omega European Masters. Left to Right: Christian Barras, Vice President of the Omega European Masters Committee, Gaston Barras, President of the Omega European Masters Committee and Crans-sur-Sierre, George O'Grady, and Yves Mittaz, Tournament Director of the Omega European Masters

Jean-François Lucquin's victory in the Omega European Masters saw him join an impressive list of players to make this event their first European Tour International Schedule victory. They are: Graham Marsh (1972), Hugh Baiocchi (1973), Nick Price (1980), Ian Woosnam (1982), Jerry Anderson (1984), Craig Stadler (1985), José Maria Olazábal (1986), Anders Forsbrand (1987), Chris Moody (1988), Jeff Hawkes (1991), Jamie Spence (1992), Mathias Grönberg (1995) and Ricardo Gonzalez (2001).

Crans-sur-Sierre

Final Results

Pos	Name		Rd1	Rd2	Rd3	Rd4	Total		€	£
1	Jean-François LUCQUIN	FRA	68	67	69	67	271	-13	333,330.00	268,010.48
2	Rory MCILROY	NIR	63	71	66	71	271	-13	222,220.00	178,673.66
3	Gary ORR	SCO	67	71	67	67	272	-12	95,000.00	76,383.75
	Miguel Angel JIMÉNEZ	ESP	68	69	68	67	272	-12	95,000.00	76,383.75
	Christian CÉVAÉR	FRA	68	71	65	68	272	-12	95,000.00	76,383.75
	Julien CLÉMENT	SUI	69	68	67	68	272	-12	95,000.00	76,383.75
7	Ross McGOWAN	ENG	67	73	66	67	273	-11	48,700.00	39,156.72
	Juan ABBATE	ARG	68	67	69	69	273	-11	48,700.00	39,156.72
	Rafa ECHENIQUE	ARG	69	70	66	68	273	-11	48,700.00	39,156.72
	Robert DINWIDDIE	ENG	76	64	64	69	273	-11	48,700.00	39,156.72
11	Julio ZAPATA	ARG	66	72	67	69	274	-10	34,466.67	27,712.56
	Alejandro CAÑIZARES	ESP	67	68	69	70	274	-10	34,466.67	27,712.56
	Francesco MOLINARI	ITA	69	70	69	66	274	-10	34,466.67	27,712.56
14	Richard STERNE	RSA	69	70	68	68	275	-9	29,400.00	23,638.76
	Michael LORENZO-VERA	FRA	70	69	71	65	275	-9	29,400.00	23,638.76
	Barry LANE	ENG	71	70	65	69	275	-9	29,400.00	23,638.76
17	Louis OOSTHUIZEN	RSA	69	68	71	68	276	-8	26,400.00	21,226.64
	Mark FOSTER	ENG	72	66	68	70	276	-8	26,400.00	21,226.64
19	Mattias ELIASSON	SWE	70	72	68	67	277	-7	24,400.00	19,618.56
	Ricardo GONZALEZ	ARG	73	68	70	66	277	-7	24,400.00	19,618.56
21	Gonzalo FDEZ-CASTAÑO	ESP	68	71	75	64	278	-6	22,900.00	18,412.50
	Thongchai JAIDEE	THA	70	71	68	69	278	-6	22,900.00	18,412.50
23	Brett RUMFORD	AUS	67	67	73	72	279	-5	19,600.00	15,759.17
	Peter LAWRIE	IRL	67	69	72	71	279	-5	19,600.00	15,759.17
	Niclas FASTH	SWE	68	73	72	66	279	-5	19,600.00	15,759.17
	Fredrik ANDERSSON HED	SWE	69	67	72	71	279	-5	19,600.00	15,759.17
	Michael CAMPBELL	NZL	69	71	68	71	279	-5	19,600.00	15,759.17
	David GRIFFITHS	ENG	70	69	68	72	279	-5	19,600.00	15,759.17
	Peter HEDBLOM	SWE	70	70	70	69	279	-5	19,600.00	15,759.17
	Robert ROCK	ENG	72	68	70	69	279	-5	19,600.00	15,759.17
	Sven STRÜVER	GER	72	69	66	72	279	-5	19,600.00	15,759.17
32	Emanuele CANONICA	ITA	67	70	68	75	280	-4	14,460.00	11,626.41
	Mikko ILONEN	FIN	67	70	70	73	280	-4	14,460.00	11,626.41
	Simon DYSON	ENG	69	67	72	72	280	-4	14,460.00	11,626.41
	Peter BAKER	ENG	70	70	69	71	280	-4	14,460.00	11,626.41
	Andrew MARSHALL	ENG	70	70	71	69	280	-4	14,460.00	11,626.41
	Andrew MCLARDY	RSA	70	72	71	67	280	-4	14,460.00	11,626.41
	Charl SCHWARTZEL	RSA	70	72	66	72	280	-4	14,460.00	11,626.41
	Paul WARING	ENG	71	71	66	72	280	-4	14,460.00	11,626.41
	Jan-Are LARSEN	NOR	71	71	67	71	280	-4	14,460.00	11,626.41
	Thomas AIKEN	RSA	72	70	65	73	280	-4	14,460.00	11,626.41
42	François DELAMONTAGNE	FRA	67	72	74	68	281	-3	12,000.00	9,648.47
	Santiago LUNA	ESP	70	71	69	71	281	-3	12,000.00	9,648.47
44	Martin ERLANDSSON	SWE	68	72	71	71	282	-2	11,000.00	8,844.43
	Scott BARR	AUS	69	68	76	69	282	-2	11,000.00	8,844.43
	Lian-wei ZHANG	CHN	71	71	71	69	282	-2	11,000.00	8,844.43
47	Garry HOUSTON	WAL	66	73	70	74	283	-1	8,800.00	7,075.55
	Felipe AGUILAR	CHI	70	69	72	72	283	-1	8,800.00	7,075.55
	Carlos RODILES	ESP	71	66	70	76	283	-1	8,800.00	7,075.55
	Fabrizio ZANOTTI	PAR	71	68	72	72	283	-1	8,800.00	7,075.55
	Miles TUNNICLIFF	ENG	71	69	71	72	283	-1	8,800.00	7,075.55
	Daniel VANCSIK	ARG	71	71	70	71	283	-1	8,800.00	7,075.55
	Tom WHITEHOUSE	ENG	72	68	68	75	283	-1	8,800.00	7,075.55
	Mads VIBE-HASTRUP	DEN	72	70	70	71	283	-1	8,800.00	7,075.55
55	Bradley DREDGE	WAL	70	70	72	73	284	0	6,450.00	5,186.05
	Hennie OTTO	RSA	69	73	72	70	284	0	6,450.00	5,186.05
	Ignacio GARRIDO	ESP	70	72	67	75	284	0	6,450.00	5,186.05
	Jarmo SANDELIN	SWE	71	66	71	76	284	0	6,450.00	5,186.05
59	Patrik SJÖLAND	SWE	69	68	73	75	285	1	5,400.00	4,341.81
	Ariel CANETE	ARG	69	72	70	74	285	1	5,400.00	4,341.81
	Eduardo ROMERO	ARG	71	68	75	71	285	1	5,400.00	4,341.81
	Steve ALKER	NZL	71	70	71	73	285	1	5,400.00	4,341.81
	Florian PRAEGANT	AUT	72	70	73	70	285	1	5,400.00	4,341.81
64	Matthew MILLAR	AUS	70	72	70	74	286	2	4,700.00	3,778.99
	Raphaël JACQUELIN	FRA	73	69	70	74	286	2	4,700.00	3,778.99
66	Robert-Jan DERKSEN	NED	69	70	76	72	287	3	4,010.00	3,224.20
	Michael JONZON	SWE	70	74	73	70	287	3	4,010.00	3,224.20
	Benoit TEILLERIA	FRA	71	69	76	71	287	3	4,010.00	3,224.20
	Francis VALERA	ESP	73	67	77	70	287	3	4,010.00	3,224.20
	Marcus FRASER	AUS	74	68	74	71	287	3	4,010.00	3,224.20
71	Simon GRIFFITHS	ENG	76	66	71	76	289	5	3,000.00	2,412.12
72	Ken BENZ (AM)	SUI	72	70	73	74	289	6		
	Pablo MARTIN	ESP	71	71	74	74	290	6	2,997.00	2,409.71
74	Craig LEE	SCO	73	69	74	75	291	7	2,994.00	2,407.29

Total Prize Fund

€2,008,991 £1,615,308

Striding Out

1	**Robert KARLSSON**		275	-13
2	Francesco MOLINARI		277	-11
3	Michael CAMPBELL		279	-9
	Ross FISHER		279	-9
	Miguel Angel JIMÉNEZ		279	-9
6	Richard FINCH		281	-7
	José Manuel LARA		281	-7
8	Søren HANSEN		282	-6
	Martin KAYMER		282	-6
	Marcel SIEM		282	-6

I f taking things in your stride is a vital attribute for a world-class sportsman, it no doubt helps if that particular characteristic would effortlessly cover most of a short par four.

That certainly applies to the six foot five inch Robert Karlsson, the tallest player on The European Tour, who had several things to ponder when he arrived at Golf Club Gut Lärchenhof on the outskirts of Cologne for the Mercedes-Benz Championship.

Coming off a three week lay-off, the towering Swede had firstly to cope with erroneous reports that he had suffered a neck injury which put his second Ryder Cup appearance the following week in jeopardy. Then there was the not inconsiderable distraction of the threat of disqualification at the end of his third round, which ultimately turned into a one stroke penalty.

Last, but by no means least, came the brilliant back nine charge in the final round from Italy's Francesco Molinari which turned the last few holes from a stroll in the late summer sunshine into a nerve-wracking battle to complete an eighth European Tour International Schedule title.

Such obstacles may have brought down a lesser man, but Karlsson is made of stern stuff - and that pun is strictly intended. The late Bengt Stern was a doctor who studied psychosomatic medicine and body psychotherapy, and who Karlsson turned to in the 1990s in a bid to revive his ailing game.

Whether he was fully aware of what he was letting himself in for is unclear, but some of the good doctor's ideas were so far off the wall as to be out the room entirely and halfway down the street.

You cannot imagine Tiger Woods submitting himself to a month of eating just bread and milk for example, but Karlsson gamely gave it a go. Then there was the wheeze of submitting to a ceremony in which he had to pretend he was reliving his birth, before he undertook a therapy workshop where those in attendance were not allowed to talk for a week. Perhaps the silence was golden for a man who also once stayed up all night practising his putting while a friend shouted abuse at him if he missed.

All of which could go some way to explain why the 39 year old from St Malm was so easily able to shrug off the penalty incurred at the end of

Saturday's third round, an incident which, for a moment, threatened to derail his bid for a first victory in two years.

One shot clear of Jean-François Lucquin at the halfway stage - the Frenchman seeking back-to-back wins following his maiden victory in the Omega European Masters the previous Sunday - Karlsson had stretched his lead to five shots as he made his way to the 18th tee.

However, a bogey five there was followed by a discussion with European Tour Senior Referee

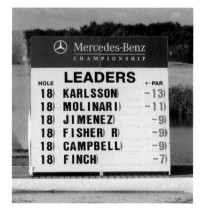

Michael Campbell

Martin Kaymer

Marc Warren

Robert Karlsson (left), receives the trophy from
Doctor Olaf Göttgens, Vice President of Brand
Communications Mercedes-Benz Car Group

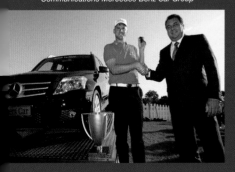

Andy McFee of a possible rules breach earlier in
the round; television footage having confirmed
that he had grounded his putter when his ball
moved fractionally on the second green.

After a review of the tape in the nearby
television compound, a one shot penalty was
administered which altered his 67 to a 68, and
his five shot lead on the 18th tee was now down
to three.

"It was definitely a one shot penalty – I'm just
happy it wasn't two shots or a disqualification,"
said the stoic Swede. "My mistake was that
I misunderstood what needed to be done. I
thought you had to be addressing the ball but
it's enough that the putter is on the ground."

Rules lesson over, Karlsson set out in the final
round and soon raced into a six shot lead, only
for Molinari – winner of the 2006 Telecom Italia
Open - to birdie four holes in a row from the
12th. When Karlsson subsequently bogeyed
the 16th, suddenly his lead was cut to just two
strokes and a major test of his resolve loomed.

It should come as no surprise it was an
examination he passed. After the Italian left a
birdie attempt agonisingly short on the 17th
green, Karlsson held his nerve to par the 18th

this time and complete the perfect preparation
for the following week's contest against the
United States.

After nine top ten finishes in 2008 – including
ending tied eighth in the Masters Tournament,
tied fourth in the US Open Championship and
tied seventh in The Open Championship -
Karlsson admitted: "It's very nice to win; it would
have felt a bit strange not to win this season
because I've been playing so well."

And he should know strange when he sees it.

Phil Casey
Press Association

Marcel Siem

Since Golf came along, gentlemen no longer duel with pistols.

www.mercedes-benz-championship.com

Mercedes-Benz

Hole	Par	Yards	Metres
1	4	362	331
2	4	426	389
3	5	555	507
4	3	191	175
5	4	437	399
6	4	439	401
7	5	583	533
8	3	241	220
9	4	469	429
OUT	**36**	**3703**	**3384**
10	4	419	383
11	3	164	150
12	4	465	425
13	5	509	465
14	4	458	419
15	5	523	478
16	3	195	178
17	4	397	363
18	4	456	417
IN	**36**	**3586**	**3278**
TOTAL	**72**	**7289**	**6662**

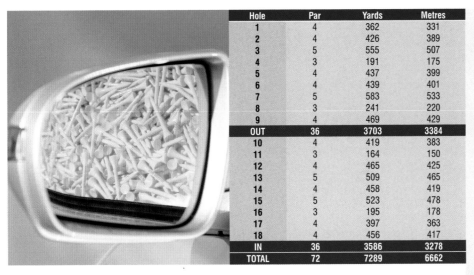

Francesco Molinari

Golf Club Gut Lärchenhof

Final Results

Pos	Name		Rd1	Rd2	Rd3	Rd4	Total		€	£
1	Robert KARLSSON	SWE	67	69	68	71	275	-13	320,000.00	258,233.20
2	Francesco MOLINARI	ITA	71	71	65	70	277	-11	220,000.00	177,535.33
3	Ross FISHER	ENG	68	73	68	70	279	-9	101,516.67	81,921.80
	Michael CAMPBELL	NZL	71	70	68	70	279	-9	101,516.67	81,921.80
	Miguel Angel JIMÉNEZ	ESP	72	73	68	66	279	-9	101,516.67	81,921.80
6	Richard FINCH	ENG	66	73	70	72	281	-7	64,000.00	51,646.64
	José Manuel LARA	ESP	73	69	67	72	281	-7	64,000.00	51,646.64
8	Marcel SIEM	GER	72	68	72	70	282	-6	44,666.67	36,045.05
	Søren HANSEN	DEN	73	67	73	69	282	-6	44,666.67	36,045.05
	Martin KAYMER	GER	74	70	68	70	282	-6	44,666.67	36,045.05
11	Marc WARREN	SCO	72	69	72	71	284	-4	34,466.67	27,813.87
	David DIXON	ENG	72	71	71	70	284	-4	34,466.67	27,813.87
	Jeev Milkha SINGH	IND	73	70	73	68	284	-4	34,466.67	27,813.87
14	Peter HANSON	SWE	69	69	73	74	285	-3	30,000.00	24,209.36
	Steve WEBSTER	ENG	73	72	68	72	285	-3	30,000.00	24,209.36
16	Jean-François LUCQUIN	FRA	66	71	70	79	286	-2	25,500.00	20,577.96
	Mikko ILONEN	FIN	72	70	67	77	286	-2	25,500.00	20,577.96
	Graeme MCDOWELL	NIR	72	73	70	71	286	-2	25,500.00	20,577.96
	Søren KJELDSEN	DEN	73	70	73	70	286	-2	25,500.00	20,577.96
	Grégory HAVRET	FRA	73	74	67	72	286	-2	25,500.00	20,577.96
	Stuart APPLEBY	AUS	74	75	68	69	286	-2	25,500.00	20,577.96
22	Paul LAWRIE	SCO	70	72	71	74	287	-1	22,000.00	17,753.53
	Richard GREEN	AUS	72	72	72	71	287	-1	22,000.00	17,753.53
	David LYNN	ENG	73	75	69	70	287	-1	22,000.00	17,753.53
25	Peter HEDBLOM	SWE	73	70	72	73	288	0	19,900.00	16,058.88
	Grégory BOURDY	FRA	76	72	71	69	288	0	19,900.00	16,058.88
	Darren CLARKE	NIR	76	74	69	69	288	0	19,900.00	16,058.88
	Gonzalo FDEZ-CASTAÑO	ESP	80	66	73	69	288	0	19,900.00	16,058.88
29	Chapchai NIRAT	THA	70	76	71	72	289	1	17,500.00	14,122.13
	Alexander NOREN	SWE	71	71	72	75	289	1	17,500.00	14,122.13
	Markus BRIER	AUT	72	74	72	71	289	1	17,500.00	14,122.13
	Johan EDFORS	SWE	74	67	73	75	289	1	17,500.00	14,122.13
33	Richard STERNE	RSA	70	73	70	77	290	2	15,700.00	12,669.57
	Maarten LAFEBER	NED	71	77	72	70	290	2	15,700.00	12,669.57
35	James KINGSTON	RSA	69	73	72	77	291	3	14,800.00	11,943.29
	Fred COUPLES	USA	75	70	74	72	291	3	14,800.00	11,943.29
37	Damien MCGRANE	IRL	70	75	75	72	292	4	13,200.00	10,652.12
	Ariel CANETE	ARG	73	72	73	74	292	4	13,200.00	10,652.12
	Paul MCGINLEY	IRL	73	74	71	74	292	4	13,200.00	10,652.12
	Thomas LEVET	FRA	75	75	70	72	292	4	13,200.00	10,652.12
	Ignacio GARRIDO	ESP	75	75	70	72	292	4	13,200.00	10,652.12
	David HOWELL	ENG	76	74	68	74	292	4	13,200.00	10,652.12
43	Felipe AGUILAR	CHI	71	77	70	75	293	5	11,800.00	9,522.35
44	David FROST	RSA	71	72	77	74	294	6	10,600.00	8,553.97
	Alvaro QUIROS	ESP	71	73	74	76	294	6	10,600.00	8,553.97
	Raphaël JACQUELIN	FRA	74	71	75	74	294	6	10,600.00	8,553.97
	Anders HANSEN	DEN	76	76	70	72	294	6	10,600.00	8,553.97
	Niclas FASTH	SWE	80	72	72	70	294	6	10,600.00	8,553.97
49	John DALY	USA	73	71	74	77	295	7	9,400.00	7,585.60
50	Prayad MARKSAENG	THA	71	73	80	72	296	8	8,800.00	7,101.41
	Mads VIBE-HASTRUP	DEN	72	75	74	75	296	8	8,800.00	7,101.41
52	Phillip PRICE	WAL	71	76	74	76	297	9	7,800.00	6,294.43
	Peter LAWRIE	IRL	72	76	74	75	297	9	7,800.00	6,294.43
	Scott STRANGE	AUS	74	74	79	70	297	9	7,800.00	6,294.43
55	Charl SCHWARTZEL	RSA	73	75	74	76	298	10	6,600.00	5,326.06
	Robert-Jan DERKSEN	NED	75	77	75	71	298	10	6,600.00	5,326.06
	Daniel CHOPRA	SWE	78	76	72	72	298	10	6,600.00	5,326.06
58	Bernhard LANGER	GER	70	76	81	73	300	12	5,800.00	4,680.48
	Per-Ulrik JOHANSSON	SWE	73	74	72	81	300	12	5,800.00	4,680.48
	Simon DYSON	ENG	76	74	76	74	300	12	5,800.00	4,680.48
61	Sven STRÜVER	GER	72	76	75	78	301	13	5,200.00	4,196.29
	Alastair FORSYTH	SCO	74	78	76	73	301	13	5,200.00	4,196.29
	Mikael LUNDBERG	SWE	80	75	70	76	301	13	5,200.00	4,196.29
64	Graeme STORM	ENG	75	71	73	83	302	14	4,800.00	3,873.50
65	Pablo LARRAZABAL	ESP	76	75	80	72	303	15	4,500.00	3,631.40
	Mardan MAMAT	SIN	76	76	74	77	303	15	4,500.00	3,631.40
67	Stephen DODD	WAL	73	76	78	79	306	18	4,100.00	3,308.61
	Mark BROWN	NZL	76	78	76	76	306	18	4,100.00	3,308.61
69	Anton HAIG	RSA	74	78	81	74	307	19	3,650.00	2,945.47
	Retief GOOSEN	RSA	76	76	78	77	307	19	3,650.00	2,945.47
	Hennie OTTO	RSA	77	78	79	73	307	19	3,650.00	2,945.47
72	Oliver FISHER	ENG	75	74	80	81	310	22	3,350.00	2,703.38
73	Pablo MARTIN	ESP	77	79	80	77	313	25	3,050.00	2,461.29
	S S P CHOWRASIA	IND	79	76	79	79	313	25	3,050.00	2,461.29
	John BICKERTON	ENG	80	76	74	83	313	25	3,050.00	2,461.29
76	Scott DRUMMOND	SCO	84	74	81	78	317	29	2,750.00	2,219.19
77	Jyoti RANDHAWA	IND	77	83	79	81	320	32	2,600.00	2,098.14
78	Daniel VANCSIK	ARG	81	WD					2,450.00	1,977.10

i The 2008 Mercerdes-Benz Championship was the 21st staging. The tournament has a rich history of champions dating back to 1987. In all, the event has produced seven Major Champions and seven European Tour Number Ones. There have been 18 different winners, who have won 268 European Tour titles between them.

Total Prize Fund

€2,000,000 £1,613,957

Compelling Contest

Swinging the Cadillac out of the hotel car park, through several lines of traffic and onto the freeway, a five hour drive north to Chicago beckoned, meaning there was more than enough time to think and to reflect on The Ryder Cup we were leaving behind in Louisville.

There was also talk, and the occasional argument, about it all with my travelling companion Jamie Corrigan, who is Welsh and very mellow as well as being the entertaining and erudite golf correspondent of The Independent newspaper.

His last day in town had started rather earlier than mine, as he had risen before dawn to hurtle to The European Team's hotel in an attempt to nab Nick Faldo for a few additional quotes. Along with a several of his colleagues he was left disappointed when the Captain departed, the only addition for their respective notebooks being the phrase: "Officially, no more."

Journalistically, however, it was worth the effort. A lot of what we do is fruitless. We cast large nets into the water in the hope of catching a bon mot worthy of Eric Cantona's great seagull revelation, but often we are left with nothing but a few strands of seaweed. It is what it is.

And what it was on this Monday morning in Kentucky was the realisation that, yes, Europe had lost after a wonderful series of victories but, then again, the United States had deservedly won, exhibiting a genuine hunger for this old battle as well as holing a host of crucial putts. As an American friend beautifully put it: "It just goes to prove that you can't lose them all!"

Best of all, in a world that was soon to be gripped by the financial equivalent to bird flu, it had been at times, competitively serious and gloriously trivial, but above all else, fun. However, to read some of the immediate analysis you would have thought that this had been a flawed campaign by Europe generally as well as an individual disaster for Faldo. The truth, of course, is that it was neither.

All losing generals are subject to post-battle scrutiny. Armed with the most cutting weapon of all, hindsight, critics pick over the bones of those left wounded on the field of play.

The European Team, with their wives and partners, prior to the Gala Dinner

The biggest small word in the language, if, is deployed relentlessly. Often it is used indiscriminately. Rarely is it parlayed into the discussion with the thing called balance.

Well, c'est la vie. These are big boys playing these games. Each of them is successful, each hardened to various degrees by the slings and arrows that outrageous sporting fortune has thrown at them.

However, to blame Faldo for everything that passed at Valhalla Golf Club is as silly as it is illogical. Did the European leader make mistakes? Of course. So, too, did Paul Azinger. Has there ever been a Ryder Cup Captain who did not make errors? No. Has there ever been a Captain who simply lacked a smidgeon of good fortune? Yes, there has, and here is where we must now file Faldo's stewardship.

When he needed them most, his pivotal players – Sergio Garcia, Padraig Harrington and Lee Westwood, who had all come into the contest bathed in well-deserved reputations – did not deliver.

Harrington's momentous summer, a memorable stint that brought him both The Open Championship and the US PGA Championship trophies, rightly marked him out as the most significant golfer of 2008. Westwood's Ryder Cup record is unsurpassed in recent times while his individual play through the course of the season suggested that here was a player caressing the very tips of his talent. Garcia, so often the whirlwind heartbeat of Europe, is an occasionally befuddled putter who has traditionally found peace and confidence on Ryder Cup greens.

If Europe were to win then it was this trio who would offer the template for victory. Yet between them they contributed just 2 ½ points to Europe's total in their 16 ½ - 11 ½ reverse. This, clearly, was crucial. Not quite at their best, they were also met by the Americans determined to reverse the humiliations suffered in the previous two matches.

Harrington was clearly lacking firepower after his Major Championship heroics. The old determination was evident enough but the steely-eyed focus he brought to both

The European Tour held a special dinner honouring recent and future Ryder Cup host countries and venues at Churchill Downs where the 2010 Breeders Cup will take place

Royal Birkdale and Oakland Hills was missing. Westwood, meanwhile, appeared a tad disconnected at times, while a subdued Garcia seemed unable to shake off the debilitating effects of illness suffered the previous week.

Shorn of his main weapons, Faldo's Team lost momentum. Much is made of this phenomenon because, especially in match play golf, it is crucial. There is little to choose between the majority of Ryder Cup golfers. Each is, by definition, a skilled practitioner, each is experienced enough one way or another. What usually marks one side out from another is the feeling that fate is sitting on their shoulders and smiling encouragingly.

To be fair, Azinger had worked hard over the previous year to encourage this feeling amongst both his players and the local fans, much of whom was made in the aftermath. But let us nail something here; this was the best American Ryder Cup crowd I have ever walked with.

The European Team, and caddies with Louisville's most famous son, Muhammad Ali

Product: Hydratech

Description:
Hydratech is a brand new golf suit incorporating new wave body-configured style with fusion fabric technology.

The sharp-cut rain suit with clean, narrow lines and deluxe styling detail configures to the golfer's body, for an athletic, fitted, standout look.

3 Year Guarantee

PERFORMANCE SYSTEM

PROQUIP

www.proquipgolf.com

Paul Casey (left) and Hunter Mahan

Yes, they were loud and supportive of their players and occasionally a few of them stepped over the line but, overwhelmingly, they were appreciative of decent play from each side. To discover that in a crowd of thousands there are a few idiots is hardly either new, or a phenomenon restricted to the United States. Sadly, out of the shadows everywhere step clowns now and then.

Firstly though, before any of this could be considered, there had been Hurricane Ike to contend with. The malevolent fringes of this colossal storm played havoc with Louisville and Valhalla Golf Club some 48 hours before the Teams were due to arrive. Trees fell, power was lost, and a television tower crashed and gouged the 12th green. It says much for the determination of the local people that much of this was put right by the time the public entered.

Tuesday, Wednesday and Thursday of a Ryder Cup week are never less than interesting. There is much practice, a prodigious amount of

Robert Karlsson (left) and Henrik Stenson

The 2008 European Ryder Cup Team

the **revenue** drivers

www.clubcar.com
info_esa@clubcar.com
(+ 44) 777 180 5463

Club Car

José Maria Olazábal

posturing and an awful lot of media work for the Captains and players to undertake. Mostly there is not a lot to say but it still has to be said, noted and mulled over, before reports are sent back across the Atlantic.

There is an opening ceremony to carry out and there is always a posse of celebrities to brighten the scene. None, however, has ever done so any more vividly than Louisville's own favourite son, Muhammad Ali, whose appearance at Valhalla reduced Faldo to at least one tear. He was not alone.

The golf, when it began, came as a blessed relief and, as ever, the old match encouraged drama from the off. Azinger had demanded that recent tradition be shredded and that the Foursomes rather than Fourballs began the first day. In the event, he was proved astute as the Americans rebounded from some early deficits to take the opening session 3-1. Not quite capturing momentum, but certainly putting an arm around its shoulder.

By the end of the first day the United States had taken a firmer grip on proceedings to lead by three points, 5 ½ - 2 ½. Europe countered by taking the Saturday morning Foursomes 2 ½ - 1 ½, the only session they were to profit from. Garcia and Westwood were rested for this one, the Englishman understandably disappointed to have to sit on the sidelines for the first time in a Ryder Cup this century. "If you look at the result, then the Captain got it right," he later wisely reflected.

And so to the Saturday afternoon Fourball matches and a flurry of astonishing golf, thrust and counter thrust from both sets of players, certainly as good as many observers have witnessed in Ryder Cup history.

No-one played better than Robert Karlsson who illuminated his stellar year with a prodigious collection of birdies over Valhalla's challenging back nine. Significantly, all this did was to garner a half point for him and partner Henrik Stenson against Hunter Mahan and Phil Mickelson, such was the quality exhibited that golden afternoon.

European Team Captain Nick Faldo (centre) and European Ryder Cup Director Richard Hills (right) present a replica of an 18th Century putter to Walt Gahm, General Chairman of The 2008 Ryder Cup and eldest son of the founding family of Valhalla Golf Club, to mark their appreciation of the biennial match between Europe and the United States being played on the Jack Nicklaus-designed course. The sterling silver putter was hand-made in the London workshops of Thomas Lyte, by the company's Master Silversmith, Kevin Williams.

The life and work of David 'Dai' Davies, one of Britain's foremost golf writers of the past 40 years who passed away in May, 2008, was celebrated during The Ryder Cup at Valhalla when the PGA of America made a special presentation to his widow, Patricia.

Joe Steranka, CEO of the PGA of America, presented a magnificent gold plaque to Patricia which, as well as featuring a replica of The Ryder Cup trophy and a gold embossed passage from Dai's 1999 book 'Beyond the Fairways', also featured the inscription; 'In Memory of Dai Davies: For his professionalism and commitment to covering the greatest spectacle in golf, The Ryder Cup.'

Steranka said: "I got to know Dai well over the years and as well as our shared love of golf we also shared a love of jazz music. We cannot help but think how much he would have enjoyed this week so much as well as looking forward to the next Ryder Cup in his beloved Wales. We all miss him very much."

Justin Rose (left) and Phil Mickelson

Ian Poulter

Ian Poulter, too, was in brilliant form. No player came to Valhalla under greater scrutiny than this Captain's pick. Many still believe it would have been preferable for him to have returned to Gleneagles at the end of August to try and qualify automatically for the Team, but his performance through the event revealed a golfer on a seriously determined mission. Before the contest began the Englishman had promised passion and commitment to the cause. He brought those qualities and much more. It might just have been the major making of him.

It all meant that, by Sunday's singles, just two points separated the Teams; the United States ahead 9-7. After consulting with his side, Faldo chose to back load his singles order with Poulter at ten, Westwood at 11 and Harrington playing the anchor role at 12. As events turned out none

was needed, the match ending when the eighth singles finished with a 2 and 1 win for Jim Furyk over Miguel Angel Jiménez.

If the result had teetered on those last three singles, then how different it all might have been? There we go again, that word 'if' once more.

What we do know is that this was a compelling three days of golf, The Ryder Cup's reputation as a must-see sporting event was greatly enhanced, and that both sides have unveiled a new core of players who will illuminate these weeks for many years to come.

For the United States there is much to applaud in the style and passion of J B Holmes, Anthony Kim and Hunter Mahan, and in the irrepressible irreverence of Boo Weekley whose daft

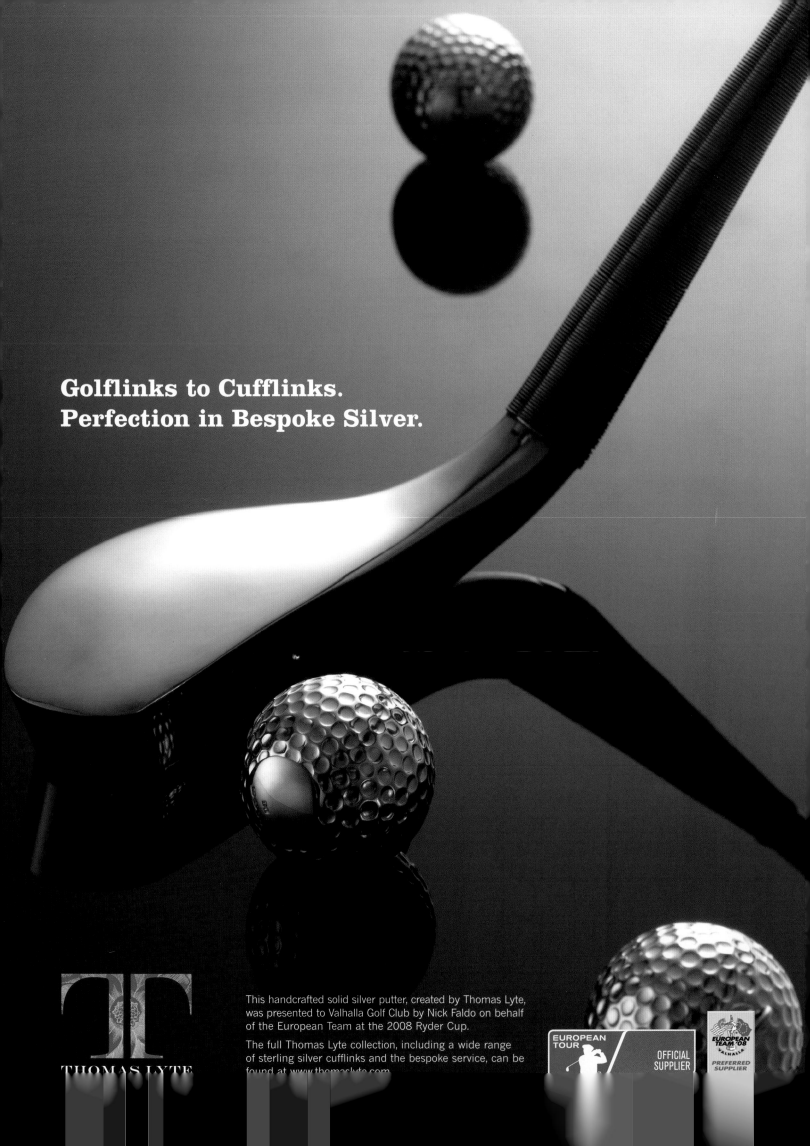

Golflinks to Cufflinks.
Perfection in Bespoke Silver.

THOMAS LYTE

This handcrafted solid silver putter, created by Thomas Lyte, was presented to Valhalla Golf Club by Nick Faldo on behalf of the European Team at the 2008 Ryder Cup.

The full Thomas Lyte collection, including a wide range of sterling silver cufflinks and the bespoke service, can be found at www.thomaslyte.com

EUROPEAN TOUR

OFFICIAL SUPPLIER

EUROPEAN TEAM '08 VALHALLA

PREFERRED SUPPLIER

The victorious United States Ryder Cup Team

Rt Hon Rhodri Morgan, First Minister for Wales, during the Wales Evening held in Louisville

gallop off the first tee on Sunday still dances deliciously in the memory. For Europe, there is the confirmation that Ian Poulter is a golfer capable of much of what he always has claimed and that in Graeme McDowell, Justin Rose and Oliver Wilson, there is a deep insertion of genuine class.

Best of all, however, is that we once again have a match. It has been fun to dismantle the United States in recent times but monotonously heavy victory is, eventually, just that – monotonous.

What Valhalla did more than anything else was to tee up the expectation for what will happen in Wales at The Celtic Manor Resort in 2010. By the time we had reached the airport in Chicago, even Jamie Corrigan agreed with that.

Bill Elliott
The Observer

Fourth Street Live: The party headquarters in downtown Louisville

Final Results

Valhalla Golf Club

Yards: Out 3694   In 3802   Total 7496
Metres: Out 3378   In 3476   Total 6854
Par: 35-36 = 71

EUROPE (Captain: Nick Faldo)		UNITED STATES: (Captain: Paul Azinger)	
FRIDAY			
Foursomes: Morning			
P Harrington & R Karlsson (halved)	½	P Mickelson & A Kim (halved)	½
H Stenson & P Casey	0	J Leonard & H Mahan (3 and 2)	1
I Poulter & J Rose	0	S Cink & C Campbell (1 hole)	1
L Westwood & S Garcia (halved)	½	K Perry & J Furyk (halved)	½
Session Score:	**1**		**3**
Match Position:	**1**		**3**
Fourballs: Afternoon			
P Harrington & G McDowell	0	P Mickelson & A Kim (2 holes)	1
I Poulter & J Rose (4 and 2)	1	S Stricker & B Curtis	0
S Garcia & M A Jiménez	0	J Leonard & H Mahan (4 and 3)	1
L Westwood & S Hansen (halved)	½	J B Holmes & B Weekley (halved)	½
Session Score:	**1½**		**2½**
Match Position:	**2½**		**5½**
SATURDAY			
Foursomes: Morning			
I Poulter & J Rose (4 and 3)	1	S Cink & C Campbell	0
M A Jiménez & G McDowell (halved)	½	J Leonard & H Mahan (halved)	½
H Stenson & O Wilson (2 and 1)	1	P Mickelson & A Kim	0
P Harrington & R Karlsson	0	J Furyk & K Perry (3 and 1)	1
Session Score:	**2½**		**1½**
Match Position:	**5**		**7**
Fourballs: Afternoon			
L Westwood & S Hansen	0	B Weekley & J B Holmes (2 and 1)	1
S Garcia & P Casey (halved)	½	S Stricker & B Curtis (halved)	½
I Poulter & G McDowell (1 hole)	1	K Perry & J Furyk	0
H Stenson & R Karlsson (halved)	½	P Mickelson & H Mahan (halved)	½
Session Score:	**2**		**2**
Match Position:	**7**		**9**
SUNDAY			
Singles			
S Garcia	0	A Kim (5 and 4)	1
P Casey (halved)	½	H Mahan (halved)	½
R Karlsson (5 and 3)	1	J Leonard	0
J Rose (3 and 2)	1	P Mickelson	0
H Stenson	0	K Perry (3 and 2)	1
O Wilson	0	B Weekley (4 and 2)	1
S Hansen	0	J B Holmes (2 and 1)	1
M A Jiménez	0	J Furyk (2 and 1)	1
G McDowell (2 and 1)	1	S Cink	0
I Poulter (3 and 2)	1	S Stricker	0
L Westwood	0	B Curtis (2 and 1)	1
P Harrington	0	C Campbell (2 and 1)	1
Session Score:	**4½**		**7½**
EUROPE	**11½**	**UNITED STATES**	**16½**

The Mighty Quinn

1	Gonzalo FDEZ-CASTAÑO		276	-12
2	Lee WESTWOOD		276	-12
3	Michael CAMPBELL		278	-10
4	Mikael LUNDBERG		280	-8
5	Charl SCHWARTZEL		282	-6
	Jeev Milkha SINGH		282	-6
7	Magnus A CARLSSON		283	-5
	Ross FISHER		283	-5
	Louis OOSTHUIZEN		283	-5
10	Alejandro CAÑIZARES		284	-4
	Michael JONZON		284	-4
	Pablo LARRAZABAL		284	-4

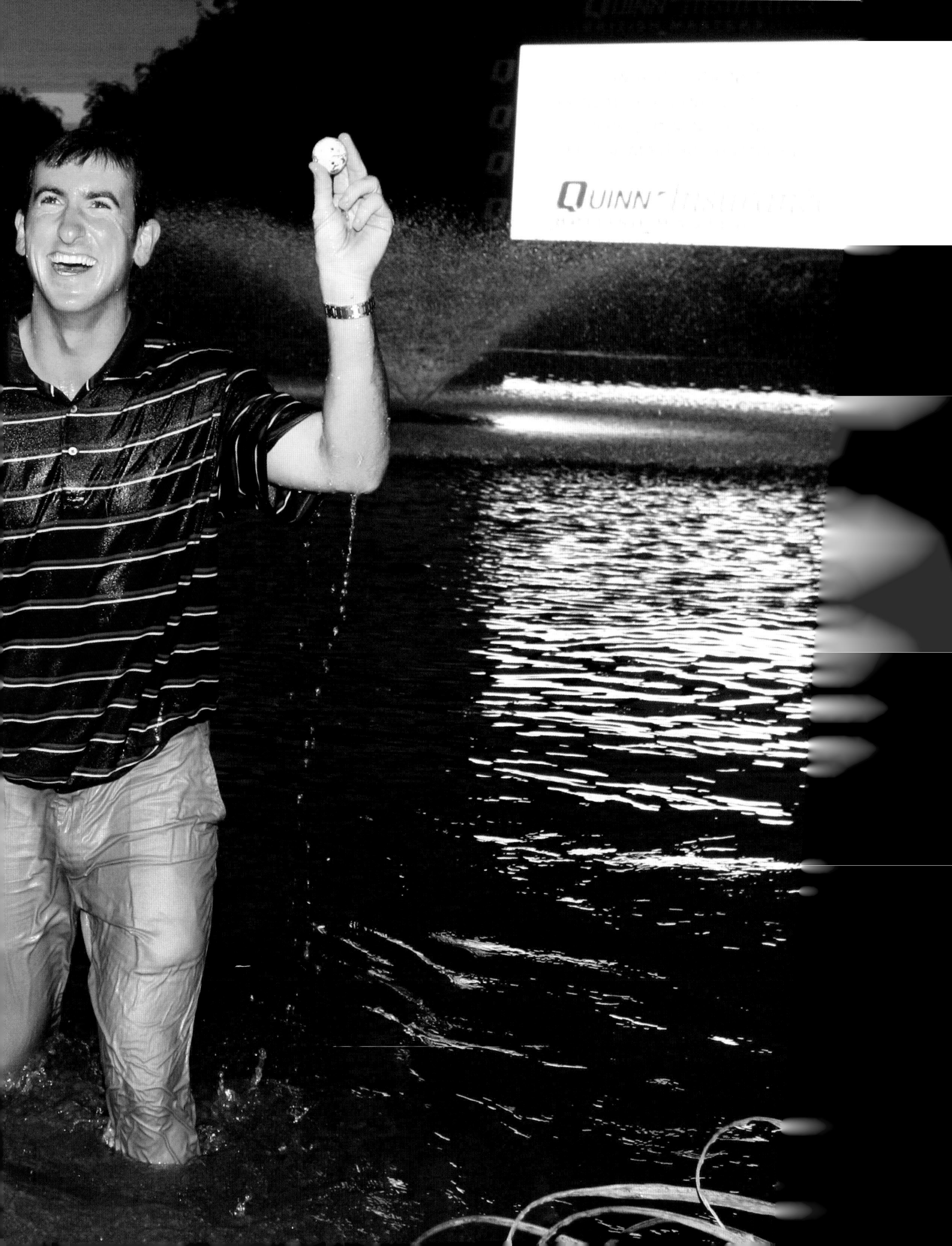
QUINN

A persistent fog might have enveloped The Belfry during large parts of The Quinn Insurance British Masters, but it could not blot out the recurring theme of the previous week's Ryder Cup at Valhalla Golf Club in Kentucky.

For hours before the golf eventually started on the Friday and Saturday, the talk on the range turned to Europe's defeat by the United States, Nick Faldo's Captaincy, and the candidates who might replace him at The Celtic Manor Resort in 2010. Players queued up to voice their opinions.

Yes, Darren Clarke had played every shot mentally in front of his television and wished he had been there. Colin Montgomerie had kept notes from the eight Ryder Cups and the five Captains he had played under. Thomas Björn wanted to play himself into the 2010 Team rather than be considered Captain. Defending champion Lee Westwood nominated the 2006 Captain Ian Woosnam to return to the role.

Thus it went on until an enthralling, if disrupted, Quinn Insurance British Masters eventually ended as dusk fell on Sunday evening with the magnificent trophy in the hands of one of the rising stars of European golf, Gonzalo Fernandez-Castaño. The Spaniard collected the winner's cheque of €381,612 (£300,000) after a dramatic play-off with Westwood which went to the third extra hole.

Once again, with reminders of previous Ryder Cups played there, the Brabazon Course made a glorious panorama of golfing terrain although preferred lies were in operation after heavy rain.

It was clear as play begun on Thursday that Westwood, one of two Ryder Cup men in the field – the other being Graeme McDowell – was not suffering any Valhalla hangover. His carefully crafted 68 brought smiles to the faces of the gallery and the promoters – his management company International Sports Management – and left him among a group of five players, all one shot behind leaders Marcus Fraser of Australia and Sweden's Mikael Lundberg.

The Belfry's second day was a parade of pink. Almost the entire field wore the colour in some shape or form to help raise awareness of breast cancer. Even spectators joined in the spirit of the day, a positive feeling not dampened by the three and a quarter hour delay for fog which left the second round incomplete at the end of the day and ensured that the final two rounds would be played in three balls from a two tee start.

By the time the second round was completed early on Saturday afternoon, after another two hours and 40 minutes lost in the Saturday morning mists, Westwood was tied with Sweden's Alexander Noren on six under par 138 while Fernandez-Castaño was back in a share of 11th place but still only three shots behind the joint leaders.

Westwood was slightly perturbed at having to start his third round from the tenth tee – the driveable but treacherously difficult hole protected by a small lake – and his fears were realised as he found the water and made bogey.

It was the beginning of a poor start for Westwood who dropped shots at his first three holes but, by the end of the round on Sunday morning, he had recovered manfully. His second 68 of the week saw him share the lead on ten under par 206 with Michael Campbell, the 2005 US Open Champion, who was enjoying a welcome return to form and who proved it by shooting up the leaderboard with a spectacular 65.

Campbell and Westwood were joined in the final threesome by Fernandez-Castaño who had moved to only three shots adrift after his own third round 68. Into the final round, Campbell gave way, leaving Fernandez-Castaño and Westwood to battle out an epic duel.

Alejandro Cañizares

Michael Jonzon

Michael Campbell

Gonzalo Fernandez-Castaño (left), receives the trophy from Sean Quinn Jnr, Operations Director of Quinn Direct Insurance

Magnus A Carlsson

Lee Westwood

The spectators saw a marvellous contest and many of them concluded that the young man from Madrid must have been brought up in the Seve Ballesteros school of big tournament survival as he repeatedly pulled off stunning iron shots, chipped in for pars and holed putts from all ranges.

As has been the case so often at The Belfry, the final drama was reserved for the famous and fabled 18th – the scene of all the play-off action. After the duo finished their regulation 72 holes on 12 under par 276, firstly the Englishman and then the Spaniard took it in turns to hole testing par putts on the first two return trips to keep the contest alive.

On the third occasion, Westwood, supporting the theory that he has become one of the best drivers in golf, sent his tee shot over the water and 70 yards past Fernandez-Castaño. Unruffled, the Spaniard simply followed his own route and played to the heart of the green.

Westwood, perhaps feeling tired after a long week that followed events in Kentucky, conjured up a poor approach shot, chipped to 15 feet and missed the putt. His bogey five to the Spaniard's careful par four saw him finally relinquish the trophy he had won a year earlier.

Fernandez-Castaño was subsequently thrown into the lake in celebration by his friends and compatriots and appeared at his Press Conference swathed in towels. It was his fourth European Tour triumph but was a performance which suggests many more.

James Mossop

A celebration of 'Pink Friday'

Jeev Milkha Singh

Mikael Lundberg

The Belfry
(The Brabazon Course)
Final Results

Pos	Name		Rd1	Rd2	Rd3	Rd4	Total		€	£
1	Gonzalo FDEZ-CASTAÑO	ESP	71	70	68	67	276	-12	381,612.00	300,000.00
2	Lee WESTWOOD	ENG	68	70	68	70	276	-12	254,408.00	200,000.00
3	Michael CAMPBELL	NZL	69	72	65	72	278	-10	143,333.47	112,680.00
4	Mikael LUNDBERG	SWE	67	75	68	70	280	-8	114,483.60	90,000.00
5	Jeev Milkha SINGH	IND	69	71	69	73	282	-6	88,610.31	69,660.00
	Charl SCHWARTZEL	RSA	72	72	66	72	282	-6	88,610.31	69,660.00
7	Ross FISHER	ENG	71	68	71	73	283	-5	59,073.54	46,440.00
	Louis OOSTHUIZEN	RSA	71	71	75	66	283	-5	59,073.54	46,440.00
	Magnus A CARLSSON	SWE	73	70	68	72	283	-5	59,073.54	46,440.00
10	Michael JONZON	SWE	70	71	72	71	284	-4	42,435.25	33,360.00
	Alejandro CAÑIZARES	ESP	71	68	72	73	284	-4	42,435.25	33,360.00
	Pablo LARRAZABAL	ESP	74	71	69	70	284	-4	42,435.25	33,360.00
13	Thomas BJÖRN	DEN	69	73	72	71	285	-3	35,184.63	27,660.00
	Anthony WALL	ENG	71	74	70	70	285	-3	35,184.63	27,660.00
	Alexander NOREN	SWE	72	66	75	72	285	-3	35,184.63	27,660.00
16	Marcus FRASER	AUS	67	73	77	69	286	-2	30,280.91	23,805.00
	Paul LAWRIE	SCO	69	71	74	72	286	-2	30,280.91	23,805.00
	David HOWELL	ENG	71	71	77	67	286	-2	30,280.91	23,805.00
	Jean VAN DE VELDE	FRA	72	74	66	74	286	-2	30,280.91	23,805.00
20	Rafa ECHENIQUE	ARG	68	77	72	70	287	-1	25,568.00	20,100.00
	Mark FOSTER	ENG	72	72	73	70	287	-1	25,568.00	20,100.00
	Bradley DREDGE	WAL	72	74	71	70	287	-1	25,568.00	20,100.00
	Phillip ARCHER	ENG	73	68	77	69	287	-1	25,568.00	20,100.00
	Sam LITTLE	ENG	73	73	70	72	287	-1	25,568.00	20,100.00
	James KAMTE	RSA	76	66	73	72	287	-1	25,568.00	20,100.00
26	Sam WALKER	ENG	68	72	78	70	288	0	22,095.33	17,370.00
	Simon WAKEFIELD	ENG	70	74	73	71	288	0	22,095.33	17,370.00
	Thongchai JAIDEE	THA	71	68	76	73	288	0	22,095.33	17,370.00
	Phillip PRICE	WAL	71	71	72	74	288	0	22,095.33	17,370.00
30	Anders HANSEN	DEN	68	78	69	74	289	1	17,884.88	14,060.00
	David DIXON	ENG	69	72	76	72	289	1	17,884.88	14,060.00
	Greg OWEN	ENG	69	76	71	73	289	1	17,884.88	14,060.00
	Graeme STORM	ENG	70	73	73	73	289	1	17,884.88	14,060.00
	Markus BRIER	AUT	71	71	74	73	289	1	17,884.88	14,060.00
	Søren KJELDSEN	DEN	73	69	74	73	289	1	17,884.88	14,060.00
	Peter HANSON	SWE	75	68	75	71	289	1	17,884.88	14,060.00
	David DRYSDALE	SCO	75	71	69	74	289	1	17,884.88	14,060.00
	Ricardo GONZALEZ	ARG	77	70	73	69	289	1	17,884.88	14,060.00
39	Paul BROADHURST	ENG	70	73	72	75	290	2	14,195.97	11,160.00
	David LYNN	ENG	71	71	77	71	290	2	14,195.97	11,160.00
	Rory MCILROY	NIR	72	73	69	76	290	2	14,195.97	11,160.00
	Graeme MCDOWELL	NIR	72	75	72	71	290	2	14,195.97	11,160.00
	Maarten LAFEBER	NED	75	72	71	72	290	2	14,195.97	11,160.00
	Henrik NYSTRÖM	SWE	76	69	71	74	290	2	14,195.97	11,160.00
45	Juan ABBATE	ARG	73	71	78	69	291	3	11,677.33	9,180.00
	Christian CÉVAËR	FRA	73	73	72	73	291	3	11,677.33	9,180.00
	Johan EDFORS	SWE	73	74	74	70	291	3	11,677.33	9,180.00
	Martin ERLANDSSON	SWE	74	70	72	75	291	3	11,677.33	9,180.00
	Alvaro QUIROS	ESP	75	72	75	69	291	3	11,677.33	9,180.00
50	Fredrik ANDERSSON HED	SWE	70	73	75	74	292	4	10,074.56	7,920.00
	Jean-François LUCQUIN	FRA	71	72	71	78	292	4	10,074.56	7,920.00
52	Francesco MOLINARI	ITA	70	76	71	76	293	5	8,700.75	6,840.00
	Peter WHITEFORD	SCO	71	75	75	72	293	5	8,700.75	6,840.00
	Paul MCGINLEY	IRL	73	73	70	77	293	5	8,700.75	6,840.00
	Peter HEDBLOM	SWE	75	72	76	70	293	5	8,700.75	6,840.00
56	Marc WARREN	SCO	68	71	78	77	294	6	7,174.31	5,640.00
	Mikko ILONEN	FIN	69	76	74	75	294	6	7,174.31	5,640.00
	Grégory BOURDY	FRA	71	76	72	75	294	6	7,174.31	5,640.00
59	Robert-Jan DERKSEN	NED	70	75	73	77	295	7	6,411.08	5,040.00
	Shiv KAPUR	IND	72	71	78	74	295	7	6,411.08	5,040.00
	Patrik SJÖLAND	SWE	72	73	74	76	295	7	6,411.08	5,040.00
62	Robert GILES	ENG	71	75	76	74	296	8	5,609.70	4,410.00
	Julien CLÉMENT	SUI	72	74	77	73	296	8	5,609.70	4,410.00
	Alastair FORSYTH	SCO	74	71	79	72	296	8	5,609.70	4,410.00
	Peter LAWRIE	IRL	74	72	74	76	296	8	5,609.70	4,410.00
66	David HORSEY	ENG	72	75	79	71	297	9	4,922.79	3,870.00
	Jamie DONALDSON	WAL	76	71	77	73	297	9	4,922.79	3,870.00
68	Simon DYSON	ENG	72	75	77	75	299	11	4,579.34	3,600.00
69	Marcel SIEM	GER	75	72	75	80	302	14	4,350.38	3,420.00
70	Grégory HAVRET	FRA	71	76	81	75	303	15	3,803.15	2,989.80
	Niclas FASTH	SWE	72	72	82	77	303	15	3,803.15	2,989.80
72	Scott DRUMMOND	SCO	74	73	81	76	304	16	3,431.00	2,697.24

Hole	Par	Yards	Metres
1	4	411	376
2	4	379	347
3	5	538	492
4	4	442	404
5	4	408	373
6	4	445	407
7	3	177	162
8	4	438	401
9	4	457	418
OUT	**36**	**3695**	**3380**
10	4	311	284
11	4	426	390
12	3	208	190
13	4	384	351
14	3	190	174
15	5	566	518
16	4	413	378
17	5	564	516
18	4	473	433
IN	**36**	**3535**	**3234**
TOTAL	**72**	**7230**	**6614**

Gonzalo Fernandez-Castaño became the fifth Spanish golfer to win a European Tour event at The Belfry. He followed Seve Ballesteros (1979 English Open), Manuel Piñero (1980 English Open), José Rivero (1984 Lawrence Batley International) and José Maria Olazábal (2000 Benson and Hedges International Open).

Total Prize Fund
€2,296,537 £1,805,396

Ghost Buster

1	**Robert KARLSSON**		**278**	**-10**
2	Ross FISHER		278	-10
	Martin KAYMER		278	-10
4	Jarmo SANDELIN		280	-8
5	Magnus A CARLSSON		281	-7
	José-Filipe LIMA		281	-7
	Anthony WALL		281	-7
8	Paul CASEY		282	-6
	Jamie DONALDSON		282	-6
	Søren HANSEN		282	-6
	Rory McILROY		282	-6
	Lee WESTWOOD		282	-6

ALFRED DUNH
LINKS CHAMPIONS

R obert Karlsson has the aura of a player you might choose to have over a short putt to win The Ryder Cup. The 39 year old Swede has a steely look about him, he exudes confidence and he did, after all, hole an eminently missable downhiller in partnership with Henrik Stenson against the formidable American pairing of Hunter Mahan and Phil Mickelson for a halved match in the 2008 biennial contest against the United States at Valhalla Golf Club during the Saturday afternoon fourball session.

Yet, appearances can be deceptive. In the Alfred Dunhill Links Championship at St Andrews, few were aware of the gremlins in his psyche when he was faced with a three foot birdie putt on the first green of the Old Course to defeat England's Ross Fisher and Germany's Martin Kaymer at the first play-off hole. For not only were the prestigious title and the colossal €545,811 (£432,970) first prize at stake, also on the line was the prospect of moving to Number One on The European Tour Order of Merit for the first time.

It was hardly the monster effort that Paul Lawrie holed from the Valley of Sin to triumph in the tournament in 2001, but in Karlsson's own mind it could have been. For, it was only five months since he failed from not much longer on the final green of Wentworth Club's West Course

to miss out on the play-off for the BMW PGA Championship with eventual winner Miguel Angel Jiménez of Spain and England's Oliver Wilson.

However here, on a sunny day at the home of golf where he had, like Fisher, produced a sparkling seven under par final round of 65 for a ten under par total of 278 to make the play-off, was a chance to lay that ghost to rest.

While Kaymer had faltered at the Road Hole 17th in regulation play – taking three from the right of the green for a bogey five to relinquish the outright lead – and Fisher took his driver on that first play-off hole and struck his ball firmly into the Swilcan Burn, Karlsson took ownership of the tournament by remaining in the present and rolling the little putt securely home.

Jamie Donaldson

Jarmo Sandelin

The 12th hole at Kingsbarns

Ross Fisher

Anthony Wall

It was the third time in a row he had birdied the first hole in a tournament also played over the daunting Championship Course at Carnoustie and the much-vaunted new links at nearby Kingsbarns. He knew a three wood from the tee would leave him his favourite 100 yard wedge distance to the pin to set up the birdie which saw him claim his ninth European Tour victory in total and his second in a row having won the Mercedes-Benz Championship in Germany the week before departing for The Ryder Cup.

While the Swede was taking the plaudits at the business end of the tournament – conceived as a celebration of links golf but now regarded by many as the best Pro-Am tournament in the world – at the other end of the spectrum, Anthony Bryan and Margaret Weder simply enchanted everyone through celebration of the human spirit.

The tournament might have been headlined by Ernie Els and Padraig Harrington, both three time Major Championship winners, and celebrities such as Samuel L Jackson and three time world heavyweight boxing champion Wladimir Klitschko, but this pair needed neither a script nor a knockout punch to make an impact.

Weder, or Maggie as she prefers to be known, is a 50 year old former American marine, a marathon runner in her younger days, but who has suffered from Multiple Sclerosis since 1991. Housebound for six years, golf has helped her to regain muscle co-ordination.

She partnered Zimbabwe's Tony Johnstone who, more than anyone, had empathy for her condition. The 52 year old Sky Sports analyst was himself told four years ago that, having contracted MS, he would never play again. He refused to believe it and, in June this year, confounded medical opinion by claiming an emotional victory in the Jersey Seniors Classic.

The duo played three rounds in tandem, much of it in strong wind, rain and extreme cold. Their combined score of level par was not good enough to make the cut in the team contest but was incidental to the fact that Maggie, who was raising money for her charity Golfin4MS, made it round.

"Golf is just a game, but it saved my life, my quality of life," she said. "I am no hero, I am just someone trying to make a difference. I just want to give a little respect to people who cannot help themselves and that's what keeps me going."

At 85, Anthony Bryan was the oldest player to ever compete in the Alfred Dunhill Links Championship. He, too, would tell you he is no hero, but the former Spitfire pilot can take you back to active service with the Royal Canadian Air Force in World War II when he was shot down behind enemy lines in France. With the help of the French resistance he made it back to England and was later awarded the Distinguished Flying Cross.

A former one handicapper and still playing off 15, he and partner Gary Orr of Scotland appeared briefly on the team leaderboard during the second round. Orr said of Bryan, still a businessman in the United States: "He's a lesson to us all. Getting around in these conditions at that age is absolutely fantastic."

Karlsson joined up with Celtic Football Club's main shareholder Dermot Desmond in the team event to be runners-up, one shot adrift of English professional John Bickerton and nine handicap Bruce Watson, a South African businessman, who returned a 27 under par total of 261.

Douglas Lowe
The Herald

Above The Kaymer family - left to right: Philip, Martin and father Horst who caddied for Philip

Rory McIlroy (left) with his amateur partner, Sir Bobby Charlton

Team Results

Pos		Rd1	Rd2	Rd3	Rd4	Total		€
1	John Bickerton and Bruce Watson	61	69	65	66	261	-27	34,113.22
2	Robert Karlsson and Dermot Desmond	65	68	69	60	262	-26	20,467.93
3	Phillip Archer and Christopher Colfer	64	69	68	63	264	-24	13,645.29
4	Nick Dougherty and Peter Dawson	67	65	70	63	265	-23	8,528.31
	Simon Dyson and Jake White	64	72	66	63	265	-23	8,528.31
6	Ross Fisher and Richard Gilberg	63	70	70	63	266	-22	3,411.32
	Peter Lawrie and Ian Lawrie	64	69	70	63	266	-22	3,411.32
	Lee Westwood and Andrew Chandler	63	67	70	66	266	-22	3,411.32
	David Howell and Sir Ian Botham	64	65	74	63	266	-22	3,411.32
10	Anthony Wall and John Sherman	63	71	69	64	267	-21	3,411.32
	Paul Broadhurst and John Tyson	70	66	65	66	267	-21	3,411.32

The winners of the 2008 Team Competition: English professional John Bickerton (left) with partner, South African businessman Bruce Watson, on the Swilcan Bridge

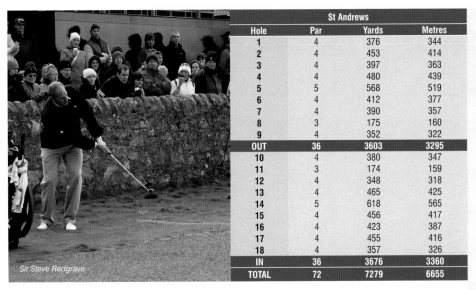

St Andrews			
Hole	Par	Yards	Metres
1	4	376	344
2	4	453	414
3	4	397	363
4	4	480	439
5	5	568	519
6	4	412	377
7	4	390	357
8	3	175	160
9	4	352	322
OUT	36	3603	3295
10	4	380	347
11	3	174	159
12	4	348	318
13	4	465	425
14	5	618	565
15	4	456	417
16	4	423	387
17	4	455	416
18	4	357	326
IN	36	3676	3360
TOTAL	72	7279	6655

Sir Steve Redgrave

Carnoustie			
Hole	Par	Yards	Metres
1	4	406	371
2	4	463	423
3	4	358	327
4	4	412	378
5	4	415	379
6	5	578	529
7	4	410	375
8	3	183	167
9	4	478	437
OUT	36	3703	3386
10	4	466	426
11	4	383	350
12	5	504	461
13	3	176	163
14	5	514	470
15	4	472	432
16	3	248	227
17	4	461	422
18	4	485	443
IN	36	3709	3394
TOTAL	72	7412	6780

Sir Ian Botham

Kingsbarns			
Hole	Par	Yards	Metres
1	4	414	379
2	3	200	183
3	5	516	472
4	4	415	379
5	4	426	390
6	4	337	308
7	4	455	416
8	3	168	154
9	5	558	510
OUT	36	3489	3191
10	4	387	354
11	4	471	431
12	5	606	554
13	3	148	135
14	4	366	335
15	3	200	183
16	5	565	517
17	4	474	433
18	4	444	406
IN	36	3661	3348
TOTAL	72	7150	6539

Samuel L Jackson (left) and Tim Henman

Following his victory in the Mercedes-Benz Championship, Robert Karlsson followed that with his second victory of the season in the Alfred Dunhill Links Championship. It was the first time in his career he has won on consecutive appearances and just the second Swede to achieve the feat, following Henrik Stenson (2007 – Dubai Desert Classic and WGC – Accenture Match Play). His win, via a sudden-death play-off against Ross Fisher and Martin Kaymer, was the 15th play-off of the season – a record for a single season, beating the 14 staged in 2005.

Old Course, St Andrews, Carnoustie and Kingsbarns
Final Results

Pos	Name		Rd1	Rd2	Rd3	Rd4	Total		€	£
1	Robert KARLSSON	SWE	67	70	76	65	278	-10	545,811.55	432,970.76
2	Ross FISHER	ENG	64	76	73	65	278	-10	284,439.46	225,634.61
	Martin KAYMER	GER	65	72	73	68	278	-10	284,439.46	225,634.61
4	Jarmo SANDELIN	SWE	66	72	72	70	280	-8	163,743.46	129,891.24
5	Anthony WALL	ENG	66	76	71	68	281	-7	117,240.32	93,002.09
	José-Filipe LIMA	POR	67	71	75	68	281	-7	117,240.32	93,002.09
	Magnus A CARLSSON	SWE	70	68	73	70	281	-7	117,240.32	93,002.09
8	Søren HANSEN	DEN	64	73	77	68	282	-6	67,462.31	53,515.18
	Rory MCILROY	NIR	68	69	78	67	282	-6	67,462.31	53,515.18
	Lee WESTWOOD	ENG	68	70	76	68	282	-6	67,462.31	53,515.18
	Jamie DONALDSON	WAL	70	70	75	67	282	-6	67,462.31	53,515.18
	Paul CASEY	ENG	72	70	72	68	282	-6	67,462.31	53,515.18
13	Marc WARREN	SCO	66	73	75	69	283	-5	47,267.28	37,495.26
	Thomas AIKEN	RSA	66	74	76	67	283	-5	47,267.28	37,495.26
	Padraig HARRINGTON	IRL	67	71	74	71	283	-5	47,267.28	37,495.26
	Michael CAMPBELL	NZL	68	70	77	68	283	-5	47,267.28	37,495.26
	Charl SCHWARTZEL	RSA	68	72	75	68	283	-5	47,267.28	37,495.26
	Robert-Jan DERKSEN	NED	72	73	72	66	283	-5	47,267.28	37,495.26
19	Markus BRIER	AUT	66	70	76	72	284	-4	38,184.98	30,290.63
	Grégory BOURDY	FRA	66	74	76	68	284	-4	38,184.98	30,290.63
	Thongchai JAIDEE	THA	69	71	72	72	284	-4	38,184.98	30,290.63
	John BICKERTON	ENG	71	72	70	71	284	-4	38,184.98	30,290.63
	Nick DOUGHERTY	ENG	74	71	74	65	284	-4	38,184.98	30,290.63
24	Marcus FRASER	AUS	66	77	71	71	285	-3	32,093.72	25,458.68
	Raphaël JACQUELIN	FRA	68	70	77	70	285	-3	32,093.72	25,458.68
	Peter HEDBLOM	SWE	69	71	77	68	285	-3	32,093.72	25,458.68
	Charley HOFFMAN	USA	69	72	75	69	285	-3	32,093.72	25,458.68
	Stephen GALLACHER	SCO	70	76	74	65	285	-3	32,093.72	25,458.68
	Damien MCGRANE	IRL	71	74	73	67	285	-3	32,093.72	25,458.68
	Jeev Milkha SINGH	IND	71	75	72	67	285	-3	32,093.72	25,458.68
31	Gary ORR	SCO	66	72	77	71	286	-2	26,264.45	20,834.55
	Miles TUNNICLIFF	ENG	68	74	77	67	286	-2	26,264.45	20,834.55
	Graeme MCDOWELL	NIR	68	75	75	68	286	-2	26,264.45	20,834.55
	Peter FOWLER	AUS	68	76	77	65	286	-2	26,264.45	20,834.55
	Ricardo GONZALEZ	ARG	70	72	77	67	286	-2	26,264.45	20,834.55
36	Gonzalo FDEZ-CASTAÑO	ESP	68	73	75	71	287	-1	22,924.09	18,184.77
	Peter LAWRIE	IRL	70	71	73	73	287	-1	22,924.09	18,184.77
	Thomas BJÖRN	DEN	70	73	76	68	287	-1	22,924.09	18,184.77
	James KINGSTON	RSA	72	75	72	68	287	-1	22,924.09	18,184.77
40	Thomas LEVET	FRA	67	74	78	69	288	0	18,994.24	15,067.38
	Alvaro QUIROS	ESP	68	74	76	70	288	0	18,994.24	15,067.38
	Mikko ILONEN	FIN	68	76	73	71	288	0	18,994.24	15,067.38
	Garry HOUSTON	WAL	69	74	75	70	288	0	18,994.24	15,067.38
	Oliver WILSON	ENG	69	76	75	68	288	0	18,994.24	15,067.38
	Louis OOSTHUIZEN	RSA	70	71	76	71	288	0	18,994.24	15,067.38
	Martin ERLANDSSON	SWE	72	74	73	69	288	0	18,994.24	15,067.38
	Joost LUITEN	NED	73	73	75	67	288	0	18,994.24	15,067.38
48	José Manuel LARA	ESP	68	75	76	70	289	1	15,064.40	11,949.99
	Darren CLARKE	NIR	73	74	72	71	289	1	15,064.40	11,949.99
	Alexander NOREN	SWE	73	73	73	70	289	1	15,064.40	11,949.99
	Robert DINWIDDIE	ENG	75	74	72	68	289	1	15,064.40	11,949.99
52	Retief GOOSEN	RSA	67	76	76	71	290	2	11,257.36	8,930.02
	Carl SUNESON	ESP	69	73	78	70	290	2	11,257.36	8,930.02
	Andrew MCLARDY	RSA	69	74	73	74	290	2	11,257.36	8,930.02
	Richard STERNE	RSA	70	75	76	69	290	2	11,257.36	8,930.02
	Matthew MILLAR	AUS	72	77	71	70	290	2	11,257.36	8,930.02
	Henrik NYSTRÖM	SWE	73	75	73	69	290	2	11,257.36	8,930.02
	Peter HANSON	SWE	75	71	75	69	290	2	11,257.36	8,930.02
	Paul BROADHURST	ENG	76	69	75	70	290	2	11,257.36	8,930.02
60	David HOWELL	ENG	66	73	80	72	291	3	8,514.66	6,754.34
	Francesco MOLINARI	ITA	68	75	78	70	291	3	8,514.66	6,754.34
	Alejandro CAÑIZARES	ESP	70	73	76	72	291	3	8,514.66	6,754.34
	Emanuele CANONICA	ITA	70	79	71	71	291	3	8,514.66	6,754.34
	Bradley DREDGE	WAL	71	73	77	70	291	3	8,514.66	6,754.34
65	Lee SLATTERY	ENG	71	75	74	72	292	4	7,532.20	5,975.00
66	Felipe AGUILAR	CHI	68	76	75	74	293	5	6,564.75	5,207.56
	Greg CHALMERS	AUS	70	75	76	72	293	5	6,564.75	5,207.56
	Steve WEBSTER	ENG	70	76	75	72	293	5	6,564.75	5,207.56
	Alastair FORSYTH	SCO	70	77	74	72	293	5	6,564.75	5,207.56
	Justin ROSE	ENG	71	74	74	74	293	5	6,564.75	5,207.56
71	Sam LITTLE	ENG	72	77	72	73	294	6	4,911.00	3,895.31
	Ignacio GARRIDO	ESP	74	72	75	73	294	6	4,911.00	3,895.31

Total Prize Fund
€3,284,691 £2,605,614

Memories and Poignancy

			TOTAL	
1	Charl SCHWARTZEL		265	-19
2	Ricardo GONZALEZ		268	-16
3	Pablo LARRAZABAL		269	-15
4	Alvaro QUIROS		270	-14
	Robert ROCK		270	-14
6	Paul WARING		272	-12
7	Carlos DEL MORAL		273	-11
8	Thongchai JAIDEE		274	-10
	Damien McGRANE		274	-10
10	Jesus Maria ARRUTI		275	-9
	Rafael CABRERA BELLO		275	-9
	Ignacio GARRIDO		275	-9

A return to the Spanish capital and to its most famous and traditional golf club was always going to stir memories and poignancy. But the inaugural Madrid Masters provided much more than that.

Ricardo Gonzalez

Jean-Baptiste Gonnet

Robert Rock

Charl Schwartzel will certainly never forget his third European Tour success, but even the young South African was moved to admit that his victory celebrations were not the main emotion felt by most people during the week.

That was because Spain's most famous golfing son, Seve Ballesteros, whose legendary feats had stirred Club de Campo Villa de Madrid so many times in the past, was in everyone's thoughts.

The five time Major winner lay stricken in the city's La Paz Hospital. He had fainted and lost consciousness at Barajas Airport not long before the tournament began. He went through tests as the week progressed and it was discovered on the Sunday night, soon after the tournament had finished, that he had a brain tumour.

The golfing world had been holding its breath - it then began to pray for The European Tour's charismatic mentor.

His close friend and protégé, José Maria Olazábal, had been checking on him daily and was distraught to hear the news coming, ironically, in a week where the double Masters Tournament Champion himself was clawing his own way back to fitness after rheumatic problems with his back allied to side effects from medication.

When, after three months away from the game altogether, he had scrambled past the cut mark and into the weekend, he gave his reason for finding such determination and short game magic to make it through. "I had a great teacher," he said. We all knew, of course, to whom he was referring.

On the plus side for Olazábal on the golf course at least, it was good news. He managed to play four rounds without further injury worries and kept largely free from pain. The resolute 42 year old appeared to have overcome his second career-threatening crisis and, understandably, he was looking ahead optimistically to a stress free 2009 season.

Of course, the 2009 season is a momentous one for The European Tour International Schedule and Schwartzel's outlook for the inaugural Race to Dubai is undeniably bright.

The 24 year old from Johannesburg achieved victory with a mixture of skill – as illustrated by his four rounds in the 60s for a 19 under par winning total of 265 – but also with a modicum of determination to overcome his own illness and injury woes.

A debilitating respiratory virus that had affected many on The European Tour over the autumn period had struck Schwartzel down the previous week. A course of antibiotics was improving his condition steadily but then, after his opening round of 69, he awoke on Friday morning with a 'frozen' shoulder-blade. Fatigue and now sharp pain caused by a pinched muscle, left him contemplating withdrawing from the tournament to avoid risking any further damage.

However, advice from his father George to give the round a go and see how he went before taking any drastic steps, persuaded him to soldier on. As soon as his first birdie went on the card, at the 13th after having started at the tenth, Schwartzel knew his father was right. By the time he had finished the day sharing the lead with Australia's Marcus Fraser after a stunning 64, he was already warning everybody; "Beware the injured golfer!"

Paul Waring

To make sure his shoulder pain did not recur, The European Tour Physiotherapy Unit staff stepped in to offer their expertise, strapping it up overnight to avoid strain on it from movement in his sleep. It worked a treat. A closing birdie on Saturday night held off a rampaging Ricardo Gonzalez and ensured he would take a one shot lead into the final round.

The Argentine, who had won the Open de Madrid on the same course in 2003, had had a memorable day once again in the city he called "my second home." Indeed a scintillating back nine of 27 in his nine under par 62 would have seen his name enter the record books but for the preferred lies in operation.

Into the final round, though, there was never any question over who would gain ownership of the trophy as Schwartzel broke the field early, maintained a firm grip all day and eased home to pocket the €166,660 (£129,795) first prize. It also continued his love affair with Madrid for, the previous April, he had claimed his second European Tour title – the 2007 Open de España – at the nearby Centro Nacional de Golf.

Gonzalez took second, three shots adrift, while another Spaniard, Open de France ALSTOM champion Pablo Larrazabal, made a mark on the week and re-established himself as the firm favourite to become the 2008 Sir Henry Cotton

Rookie of the Year with closing rounds of 62-67 to take third.

While the home fans rightly rejoiced at Larrazabal's showing – as they did for Alvaro Quiros whose closing 64 saw him move from 11th to share fourth with England's Robert Rock – everyone knew where their thoughts, and those of everyone in the world of golf, were truly directed that Sunday night.

Norman Dabell

Left to right: Santiago Fisas, Ministry of Culture and Tourism, Charl Schwartzel and Juan Astorqui, Communications Director of Caja Madrid

Sam Little

Pablo Larrazabal

Hole	Par	Yards	Metres
1	4	467	427
2	4	442	404
3	3	207	189
4	5	518	474
5	4	407	372
6	4	442	404
7	5	540	494
8	4	385	352
9	3	177	162
OUT	**36**	**3565**	**3278**
10	4	411	376
11	3	210	192
12	4	445	407
13	4	467	427
14	5	526	481
15	4	375	343
16	4	422	386
17	3	167	153
18	4	362	331
IN	**35**	**3385**	**3096**
TOTAL	**71**	**6950**	**6374**

i Charl Schwartzel is the third South African to win at the Club de Campo Villa de Madrid. He follows Retief Goosen (2001 Open de Madrid) and Richard Sterne (2004 Open de Madrid).

Club de Campo Villa de Madrid

Final Results

Pos	Name		Rd1	Rd2	Rd3	Rd4	Total		€	£
1	Charl SCHWARTZEL	RSA	69	64	66	66	265	-19	166,660.00	129,795.49
2	Ricardo GONZALEZ	ARG	69	69	62	68	268	-16	111,110.00	86,532.92
3	Pablo LARRAZABAL	ESP	68	72	62	67	269	-15	62,600.00	48,753.13
4	Robert ROCK	ENG	70	65	71	64	270	-14	46,200.00	35,980.75
	Alvaro QUIROS	ESP	74	66	66	64	270	-14	46,200.00	35,980.75
6	Paul WARING	ENG	69	67	67	69	272	-12	35,000.00	27,258.14
7	Carlos DEL MORAL	ESP	69	67	67	70	273	-11	30,000.00	23,364.12
8	Damien MCGRANE	IRL	69	68	68	69	274	-10	23,700.00	18,457.66
	Thongchai JAIDEE	THA	69	69	67	69	274	-10	23,700.00	18,457.66
10	Ignacio GARRIDO	ESP	70	68	67	70	275	-9	18,533.33	14,433.84
	Jesus Maria ARRUTI	ESP	72	67	70	66	275	-9	18,533.33	14,433.84
	Rafael CABRERA BELLO	ESP	74	68	66	67	275	-9	18,533.33	14,433.84
13	Steve WEBSTER	ENG	68	69	71	68	276	-8	15,366.67	11,967.62
	Sion E BEBB	WAL	69	68	68	71	276	-8	15,366.67	11,967.62
	Andrew TAMPION	AUS	75	63	65	73	276	-8	15,366.67	11,967.62
16	James KAMTE	RSA	68	70	72	67	277	-7	12,980.00	10,108.88
	Kyron SULLIVAN	WAL	71	68	68	70	277	-7	12,980.00	10,108.88
	Martin KAYMER	GER	71	69	67	70	277	-7	12,980.00	10,108.88
	Tom WHITEHOUSE	ENG	71	70	66	70	277	-7	12,980.00	10,108.88
	Fredrik ANDERSSON HED	SWE	72	69	71	65	277	-7	12,980.00	10,108.88
21	Marcus FRASER	AUS	67	66	74	71	278	-6	10,550.00	8,216.38
	Magnus A CARLSSON	SWE	67	70	73	68	278	-6	10,550.00	8,216.38
	Steven JEPPESEN	SWE	68	67	71	72	278	-6	10,550.00	8,216.38
	Patrik SJÖLAND	SWE	70	69	70	69	278	-6	10,550.00	8,216.38
	Joakim BÄCKSTRÖM	SWE	70	69	71	68	278	-6	10,550.00	8,216.38
	Angel CABRERA	ARG	71	69	70	68	278	-6	10,550.00	8,216.38
	Sam LITTLE	ENG	71	70	71	66	278	-6	10,550.00	8,216.38
	Pelle EDBERG	SWE	72	70	67	69	278	-6	10,550.00	8,216.38
29	Paul BROADHURST	ENG	67	72	69	71	279	-5	8,187.50	6,376.46
	José Manuel LARA	ESP	69	69	72	69	279	-5	8,187.50	6,376.46
	Francis VALERA	ESP	69	70	71	69	279	-5	8,187.50	6,376.46
	Miguel Angel JIMÉNEZ	ESP	69	71	72	67	279	-5	8,187.50	6,376.46
	Eduardo DE LA RIVA	ESP	71	71	65	72	279	-5	8,187.50	6,376.46
	Paul LAWRIE	SCO	72	68	72	67	279	-5	8,187.50	6,376.46
	Steve ALKER	NZL	73	66	71	69	279	-5	8,187.50	6,376.46
	Leif WESTERBERG	SWE	75	66	72	66	279	-5	8,187.50	6,376.46
37	François DELAMONTAGNE	FRA	70	72	71	67	280	-4	6,600.00	5,140.11
	Stephen GALLACHER	SCO	71	65	71	73	280	-4	6,600.00	5,140.11
	Phillip ARCHER	ENG	71	69	69	71	280	-4	6,600.00	5,140.11
	Mattias ELIASSON	SWE	72	69	70	69	280	-4	6,600.00	5,140.11
	Bradley DREDGE	WAL	73	66	70	71	280	-4	6,600.00	5,140.11
	Lee SLATTERY	ENG	73	66	69	72	280	-4	6,600.00	5,140.11
43	Santiago LUNA	ESP	68	68	71	74	281	-3	5,200.00	4,049.78
	Jean-Baptiste GONNET	FRA	69	68	73	71	281	-3	5,200.00	4,049.78
	Joel SJOHOLM	SWE	71	68	75	67	281	-3	5,200.00	4,049.78
	Emanuele CANONICA	ITA	71	70	74	66	281	-3	5,200.00	4,049.78
	Benoit TEILLERIA	FRA	71	71	69	70	281	-3	5,200.00	4,049.78
	Rafa ECHENIQUE	ARG	72	70	68	71	281	-3	5,200.00	4,049.78
	Miles TUNNICLIFF	ENG	74	66	71	70	281	-3	5,200.00	4,049.78
	Jarmo SANDELIN	SWE	75	67	73	66	281	-3	5,200.00	4,049.78
51	Ariel CANETE	ARG	69	71	70	72	282	-2	4,200.00	3,270.98
	Gabriel CANIZARES	ESP	71	71	73	67	282	-2	4,200.00	3,270.98
53	Peter O'MALLEY	AUS	70	71	72	70	283	-1	3,600.00	2,803.69
	Pedro LINHART	ESP	71	70	74	68	283	-1	3,600.00	2,803.69
	Richard STERNE	RSA	72	67	73	71	283	-1	3,600.00	2,803.69
	Lee S JAMES	ENG	73	69	75	66	283	-1	3,600.00	2,803.69
57	Miguel Angel MARTIN	ESP	71	70	70	73	284	0	3,000.00	2,336.41
	Simon WAKEFIELD	ENG	72	69	71	72	284	0	3,000.00	2,336.41
	Edoardo MOLINARI	ITA	75	67	68	74	284	0	3,000.00	2,336.41
60	Julio ZAPATA	ARG	70	69	74	72	285	1	2,600.00	2,024.89
	Gary MURPHY	IRL	70	71	72	72	285	1	2,600.00	2,024.89
	Jean-François LUCQUIN	FRA	70	72	76	67	285	1	2,600.00	2,024.89
	Stuart MANLEY	WAL	71	70	70	74	285	1	2,600.00	2,024.89
	Alfredo GARCIA-HEREDIA	ESP	72	70	70	73	285	1	2,600.00	2,024.89
65	José Maria OLAZÁBAL	ESP	70	72	71	73	286	2	2,250.00	1,752.31
	Carlos BALMASEDA	ESP	71	71	73	71	286	2	2,250.00	1,752.31
67	Paolo TERRENI	ITA	71	65	72	82	290	6	2,050.00	1,596.55
	Peter FOWLER	AUS	72	70	76	72	290	6	2,050.00	1,596.55
69	Peter BAKER	ENG	69	73	76	73	291	7	1,865.00	1,452.47
	Pablo MARTIN	ESP	73	67	80	71	291	7	1,865.00	1,452.47

Total Prize Fund

€1,000,000 £778,804

Majestic Conclusion

1	**Alvaro QUIROS**		**269**	**-19**
2	Paul LAWRIE		272	-16
3	Ross FISHER		273	-15
	Robert KARLSSON		273	-15
	Steve WEBSTER		273	-15
6	James KINGSTON		274	-14
7	Grégory BOURDY		275	-13
	Simon DYSON		275	-13
	Søren HANSEN		275	-13
10	Rory McILROY		276	-12
	Anthony WALL		276	-12
	Chris WOOD		276	-12

As the world of golf collectively said a silent prayer for Seve Ballesteros, further impressive evidence of his influence on the sport in his homeland was seen at Vilamoura in Portugal when another young Spaniard triumphed on The European Tour.

This time it was the turn of 25 year old Alvaro Quiros to receive the plaudits, following on from Pablo Larrazabal's splendid success in June's Open de France ALSTOM and Gonzalo Fernandez-Castaño's battling victory in The Quinn Insurance British Masters last month.

Quiros' ability to fire balls like a human bazooka reminded Dave McNeilly – the Spaniard's caddie at the Oceânico Victoria Golf Course – of the time he explored golf's outer limits during a three week stint with a young John Daly.

Let it be clear that we are talking about Daly's distance here, not his capacity to party. Quiros certainly likes to 'Grip It and Rip It' but even if Ulsterman McNeilly, a 26 year Tour veteran, cheerfully describes him as "a free spirit", Alvaro is certainly no 'Wild Thing.'

Instead, he impresses friends and rivals alike with his affable nature and ready smile. For example, Englishman Ross Fisher relished playing alongside him and Robert Karlsson in the final group on Sunday, admitting: "Alvaro is so funny, he really is a breath of fresh air."

Fisher also found himself in an unfamiliar situation in that towering three ball. "At six feet two inches, being the shortest person in the group as well as the shortest off the tee takes some beating!" he exclaimed.

Quiros swings with such force – the guys on the Callaway truck say he goes through more drivers than any of their other clients – that he always travels with a spare, just in case.

The Spaniard has also damaged himself. After opening the 2007 season with his maiden European Tour victory in the Alfred Dunhill Championship in South Africa – his first tournament as a full European Tour Member – he injured his wrist so badly on the driving range that May, it took five months to recover from surgery.

Physically now, the joint is as strong as ever, as he proved when he sped back to the top of the long driving charts in 2008. In professional golf, length is important and also exhilarating for the spectators who want to be thrilled when they turn up alongside the fairway ropes.

Alexander Noren

Alvaro Quiros (right), receives the trophy from Manuel Pinho, Minister for Economy and Innovation

James Kingston

Paul Lawrie

Steve Webster

Søren Hansen

Quiros certainly gave fans their money's worth on the Algarve as he swept home three ahead of the 1999 Open Champion Paul Lawrie of Scotland, with Karlsson falling just short of a hat-trick of tournament wins in a tie for third with defending champion Steve Webster of England and Fisher.

According to the Genworth Financial Statistics, Quiros' average drive on Tour is just over 310 yards, more than the width of the Thames at Westminster. In dead calm, on a flat course, he can drive his ball around 330 yards. Downwind, it will travel 350 yards or more.

One might expect a chap who pushes new technology to the limit to take at least a passing interest in the astonishing numbers he crunches. Not the young Spaniard. Asked what his believed his clubhead speed might be, he shrugged and smiled: "I have no idea. When I pick up a club, I just know 'this one I like, this one I don't!'"

After three days of hitting the ball satisfyingly straight, Quiros led Fisher and Karlsson by one shot going into the last round, which would become a more searching test of nerve than the final tally suggests.

Though the gloss disappeared from his long game early on Sunday, Quiros found the Midas touch with his putter. After toughing it out for much of the day, he underlined his class by finishing with two birdies, bringing a heavenly week on the Algarve to a majestic conclusion.

The €500,000 (£395,344) he won also guaranteed him a place in the Volvo Masters, a major milestone for a young man born and reared in the Andalusian village of Guadiaro, less than five minutes from Valderrama.

"This guy is going to be an absolute superstar," enthused McNeilly, who intimated he would like to make permanent his temporary partnership with The European Tour's latest champion.

"For sheer natural talent, he's as good as anyone I've worked with," he added. "I mean, Padraig Harrington is an incredibly gifted player. He's the second best player in the world, could even be the best, but Alvaro can do stuff Padraig can't. He's got so much game, he can do things not many people can.

"When somebody hits it that far and straight as well, course design doesn't cater for it. So, all of a sudden, you can start being way more adventurous and creative out there."

The swashbuckling Quiros could not have chosen a better time to underline the strength of the game in Spain. Keep an eye out for him in the future.

Karl MacGinty
Irish Independent

293

Portugal

Portraits by Nick Knight

"My country is the best golf destination in the world"

Find out international football star Cristiano Ronaldo's suggestions on **www.visitportugal.com**

Portugal

Europe's West Coast

TURISMO DE
PORTUGAL

Ross Fisher

Oceânico Victoria Golf Course

Final Results

Pos	Name		Rd1	Rd2	Rd3	Rd4	Total		€	£
1	Alvaro QUIROS	ESP	66	68	67	68	269	-19	500,000.00	395,344.42
2	Paul LAWRIE	SCO	70	65	70	67	272	-16	333,330.00	263,560.31
3	Ross FISHER	ENG	67	70	65	71	273	-15	155,000.00	122,556.77
	Robert KARLSSON	SWE	69	67	66	71	273	-15	155,000.00	122,556.77
	Steve WEBSTER	ENG	72	67	66	68	273	-15	155,000.00	122,556.77
6	James KINGSTON	RSA	69	71	64	70	274	-14	105,000.00	83,022.33
7	Grégory BOURDY	FRA	69	67	68	71	275	-13	77,400.00	61,199.32
	Simon DYSON	ENG	71	69	67	68	275	-13	77,400.00	61,199.32
	Søren HANSEN	DEN	73	65	65	72	275	-13	77,400.00	61,199.32
10	Rory MCILROY	NIR	69	69	69	69	276	-12	55,600.00	43,962.30
	Anthony WALL	ENG	72	66	70	68	276	-12	55,600.00	43,962.30
	Chris WOOD	ENG	73	70	68	65	276	-12	55,600.00	43,962.30
13	Andrew MCLARDY	RSA	67	75	66	69	277	-11	48,300.00	38,190.27
14	Stuart MANLEY	WAL	65	68	73	72	278	-10	45,000.00	35,581.00
	David LYNN	ENG	70	69	68	71	278	-10	45,000.00	35,581.00
16	Søren KJELDSEN	DEN	67	74	72	66	279	-9	38,940.00	30,789.42
	Bradley DREDGE	WAL	70	70	67	72	279	-9	38,940.00	30,789.42
	Robert-Jan DERKSEN	NED	71	68	67	73	279	-9	38,940.00	30,789.42
	Alexander NOREN	SWE	71	69	67	72	279	-9	38,940.00	30,789.42
	Lee WESTWOOD	ENG	72	67	72	68	279	-9	38,940.00	30,789.42
21	Sam WALKER	ENG	67	73	69	71	280	-8	34,350.00	27,160.16
	Garry HOUSTON	WAL	73	66	73	68	280	-8	34,350.00	27,160.16
23	Mark FOSTER	ENG	66	71	73	71	281	-7	30,300.00	23,957.87
	Martin ERLANDSSON	SWE	67	73	73	68	281	-7	30,300.00	23,957.87
	Felipe AGUILAR	CHI	68	68	72	73	281	-7	30,300.00	23,957.87
	Peter LAWRIE	IRL	72	69	71	69	281	-7	30,300.00	23,957.87
	Darren CLARKE	NIR	72	69	74	66	281	-7	30,300.00	23,957.87
	Angel CABRERA	ARG	73	69	66	73	281	-7	30,300.00	23,957.87
	Gary ORR	SCO	74	68	68	71	281	-7	30,300.00	23,957.87
30	Jyoti RANDHAWA	IND	66	70	74	72	282	-6	23,775.00	18,798.63
	Jean-François LUCQUIN	FRA	67	69	73	73	282	-6	23,775.00	18,798.63
	Marc WARREN	SCO	68	73	70	71	282	-6	23,775.00	18,798.63
	Magnus A CARLSSON	SWE	69	66	72	75	282	-6	23,775.00	18,798.63
	Paul WARING	ENG	71	71	68	72	282	-6	23,775.00	18,798.63
	Martin KAYMER	GER	72	65	73	72	282	-6	23,775.00	18,798.63
	David DIXON	ENG	72	69	72	69	282	-6	23,775.00	18,798.63
	David HOWELL	ENG	74	70	67	71	282	-6	23,775.00	18,798.63
38	Jamie DONALDSON	WAL	69	70	74	70	283	-5	19,800.00	15,655.64
	Francesco MOLINARI	ITA	72	72	71	68	283	-5	19,800.00	15,655.64
	Miguel Angel JIMÉNEZ	ESP	73	71	69	70	283	-5	19,800.00	15,655.64
	Oliver FISHER	ENG	73	71	71	68	283	-5	19,800.00	15,655.64
42	Graeme MCDOWELL	NIR	67	74	73	70	284	-4	17,700.00	13,995.19
	Phillip PRICE	WAL	69	70	74	71	284	-4	17,700.00	13,995.19
	Richard GREEN	AUS	71	69	72	72	284	-4	17,700.00	13,995.19
45	Jesus Maria ARRUTI	ESP	69	72	72	72	285	-3	15,900.00	12,571.95
	Johan EDFORS	SWE	70	71	72	72	285	-3	15,900.00	12,571.95
	Peter HANSON	SWE	73	69	70	73	285	-3	15,900.00	12,571.95
48	Stephen GALLACHER	SCO	69	71	72	74	286	-2	13,500.00	10,674.30
	Gary MURPHY	IRL	69	74	68	75	286	-2	13,500.00	10,674.30
	John BICKERTON	ENG	71	73	69	73	286	-2	13,500.00	10,674.30
	Ricardo GONZALEZ	ARG	72	70	72	72	286	-2	13,500.00	10,674.30
	Maarten LAFEBER	NED	74	68	73	71	286	-2	13,500.00	10,674.30
53	Thomas LEVET	FRA	71	73	73	70	287	-1	11,100.00	8,776.65
	Patrik SJÖLAND	SWE	72	72	69	74	287	-1	11,100.00	8,776.65
	Robert ROCK	ENG	72	72	72	71	287	-1	11,100.00	8,776.65
56	David FROST	RSA	69	72	73	74	288	0	9,400.00	7,432.48
	Henrik NYSTRÖM	SWE	70	73	73	72	288	0	9,400.00	7,432.48
	Alvaro VELASCO	ESP	73	71	73	71	288	0	9,400.00	7,432.48
59	Marcel SIEM	GER	68	71	73	78	290	2	8,400.00	6,641.79
	António SOBRINHO	POR	70	73	73	74	290	2	8,400.00	6,641.79
	Grégory HAVRET	FRA	71	71	71	77	290	2	8,400.00	6,641.79
62	Rafa ECHENIQUE	ARG	72	71	71	77	291	3	7,800.00	6,167.37
63	Nick DOUGHERTY	ENG	70	70	73	79	292	4	7,350.00	5,811.56
	Jean-Baptiste GONNET	FRA	73	71	74	74	292	4	7,350.00	5,811.56
65	Sion E BEBB	WAL	68	74	72	79	293	5	6,600.00	5,218.55
	Robert DINWIDDIE	ENG	72	68	72	81	293	5	6,600.00	5,218.55
	Jarmo SANDELIN	SWE	73	69	74	77	293	5	6,600.00	5,218.55
68	Graeme STORM	ENG	69	69	72	85	295	7	6,000.00	4,744.13
69	Barry LANE	ENG	68	70	78	81	297	9	5,585.00	4,416.00
	Raphaël JACQUELIN	FRA	72	69	73	83	297	9	5,585.00	4,416.00

Hole	Par	Yards	Metres
1	4	446	408
2	4	358	327
3	5	566	517
4	4	407	372
5	5	579	529
6	3	218	199
7	4	510	466
8	3	168	154
9	4	442	404
OUT	36	3694	3376
10	4	406	371
11	4	385	352
12	5	547	500
13	3	200	183
14	4	424	388
15	4	315	288
16	3	208	190
17	5	589	538
18	4	463	423
IN	36	3537	3233
TOTAL	72	7231	6609

Alvaro Quiros maintained his outstanding record in the Portugal Masters. In the inaugural event in 2007, he was 11th. Twelve months later he followed that up with his second European Tour victory. For his eight rounds in the event he is a total of 35 under par. He was 17 under in 2007 and 19 below par in winning, with all eight being under par and six of them sub-70.

Total Prize Fund

€3,000,000 £2,372,066

Done and Dusted

1	Sergio **GARCIA**		264	-20
2	Peter HEDBLOM		267	-17
3	Alexander NOREN		269	-15
4	Simon DYSON		270	-14
	Søren KJELDSEN		270	-14
	David LYNN		270	-14
7	Richard FINCH		271	-13
	Peter HANSON		271	-13
9	Paul CASEY		272	-12
	Stephen GALLACHER		272	-12
	Mikael LUNDBERG		272	-12
	Rory McILROY		272	-12

The fact that Sergio Garcia cleaned up on his own doorstep by winning the CASTELLÓ MASTERS Costa Azahar will have come as no great surprise to his doting mother, Consuelo. For, at the age of three, the tiny tot could be found wandering around the family home adjacent to the eighth hole at Club de Campo del Mediterráneo wielding a feather duster in his hands.

However, do not get the strange idea that little Sergio had an abnormal cleaning fetish! It was just that, in the absence of the real thing, the golf-obsessed youngster borrowed his mum's duster on a stick as an ersatz golf club - the only means of trying to mimic the swing of his father, Victor, down at the end of the practice range.

A quarter of a century later, the feather implement has been replaced by the most high-tech equipment money can buy and Garcia is one of the world's most gifted and successful professional golfers. But the anecdote of how the little boy first grooved his golf swing still makes his proud parents smile contentedly.

"Sergio loved golf from a very early age," recalled Victor, the first teaching professional at the Club de Campo del Mediterráneo, set among the olive and carob trees high in the hills above Castellón where the family have lived for 30 years.

Garcia Snr, who still fills that role to this day with Consuelo running the club shop, recounted: "When he was about three, he used to watch me

teaching on the range and he would go home and try to make a swing himself. The only thing he could find was the duster to imitate the golf swing and, of course, when Consuelo wanted to clean the house and could not find the duster, she knew where it would be!"

Fast forward 25 years and little has changed at Club de Campo del Mediterráneo, other than the refinements to the course suggested and overseen by father and son, and the refurbishment of the clubhouse and facilities for the inaugural edition of the CASTELLÓ MASTERS Costa Azahar.

The family still live on the complex. Sergio, as the club's Touring Professional, travels the world while his two siblings, Victor Jnr and sister, Mar, are involved in the promotion of golf in the region. Sergio's parents met and married when Victor was teaching professional at La Manga where Consuelo worked. By good fortune, the President of the new club in Castellón played golf socially at La Manga and invited the couple to move there.

Sergio Garcia (right), receives the trophy from Francisco Camps, President of the Comunitat Valenciana

Below left Stephen Gallacher

David Lynn

Paul Casey

Simon Dyson

Peter Hedblom

Since then, Victor has been father, coach, mentor, caddie and adviser to his hugely talented son. As a partnership they have been unbreakable, despite some glitches along the way when Sergio's detractors felt he needed a more recognised coach to help him progress. That strong bond exists to this day, and there was no mistaking the rosy glow of contentment on Victor's rumpled features when his son sank the putt which secured his seventh European Tour title in front of family, friends and well-wishers on his home course.

"My dad has always been there to offer me advice," said Garcia, whose brilliance has taken him to the brink of Major Championship glory on several occasions in his first decade as a professional. "He has always told me to enjoy what I do on and off the golf course but, most importantly, he told me to be myself. That is always what I try to do."

Although not able to replicate his own personal best of 62 over the par 71 layout, he did achieve impressive rounds of 66-65-66-67 for a 20 under par total of 264, comfortably ahead of a pair of Swedes; second placed Peter Hedblom on 267

and third placed Alexander Noren on 269.

"It almost feels like winning a Major to me," he declared. "I grew up here, I've lived here all my life and every time I looked up, I saw somebody I knew. It was difficult not to stop and say hello! I just tried to focus on my game and not be distracted."

There were some other special moments during the week, too, none more so than when Colombia's new star, Camilo Villegas, who had travelled over to join in the fun with his good friend Garcia, holed in one at the 12th during the second round.

However, the week – and the tournament – belonged to one man, a player who had not won in Europe for three years. Typically though, Garcia picked himself up, dusted himself down, and showed what a great champion can achieve with a proper golf club in his hands!

Gordon Simpson

299

Preparing the ground
for innovation

Victor Garcia (left) with tennis star Rafael Nadal during the tournament Pro-Am

Hole	Par	Yards	Metres
1	4	377	345
2	3	228	208
3	4	458	419
4	5	634	580
5	4	447	409
6	3	195	178
7	4	339	310
8	5	554	506
9	4	444	406
OUT	36	3676	3361
10	4	368	337
11	4	336	307
12	3	223	204
13	5	596	545
14	4	366	335
15	4	428	391
16	3	186	170
17	4	503	460
18	4	429	392
IN	35	3435	3141
TOTAL	71	7111	6502

Sergio Garcia's victory in the CASTELLÓ MASTERS Costa Azahar was the fifth by a Spanish golfer on The 2008 European Tour International Schedule. The five are: Miguel Angel Jiménez (UBS Hong Kong Open and BMW PGA Championship), Pablo Larrazabal (Open de France ALSTOM), Gonzalo-Fernandez-Castaño (The Quinn Insurance British Masters), Alvaro Quiros (Portugal Masters) and Garcia (CASTELLÓ MASTERS Costa Azahar). This marks the first time since 1992, five different players from that country have won in the same European Tour season.

Club de Campo del Mediterráneo

Final Results

Pos	Name		Rd1	Rd2	Rd3	Rd4	Total		€	£
1	Sergio GARCIA	ESP	66	65	66	67	264	-20	333,330.00	258,115.22
2	Peter HEDBLOM	SWE	68	65	68	66	267	-17	222,220.00	172,076.82
3	Alexander NOREN	SWE	68	68	68	65	269	-15	125,200.00	96,949.05
4	Søren KJELDSEN	DEN	64	67	70	69	270	-14	84,933.33	65,768.42
	Simon DYSON	ENG	66	67	68	69	270	-14	84,933.33	65,768.42
	David LYNN	ENG	67	66	68	69	270	-14	84,933.33	65,768.42
7	Richard FINCH	ENG	65	66	71	69	271	-13	55,000.00	42,589.44
	Peter HANSON	SWE	65	73	67	66	271	-13	55,000.00	42,589.44
9	Mikael LUNDBERG	SWE	67	68	68	69	272	-12	39,000.00	30,199.78
	Stephen GALLACHER	SCO	67	70	65	70	272	-12	39,000.00	30,199.78
	Rory MCILROY	NIR	68	67	69	68	272	-12	39,000.00	30,199.78
	Paul CASEY	ENG	69	67	69	67	272	-12	39,000.00	30,199.78
13	Alvaro QUIROS	ESP	67	66	76	64	273	-11	31,400.00	24,314.70
	Jeev Milkha SINGH	IND	71	66	69	67	273	-11	31,400.00	24,314.70
15	Ignacio GARRIDO	ESP	65	70	69	70	274	-10	27,040.00	20,938.52
	Angel CABRERA	ARG	65	72	69	68	274	-10	27,040.00	20,938.52
	Alvaro VELASCO	ESP	66	71	69	68	274	-10	27,040.00	20,938.52
	José María OLAZÁBAL	ESP	66	72	67	69	274	-10	27,040.00	20,938.52
	Sam LITTLE	ENG	72	69	66	67	274	-10	27,040.00	20,938.52
20	Thomas LEVET	FRA	66	68	73	68	275	-9	22,950.00	17,771.41
	Phillip ARCHER	ENG	67	68	70	70	275	-9	22,950.00	17,771.41
	Jarmo SANDELIN	SWE	69	67	67	72	275	-9	22,950.00	17,771.41
	Maarten LAFEBER	NED	70	66	69	70	275	-9	22,950.00	17,771.41
24	Thomas BJÖRN	DEN	69	68	68	71	276	-8	20,200.00	15,641.94
	Camilo VILLEGAS	COL	70	66	71	69	276	-8	20,200.00	15,641.94
	Gary ORR	SCO	70	67	69	70	276	-8	20,200.00	15,641.94
	Jesus Maria ARRUTI	ESP	70	68	67	71	276	-8	20,200.00	15,641.94
	Felipe AGUILAR	CHI	71	67	68	70	276	-8	20,200.00	15,641.94
29	Nick DOUGHERTY	ENG	68	69	72	68	277	-7	17,200.00	13,318.88
	Chris WOOD	ENG	68	72	69	68	277	-7	17,200.00	13,318.88
	Gonzalo FDEZ-CASTAÑO	ESP	69	68	68	72	277	-7	17,200.00	13,318.88
	José-Filipe LIMA	POR	70	70	67	70	277	-7	17,200.00	13,318.88
	Francesco MOLINARI	ITA	72	65	70	70	277	-7	17,200.00	13,318.88
34	John BICKERTON	ENG	66	70	73	69	278	-6	14,400.00	11,150.69
	Justin ROSE	ENG	67	70	70	71	278	-6	14,400.00	11,150.69
	Jean VAN DE VELDE	FRA	68	70	68	72	278	-6	14,400.00	11,150.69
	Bradley DREDGE	WAL	71	68	68	71	278	-6	14,400.00	11,150.69
	Martin ERLANDSSON	SWE	71	69	67	71	278	-6	14,400.00	11,150.69
	Mark FOSTER	ENG	72	70	68	68	278	-6	14,400.00	11,150.69
40	David GRIFFITHS	ENG	67	71	70	71	279	-5	11,800.00	9,137.37
	Alastair FORSYTH	SCO	68	70	73	68	279	-5	11,800.00	9,137.37
	Stuart MANLEY	WAL	69	68	73	69	279	-5	11,800.00	9,137.37
	Paul LAWRIE	SCO	71	70	71	67	279	-5	11,800.00	9,137.37
	Christian CÉVAÉR	FRA	72	68	69	70	279	-5	11,800.00	9,137.37
	Ross McGOWAN	ENG	72	69	70	68	279	-5	11,800.00	9,137.37
	Markus BRIER	AUT	74	67	76	62	279	-5	11,800.00	9,137.37
47	François DELAMONTAGNE	FRA	66	67	73	74	280	-4	9,600.00	7,433.79
	Richard STERNE	RSA	71	69	71	69	280	-4	9,600.00	7,433.79
	Anthony WALL	ENG	71	69	67	73	280	-4	9,600.00	7,433.79
	Barry LANE	ENG	71	69	72	68	280	-4	9,600.00	7,433.79
51	Grégory BOURDY	FRA	68	70	67	76	281	-3	8,200.00	6,349.70
	Pedro LINHART	ESP	68	72	70	71	281	-3	8,200.00	6,349.70
	Pablo LARRAZABAL	ESP	71	68	71	71	281	-3	8,200.00	6,349.70
54	Ricardo GONZALEZ	ARG	67	71	73	71	282	-2	6,800.00	5,265.60
	Garry HOUSTON	WAL	67	71	71	73	282	-2	6,800.00	5,265.60
	Magnus A CARLSSON	SWE	71	68	70	73	282	-2	6,800.00	5,265.60
	Jean-François REMESY	FRA	73	69	71	69	282	-2	6,800.00	5,265.60
58	Benn BARHAM	ENG	68	72	75	68	283	-1	5,600.00	4,336.38
	Fredrik ANDERSSON HED	SWE	69	73	71	70	283	-1	5,600.00	4,336.38
	David HOWELL	ENG	69	73	72	69	283	-1	5,600.00	4,336.38
	Johan EDFORS	SWE	70	71	72	70	283	-1	5,600.00	4,336.38
	Simon WAKEFIELD	ENG	72	68	73	70	283	-1	5,600.00	4,336.38
63	Lee SLATTERY	ENG	71	71	69	74	285	1	4,900.00	3,794.33
	Shiv KAPUR	IND	72	70	73	70	285	1	4,900.00	3,794.33
65	Peter O'MALLEY	AUS	72	70	75	70	287	3	4,600.00	3,562.03
66	Pelle EDBERG	SWE	70	72	74	77	293	9	4,400.00	3,407.16

Total Prize Fund

€1,984,350 £1,536,588

Inspiration and Incentive

1	**Søren KJELDSEN**	**276**	**-8**
2	Martin KAYMER	278	-6
	Anthony WALL	278	-6
4	Sergio GARCIA	280	-4
	Lee WESTWOOD	280	-4
6	David LYNN	281	-3
7	Richard GREEN	282	-2
8	Anders HANSEN	283	-1
	Graeme McDOWELL	283	-1
10	Peter HEDBLOM	284	0

N o-one needed to tell the Volvo Masters what to do when the curtain fell. For two decades the tournament showed what is meant by the term 'showstopper' as events at Club de Golf Valderrama provided the annual conclusion of drama and excitement on The European Tour International Schedule.

So when it was finally time for the Volvo Masters to say goodbye it did so like the old trouper it has always been. In its determination to give one last performance worthy of its reputation, the tournament refused to be wrecked by two days of persistent rain that could have troubled a rowing regatta never mind a golfing extravaganza.

Undaunted, it mopped itself down, dried itself off, shone the spotlight back on the heroes on centre stage and, as it has always liked to, gave the audience not just one, but two lead characters to applaud.

Søren Kjeldsen's display in winning the €708,000 (£562,485) first prize with an eight under par total of 276 impressed everyone who witnessed it. "That is some score around this course," commented Colin Montgomerie who knows a thing or two about Valderrama having won two Volvo Masters and sealed five Order of Merit titles there. "You deserve to win any tournament anywhere with golf like that," he added.

Indeed, the Dane's two stroke triumph over Germany's Martin Kaymer and Anthony Wall of England was doused in brilliance right from the outset with a remarkable opening 65. Despite having players of the calibre of Sergio Garcia and Lee Westwood in close proximity for much of the week, the 33 year old from Aalborg led from wire to wire, barely looking over his shoulder in the process. It was sweet revenge for Kjeldsen after the 2007 Volvo Masters where he, and Englishman Simon Dyson, had to give way in a play-off to Dyson's compatriot Justin Rose.

"The weather had been troubling us so it was fantastic to finish the tournament like this in the sunshine," reflected Kjeldsen, after lifting his second European Tour title. "The tournament deserved a finish like today with all the people sitting out watching. It was a very special atmosphere and a very special day."

As he secured his first Harry Vardon Trophy, Robert Karlsson concurred. Defending an overnight lead is one thing, but defending a lead in an Order of Merit you have taken 12 months to compile is another thing entirely. "It's one of those situations where you have it in your own

hands - but not really," said the Swede. "Because the prize money is so big here, both Padraig (Harrington) and Lee, could have gone on to win."

With Harrington never threatening the top two position he needed to leapfrog his Ryder Cup foursomes partner, it was left to Westwood to challenge meaningfully for the win he required. But, as commendable as his effort was, he could only finish tied for fourth with Garcia, four shots behind Kjeldsen. It would have been nail-biting for Karlsson – who eventually finished in a tie for 32nd place – had Westwood seriously pushed Kjeldsen down the stretch but, realistically, nothing could, nor should, be taken away from the Swede.

Karlsson has been regarded as an imposing talent on Tour since his rookie year in 1991 but in this, his stellar season, he was positively relentless in his presence on leaderboards. During any other campaign it would have been considered scandalous for Harrington, with his consecutive Major victories in The Open Championship and the US PGA Championship under his belt, not to be crowned European Number One. But it says much for the strength in depth of The European Tour, not to say the talent of Karlsson himself, that Harrington himself immediately recognised his quality.

Martin Kaymer

Sergio Garcia

Anthony Wall

Richard Green

VOLVO MASTERS
LEADER BOARD

HOLE	1	2	3	4	5	6	7	8	9	10	11	12	13	14	15	16	17	18	TOTAL
PAR	4	4	3	5	4	3	4	4	4	4	4	5	3	4	4	3	5	4	
SEN												9	10	10	10	9	9	8	284
WOOD	5	5	5	5	5	5	4	3	3	3	3	3	3	3	3	4	4		276
A	5	5	4	4	4	4	4	4	4	4	5	5	5	5	4	4			280
ER	4	4	5	4	4	4	4	4	4	6	6	6	7	6	6	6			278
KE	1	1	2	2	2	2	2	1	1	L	1	L	L	L	L	L	1		285
EN A	1	1	L	1	1	1	1	1	1	2	2	2	2	2	1	1	1		283
N	1	1	1	1	2	2	2	3	4	5	5	5	3	3	3				281
WELL	2	2	1	L	1	1	1	1	1	2	2	2	1	1	1	1			283
LOM	4	4	3	3	3	3	4	3	2	1	1	2	1	1	L	1	L		283
	3	3	3	3	3	3	3	3	3	2	2	2	2	2	1	1			285

Left to right: Felipe Ortiz-Patiño, President of Valderrama, Robert Karlsson with the Harry Vardon trophy, Søren Kjeldsen with the Volvo Masters trophy and Jaime Ortiz-Patiño, Honorary President of Valderrama

"Robert fully deserves this," said Harrington. "He has been a paragon of consistency all year and none of his fellow players are surprised how good a player he has become. It was always a question of 'when' and not 'if' with him."

Karlsson's next challenge, of course, will be to replicate the Dubliner, who famously built on the foundations of his own Order of Merit triumph in 2006 to collect three Majors in the next two years. However, as he left Valderrama, Karlsson, already the most prolific Swedish winner in European Tour history with nine wins, was content to bask in the additional glory of becoming the first Swedish player to top the Order of Merit. "I hope my success will serve to increase my country's growing passion for golf," he said.

Kjeldsen felt the same as he became the first Danish golfer to win the Volvo Masters and, with such an unmistakable whiff of a changing era in the air, it was recognised by both men as a special time to be prominent on The European Tour International Schedule.

For, in November 2009, the end of season finale will be the inaugural Dubai World Championship on the Earth course at Jumeirah Golf Estates where the top 60 will battle, not for the Order of Merit, but for The Race to Dubai, where a US$10 million bonus pool will be on offer in addition to the US$10 million prize fund for the tournament itself.

Those ambitious visionaries in the Emirates are to be congratulated on their commitment but they would, no doubt, be amongst the first to raise a toast to the Volvo Masters for providing the inspiration and the incentive. The old trouper has given them a hard act to follow.

Jamie Corrigan
The Independent

OSCAR JACOBSON
GOLF

BY APPOINTMENT TO H.M.
THE KING OF SWEDEN
SINCE 1903

FOR MORE INFORMATION CALL OSCAR JACOBSON ON +44 (0)207 402 0797 OR VISIT WWW.OSCARJACOBSON.COM

Lee Westwood

Hole	Par	Yards	Metres
1	4	399	365
2	4	421	385
3	3	196	179
4	5	563	515
5	4	381	348
6	3	163	149
7	4	497	454
8	4	350	320
9	4	441	403
OUT	**35**	**3411**	**3118**
10	4	389	356
11	5	547	500
12	3	212	194
13	4	411	376
14	4	370	338
15	3	225	206
16	4	433	396
17	5	536	490
18	4	454	415
IN	**36**	**3577**	**3271**
TOTAL	**71**	**6988**	**6389**

By virtue of winning the Volvo Masters, Søren Kjeldsen broke into the top ten of The European Tour Order for the first time in his career, with earnings of €1,437,979. The 2008 season represents his third consecutive season he has improved his Order of Merit position. The Dane finished 36th in 2006, 17th in 2007 and tenth in 2008.

Club de Golf Valderrama

Final Results

Pos	Name		Rd1	Rd2	Rd3	Rd4	Total		€	£
1	Søren KJELDSEN	DEN	65	71	69	71	276	-8	708,000.00	562,485.10
2	Anthony WALL	ENG	69	69	71	69	278	-6	369,000.00	293,159.61
	Martin KAYMER	GER	73	70	67	68	278	-6	369,000.00	293,159.61
4	Sergio GARCIA	ESP	68	70	70	72	280	-4	196,000.00	155,716.22
	Lee WESTWOOD	ENG	70	68	70	72	280	-4	196,000.00	155,716.22
6	David LYNN	ENG	69	73	70	69	281	-3	148,400.00	117,899.42
7	Richard GREEN	AUS	73	70	72	67	282	-2	127,000.00	100,897.75
8	Graeme MCDOWELL	NIR	72	70	74	67	283	-1	100,500.00	79,844.28
	Anders HANSEN	DEN	74	69	69	71	283	-1	100,500.00	79,844.28
10	Peter HEDBLOM	SWE	71	74	72	67	284	0	85,000.00	67,529.99
11	Darren CLARKE	NIR	71	69	72	73	285	1	76,350.00	60,657.82
	Ross FISHER	ENG	76	70	70	69	285	1	76,350.00	60,657.82
13	Markus BRIER	AUT	72	69	74	71	286	2	61,285.71	48,689.69
	Peter HANSON	SWE	72	69	73	72	286	2	61,285.71	48,689.69
	Robert-Jan DERKSEN	NED	72	70	72	72	286	2	61,285.71	48,689.69
	Steve WEBSTER	ENG	72	71	73	70	286	2	61,285.71	48,689.69
	Søren HANSEN	DEN	74	71	70	71	286	2	61,285.71	48,689.69
	Andres ROMERO	ARG	74	72	68	72	286	2	61,285.71	48,689.69
	Padraig HARRINGTON	IRL	76	71	71	68	286	2	61,285.71	48,689.69
20	Francesco MOLINARI	ITA	74	73	74	66	287	3	53,600.00	42,583.62
21	Alexander NOREN	SWE	74	74	73	67	288	4	52,200.00	41,471.36
22	Gonzalo FDEZ-CASTAÑO	ESP	73	74	67	75	289	5	50,100.00	39,802.97
	Colin MONTGOMERIE	SCO	73	76	68	72	289	5	50,100.00	39,802.97
24	Miguel Angel JIMÉNEZ	ESP	73	80	70	67	290	6	48,000.00	38,134.58
25	Thomas LEVET	FRA	71	68	75	77	291	7	44,500.00	35,353.94
	David HOWELL	ENG	73	71	75	72	291	7	44,500.00	35,353.94
	Oliver FISHER	ENG	73	71	73	74	291	7	44,500.00	35,353.94
	Grégory BOURDY	FRA	73	75	71	72	291	7	44,500.00	35,353.94
29	Paul CASEY	ENG	73	68	73	78	292	8	40,000.00	31,778.82
	Felipe AGUILAR	CHI	74	72	70	76	292	8	40,000.00	31,778.82
	Ian POULTER	ENG	76	76	67	73	292	8	40,000.00	31,778.82
32	Robert KARLSSON	SWE	73	73	72	75	293	9	37,500.00	29,792.64
	Paul LAWRIE	SCO	76	72	75	70	293	9	37,500.00	29,792.64
34	Simon DYSON	ENG	72	68	81	73	294	10	34,000.00	27,012.00
	Ignacio GARRIDO	ESP	74	75	73	72	294	10	34,000.00	27,012.00
	Jean-François LUCQUIN	FRA	77	74	70	73	294	10	34,000.00	27,012.00
	Nick DOUGHERTY	ENG	78	73	70	73	294	10	34,000.00	27,012.00
	Alvaro QUIROS	ESP	78	76	71	69	294	10	34,000.00	27,012.00
39	Hennie OTTO	RSA	70	77	74	74	295	11	29,500.00	23,436.88
	Pablo LARRAZABAL	ESP	73	79	73	70	295	11	29,500.00	23,436.88
	Rory MCILROY	NIR	74	73	75	73	295	11	29,500.00	23,436.88
	Peter LAWRIE	IRL	75	79	69	72	295	11	29,500.00	23,436.88
43	Grégory HAVRET	FRA	76	75	67	78	296	12	27,000.00	21,450.70
44	Mark BROWN	NZL	75	77	71	74	297	13	26,000.00	20,656.23
45	Henrik STENSON	SWE	74	75	72	77	298	14	25,000.00	19,861.76
46	Oliver WILSON	ENG	75	77	75	72	299	15	24,000.00	19,067.29
47	John BICKERTON	ENG	74	73	75	78	300	16	22,550.00	17,915.31
	Paul MCGINLEY	IRL	76	78	76	70	300	16	22,550.00	17,915.31
49	Damien MCGRANE	IRL	74	75	73	79	301	17	21,200.00	16,842.77
50	Scott STRANGE	AUS	76	74	73	79	302	18	19,850.00	15,770.24
	James KINGSTON	RSA	76	78	75	73	302	18	19,850.00	15,770.24
52	Richard FINCH	ENG	74	77	76	76	303	19	18,500.00	14,697.70
53	José Manuel LARA	ESP	77	76	77	75	305	21	17,900.00	14,221.02
54	Jeev Milkha SINGH	IND	74	77	75	82	308	24	16,700.00	13,267.66
	Charl SCHWARTZEL	RSA	77	76	76	79	308	24	16,700.00	13,267.66
	Graeme STORM	ENG	77	79	71	81	308	24	16,700.00	13,267.66
57	Justin ROSE	ENG	80	81	WD					

Total Prize Fund

€4,190,600 £3,329,307

Tradition and Romance

When the World Cup returned to Mission Hills Golf Club in China in 2007 where it had been previously played in 1995 and where it will now continue through to 2018, it was inevitable that the atmosphere would be electric. That was most certainly the case over four enthralling days which concluded with Scotland overcoming the United States in a thrilling play-off.

It was the 53rd edition of this prestigious event and the result meant that, in 2008, Scotland – following several near misses which included losing a play-off to Germany in 2006 – would defend the title which the United States have won a record 23 times.

Even so Scotland's win in the 2007 Omega Mission Hills World Cup continued a more recent trend of nations outside the United States triumphing, with teams from South Africa (1996, 2001 and 2003), Ireland's (1997), England (1998 and 2004), Japan (2002), Wales (2005) and Germany (2006) among those having claimed the impressive trophy over the past dozen years.

That trophy was first provided for competition in 1953 when John Jay Hopkins, the noted Canadian industrialist, realised a dream that the game of golf could promote goodwill between nations. The first event took place in Montreal – the winners were Argentina – and it was called the Canada Cup. This founded the International Golf Association and they grew the event that would become recognised throughout sport as 'The Olympics of Golf' as the game gathered popularity around the world.

The international image of the event was reflected by the name change to The World Cup in 1967 and with that its reputation, harnessed by tradition and romance, was further developed as earlier victories by the likes of Kel Nagle and Peter Thomson (Australia), Ben Hogan and Sam Snead (United States) and Jack Nicklaus and Arnold Palmer (United States) were followed by Seve Ballesteros and Manuel Piñero (Spain), Fred Couples and Davis Love III (United States), Padraig Harrington and Paul McGinley (Ireland), Nick Faldo and David Carter (England), Mark O'Meara and Tiger Woods (United States), Ernie Els and Retief Goosen (South Africa) and Paul Casey and Luke Donald (England) to name but a few.

Justin Rose (left) and Ian Poulter

Zhang Lian-wei (left) and Liang Wen-chong

Søren Hansen (left) and Anders Hansen

Martin Kaymer (left) and Alex Cejka

311

MISSION HILLS
觀瀾湖

World's No.1
GUINNESS WORLD RECORDS

Left to right: Marc Warren, Stephen Urquhart, President of Omega, Colin Montgomerie and Dr David Chu, Group Chairman, Mission Hills Group

The Scottish victory in the Omega Mission Hills World Cup by Colin Montgomerie and Marc Warren saw Montgomerie become the first European player to be on a winning side in five different team competitions. They are: The Ryder Cup (1995, 97, 02, 04 and 06), Alfred Dunhill Cup (1995), 4 Tours World Championship (1991), the Seve Trophy (2002, 03 and 05) and now the Omega Mission Hills World Cup (2007).

The International Federation of PGA Tours became the custodians of the event in 2000 while the 2008 tournament unfolded little more than two months after the staging of the Beijing Olympic Games at which Omega enjoyed the unique role as Official Timekeeper.

Stephen Urquhart, President of Omega, stated: "Omega has an unparalleled position in China and recently celebrated 112 years presence in this significant market. The Omega Mission Hills World Cup has sealed our commitment to the world of golf and provided an exciting opportunity to further develop our activities in this sport."

Dr David Chu, Group Chairman, Mission Hills Group, said: "Being the largest golf facility in the world we were delighted to welcome the Omega Mission Hills World Cup back in 2007 in the knowledge that we will be the hosts through 2018. We are making history in the fine chronicle of golf.

"China has a population of 1.4 billion with 400 million youths. I believe hosting the World Cup of Golf in China together with partners like Omega, the IGA, the China Golf Federation and the International Federation of PGA Tours, under The European Tour's guidance; will go beyond just influencing sports and commercial development. It will create an impact so big it will truly turn golf into a global sport."

The European Tour has an excellent relationship with Omega through their sponsorship of the Omega European Masters on The European Tour International Schedule and it is interesting to note how many players who have enjoyed success in that event high in the Swiss Alps have also enjoyed high times in the Omega Mission Hills World Cup – Seve Ballesteros, Bradley Dredge, Luke Donald, Ernie Els, Nick Faldo, Anders Forsbrand, Dale Hayes, Harold Henning, Colin Montgomerie, Kel Nagle, Manuel Piñero and Ian Woosnam – a very impressive group to have their names engraved on both the Omega European Masters and the Omega Mission Hills World Cup trophies.

Mitchell Platts

Martin Wiegele (right), receives the trophy
from Qualifying School Director Mike Stewart

Impressive Consistency

The impressive consistency with which players emerging from The European Tour Qualifying School raise their profiles by immediately claiming success at the highest level was further demonstrated in 2008 by England's David Dixon and Spain's Pablo Larrazabal.

The duo became the 28th and 29th players respectively to rubber stamp their graduation from the Qualifying School with wins on The European Tour International Schedule the following season. Dixon captured the SAINT OMER OPEN presented by Neuflize OBC at the Aa Saint Omer Golf Club, Lumbres, France, while Larrazabal, later named the 2008 Sir Henry Cotton Rookie of the Year, won the Open de France ALSTOM only two weeks later and little more than 150 miles along the road at Le Golf National on the outskirts of Paris.

For Dixon, victory at the age of 31 came as a reward for his endeavours as he finally fulfilled the promise shown in The Open Championship at Royal Lytham & St Annes in 2001 where he won the Silver Medal as the leading amateur. Larrazabal's triumph meant he followed in the footsteps of the likes of José Maria Olazábal

(1986), Vijay Singh (1989) and Padraig Harrington (1996) who stood on the winner's rostrum in their rookie seasons. Larrazabal, of course, will take encouragement from the fact that Olazábal, Singh and Harrington, with more than 100 victories between them, all went on to become Major Champions too.

Austria's Martin Wiegele led the 30 qualifiers – Dixon and Larrazabal included – onto The 2008 European Tour International Schedule by winning the Qualifying School – Final Stage on a day fuelled by tension and drama at the San Roque Club.

The nature of the sixth round at the Final Stage once more ensured phenomenal finishes, lucky escapes and shattered dreams as the 71 remaining players – from an original entry of 879 – did battle for the 30 available European Tour cards.

Pablo Larrazabal

David Dixon

Wiegele finished with a six round aggregate of 11 under par 421 and a two stroke victory over Spain's Pedro Linhart and England's Lee Slattery, whose success tasted sweeter than most after he missed out on retaining his card via the 2007 Order of Merit by the mere figure of €77.

But the week belonged to Wiegele, who collected the €21,388 first prize from European Tour Qualifying School Director Mike Stewart and said: "It's a beautiful feeling. I won for the first time on the Challenge Tour in Norway this year but it feels even better to win the Tour School and regain my card. It's a great day for Austrian golf with Florian Praegant finishing fourth too. We will have three players on The European Tour next year which has never happened before."

Few events can rival the drama and the tension of The European Tour Qualifying School. The pressure, with the ultimate dream of Membership of The European Tour at stake, warmed-up in 2008 at the First Stage – held at six venues across England, France, Germany, Italy and Scotland – and the Second Stage – held at Arcos Gardens, Golf Costa Ballena, Sherry Golf Jerez and Montenmedio Golf and Country Club in Spain – prior to 156 players contesting the Final Stage at PGA Golf de Catalunya.

In November 2008, PGA Golf de Catalunya, situated in the north east of Spain in the town of Caldas between Barcelona and Girona, became the 14th venue in total to stage the event. PGA Golf de Catalunya features two courses – the Green Course and the Red Course – both of which were designed by two of the most renowned figures in European golf, England's Neil Coles MBE and Spain's Angel Gallardo, respectively Chairman and Vice-Chairman of The PGA European Tour Board of Directors. The club is no stranger to hosting top level competition either – Thomas Björn having won the 1999 Gene Sarazen World Open there, Brian Davis the 2000 Peugeot Open de España, and Jerry Bruner the 2001 European Seniors Tour Championship.

"PGA Golf de Catalunya has not only hosted events on The European Tour International Schedule but it has also been a superb supporter of the Qualifying School having, for four of the last six years, been one of the venues for the event's Second Stage," said Mike Stewart. "It presents an excellent challenge for the players striving to finish in the top 30 to gain that highly regarded status of Membership of The European Tour."

Mitchell Platts

San Roque Club, Spain, November 15-20, 2007
Final Results

Pos	Name	Ctry	PQ	R1	R2	R3	R4	R5	R6	Agg	Par	€
1	Martin WIEGELE	AUT	EX	71	69	69	72	64	76	421	-11	21,388.65
2	Pedro LINHART	ESP	EX	71	72	71	69	70	70	423	-9	13,902.62
3	Lee SLATTERY	ENG	EX	69	76	72	64	70	72	423	-9	13,902.62
4	Florian PRAEGANT	AUT	286	73	69	67	72	71	72	424	-8	8,797.86
5	Luis CLAVERIE	ESP	282	69	71	68	73	71	72	424	-8	8,797.86
6	François DELAMONTAGNE	FRA	EX	73	74	72	69	69	68	425	-7	6,379.52
7	Lee S JAMES	ENG	276	72	69	74	73	68	69	425	-7	6,379.52
8	Alan MCLEAN	SCO	EX	71	69	69	74	72	70	425	-7	6,379.52
9	Sion E BEBB	WAL	276	71	71	69	69	74	71	425	-7	6,379.52
10	Pablo LARRAZABAL	ESP	282	71	66	71	70	71	76	425	-7	6,379.52
11	Richard BLAND	ENG	EX	73	69	71	73	71	70	427	-5	4,776.80
12	Birgir HAFTHORSSON	ISL	274	71	70	73	70	71	72	427	-5	4,776.80
13	Joakim BÄCKSTRÖM	SWE	EX	69	74	68	70	74	72	427	-5	4,776.80
14	Sven STRÜVER	GER	EX	71	71	68	72	72	73	427	-5	4,776.80
15	Paolo TERRENI	ITA	278	72	71	71	67	71	75	427	-5	4,776.80
16	Benoit TEILLERIA	FRA	277	76	71	71	69	71	70	428	-4	3,548.14
17	Juan ABBATE	ARG	EX	74	71	73	70	68	72	428	-4	3,548.14
18	David DRYSDALE	SCO	282	70	75	73	70	67	73	428	-4	3,548.14
19	David DIXON	ENG	280	70	72	74	68	71	73	428	-4	3,548.14
20	Matthew MILLAR	AUS	EX	71	73	69	71	71	73	428	-4	3,548.14
21	Craig LEE	SCO	276	72	68	75	70	69	74	428	-4	3,548.14
22	Patrik SJÖLAND	SWE	EX	75	72	73	69	72	68	429	-3	2,588.82
23	Marcel SIEM	GER	EX	71	72	74	70	71	71	429	-3	2,588.82
24	James KAMTE	RSA	EX	71	70	73	73	70	72	429	-3	2,588.82
25	Gareth PADDISON	NZL	EX	74	72	70	73	67	73	429	-3	2,588.82
26	Philip GOLDING	ENG	EX	75	69	69	69	74	73	429	-3	2,588.82
27	Paul WARING	ENG	283	74	70	72	70	68	75	429	-3	2,588.82
28	Jan-Are LARSEN	NOR	EX	72	70	73	70	69	75	429	-3	2,588.82
29	Ulrich VAN DEN BERG	RSA	284	70	71	72	71	70	75	429	-3	2,588.82
30	Thomas AIKEN	RSA	283	70	68	72	68	71	80	429	-3	2,588.82
31	Scott BARR	AUS	EX	71	69	76	71	70	73	430	-2	998.14
32	Doug McGUIGAN	RSA	EX	72	69	73	68	75	73	430	-2	998.14
33	Matthew CORT	ENG	285	70	74	73	69	70	74	430	-2	998.14
34	Tiago CRUZ	POR	284	68	70	74	68	72	77	430	-2	998.14
35	Alessandro TADINI	ITA	EX	70	73	72	69	77	70	431	-1	998.14
36	Miguel RODRIGUEZ	ARG	EX	74	71	76	68	69	73	431	-1	998.14
37	Peter SENIOR	AUS	EX	73	67	73	75	69	74	431	-1	998.14
38	Adilson DA SILVA	BRA	EX	71	72	74	69	71	74	431	-1	998.14
39	Alessio BRUSCHI	ITA	285	71	71	72	71	74	72	431	-1	998.14
40	Terry PILKADARIS	AUS	EX	72	75	70	66	73	75	431	-1	998.14
41	Colm MORIARTY	IRL	EX	70	73	71	75	72	71	432	0	998.14
42	Renaud GUILLARD	FRA	285	72	70	71	72	72	75	432	0	998.14
43	Stuart DAVIS	ENG	EX	70	75	73	70	67	77	432	0	998.14
44	James MORRISON	ENG	278	73	71	71	71	70	77	433	1	998.14
45	Ben MASON	ENG	EX	70	74	74	66	69	80	433	1	998.14
46	Manuel QUIROS	ESP	282	71	74	69	75	71	74	434	2	998.14
47	Christopher HANELL	SWE	EX	70	73	75	70	72	74	434	2	998.14
48	Mikko KORHONEN	FIN	285	71	72	73	70	73	75	434	2	998.14
49	John E MORGAN	ENG	284	71	72	73	69	72	77	434	2	998.14
50	Eric RAMSAY	SCO	EX	70	73	74	71	68	78	434	2	998.14
51	Stephen BROWNE	IRL	EX	75	74	70	70	71	75	435	3	998.14
52	Anders Schmidt HANSEN	DEN	EX	72	73	73	71	71	75	435	3	998.14
53	Lawrence DODD	ENG	283	73	71	72	71	71	77	435	3	998.14
54	Fredrik WIDMARK	SWE	280	70	73	77	66	78	72	436	4	998.14
55	Robert ROCK	ENG	EX	70	72	75	72	72	75	436	4	998.14
56	Olivier DAVID	FRA	283	70	73	74	72	71	76	436	4	998.14
57	Gabriel CANIZARES	ESP	276	73	74	70	69	73	77	436	4	998.14
58	Marco SOFFIETTI	ITA	283	73	71	72	67	75	78	436	4	998.14
59	Andreas HÖGBERG	SWE	281	73	75	71	70	73	75	437	5	998.14
60	Benjamin MIARKA	GER	280	71	73	74	70	74	75	437	5	998.14
61	Mattias ELIASSON	SWE	EX	72	75	75	67	71	77	437	5	998.14
62	Graeme A CLARK	ENG	282	71	71	74	71	72	78	437	5	998.14
63	Gary LOCKERBIE	ENG	EX	72	72	73	72	69	79	437	5	998.14
64	John MELLOR	ENG	285	71	69	72	74	75	78	439	7	998.14
65	Chris GANE	ENG	279	70	73	71	74	72	79	439	7	998.14
66	Ben EVANS (AM)	ENG	285	71	69	74	72	74	79	439	7	998.14
67	Gary BOYD (AM)	ENG	278	71	71	75	71	73	79	440	8	
68	Roland STEINER	AUT	282	68	71	71	73	75	82	440	8	998.14
69	Jordi G DEL MORAL	ESP	283	71	75	72	70	77	76	441	9	998.14
70	Gary EMERSON	ENG	EX	72	71	71	71	76	80	441	9	998.14
71	Juan PARRON	ESP	277	70	72	72	74	DISQ		288	1	

The first 30 players became eligible for
Category 11 Membership on The 2008
European Tour International Schedule

Tremendous Impact

Padraig Harrington (right) became the first Irishman and only the second European player in history to win The PGA Player of the Year Award. Brian Whitcomb (right), President of the PGA of America, presented the trophy to Harrington during the PGA Grand Slam of Golf in Bermuda in October

Wins Around The World

If there was one moment which symbolised the tremendous impact European Tour Members have had on the global golfing scene in 2008, it came in Bermuda in October when Padraig Harrington was honoured with The PGA Player of the Year award.

The Irishman followed England's Nick Faldo in 1990 as the only European golfer in history to earn the prestigious accolade which was first presented by The PGA of America 60 years ago in 1948 and which is given to the top PGA TOUR player based on a mathematical formula that weighs tournament wins, official money and scoring averages.

Harrington came out on top due to his superb victories in both The Open Championship at Royal Birkdale and the US PGA Championship at Oakland Hills and would dearly have loved to have rounded the season off in style in Bermuda with victory in the PGA Grand Slam of Golf at the Mid Ocean Course.

However, despite a closing 68 to match Jim Furyk, Harrington had to concede defeat at the first play-off hole when the American rolled in a ten foot putt for a winning eagle three. Although disappointed, it was another fine week for the Irishman and The European Tour in general, with the field being completed by Members Retief Goosen in third and Masters Tournament Champion Trevor Immelman in fourth.

Staying in America is appropriate for it was across 'The Pond' that European Tour Members gained some of the most significant victories of 2008 – and none more so than Sergio Garcia who claimed the flagship event on the US PGA Tour; The Players Championship at the TPC Sawgrass course, Ponte Vedra Beach, Florida, in May.

After tying with American professional Paul Goydos on five under par 283 at the end of regulation play, the Spaniard took the title on the first play-off hole – the intimidating par three 17th – with a three after Goydos found trouble.

"The goal is to keep getting better and the only thing this victory tells me is to keep working hard and to believe in myself because when I do that, I don't think there are a lot of guys out there who can beat me," said Garcia. "So it is just a matter of doing that and knowing the capability that I have within myself." Indeed, Garcia demonstrated his talent again in both the US PGA Championship and the US Tour Champioship in which he was runner-up each time.

Outwith the flagship event, the biggest occasion in the US PGA Tour calendar was the end-of-season FedEx Cup Series which was also claimed by a European Tour Member – Honorary Member Vijay Singh, thanks largely to successive victories in the first two of the four tournament series in August; The Barclays at the Ridgewood Country Club, Paramus, New Jersey, and the Deutsche Bank Championship at the TPC Boston, Norton, Massachusetts.

In the former tournament the 45 year old Fijian – a 12 time winner on The European Tour International Schedule – took the title for the fourth time at the second hole of a play-off which also featured Garcia and former WGC – Accenture Match Play champion Kevin Sutherland; while the latter tournament was claimed in more orthodox fashion when a fine closing 63 gave him a 22 under par total of 262 and a five shot victory over Canada's Mike Weir.

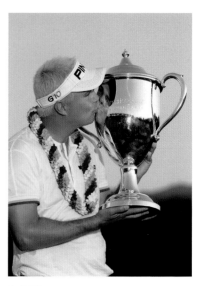
Daniel Chopra

Sergio Garcia

Ernie Els with The Honda Classic trophy

Vijay Singh with the Deutsche Bank Championship trophy

If Singh ended the US PGA Tour year in style – capturing the Money List with earnings of $6,601,094 – then Daniel Chopra started it in exactly the same fashion with victory in the curtain-raising Mercedes-Benz Championship in January at The Plantation Course, Kapalua Resort, Hawaii.

The 34 year old Swede ended the 72 holes level with American veteran Steve Stricker on 18 under par 274 but claimed the title and a US$100,000 Mercedes-Benz CL550 at the fourth play-off hole.

Ironically, Chopra's place in the field was earned when he won the 2007 Ginn Sur Mer Classic at Tesoro which, aside from The Plantation Course, is the only par 73 layout used on the regular US PGA Tour. "How about that?" proclaimed the Swede when told of the coincidence. "But, in truth, there's not a golf course out there which

suits me more than this one – I loved it from the moment I saw it."

Chopra was not the only Swede to enjoy success Stateside in 2008, the Scandinavian country also providing the winner of the Wyndham Championship at Sedgefield Country Club in Greensboro, North Carolina in August, namely Carl Pettersson.

The victory – garnered via a 21 under par total of 259 to finish two shots clear of American Scott McCarron – had extra significance for Pettersson for it came in his adopted home town of Greensboro, having decided to stay there after having attended North Carolina State University.

The win was Pettersson's third on the US PGA Tour, but 2008 also saw the return to the winners' circle in America of a European Tour Member who has enjoyed more than five times that success rate, one Ernie Els.

The 38 year old South African had not triumphed in America for over three years but ended that drought in emphatic style at the beginning of March when a final round 67 saw him come from three shots behind at the start of the day to pip England's Luke Donald and win The Honda Classic at the PGA National Resort and Spa Champion Course at Palm Beach Gardens in Florida by a shot – six under par 274 to Donald's 275.

"We play out here to win," said Els, who also won the King Hassan II Trophy in Morocco in November. "I guess we get addicted to that feeling and, when you don't get your rush, so to speak, you miss it. I definitely missed winning."

Carl Pettersson

Wins Around The World

From one multiple winner, three weeks later the US PGA Tour through up a European Tour Member enjoying his first taste of silverware in the United States, Andres Romero of Argentina.

The 27 year old from Tucuman cemented his reputation as one of the most exciting stars of world golf when he captured the Zurich Classic of New Orleans at the TPC Louisiana course in Avondale, Louisiana.

Romero carded weekend rounds of 65-68 for a 13 under par total of 275 to win by a shot from Australia's Peter Lonard and continue a remarkable statistic for the tournament which has now seen six of the last seven winners being first time champions on the US PGA Tour, the only man to break that sequence being Vijay Singh in 2004.

Completing the Roll of Honour on the main tour in the United States in 2008 were American Zach Johnson and Adam Scott of Australia.

Johnson, the former Masters Tournament Champion won the Valero Texas Open at La Cantera Golf Club in San Antonio, Texas in October by two shots from Charlie Wi with a 19 under par total of 261; while Scott took the plaudits in the EDS Byron Nelson Classic in April in dramatic fashion in a play-off with American Ryan Moore after both players finished on seven under par 273.

That he did just that was impressive, as the six time winner on The European Tour International Schedule had to hole a nine foot birdie putt on the final green to make the play-off before bringing the curtain down on proceedings with a 50 footer for birdie on the same green at the third time of asking. "I got away with one today," admitted the Australian. "I was a bit lucky."

While that may have been the case, there was certainly nothing fortuitous about the form of the 2004 European Ryder Cup Captain Bernhard Langer on the US Champions Tour. Quite simply the 50 year old German was sensational as he won three times and stormed to victory on both the Money List with $2,035,073 and in the season-long Charles Schwab Cup, a points programme designed to recognise the Tour's best player and for which Langer received the additional bonus of $1 million.

Bernhard Langer after his victory in the Toshiba Classic

Andres Romero

James Kingston

First victory of the year, and his second on the over-50's circuit in the United States came in the Toshiba Classic at the Newport Beach Country Club in Newport Beach, California at the beginning of March, and paid testament to Langer's legendary fitness as well as his golfing prowess as he beat American Jay Haas at the seventh extra hole of a play-off after both players had ended on 14 under par 199.

Two weeks later at the end of March, Langer was back in the winners' circle in vastly different circumstances at the Ocean Course in Palm

Coast, Florida, when a battling final round 71 in treacherously windy conditions saw him finish on 12 under par 204 and wrap up an eight shot victory over Americans Lonnie Nielsen and Tim Simpson in the Ginn Championship Hammock Beach Resort.

His third win in October saw him successfully defend the first US Champions Tour title he won in 2007, the Administaff Small Business Classic at The Woodlands Country Club in Texas where he carded a final round 69 for a 12 under par total of 204 to win by two shots from American Lonnie Nielsen.

The achievements proved to the 42 time winner on The European Tour International Schedule that he had unquestionably recovered from a bout of the Epstein-Barr virus he contracted mid-season, one which saw him lose energy, run fevers and endure an elevated heart rate for a spell.

Like Langer, Argentine Eduardo Romero – his old sparring partner from many European Tour events over the years – also won three times on the US Champions Tour in 2008.

The highlight of the three unquestionably came in August when, a week after missing out by a shot on a play-off for The Senior Open Championship, presented by MasterCard, at Royal Troon, the 54 year old Argentine captured the US Senior Open at The Broadmoor Resort in Colorado Springs, Colorado.

Romero carded a one over par final round 73 for a six under par total of 274, but was never seriously challenged by runner-up, American Fred Funk, who ended the day four shots adrift with Ireland's Mark McNulty third and Greg Norman of Australia fourth, the only players in the field to match or better par over the four rounds.

Straddling that memorable success were two other victories for the man affectionately known as "El Gato" and Romero was certainly smiling like the cat who got the cream when he won the Dick's Sporting Goods Open at the En-Joie Golf Course in Endicott, New York in July; and the SAS Championship at the Prestonwood Country Club in Cary, North Carolina in September.

In Endicott, a final round 69 for a 17 under par total of 199 was good enough for a one shot victory over American Gary Koch, while in Cary, 1992 US Open Champion Tom Kite was Romero's

Adam Scott

Wins Around The World

nearest challenger but could not get within three shots as progressively improving rounds of 68-67-66 gave the Argentine victory on 15 under par 201.

Completing a highly successful year in the United States was India's Arjun Atwal who won the Nationwide Tour's Chattanooga Classic at the Black Creek Club in Tennessee, a birdie at the first play-off hole good enough to see off the challenge of America's Webb Simpson after both players ended the tournament on 24 under par 264.

Of course, as with The European Tour International Schedule itself, the performances of Tour Members stretches worldwide and, once again, it was not simply in the United States that they excelled. As in previous years, South Africa in particular, proved a fertile hunting ground for trophies throughout the year.

Proving that point conclusively was South African James Kamte who enjoyed his first success in January in the Dimension Data Pro-Am at the Gary Player Country Club, winning by three shots from James Kingston with an 11 under par total of 277; and his second success in October when stunning final rounds of 63-64 saw him come from behind to win the Metmar Highveld Classic at the Witbank Golf Club, finishing on 20 under par 196, five shots clear of the trio of Desvonde Botes, Doug McGuigan and Brandon Pieters. It was also two weeks before Thomas Aiken claimed the Platinum Classic at the Mooinooi Golf Club, finishing five shots clear of the field after a fine showing which brought him a 19 under par winning total of 197.

Kamte's storming finish in the Metmar Highveld Classic put paid to hopes of a back-to-back triumph for his compatriot McGuigan, who, the week previously, had triumphed in the BMG Classic at the Ebotse Golf and Country Estate, a closing 68 giving him a ten under par total of 206 and a one shot victory over his fellow countryman Jaco Van Zyl.

Although the majority of success in South Africa was enjoyed by home country players, it was not exclusively thus, and bucking the trend at the beginning of February was Zimbabwe's Marc Cayeux whose ultra consistent rounds of 66-67-67-68 for a 12

under par total of 268 was good enough for a two shot victory over South African Bradford Vaughan in the Nashua Masters at the Wild Coast Sun Country Club.

However, the rest of the month revered to type with victories for host country players James Kingston in the Vodacom Championship at the Pretoria Country Club; and Louis Oosthuizen in the Telkom PGA Championship at the Country Club Johannesburg.

A storming finish, which included birdies at the final three holes saw Kingston end with a 65 for a 17 under par total of 271

and a two shot triumph over Brazil's Adilson da Silva; while, a week later, Oosthuizen gave new meaning to the phrase 'runaway winner' when he captured the Telkom PGA Championship by a whopping 14 shot margin with a sensational 28 under par total of 260 – the biggest 72 hole winning margin since the Sunshine Tour came into existence in 1967.

The same day – Sunday February 24 – Oosthuizen was cruising to victory in South Africa, another European Tour Member, New Zealand's Mark Brown was triumphing on the Asian Tour, winning the Sail Open presented by Jaypee Greens in Noida, India.

Eduardo Romero with the US Senior Open trophy

Louis Oosthuizen

Marc Cayeux

James Kamte after his victory in the Dimension Data Pro-Am

A final round 69 gave the 33 year old from Auckland a 14 under par total of 274 and a comfortable four shot victory. It also laid the foundations for his sensational victory in the Johnnie Walker Classic on The European Tour the following week, a 14 day spell which deservedly saw him win The European Tour Golfer of the Month award for February.

Continuing the success in Asia was Thailand's Thaworn Wiratchant, who claimed the Bangkok Airways Open at the Santiburi Samui Country Club in his home country in June; China's Liang Wen-chong who enjoyed a wire-to-wire win in the Hero Honda Indian Open at the Delhi Golf Club in October; while South Africa's Retief Goosen won the Iskandar Johor Open at Royal Johor International Golf Club in Johor Bahru, Malaysia, in November.

Thai players did not, however, reserve success solely for their own country, Prayad Marksaeng proving that point conclusively with two victories in consecutive tournaments on the Japan Golf Tour; firstly in the Mitsubishi Diamond Cup at the Higashi Hirono Golf Club in Hyogo

at the end of May before following that with another triumph in the Gateway to The Open Mizuno Open Yomiuri Classic at the Yomiuri Country Club in Hyogo in mid June – winning on both occasions by a shot with respective totals of ten under par 274 and 15 under par 269.

Completing the roll of honour in Japan was India's Jeev Milkha Singh who followed up his two victories in the country in 2006 with another in July 2008 when his 13 under par total of 275 was good enough for a two shot victory in the Nagashima Shigeo Invitational Sega Sammy Cup at The North Country Golf Club in Hokkaido.

While it is unquestionably joyous to win anywhere in the world, there is nothing like the feeling of winning in your own back yard and two other players to enjoy that special moment in 2008 were Felipe Aguilar and Padraig Harrington.

Although not quite matching the achievement of Louis Oosthuizen in Johannesburg, Aguilar nevertheless enjoyed a fairly comfortable ride on Sunday April 20 when he cruised to an 11 shot victory in Chile's national open on the Tour de las Americas – the 82nd Abierto de Chile VISA.

The man who, two months earlier had claimed his maiden European Tour title in the Enjoy Jakarta Astro Indonesia Open, carded a final round 68 to record an overall score of 23 under par 265 at the Club de Golf Hacienda de Chicureo to finish comfortably ahead of runner up, Sebastian Saavedra of Argentina.

Having started this 2008 global odyssey with Padraig Harrington, it seems only fitting that it ends with the Irishman too who, for the second year running, warmed up for his Open Championship triumph at home by winning the Ladbrokes Irish PGA Championship.

This time he did it at The European Club, the majestic Pat Ruddy designed links between the coastal towns of Wicklow and Arklow about 30 miles south of Dublin, winning by four shots from Philip Walton, despite carding a final round one over par 72.

What price a hat-trick in 2009 – both in the Irish PGA Championship and in The Open Championship on the Ailsa Course at Turnberry? It would take a brave man to bet against him.

Scott Crockett

Welsh
Wizard

It was heralded as a watershed year for Senior golf, one when three of Europe's 'Famous Five' from the 1980s all came of age, yet few could have quite predicted the drama that was to unfold in 2008.

Domingo Hospital

Gordon J Brand

A season which began when Bernhard Langer, Sandy Lyle and Ian Woosnam joined the ranks of the European Senior Tour, and which was punctuated by Greg Norman setting a new benchmark for the over 50s club in The Open Championship at Royal Birkdale, ultimately ended with Woosnam topping the class of new recruits.

Woosnam claimed two titles and finished runner up three times in his rookie season to break up the five year monopoly of Carl Mason and Sam Torrance. He won the Order of Merit with €320,120 and received the coveted John Jacobs Trophy, awarded each year to the Number One player, for the first time.

World Number One for 50 weeks in 1991 and winner of 44 titles worldwide, Woosnam will point to his Masters Tournament victory being the highlight of his career, but while that occurred on American soil, the foundation for his success in 2008 was undoubtedly his form in the old Eastern Bloc countries.

The Welshman claimed the silverware in both Poland and Russia, and finished runner up behind Langer in the Czech Republic as the Senior Tour visited all three countries for the first time.

"It was obviously a great feeling to win again and once I had done that, I set myself the goal of winning the Order of Merit," he said. "John Jacobs has been so influential in my career and therefore I am doubly proud to receive The John Jacobs Trophy.

"It was fantastic to be back playing amongst old friends but we are all out here on the Senior Tour to compete and I will need to work on my

Juan Quiros

Eduardo Romero

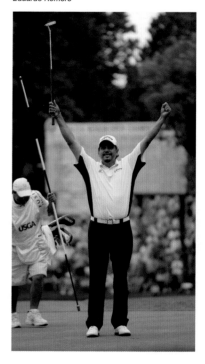

game and fitness if I am to win the Order of Merit again.

"It is great to be able to contend again on a level, certainly when it comes to driving distance – I am once again one of the longest hitters on Tour. I am also playing in countries that I have never visited before and hopefully this is helping open up golf in these territories."

After beginning life on the Senior Tour with a solid fifth place in the DGM Barbados Open, a week after celebrating his 50th birthday, and a share of 16th in the US Senior PGA Championship, it was to be third time lucky for Woosnam when the Senior Tour arrived in Poland.

Europe's 2006 Ryder Cup winning Captain lit the blue touch-paper for his Order of Merit aspirations with his best round of his year – a closing 63 – to smash the course record at

Krakow Valley Golf and Country Club, Krakow, Poland, and claim his maiden Senior Tour title, the Parkridge Polish Seniors Championship.

Ten birdies on the final day ensured Woosnam finished one shot clear of Spain's Domingo Hospital, who pushed him all the way with a fine 64, to claim his first stroke play title since 1997 in which year he won the PGA Championship at Wentworth Club.

Just six weeks separated Woosnam's first victory from his second, when he returned to eastern Europe to win another inaugural event, the Russian Seniors Open, in markedly contrasting conditions.

While his victory in Poland was sun-drenched, his success at the Pestovo Golf and Yacht Club, Moscow, Russia, came in driving rain but, having replaced Langer at the top of the Order of Merit with a share of ninth place in Ireland

Costantino Rocca

Craig Stadler won 123 bottles of Hardys wine after holing in one at Royal Troon's famous Postage Stamp eighth hole during The Senior Open Championship, presented by MasterCard. Stadler received a bottle of wine for every yard of the hole's length

Peter Mitchell

the previous week, Woosnam showed all of his renowned battling qualities to finish three shots ahead of another rookie, Paraguay's Angel Franco.

Having acquired a stranglehold on the John Jacobs Trophy at an early stage in the season, Woosnam's consistent presence at the top end of leaderboards meant he did not relinquish it, although the form of Langer and two Englishmen meant the remainder of the season was far from a victory stroll.

Both Gordon J Brand and Peter Mitchell joined Woosnam as multiple winners in 2008, and it was Mitchell who actually recorded the most number of victories in the season, winning three times in a fine rookie campaign.

After taking five years off from playing to run his own golf academies, Mitchell showed no signs of ring rust when he opened his Senior Tour account in the Ryder Cup Wales Seniors

Open at Conwy (Caernarvonshire) Golf Club, Wales, in June.

With Woosnam back on home turf and Lyle setting the pace in the first round, few would have bet against one of the former Shropshire county rivals landing the title but it was Mitchell who came through the field to win by two strokes from Woosnam and clinch the €93,899 first prize, the biggest pay cheque of his career to date.

Having edged out one Ryder Cup winning Captain in his home open, Mitchell also delivered the same fate to Sam Torrance in the Scottish Seniors Open in September over the East Course at the Marriott Dalmahoy Hotel and Country Club, Edinburgh, Scotland. Mitchell won by two strokes, despite Torrance's excellent closing 69.

Not content with matching Woosnam's season haul, Mitchell then went one better when he won his second consecutive tournament against

Ryder Cup Wales 2010

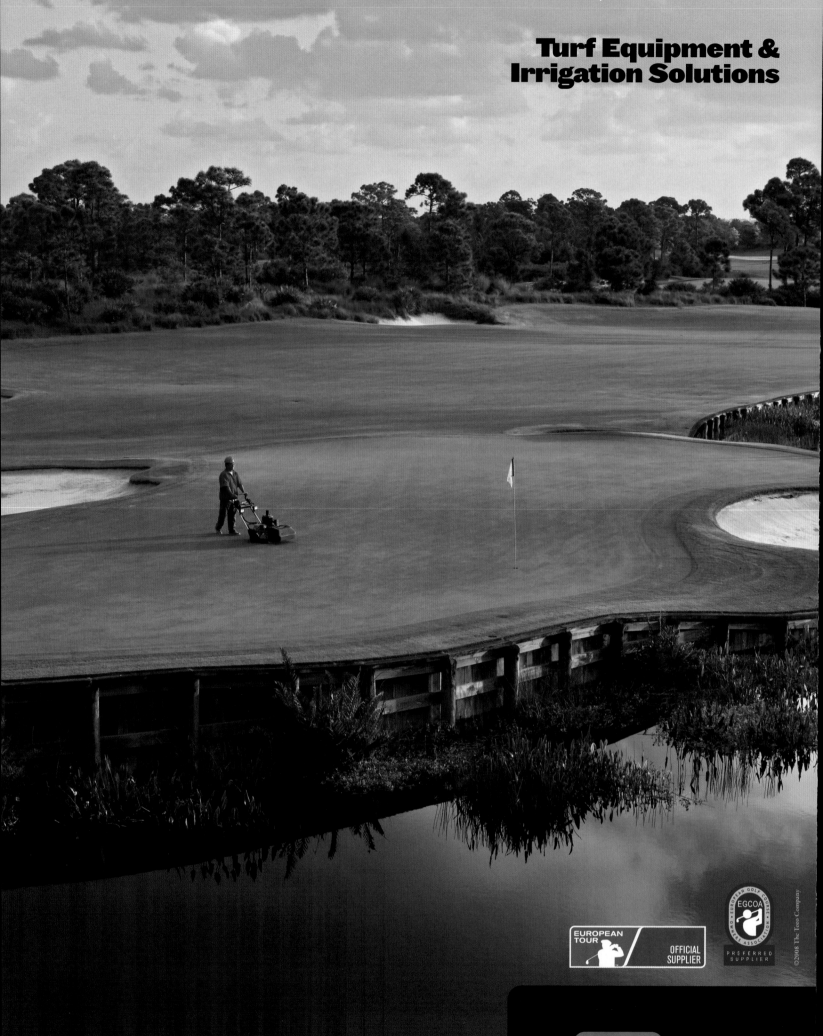

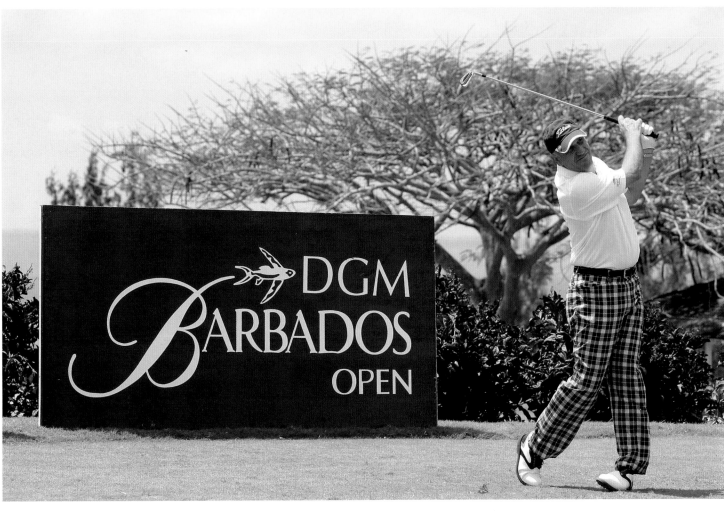

Bill Longmuir

Angel Franco

Jerry Bruner

one of the most picturesque backdrops on the Senior Tour Schedule.

The 50 year old from Kent held off strong challenges from both Gordon J Brand and Woosnam to cap a marvellous first few months as a Senior professional by winning the Lake Garda Italian Seniors Open at the Palazzo Arzaga Hotel, Spa and Golf Resort, Lake Garda, Italy, by a single stroke in one of most exciting finishes of the season.

If Woosnam dominated the early season and Mitchell the latter part, the middle certainly belonged to Gordon J Brand.

While Mitchell's finish to hold off the pair in Italy was dramatic, Brand's own finale to clinch The De Vere Collection PGA Seniors Championship in August can only be described as epic. The Hunting Course at De Vere Slaley Hall, Northumberland, England, played host to the Battle of the Brands, with Gordon J eventually defeating namesake Gordon Brand Jnr on the sixth extra hole of a play-off.

After 90 minutes of deadlock, having replayed the 18th five times and with light fading fast, it was Brand Jnr, making his Senior Tour debut, who was first to falter at the par three 17th, leaving Brand with two putts to secure his fourth Senior Tour title overall.

The former Ryder Cup player then achieved back-to-back victories in his homeland when

Greg Norman (left) and Bernhard Langer

THE SENIOR
OPEN CHAMPIONSHIP
Royal Troon 2008

1

MasterCard

Flying high with the birdies and eagles.
Priceless.

MasterCard

www.priceless.com/golf

Bob Cameron

José Rivero

Stewart Ginn

he lifted the silverware in the Travis Perkins plc Senior Masters over the Duke's Course at Woburn Golf Club, England, seven days later, finishing two strokes clear of Spain's Juan Quiros and three ahead of defending champion Carl Mason.

Both Mason and Quiros had been winners themselves earlier in the season, with Mason claiming the 20th victory of his Senior Tour career in the Bad Ragaz PGA Seniors Open at the beginning of August.

The all time leading Senior Tour career money winner - he has now earned €1,794,456 in six seasons - equalled the lowest round in Senior Tour history with a superb second day nine under par 61 and duly finished the job off with a final round 63 to successfully defend his title at the Golf Club Bad Ragaz, Switzerland.

That stunning victory was the first of six top ten finishes in the final eight events of the season as the 2007 Order of Merit winner ended the year in style, but ultimately it was not enough to stop Woosnam succeeding him as the Number One player.

Similarly Quiros' victory in the Irish Seniors Open in association with Fáilte Ireland and Allied Irish Bank sparked a run of four top ten finishes in his next six events but more importantly it gave the Spaniard his third Senior Tour title in as many years.

Quiros produced one of the shots of the year on the 18th hole to snatch the trophy from home favourite Des Smyth following a fascinating final round battle at Ballyliffin Golf Club, Co. Donegal, Ireland. His stunning 132 yard approach shot landed just 18 inches from the pin to leave him with a simple birdie putt for victory.

That win prompted understandable scenes of jubilation from the Spaniard but even the most hardened of golf fans would have struggled to keep a dry eye when Tony Johnstone sealed his maiden title at the tournament which had kicked off three weeks of links golf prior to Mitchell's win in Wales and Quiros' in Ireland.

In the most heart-warming story of the season, Johnstone defied the odds to win the Jersey Seniors Classic in June by two strokes, four years after doctors diagnosed him with Multiple Sclerosis and told him he would never play golf again.

The Zimbabwean, who had to re-learn large parts of his game affected by the debilitating condition, including his putting, understandably fought back the tears after sealing a superb wire-to-wire victory at La Moye Golf Club, Channel Islands.

"It was a massive victory for me," said Johnstone. "In terms of personal satisfaction no other win has meant as much to me. Four years ago when I was diagnosed I could never have dreamed of winning – I didn't even think I would play golf again. It's only when they tell you that you'll never do it again that you realise how much you love it."

It was also a joyous occasion for Langer when he claimed his own maiden European Senior Tour title in the inaugural Casa Serena Open in September which signalled the Tour's first visit to the Czech Republic and brought together Europe's last three Ryder Cup winning Captains – Langer, Torrance and Woosnam – two weeks before Nick Faldo's Team flew out to Valhalla.

Fittingly it was Langer and Woosnam who grabbed the limelight with the German ultimately

holding the silverware – at the tournament staged by his brother Erwin – courtesy of a three stroke victory over the Welshman. Langer dropped only one shot in 54 holes at Casa Serena Golf, Kutna Hora, Czech Republic, to emerge on top.

Another captivating contest of old friends ensued when the Senior Tour returned to the British Isles later in September for the Weston Homes PGA International Seniors at The Stoke By Nayland Club, Suffolk, England. This time it was the home pairing of Nick Job and Carl Mason who locked horns, with Job surviving a late surge by his good friend to win his fifth Senior Tour title by two strokes.

Job had started the season in style, finishing third and second respectively in the first two events of the year, behind Bill Longmuir in the DGM Barbados Open and Stewart Ginn in the Azores Senior Open.

Scotsman Longmuir set the early Order of Merit pace at the season curtain raiser on the leisurely Caribbean island back in March when he produced a final day birdie blitz at Royal Westmoreland, Barbados, to win the DGM Barbados Open, his seventh Senior Tour title.

Australian Ginn then paved the way for the spate of maiden winners – which subsequently included Johnstone, Langer, Mitchell and

Jay Haas

Katsuyoshi Tomori

Des Smyth

Luis Carbonetti

Tony Johnstone

Bruce Vaughan

Nick Job

Woosnam – when he surged through the field in the Azores Senior Open, at the Batalha Golf Course, Azores, Portugal, finishing two strokes clear of Job after starting the final day five strokes behind overnight leader Martin Gray of Scotland.

The first Senior Major Championship of the year saw American Jay Haas pip Langer on the line in the US Senior PGA Championship at Oak Hill Country Club, Rochester, New York, USA, finishing one stroke clear of the German. There was also a glimpse of the Major form that was to come from Greg Norman, who harboured real hopes of winning the tournament until he dropped three shots in the last two holes to finish in a tie for sixth place.

By the time Norman headed to Royal Troon Golf Club, Ayrshire, Scotland, for The Senior Open Championship presented by MasterCard in July, the Australian had enthralled the golfing world with his captivating performance in The 137th Open Championship the previous week.

Having rolled back the years at Royal Birkdale, where he led going into the back nine on Sunday before finishing in a share of third place, Norman helped attract record crowds to Royal Troon, where he started as firm favourite to land the title, along with defending champion Tom Watson, Langer and Woosnam.

However, amidst such stellar competition, it was the relatively unheralded American Bruce Vaughan who stole the show, holding his nerve to defeat compatriot John Cook at the first hole of a sudden death play-off for the unlikely first tournament victory of his career.

Argentine Eduardo Romero, a runner up in The Senior Open Championship in both 2004 and 2006, came close once again, missing an eight foot par putt on the last hole to drop out of a share of the lead and the subsequent play-off, but his wait for his second Senior Major Championship would not last too much longer, as he won the US Senior Open at The Broadmoor Resort, Colorado Springs, USA, the following week.

All of which left the season finale, the OKI Castellón Open España – Senior Tour Championship. Torrance left it late to continue his run of winning at least one tournament each year since his first full season in 2004 when he claimed his 10th Senior Tour title at Club de Campo del Mediterráneo, Spain. Torrance, who

had struggled for most of the year with a hand injury, finished two strokes clear of Chilean Angel Fernandez and Japan's Katsuyoshi Tomori to end 2008 on a high and finish eighth in the Order of Merit and intimate at another possible challenge for the John Jacobs Trophy in 2009.

With Langer, Mitchell and Woosnam setting new standards in 2008, there was a definite sense of a changing of the guard – something perhaps brought to the fore even more so by the official retirement of Senior Tour legend Tommy Horton after a 51 year playing career that saw him win 31 titles.

The 67 year old Englishman's haul of 23 Senior Tour titles makes him the most successful player in Senior Tour history, still three clear of the prolific Mason, and he finished Number One on the Order Of Merit for four successive seasons from 1996 and five times overall.

That baton, of course, is now firmly in the hands of Woosnam. The challenge now is to wrest it from the Welshman.

Steve Todd

Eamonn Darcy

Ross Drummond

Sandy Lyle

Carl Mason

Sam Torrance

European Senior Tour
Order of Merit 2008

Pos	Name	Country	Played	€	£
1	Ian WOOSNAM	(WAL)	(13)	320119.51	249742.17
2	Gordon J BRAND	(ENG)	(17)	257743.59	201079.41
3	Peter MITCHELL	(ENG)	(10)	217487.69	169673.65
4	Juan QUIROS	(ESP)	(15)	190164.29	148357.23
5	Bill LONGMUIR	(SCO)	(17)	177033.34	138113.08
6	Nick JOB	(ENG)	(17)	162682.83	126917.49
7	Carl MASON	(ENG)	(16)	156414.43	122027.17
8	Sam TORRANCE	(SCO)	(13)	152753.19	119170.85
9	Costantino ROCCA	(ITA)	(16)	140531.79	109636.28
10	Domingo HOSPITAL	(ESP)	(13)	124660.37	97254.15
11	Angel FRANCO	(PAR)	(11)	121252.15	94595.22
12	Tony JOHNSTONE	(ZIM)	(13)	118909.62	92767.69
13	Jerry BRUNER	(USA)	(15)	118543.43	92482.00
14	Katsuyoshi TOMORI	(JPN)	(12)	113251.71	88353.65
15	Luis CARBONETTI	(ARG)	(16)	110250.77	86012.46
16	Bob CAMERON	(ENG)	(17)	106700.15	83242.43
17	Ross DRUMMOND	(SCO)	(16)	106343.08	82963.87
18	Eamonn DARCY	(IRL)	(13)	105632.31	82409.36
19	José RIVERO	(ESP)	(15)	103851.82	81020.30
20	Stewart GINN	(AUS)	(10)	102222.66	79749.31
21	Des SMYTH	(IRL)	(7)	98588.85	76914.38
22	David MERRIMAN	(AUS)	(14)	93428.55	72888.55
23	Bob BOYD	(USA)	(16)	91311.86	71237.21
24	Angel FERNANDEZ	(CHI)	(14)	81595.20	63656.74
25	John CHILLAS	(SCO)	(17)	81400.04	63504.48
26	Denis O'SULLIVAN	(IRL)	(16)	76874.58	59973.93
27	Giuseppe CALI	(ITA)	(16)	74406.49	58048.44
28	Simon OWEN	(NZL)	(14)	72814.01	56806.06
29	Pete OAKLEY	(USA)	(17)	69892.94	54527.18
30	Martin GRAY	(SCO)	(15)	65537.75	51129.46
31	Delroy CAMBRIDGE	(JAM)	(15)	60307.58	47049.13
32	Guillermo ENCINA	(CHI)	(16)	56681.43	44220.19
33	Horacio CARBONETTI	(ARG)	(16)	56200.42	43844.92
34	Emilio RODRIGUEZ	(ESP)	(13)	55458.48	43266.09
35	Andrew MURRAY	(ENG)	(10)	55042.80	42941.80
36	David GOOD	(AUS)	(15)	54037.86	42157.80
37	John BLAND	(RSA)	(10)	52127.42	40667.36
38	Bobby LINCOLN	(RSA)	(15)	49880.40	38914.34
39	Gery WATINE	(FRA)	(11)	49388.89	38530.89
40	David J RUSSELL	(ENG)	(15)	49342.04	38494.34
41	Jeff HALL	(ENG)	(16)	48922.62	38167.12
42	Gordon BRAND JNR	(SCO)	(3)	47601.85	37136.72
43	Jim RHODES	(ENG)	(14)	44929.35	35051.76
44	Bob CHARLES	(NZL)	(9)	40091.61	31277.59
45	Tony ALLEN	(ENG)	(15)	36189.75	28233.54
46	Kevin SPURGEON	(ENG)	(14)	34669.24	27047.31
47	Philippe DUGENY	(FRA)	(13)	33462.01	26105.48
48	Adan SOWA	(ARG)	(10)	31566.76	24626.90
49	Seiji EBIHARA	(JPN)	(6)	31126.69	24283.58
50	Bruce HEUCHAN	(CAN)	(13)	30479.01	23778.29
51	Mark JAMES	(ENG)	(5)	29508.13	23020.86
52	Bob LARRATT	(ENG)	(14)	26964.98	21036.81
53	Manuel PIÑERO	(ESP)	(12)	26791.26	20901.28
54	Noel RATCLIFFE	(AUS)	(9)	25752.48	20090.87
55	Martin POXON	(ENG)	(15)	24866.31	19399.53
56	Bertus SMIT	(RSA)	(8)	23812.81	18577.63
57	Matt BRIGGS	(ENG)	(7)	23365.56	18228.71
58	John HOSKISON	(ENG)	(13)	23229.17	18122.30
59	Mike MILLER	(SCO)	(14)	23204.25	18102.86
60	Jimmy HEGGARTY	(NIR)	(15)	23020.23	17959.30
61	Sandy LYLE	(SCO)	(5)	21700.07	16929.37
62	Steve STULL	(USA)	(7)	20952.91	16346.48
63	Terry GALE	(AUS)	(11)	20359.63	15883.63
64	Jim LAPSLEY	(NZL)	(7)	20177.33	15741.40
65	Maurice BEMBRIDGE	(ENG)	(14)	19909.21	15532.23
66	John MASHEGO	(RSA)	(6)	16660.63	12997.84
67	Philip HARRISON	(ENG)	(5)	16464.89	12845.13
68	Denis DURNIAN	(ENG)	(12)	15975.65	12463.45
69	Eddie POLLAND	(NIR)	(11)	15403.18	12016.83
70	Graham BANISTER	(AUS)	(4)	15399.28	12013.79
71	John BENDA	(USA)	(10)	14533.01	11337.97
72	Jean Pierre SALLAT	(FRA)	(8)	13970.19	10898.89
73	Tommy HORTON	(ENG)	(11)	12394.05	9669.25
74	Ian MOSEY	(ENG)	(13)	11935.07	9311.18
75	Torsten GIEDEON	(GER)	(11)	11915.95	9296.26
76	Tim RASTALL	(ENG)	(14)	11755.32	9170.95
77	Tony PRICE	(WAL)	(15)	11396.83	8891.27
78	Alfonso BARRERA	(ARG)	(11)	11390.04	8885.97
79	Antonio GARRIDO	(ESP)	(14)	10055.84	7845.10
80	Tony CHARNLEY	(ENG)	(11)	9368.49	7308.85
81	Ian PALMER	(RSA)	(4)	8906.15	6948.16
82	Bill MCCOLL	(SCO)	(7)	8569.36	6685.41
83	Victor GARCIA	(ESP)	(11)	7736.26	6035.47
84	Liam HIGGINS	(IRL)	(5)	7056.72	5505.32
85	Ronald STELTEN	(USA)	(5)	6930.00	5406.46
86	Gavan LEVENSON	(RSA)	(5)	6401.92	4994.48
87	Steve MARTIN	(SCO)	(5)	5672.36	4425.31
88	Alberto CROCE	(ITA)	(4)	4853.65	3786.59
89	Peter TERAVAINEN	(USA)	(6)	4699.25	3666.14
90	Martin GALWAY	(ENG)	(6)	4615.84	3601.06
91	Bill HARDWICK	(CAN)	(6)	4076.33	3180.16
92	Bob LENDZION	(USA)	(4)	3436.78	2681.21
93	Ray CARRASCO	(USA)	(5)	3134.20	2445.16
94	Gordon TOWNHILL	(ENG)	(5)	2668.68	2081.98
95	Mike GALLAGHER	(ENG)	(3)	2507.61	1956.32
96	Mitch KIERSTENSON	(ENG)	(4)	2494.81	1946.33
97	Greg HOPKINS	(USA)	(4)	1449.93	1131.17
98	Baldovino DASSU	(ITA)	(1)	1444.00	1126.54
99	Andy BOWNES	(ENG)	(4)	838.59	654.23
100	Robin MANN	(ENG)	(3)	834.50	651.04
101	Peter DAHLBERG	(SWE)	(1)	756.86	590.47
102	Helmuth SCHUMACHER	(SUI)	(1)	305.50	238.34

Success and Consistency

David Horsey

W ith so much at stake for those finishing in the top 20, it was perhaps hardly surprising that the 2008 European Challenge Tour season proved to be one of the hardest fought in its 20 year history.

Marco Ruiz

Gary Lockerbie

Going into the season ending Apulia San Domenico Grand Final, up to ten players in the 45-man field were still in with a chance of securing the coveted Number One spot on the Challenge Tour Rankings, and with it a place in November's HSBC Champions on The European Tour.

The rest of the field, meanwhile, focused their efforts on claiming one of the 19 remaining spots which would assure them a place amongst the elite on The 2009 European Tour International Schedule and, of course, The Race to Dubai.

As it was, England's David Horsey finished on top with record earnings of €144,118 – some €15,191 more than was garnered by the 2007 Rankings winner Michael Lorenzo-Vera – whilst his compatriot Stuart Davis took 20th place by a mere €260 from the unfortunate Marco Ruiz of Paraguay. Such are the fine margins.

Horsey owed his triumph to an astonishingly consistent maiden season during which he claimed two titles in a glorious three week spell in mid-summer – first at the Telenet Trophy at the Limburg Golf and Country Club in Houthalen, Belgium; and then at the AGF-Allianz EurOpen de Lyon at Golf du Gouverneur, Monthieux, France – and missed just one cut in his 22 outings.

The 23 year old finished in the top ten for the ninth time in the Apulia San Domenico Grand Final at San Domenico Golf, Savalletri, Puglia, Italy, which was won in thrilling fashion by Argentina's Estanislao Goya.

Having come into the tournament in need of a big week to guarantee his European Tour playing privileges after slipping to 18th place on the Rankings, Goya proved his mettle by notching four birdies in the final five holes to pip the English duo of Richard Bland and John E Morgan to the €48,000 first prize.

Richard Bland

Estanislao Goya

It helped Goya finish fifth on the Rankings while Bland took 13th place and Morgan 17th, but the year, and the end of season plaudits, belonged to Horsey. "Winning the Challenge Tour means everything to me, but it means just as much to my friends and family back home," he said. "In fact it's dedicated to my gran, who passed away earlier this year. Hopefully she was looking down and had a smile on her face.

"I set my sights high at the start of the season and I've achieved them and more. I got off to a bit of a slow start and got into winning positions a couple of times without pulling it off, but the win in Belgium really got me going. It gave me the confidence to win again a couple of weeks later in France, which basically got me my card. It was a great feeling, knowing I could relax a bit more and play the rest of the season without too many worries.

"It's been a fantastic experience. In a way I am sorry to leave the Challenge Tour, because the

camaraderie was great. Everybody gets along which makes for a more relaxed environment. So I will be sad to see the back of it but, as much as I've loved it, I want to keep my European Tour card and keep improving every year from now on."

In total there were 26 winners on the 2008 Schedule, with Finland's Antti Ahokas, England's Seve Benson and Richie Ramsay of Scotland joining Messrs Goya and Horsey in the double winners' club.

While the quintet's haul was impressive, it was shaded by Taco Remkes of the Netherlands who became the first player since Australian Marcus Fraser in 2003 to claim three Challenge Tour titles in a single season.

The Flying Dutchman got off the mark with victory in the Scottish Challenge at the Macdonald Cardrona Hotel, Golf and Country Club, Peebles, Scotland, in June, before proving

Jeppe Huldahl

Klas Eriksson

Antti Ahokas

an extremely popular home winner of The Dutch Futures, presented by The Royal Bank of Scotland, at Golfclub Houtrak, Halfweg, Netherlands, in September.

There, the 24 year old from Amsterdam stormed home in figures of seven under par for the last ten holes to tie Denmark's Jeppe Huldahl before winning the title at the first play-off hole, an extra time feat he repeated three weeks later in the Margara Diehl-Ako Platinum Open at Margara Golf Club, Italy, where he recovered from a late wobble to see off Finland's Roope Kakko.

Remkes ended the season with €137,331 to his name, good enough only for third place on the Rankings behind Horsey and second placed Gary Lockerbie of England who finished with €138,509 thanks largely to his victory in the Kazakhstan Open at Nurtau Golf Club, Almaty, Kazakhstan, in September. The fact that the top three on the Rankings all finished the season with higher earnings than last year's winner Lorenzo-Vera further outlined the all-round progress the European Challenge Tour continues to make.

Behind Remkes in fourth place on the Rankings was Northern Ireland's Gareth Maybin whose season highlight came a week before Lockerbie's triumph when, after a series of near misses, he won the historic Qingdao Golf Open at the Qingdao Huashan Golf and Resort, Qingdao, China – the Challenge Tour's first visit to the People's Republic.

In fifth place at the end of the season was the second of the year's double winners, Goya. The 20 year old from Cordoba had exhibited his exciting talent with that thrilling victory in the Apulia San Domenico Grand Final and earlier he showed his resilience in March by prevailing in

San Domenico Golf

72010 Savelletri di Fasano (BR) - Puglia - ITALY
e-mail: info@sandomenicogolf.com

Tel. +39 (0)80 4829200 - Fax +39 (0)80 4827944
www.sandomenicogolf.com

Masseria Cimino
Guest House San Domenico Golf

72010 Savelletri di Fasano (BR) - Puglia - ITALY
e-mail: info@masseriacimino.com

Tel. +39 (0)80 4827886 - Fax +39 (0)80 4827950
www.masseriacimino.com

Seve Benson

Alessandro Tadini

Michael Hoey

Wil Besseling

Mark Haastrup

Rafael Cabrera Bello

a play-off with England's Gary Boyd in the 77° Abierto VISA del Centro 2008 presentado por Personal at the Córdoba Golf Club, Córdoba, Argentina.

In so doing, Goya franked the form which had, the previous year, seen him win the Tour de las Americas Qualifying School by nine shots, and in the process break Johnny Miller's 32 year course record at the Bonaventure Country Club in Florida with a sublime round of 61.

The third double winner of the season, Benson, finished the year in sixth place on the Rankings thanks to two victories on European soil. The Wentworth Club attached professional claimed his first victory in the Piemonte Open at the Circolo Golf Torino and Royal Park Golf and Country Club, Torino, Italy, in May; a result which marked the start of a consistent run of form

which culminated in a second title in the Ypsilon Golf Challenge by Alex Cejka in August.

In testing conditions at the Ypsilon Golf Resort, Liberec, Czech Republic, Benson clinched victory at the third hole of a play-off, dispatching Spain's Rafael Cabrera Bello and Branden Grace of South Africa with the sort of touch around the greens which would have made his famous Spanish namesake proud.

Completing the double winners' roll of honour were Richie Ramsay and Ahokas, who both profited largely towards the end of the season.

Ramsay, the 2006 US Amateur Championship winner, showed he had discovered the knack of winning in the professional ranks too when he claimed the Vodafone Challenge at Golf and Country Club An der Elfrather Mühle, Dusseldorf, Germany, in mid-August before, six weeks later at the start of October, he won the AGF-Allianz Golf Open Grand Toulouse at Golf de Toulouse-Seilh, Seilh, France; performances which helped the Scot finish eighth on the Rankings.

In between Ramsay's two victories, big-hitting left hander Ahokas won the ECCO Tour Championship at the Kokkedal Golfklub, Copenhagen, Denmark, at the end of August to add to his maiden Challenge Tour triumph in the

Stuart Davis

Steven O'Hara

European Challenge Tour

103° Abierto VISA de la Republica presentado por Peugeot at the Hurlingham Club, Buenos Aires, Argentina, at the beginning of April.

The two wins saw the 23 year old Finn take the 19th of the 20 cards on offer for The 2009 European Tour International Schedule, further proof of the growing strength in depth of the Challenge Tour.

Like The European Tour, the Challenge Tour continues to travel around the globe and the start of the season was given a distinctly Latin flavour as South American golfers took the first two tournaments on the schedule.

Firstly Argentina's Miguel Rodriguez delighted the home fans with victory in the Abierto del Litoral Personal 2007, at Rosario Golf Club, Rosario, Argentina; before Paraguay's Marco

Andrew McArthur

Taco Remkes

Ruiz held off the challenge of the then US Open Champion Angel Cabrera to triumph in the 102° Abierto VISA de la Republica presentado por Peugeot at Buenos Aires Golf Club, Buenos Aires, Argentina.

"It was like a dream," said Ruiz of his memorable triumph. Sadly, for the 34 year old godson of one of Argentina's most celebrated golfers, Vicente Fernandez, there was to be no fairytale ending to the season as, such are the high demands of the modern day Challenge Tour, even with a victory under his belt in the course of a season, he, like Rodriguez, did not finish within the top 20 on the final Rankings.

Indeed, 12 players in total found themselves in that situation over the course of 2008; the days where one victory during the year was a guarantee of progression, long gone.

Following Rodriguez and Ruiz in that group was England's Iain Pyman, who claimed a record-

breakding eighth Challenge Tour success in the Tusker Kenya Open at the Karen Golf Club, Nairobi, Kenya at the beginning of March. He was joined, in the first half of the year, by Sweden's Joakim Haeggman (AGF-Allianz Open Côtes d'Armor Bretagne at Golf Blue Green de Pléneuf Val Andre, France); Northern Ireland's Michael Hoey (Banque Populaire Moroccan Classic 2008 at the El Jadida Sofitel Golf Resort, El Jadida, Morocco); England's Gary Clark (DHL Wroclaw Open at the Toya Golf and Country Club, Wroclaw, Poland); Scotland's Andrew McArthur (Reale Challenge de España at Casino Club de Golf Retamares, Madrid, Spain); and

Chris Gane

European Challenge Tour

Christian Nilsson

Andrew Tampion

Richie Ramsay

Simon Robinson of England (SK Golf Challenge at St Laurence Golf, Lohja, Finland).

Completing the group from July onwards were Switzerland's André Bossert (MAN NÖ Open at Golf Club Adamstal, Ramsau, Austria); Ireland's Michael McGeady (SWALEC Wales Challenge at the Vale Hotel Golf and Spa Resort, Cardiff, Vale of Glamorgan, Wales); Australia's Andrew Tampion (Challenge of Ireland presented by Glasson at the Glasson Golf Hotel and Country Club, Athlone, Ireland); and Mark Haastrup of Denmark (The Dubliner Challenge at the Hills Golf Club, Gothenburg, Sweden).

Of course, for some, victory did provide the impetus for a top 20 finish, beginning with Wil Besseling of The Netherlands who won the II Club Colombia Masters at the Country Club de Bogotá, Bogotá, Colombia, in April on his way to claiming the 15th card on offer.

The first day of June saw Italy's Alessandro Tadini – who eventually finished seventh on the Rankings –win the Oceânico Group Pro-Am Challenge at the Marriott Worsley Park Hotel and Country Club in Manchester, England; two weeks before European Tour professional David Dixon of England won the SAINT-OMER OPEN, presented by Neuflize OBC at the Aa St Omer Golf Club, Lumbres, France – the only event in 2008 to have a dual ranking between The European Tour and the Challenge Tour.

Alexandre Rocha

John E Morgan

The 13th day of July certainly did not prove unlucky for Spain's Rafael Cabrera Bello as he won the Credit Suisse Challenge at the Wylihof Golf Club, Luterbach, Switzerland, on his way to 14th place on the Rankings; while the final two winners of the season to finish in the top 20 – Denmark's Jeppe Huldahl and the experienced Klas Eriksson of Sweden – both triumphed in August on their way to tenth and 11th place respectively.

First onto the winners' podium was Huldahl in the Lexus Open at the Moss and Rygge Golfklub, Dilling, Norway, and he was succeeded the following week by Eriksson who claimed his fifth Challenge Tour success in the Trophée du Golf Club de Genève at the Golf Club de Genève, Genève, Switzerland following a play-off with Wil Besseling and Alexandre Rocha of Brazil, to ensure a return to The European Tour where he was a fixture in the 1990s and early 2000s.

While all professional golfers strive for success, consistency is equally as important a trait to possess and that was proved by the seven players who booked their places in the top 20 of the Challenge Tour Rankings at the end of the season without a tournament success to their name, but following a season where many weekend appearances paid dividends.

Leading the way was Scotland's Steven O'Hara, who took ninth place, and he was followed by Brazil's Alexandre Rocha (12th), Englishmen Richard Bland (13th), Marcus Higley (16th) and John E Morgan (17th), Sweden's Christian Nilsson (18th) and Stuart Davis of England (20th).

The seven, and indeed all 20 graduates from the European Challenge Tour, deserve praise and congratulations for their achievements during 2008, coupled with a wish of good fortune as they begin the next stage of their own golfing odysseys on The Race to Dubai in 2009.

Paul Symes

Carlos Cardeza

The 2008 European Challenge Tour season was tinged with sadness at the death of promising young Argentine golfer Carlos Cardeza as a result of a car accident in his hometown of Villa Allende, near Cordoba. The 24 year old played 12 times on the Challenge Tour in 2008 and was also scheduled to compete in The European Tour Qualifying School. Alain de Soultrait, Managing Director of the European Challenge Tour, paid tribute to player widely recognised as one of the friendliest players on Tour. "It is always very sad to lose such a young person and Carlos was a young man who was also very talented," he said. "He was a very nice person who was well thought of among the other players and was very enjoyable to be around. Our thoughts go to everyone connected with the Tour de las Americas but most of all to Carlos' family."

Born in Entre Ríos but raised in Córdoba, Cardeza first began to showcase his talent at Córdoba Golf Club, the home club of his golfing hero, Angel Cabrera. As a junior player he won national championships in 2002 and 2003 and represented his nation at the Junior Golf World Cup in Japan. He entered the Tour de las Americas in October 2004 and, since then, played 26 official tournaments, including a tie for third at the 2006 Mexico Open for his best TLA finish. His best finish of the 2008 European Challenge Tour was a tie for tenth place in the 77° Abierto VISA del Centro 2008 presentado por Personal at his home Cordoba Golf Club in March.

Back row, from from left to right: Stuart Davis, John E Morgan, Klas Eriksson, Antti Ahokas, Christian Nilsson, Marcus Higley, Rafael Cabrera Bello, Richard Bland, Seve Benson, Alexandre Rocha, Alessandro Tadini, Gareth Maybin, Richie Ramsay, Steven O'Hara, Gary Lockerbie, Jeppe Huldahl, Taco Remkes, Wil Besseling. Front row, from left to right: Estanislao Goya, David Horsey

Gareth Maybin

Marcus Higley

Estanislao Goya's victory in the season ending Apulia San Domenico Grand Final lifted him from 18th to fifth in the Challenge Tour Rankings. Left to right at the trophy presentation: Sergio Melpignano, owner and President of San Domenico Golf, Franco Chimenti, President of the Italian Golf Federation, Goya, Aldo Melpignano and Alain de Soultrait, Director of Challenge Tour

European Challenge Tour Rankings 2008

Pos	Name	Country	Played	€
1	David HORSEY	(ENG)	(22)	144118.30
2	Gary LOCKERBIE	(ENG)	(19)	138508.52
3	Taco REMKES	(NED)	(25)	137330.76
4	Gareth MAYBIN	(NIR)	(20)	117719.04
5	Estanislao GOYA	(ARG)	(24)	113336.38
6	Seve BENSON	(ENG)	(16)	111529.12
7	Alessandro TADINI	(ITA)	(19)	106892.98
8	Richie RAMSAY	(SCO)	(21)	106655.63
9	Steven O'HARA	(SCO)	(16)	103211.64
10	Jeppe HULDAHL	(DEN)	(26)	96818.22
11	Klas ERIKSSON	(SWE)	(16)	96514.25
12	Alexandre ROCHA	(BRA)	(24)	93684.29
13	Richard BLAND	(ENG)	(15)	92645.45
14	Rafael CABRERA BELLO	(ESP)	(17)	89846.82
15	Wil BESSELING	(NED)	(22)	89358.16
16	Marcus HIGLEY	(ENG)	(25)	85946.37
17	John E MORGAN	(ENG)	(20)	77253.53
18	Christian NILSSON	(SWE)	(10)	75200.00
19	Antti AHOKAS	(FIN)	(20)	74866.65
20	Stuart DAVIS	(ENG)	(22)	67104.90
21	Marco RUIZ	(PAR)	(22)	66845.17
22	Andrew MCARTHUR	(SCO)	(20)	64559.75
23	Raphaël DE SOUSA	(SUI)	(20)	63132.99
24	Gary CLARK	(ENG)	(19)	62161.28
25	Chris GANE	(ENG)	(21)	61768.81
26	Mark F HAASTRUP	(DEN)	(24)	61625.08
27	Roope KAKKO	(FIN)	(19)	57318.52
28	Michael HOEY	(NIR)	(23)	52424.33
29	Gary BOYD	(ENG)	(18)	51295.91
30	Andrew TAMPION	(AUS)	(18)	51020.52
31	Richard MCEVOY	(ENG)	(24)	49265.06
32	Mikko KORHONEN	(FIN)	(19)	48288.46
33	David DRYSDALE	(SCO)	(9)	46845.82
34	Inder VAN WEERELT	(NED)	(25)	46671.36
35	Branden GRACE	(RSA)	(22)	46540.27
36	Greig HUTCHEON	(SCO)	(18)	46292.60
37	Julien QUESNE	(FRA)	(23)	46144.41
38	Bernd WIESBERGER	(AUT)	(23)	45452.14
39	Joakim HAEGGMAN	(SWE)	(19)	44898.52
40	Robert COLES	(ENG)	(19)	44589.50
41	Roland STEINER	(AUT)	(21)	44220.80
42	Michael McGEADY	(IRL)	(18)	42944.71
43	Liam BOND	(WAL)	(18)	41611.27
44	Thomas FEYRSINGER	(AUT)	(19)	41005.00
45	Matthew MORRIS	(ENG)	(13)	40563.00
46	Simon ROBINSON	(ENG)	(18)	38550.00
47	Andrew WILLEY	(ENG)	(21)	38503.50
48	Carlos DEL MORAL	(ESP)	(22)	35946.84
49	Mark TULLO	(CHI)	(24)	35250.72
50	Ricardo SANTOS	(POR)	(18)	35001.00
51	Björn PETTERSSON	(SWE)	(15)	34535.64
52	Joel SJOHOLM	(SWE)	(11)	32811.25
53	Anders Schmidt HANSEN	(DEN)	(25)	32780.53
54	Gregory MOLTENI	(ITA)	(18)	32167.82
55	Colm MORIARTY	(IRL)	(20)	31527.05
56	George MURRAY	(SCO)	(21)	30517.90
57	André BOSSERT	(SUI)	(15)	30141.50
58	Benjamin MIARKA	(GER)	(23)	29575.30
59	Eirik Tage JOHANSEN	(NOR)	(12)	28772.00
60	Nicolas VANHOOTEGEM	(BEL)	(19)	28680.19
61	Richard TREIS	(GER)	(23)	27862.11
62	Lorenzo GAGLI	(ITA)	(25)	27454.01
63	Adam GEE	(ENG)	(22)	27328.19
64	Jan-Are LARSEN	(NOR)	(8)	25477.04
65	Miguel RODRIGUEZ	(ARG)	(19)	25065.22
66	Eric RAMSAY	(SCO)	(21)	24480.06
67	Matthew CORT	(ENG)	(19)	23970.14
68	James MORRISON	(ENG)	(21)	23924.26
69	Andreas HÖGBERG	(SWE)	(24)	23443.03
70	Julien CLÉMENT	(SUI)	(17)	23312.88
71	Christophe BRAZILLIER	(FRA)	(22)	23089.86
72	Anthony SNOBECK	(FRA)	(24)	23088.89
73	Edward RUSH	(ENG)	(21)	22854.01
74	Lars BROVOLD	(NOR)	(10)	22797.71
75	François CALMELS	(FRA)	(21)	22258.63
76	Andrew MARSHALL	(ENG)	(16)	21465.14
77	Kasper Linnet JORGENSEN	(DEN)	(16)	20710.99
78	Ian GARBUTT	(ENG)	(13)	20543.89
79	Adrien BERNADET	(FRA)	(23)	20533.18
80	Jaakko MAKITALO	(FIN)	(10)	19873.52
81	Johan SKÖLD	(SWE)	(16)	19459.37
82	Marco SOFFIETTI	(ITA)	(17)	19444.01
83	Michele REALE	(ITA)	(18)	19321.86
84	Soren JUUL	(DEN)	(16)	19064.33
85	Steven JEPPESEN	(SWE)	(15)	18501.30
86	Andrew BUTTERFIELD	(ENG)	(21)	18309.88
87	Cesar MONASTERIO	(ARG)	(13)	17979.20
88	Matthew ZIONS	(AUS)	(20)	17460.47
89	Jamie LITTLE	(ENG)	(24)	17444.26
90	Tiago CRUZ	(POR)	(20)	17156.50
91	Sébastien DELAGRANGE	(FRA)	(15)	16743.71
92	Ben MASON	(ENG)	(17)	16291.50
93	Tyrone FERREIRA	(RSA)	(12)	16029.42
94	Lloyd SALTMAN	(SCO)	(11)	15707.50
95	James HEATH	(ENG)	(19)	15385.58
96	Sebastian L SAAVEDRA	(ARG)	(14)	15381.13
97	Gustavo ROJAS	(ARG)	(14)	15219.76
98	Martin MONGUZZI	(ARG)	(11)	15168.37
99	Peter KAENSCHE	(NOR)	(22)	14972.64
100	Rikard KARLBERG	(SWE)	(18)	14937.56

The European Tour Golfer of the Month Awards are presented throughout the year followed by an Annual Award

Martin Kaymer - *January*

Mark Brown - *February*

Graeme McDowell - *March*

Sergio Garcia - *May*

Padraig Harrington (July & August) became in 2008 The European Tour Golfer of the Year for the second successive time

Trevor Immelman - *April*

Pablo Larrazabal - *June*

Robert Karlsson - *September & October*

ANNUAL WINNERS

Year	Winner		Year	Winner	
2008	Padraig Harrington		1996	Colin Montgomerie	
2007	Padraig Harrington		1995	Colin Montgomerie	
2006	Paul Casey		1994	Ernie Els	
2005	Michael Campbell		1993	Bernhard Langer	
2004	Vijay Singh		1992	Nick Faldo	
2003	Ernie Els		1991	Severiano Ballesteros	
2002	Ernie Els		1990	Nick Faldo	
2001	Retief Goosen		1989	Nick Faldo	
2000	Lee Westwood		1988	Severiano Ballesteros	
1999	Colin Montgomerie		1987	Ian Woosnam	
1998	Lee Westwood		1986	Severiano Ballesteros	
1997	Colin Montgomerie		1985	Bernhard Langer	

The European Tour Shot of the Month Awards are presented throughout the year followed by an Annual Award

Padraig Harrington (July & August) also captured the annual Award for his five wood at the 17th hole in the final round of The 137th Open Championship at Royal Birkdale. He is pictured receiving a monthly award from George O'Grady, Chief Executive of The European Tour

Richard Sterne - *January*

Mark Brown - *February*

Graeme McDowell - *March*

Darren Clarke - *April*

Richard Finch - *May*

Martin Kaymer - *June*

Gonzalo Fernandez-Castaño
- *September*

Sergio Garcia - *October*

ANNUAL WINNERS

2008	Padraig Harrington	
2007	Angel Cabrera	
2006	Paul Casey	
2005	Paul McGinley	
2004	David Howell	
2003	Fredrik Jacobson	

Stroke Average

Pos	Name	Stroke Average	Total Strokes	Total Rounds	Pos	Name	Stroke Average	Total Strokes	Total Rounds	Pos	Name	Stroke Average	Total Strokes	Total Rounds
1	**Robert KARLSSON**	**70.08**	**6027**	**86**	51	Jarmo SANDELIN	71.43	6357	89	102	Alessandro TADINI	71.91	2373	33
2	Lee WESTWOOD	70.44	5283	75	52	Damien MCGRANE	71.44	7144	100	103	Paul SHEEHAN	71.92	1726	24
3	Sergio GARCIA	70.63	3249	46	53	Matthew MILLAR	71.46	4788	67	103	Lian-wei ZHANG	71.92	1870	26
4	Jeev Milkha SINGH	70.73	6295	89	54	Johan EDFORS	71.48	6219	87	105	Prom MEESAWAT	71.93	2158	30
5	Gary ORR	70.74	5518	78	55	Jan-Are LARSEN	71.49	3789	53	106	Alvaro QUIROS	71.95	5828	81
6	David LYNN	70.79	6867	97	55	Anders HANSEN	71.49	5004	70	107	Ian POULTER	71.96	3814	53
6	Graeme MCDOWELL	70.79	7008	99	57	Retief GOOSEN	71.52	4005	56	107	Richard BLAND	71.96	3670	51
8	Thongchai JAIDEE	70.81	5311	75	57	Gonzalo FDEZ-CASTAÑO	71.52	5865	82	107	Miles TUNNICLIFF	71.96	5901	82
9	Alexander NOREN	70.82	7082	100	57	Oliver WILSON	71.52	6151	86	107	Richard GREEN	71.96	5253	73
10	Francesco MOLINARI	70.83	7154	101	60	Thaworn WIRATCHANT	71.54	2003	28	111	Louis OOSTHUIZEN	71.97	5542	77
11	Darren CLARKE	70.84	6659	94	60	Ben MASON	71.54	1860	26	112	Per-Ulrik JOHANSSON	71.98	3527	49
12	Miguel Angel JIMÉNEZ	70.87	6095	86	60	Steve WEBSTER	71.54	5866	82	113	David BRANSDON	72.00	2160	30
13	Paul MCGINLEY	70.88	6450	91	63	Peter HEDBLOM	71.57	6584	92	113	Chris RODGERS	72.00	1728	24
14	Padraig HARRINGTON	70.90	3545	50	64	Mikko ILONEN	71.58	6156	86	113	Robert DINWIDDIE	72.00	6624	92
15	Søren KJELDSEN	70.95	7450	105	64	Oliver FISHER	71.58	6943	97	113	Gary MURPHY	72.00	6192	86
16	Martin ERLANDSSON	70.97	7026	99	66	Liam BOND	71.59	1933	27	117	Jean-François LUCQUIN	72.01	7345	102
16	Danny WILLETT	70.97	2129	30	66	Fredrik ANDERSSON HED	71.59	6085	85	117	Graeme STORM	72.01	5761	80
18	Robert ROCK	71.00	5396	76	66	Chris WOOD	71.59	2076	29	119	Patrik SJÖLAND	72.02	5834	81
19	Henrik STENSON	71.03	4759	67	69	John BICKERTON	71.60	6158	86	119	Wen-chong LIANG	72.02	3025	42
19	Adam SCOTT	71.03	2699	38	69	Jamie DONALDSON	71.60	6372	89	121	Thomas AIKEN	72.03	5258	73
21	Martin KAYMER	71.05	6110	86	72	Nick DOUGHERTY	71.62	6159	86	122	Garry HOUSTON	72.04	6844	95
22	Ricardo GONZALEZ	71.06	5827	82	72	Scott BARR	71.62	4154	58	122	Peter BAKER	72.04	5691	79
23	Bradley DREDGE	71.08	5544	78	74	Simon YATES	71.63	2292	32	122	Kyron SULLIVAN	72.04	3962	55
24	Christian NILSSON	71.11	1920	27	75	Alvaro VELASCO	71.66	5948	83	122	Scott HEND	72.04	1873	26
25	Anthony WALL	71.14	6901	97	76	Gary CLARK	71.67	1720	24	126	Peter O'MALLEY	72.07	5261	73
25	Mark FOSTER	71.14	6047	85	77	Paul LAWRIE	71.68	6093	85	126	Ian GARBUTT	72.07	2090	29
27	Thomas LEVET	71.15	6261	88	77	Ross McGOWAN	71.68	6523	91	128	Marc WARREN	72.08	5622	78
28	Søren HANSEN	71.17	6334	89	79	Lee SLATTERY	71.70	5664	79	129	Hennie OTTO	72.09	5335	74
28	Felipe AGUILAR	71.17	5551	78	79	Gareth PADDISON	71.70	5306	74	129	Rafael CABRERA BELLO	72.09	2523	35
28	Maarten LAFEBER	71.17	6832	96	79	Shiv KAPUR	71.70	5879	82	131	Prayad MARKSAENG	72.10	2091	29
31	Andrew MCLARDY	71.18	5837	82	82	Michael JONZON	71.71	5163	72	132	Jyoti RANDHAWA	72.11	5336	74
32	Stephen GALLACHER	71.21	6338	89	83	David FROST	71.72	5953	83	132	Manuel QUIROS	72.11	2019	28
33	Robert-Jan DERKSEN	71.24	6982	98	83	Paul BROADHURST	71.72	5881	82	132	Mattias ELIASSON	72.11	2740	38
34	Paul CASEY	71.25	3705	52	85	David HOWELL	71.73	6743	94	135	James KINGSTON	72.13	5482	76
35	Charl SCHWARTZEL	71.26	6413	90	86	Grégory HAVRET	71.74	6672	93	135	Rafa ECHENIQUE	72.13	6131	85
36	Santiago LUNA	71.27	3207	45	87	José Manuel LARA	71.75	7103	99	135	Adam GROOM	72.13	1731	24
36	Peter HANSON	71.27	6984	98	88	Peter LAWRIE	71.76	7176	100	138	Mikael LUNDBERG	72.14	5843	81
36	Ignacio GARRIDO	71.27	6129	86	89	Sam LITTLE	71.78	6532	91	138	Andres ROMERO	72.14	3174	44
36	Rory MCILROY	71.27	6129	86	89	Alastair FORSYTH	71.78	5886	82	140	Henrik NYSTRÖM	72.17	5629	78
40	Markus BRIER	71.32	6062	85	89	Steve ALKER	71.78	2656	37	140	Richard STERNE	72.17	4763	66
40	Daniel CHOPRA	71.32	2710	38	92	Joost LUITEN	71.80	3159	44	142	Pelle EDBERG	72.20	6281	87
42	Simon DYSON	71.33	7347	103	93	Scott STRANGE	71.83	6177	86	142	Pablo LARRAZABAL	72.20	6354	88
42	Grégory BOURDY	71.33	7133	100	93	Kane WEBBER	71.83	2083	29	144	Justin ROSE	72.22	3322	46
44	Ross FISHER	71.34	7134	100	95	Edoardo MOLINARI	71.84	5316	74	145	Phillip ARCHER	72.24	6574	91
45	Paul WARING	71.38	5139	72	96	Ernie ELS	71.86	3665	51	145	Richard FINCH	72.24	6574	91
46	Christian CÉVAËR	71.39	5640	79	96	Robert ALLENBY	71.86	2012	28	147	Tony CAROLAN	72.25	1734	24
46	Thomas BJÖRN	71.39	4783	67	96	François DELAMONTAGNE	71.86	6180	86	147	Adilson DA SILVA	72.25	2023	28
48	Alejandro CAÑIZARES	71.41	3642	51	99	Magnus A CARLSSON	71.87	6181	86	149	Daniel VANCSIK	72.26	5347	74
48	Marcus FRASER	71.41	5570	78	100	Raphaël JACQUELIN	71.89	6686	93	149	Fabrizio ZANOTTI	72.26	5275	73
50	Steven O'HARA	71.42	2214	31	101	Sion E BEBB	71.90	4961	69					

Driving Distance (yds)

Pos	Name	Average Yards	Stats Rounds
1	**Alvaro QUIROS**	**309.7**	**77**
2	Rafael CABRERA BELLO	303.2	35
3	Christian NILSSON	302.9	27
4	Emanuele CANONICA	301.9	75
5	Joakim BÄCKSTRÖM	301.3	55
6	Paul WARING	300.6	60
6	Paolo TERRENI	300.6	41
8	Mattias ELIASSON	300.4	36
9	Daniel VANCSIK	300.2	75
10	Anton HAIG	299.7	72
11	Ernie ELS	298.0	26
12	Ricardo GONZALEZ	297.4	77
12	Robert ROCK	297.4	69
14	Thomas AIKEN	297.0	62
15	Pelle EDBERG	296.9	82
16	Rafa ECHENIQUE	296.6	81
17	Johan EDFORS	296.4	79
18	James KAMTE	295.5	58
19	Edoardo MOLINARI	295.3	66
19	Rory MCILROY	295.3	82
21	Louis OOSTHUIZEN	295.0	61
22	Alan MCLEAN	293.5	26
23	Paul CASEY	293.4	24
24	Retief GOOSEN	293.3	27
24	Peter WHITEFORD	293.3	85

Greens In Regulation (%)

Pos	Name	%	Stats Rounds
1	**Steven O'HARA**	**75.3**	**29**
2	Johan EDFORS	75.2	79
2	Lee WESTWOOD	75.2	48
4	Thomas LEVET	75.1	82
4	Rafael CABRERA BELLO	75.1	35
6	Søren HANSEN	73.4	64
7	Peter O'MALLEY	73.2	70
8	Francesco MOLINARI	73.1	97
8	Stephen GALLACHER	73.1	81
10	Bradley DREDGE	72.9	74
11	Robert ROCK	72.4	69
12	Jeev Milkha SINGH	72.0	72
13	Gary MURPHY	71.8	83
14	Darren CLARKE	71.5	81
14	José Manuel LARA	71.5	95
16	Ernie ELS	71.4	26
16	Mark FOSTER	71.4	82
18	Peter HANSON	71.3	82
18	Robert KARLSSON	71.3	58
18	Gary ORR	71.3	74
21	Alastair FORSYTH	71.1	70
21	Martin KAYMER	71.1	62
23	Ulrich VAN DEN BERG	70.9	26
24	Graeme STORM	70.8	69
25	Jarmo SANDELIN	70.7	84
25	Steve WEBSTER	70.7	70

Scrambles

Pos	Name	%	AVE SPR	AVE Missed GPR	Total Missed GIR	Total Scrambles	Stats Rounds
1	**Paul CASEY**	**64.0**	**3.6**	**6**	**136**	**87**	**24**
2	Robert KARLSSON	63.7	3.3	5	300	191	58
3	Sergio GARCIA	63.1	3.4	5	130	82	24
4	Richard GREEN	62.5	4.0	6	331	207	52
5	David LYNN	62.0	3.6	6	542	336	94
5	Wen-chong LIANG	62.0	3.9	6	150	93	24
7	Paul BROADHURST	61.4	4.3	7	552	339	78
8	Christian CÉVAËR	61.3	4.1	7	506	310	76
8	Maarten LAFEBER	61.3	3.7	6	556	341	93
10	Henrik STENSON	61.1	3.6	6	247	151	42
10	Padraig HARRINGTON	61.1	3.9	6	167	102	26
12	Lee SLATTERY	60.7	3.5	6	427	259	75
13	Martin ERLANDSSON	60.3	3.5	6	551	332	95
14	Graeme MCDOWELL	60.1	3.2	5	416	250	78
14	Søren KJELDSEN	60.1	3.4	6	534	321	94
16	Martin KAYMER	59.8	3.1	5	323	193	62
17	Thongchai JAIDEE	59.6	3.5	6	413	246	71
18	Francesco MOLINARI	59.4	2.9	5	470	279	97
18	Simon DYSON	59.4	3.5	6	552	328	95
20	Colin MONTGOMERIE	59.1	3.6	6	345	204	56
20	Damien MCGRANE	59.1	3.8	6	597	353	94
22	David FROST	58.8	3.6	6	478	281	74
22	Robert-Jan DERKSEN	58.8	3.6	6	570	335	94
24	Ricardo GONZALEZ	58.5	3.5	6	460	269	77
24	Grégory BOURDY	58.5	3.6	6	559	327	92

Driving Accuracy (%)

Pos	Name	%	Stats Rounds
1	**Pedro LINHART**	**76.5**	**52**
2	Peter O'MALLEY	72.8	70
3	Henrik NYSTRÖM	71.3	74
4	John BICKERTON	70.3	82
5	Ian GARBUTT	70.2	25
5	Francesco MOLINARI	69.0	97
6	Andrew COLTART	69.0	32
8	Darren CLARKE	68.8	81
9	Simon WAKEFIELD	68.4	91
9	Alessandro TADINI	68.4	30
11	Jean-François LUCQUIN	68.2	99
12	Gary ORR	67.7	74
12	Matthew MILLAR	67.7	63
14	Søren KJELDSEN	67.5	94
15	Paul MCGINLEY	67.2	84
16	Per-Ulrik JOHANSSON	67.1	49
16	Barry LANE	67.1	68
18	Garry HOUSTON	67.0	90
18	Mark BROWN	67.0	51
20	Peter LAWRIE	66.9	96
21	Gary MURPHY	66.8	83
22	Steve WEBSTER	66.5	70
23	Ian POULTER	66.3	32
24	David FROST	66.0	74
25	Edoardo MOLINARI	65.9	66
25	Steven O'HARA	65.9	29

Sand Saves (%)

Pos	Name	%	Stats Rounds
1	**James KINGSTON**	**77.8**	**54**
2	Danny WILLETT	72.7	30
3	Jeev Milkha SINGH	70.9	72
4	Ernie ELS	68.4	26
5	Robert KARLSSON	67.8	58
6	Francesco MOLINARI	67.2	97
7	Retief GOOSEN	66.7	27
7	Steve ALKER	66.7	34
9	Jean-François REMESY	66.1	47
10	Paul BROADHURST	66.0	78
11	José Manuel LARA	65.4	95
12	Gonzalo FDEZ-CASTAÑO	65.3	78
13	John BICKERTON	65.1	82
14	S S P CHOWRASIA	64.9	32
15	Iain PYMAN	64.0	60
16	Darren FICHARDT	63.6	24
16	Martin KAYMER	63.6	62
18	Ignacio GARRIDO	63.4	82
19	Robert ROCK	63.1	69
19	Ariel CANETE	63.1	76
21	Santiago LUNA	63.0	38
22	Andrew COLTART	62.5	32
22	Grégory BOURDY	62.5	92
22	Oliver WILSON	62.5	70
25	Philip GOLDING	62.0	43
25	Mads VIBE-HASTRUP	62.0	66

Average Putts Per Round

Pos	Name	Putts per Round	Stats Rounds
1	**S S P CHOWRASIA**	**27.4**	**32**
2	David HOWELL	28.1	82
3	Paul BROADHURST	28.3	78
4	Padraig HARRINGTON	28.4	26
5	Christian CÉVAËR	28.6	76
5	Rafa ECHENIQUE	28.6	81
5	Kyron SULLIVAN	28.6	51
8	David FROST	28.7	74
8	Henrik STENSON	28.7	42
8	Wen-chong LIANG	28.7	24
11	Michael CAMPBELL	28.8	45
11	Mikael LUNDBERG	28.8	77
13	Robert KARLSSON	28.9	58
13	Marc WARREN	28.9	74
13	Marcus FRASER	28.9	73
13	Sergio GARCIA	28.9	24
13	Richard GREEN	28.9	52
18	Danny WILLETT	29.0	30
18	Damien MCGRANE	29.0	94
20	Andrew MCLARDY	29.1	70
20	Miguel Angel JIMÉNEZ	29.1	64
20	Simon DYSON	29.1	95
20	Shiv KAPUR	29.1	77
20	Robert-Jan DERKSEN	29.1	94
25	David LYNN	29.2	94
25	Benn BARHAM	29.2	74
25	Mikko ILONEN	29.2	82
25	Gareth PADDISON	29.2	66
25	Grégory BOURDY	29.2	92
25	Michael LORENZO-VERA	29.2	70
31	Peter LAWRIE	29.3	96
31	Graeme MCDOWELL	29.3	78
31	Louis OOSTHUIZEN	29.3	61
31	Pablo LARRAZABAL	29.3	71
31	Paul WARING	29.3	60
31	Søren KJELDSEN	29.3	94
31	Maarten LAFEBER	29.3	93
38	Martin ERLANDSSON	29.4	95
38	Pelle EDBERG	29.4	82
38	Markus BRIER	29.4	80
38	Patrik SJÖLAND	29.4	74
38	François DELAMONTAGNE	29.4	79
38	Thongchai JAIDEE	29.4	71
38	Gonzalo FDEZ-CASTAÑO	29.4	78
38	Peter FOWLER	29.4	60

Putts Per Green In Regulation

Pos	Name	Putts per GIR	Stats Rounds
1	**Danny WILLETT**	**1.719**	**30**
2	David HOWELL	1.723	82
3	S S P CHOWRASIA	1.730	32
4	Rafa ECHENIQUE	1.734	81
5	Miguel Angel JIMÉNEZ	1.736	64
6	Padraig HARRINGTON	1.744	26
7	Sergio GARCIA	1.745	24
8	Robert KARLSSON	1.746	58
9	Michael CAMPBELL	1.748	45
10	Ernie ELS	1.749	26
11	Andrew MCLARDY	1.750	70
12	Christian CÉVAËR	1.751	76
13	Nick DOUGHERTY	1.753	62
14	David FROST	1.756	74
15	Lee WESTWOOD	1.757	48
15	Marcus FRASER	1.757	73
17	Pablo LARRAZABAL	1.759	71
18	Henrik STENSON	1.760	42
19	Mikael LUNDBERG	1.761	77
20	Wen-chong LIANG	1.762	24
20	Oliver WILSON	1.762	70
22	Jeev Milkha SINGH	1.765	72
23	Marc WARREN	1.766	74
24	Graeme MCDOWELL	1.767	78
24	Gareth PADDISON	1.767	66
24	Charl SCHWARTZEL	1.767	77
24	Paul WARING	1.767	60
28	Paul BROADHURST	1.768	78
28	François DELAMONTAGNE	1.768	79
30	Shiv KAPUR	1.769	77
31	Mikko ILONEN	1.770	82
32	Gonzalo FDEZ-CASTAÑO	1.771	78
33	Benn BARHAM	1.772	74
33	Joost LUITEN	1.772	40
35	Markus BRIER	1.774	80
35	Alexander NOREN	1.774	91
37	Kyron SULLIVAN	1.775	51
37	Damien MCGRANE	1.775	94
39	Søren HANSEN	1.776	64
39	Scott STRANGE	1.776	75

Pos	Name	Country	Played	€	£	Pos	Name	Country	Played	€	£
1	Robert KARLSSON	(SWE)	(23)	2732747.83	2171087.50	51	Oliver FISHER	(ENG)	(30)	594587.18	472381.97
2	Padraig HARRINGTON	(IRL)	(14)	2459108.73	1953689.31	52	Jean-François LUCQUIN	(FRA)	(31)	592104.45	470409.51
3	Lee WESTWOOD	(ENG)	(21)	2424641.58	1926306.17	53	Mark BROWN	(NZL)	(23)	585670.52	465297.94
4	Miguel Angel JIMÉNEZ	(ESP)	(26)	2066596.11	1641849.62	54	Robert-Jan DERKSEN	(NED)	(28)	577074.03	458468.28
5	Graeme MCDOWELL	(NIR)	(28)	1859346.26	1477195.73	55	Simon DYSON	(ENG)	(30)	570949.29	453602.36
6	Ross FISHER	(ENG)	(27)	1836529.69	1459068.63	56	José Manuel LARA	(ESP)	(32)	564407.79	448405.33
7	Henrik STENSON	(SWE)	(19)	1798616.76	1428947.93	57	Angel CABRERA	(ARG)	(15)	559625.43	444605.89
8	Martin KAYMER	(GER)	(25)	1794499.96	1425677.25	58	Markus BRIER	(AUT)	(28)	553960.97	440105.64
9	Sergio GARCIA	(ESP)	(13)	1591916.99	1264731.07	59	Ignacio GARRIDO	(ESP)	(27)	545822.41	433639.80
10	Søren KJELDSEN	(DEN)	(29)	1440979.05	1144815.33	60	Thomas LEVET	(FRA)	(26)	539390.91	428530.16
11	Oliver WILSON	(ENG)	(26)	1270705.50	1009538.02	61	Alastair FORSYTH	(SCO)	(26)	489359.18	388781.42
12	Jeev Milkha SINGH	(IND)	(26)	1218208.91	967831.02	62	Louis OOSTHUIZEN	(RSA)	(23)	485035.99	385346.78
13	Darren CLARKE	(NIR)	(29)	1151038.08	914465.78	63	Mikael LUNDBERG	(SWE)	(25)	476929.82	378906.67
14	Søren HANSEN	(DEN)	(25)	1123897.15	892903.12	64	Gary ORR	(SCO)	(23)	472033.36	375016.57
15	Retief GOOSEN	(RSA)	(15)	1051334.71	835254.40	65	Johan EDFORS	(SWE)	(25)	456695.55	362831.13
16	Peter HANSON	(SWE)	(28)	992621.81	788608.73	66	Maarten LAFEBER	(NED)	(29)	451975.13	359080.90
17	James KINGSTON	(RSA)	(22)	973594.38	773492.00	67	Jyoti RANDHAWA	(IND)	(25)	449401.82	357036.49
18	Pablo LARRAZABAL	(ESP)	(28)	960857.53	763372.95	68	Thongchai JAIDEE	(THA)	(22)	446505.37	354735.34
19	Ian POULTER	(ENG)	(16)	946806.18	752209.57	69	Michael CAMPBELL	(NZL)	(21)	430147.03	341739.12
20	Richard FINCH	(ENG)	(29)	937437.76	744766.63	70	Ross McGOWAN	(ENG)	(29)	429172.95	340965.24
21	Paul CASEY	(ENG)	(15)	930347.05	739133.27	71	Raphaël JACQUELIN	(FRA)	(30)	427575.90	339696.43
22	Anthony WALL	(ENG)	(30)	914779.46	726765.28	72	Robert DINWIDDIE	(ENG)	(31)	426811.05	339088.79
23	Richard GREEN	(AUS)	(22)	888792.72	706119.59	73	Martin ERLANDSSON	(SWE)	(29)	416896.73	331212.15
24	Francesco MOLINARI	(ITA)	(30)	880240.87	699325.40	74	Bradley DREDGE	(WAL)	(23)	416720.23	331071.92
25	Alvaro QUIROS	(ESP)	(28)	833799.52	662429.11	75	Richard STERNE	(RSA)	(22)	415039.62	329736.73
26	Paul MCGINLEY	(IRL)	(27)	824725.96	655220.43	76	David FROST	(RSA)	(23)	413794.81	328747.76
27	Colin MONTGOMERIE	(SCO)	(24)	815153.09	647615.07	77	Stephen GALLACHER	(SCO)	(29)	413367.27	328408.10
28	Charl SCHWARTZEL	(RSA)	(27)	797224.94	633371.69	78	Andrew MCLARDY	(RSA)	(27)	411416.50	326858.27
29	Peter HEDBLOM	(SWE)	(28)	796219.92	632573.22	79	Magnus A CARLSSON	(SWE)	(29)	405997.59	322553.10
30	Damien MCGRANE	(IRL)	(31)	748289.40	594493.84	80	Jarmo SANDELIN	(SWE)	(29)	395254.91	314018.36
31	Alexander NOREN	(SWE)	(28)	742090.82	589569.26	81	Justin ROSE	(ENG)	(14)	392562.24	311879.11
32	Scott STRANGE	(AUS)	(26)	739368.16	587406.18	82	Mark FOSTER	(ENG)	(28)	377429.81	299856.84
33	Grégory HAVRET	(FRA)	(26)	725270.95	576206.37	83	Ricardo GONZALEZ	(ARG)	(25)	369736.91	293745.06
34	Gonzalo FDEZ-CASTAÑO	(ESP)	(25)	711545.60	565301.98	84	Simon KHAN	(ENG)	(27)	368037.71	292395.10
35	David LYNN	(ENG)	(29)	705766.87	560710.95	85	Pelle EDBERG	(SWE)	(30)	366000.67	290776.73
36	Rory MCILROY	(NIR)	(28)	696334.83	553217.47	86	Greg NORMAN	(AUS)	(3)	363976.30	289168.43
37	Hennie OTTO	(RSA)	(21)	683368.78	542916.32	87	Robert ALLENBY	(AUS)	(8)	359991.54	286002.66
38	Peter LAWRIE	(IRL)	(31)	682180.63	541972.38	88	Simon WAKEFIELD	(ENG)	(32)	359428.25	285555.14
39	Andres ROMERO	(ARG)	(13)	680601.39	540717.72	89	Jamie DONALDSON	(WAL)	(29)	350285.77	278291.71
40	Paul LAWRIE	(SCO)	(26)	679530.38	539866.83	90	Rafa ECHENIQUE	(ARG)	(29)	346344.11	275160.17
41	Felipe AGUILAR	(CHI)	(24)	676182.34	537206.91	91	Mikko ILONEN	(FIN)	(25)	329916.26	262108.73
42	Ernie ELS	(RSA)	(15)	674097.71	535550.73	92	Daniel CHOPRA	(SWE)	(13)	329319.13	261634.33
43	Adam SCOTT	(AUS)	(11)	671436.99	533436.87	93	S S P CHOWRASIA	(IND)	(14)	327283.04	260016.72
44	Nick DOUGHERTY	(ENG)	(26)	658973.64	523535.10	94	Niclas FASTH	(SWE)	(24)	322369.14	256112.77
45	David HOWELL	(ENG)	(27)	652491.48	518385.23	95	Christian CÉVAËR	(FRA)	(27)	318230.52	252824.75
46	Grégory BOURDY	(FRA)	(28)	648923.75	515550.77	96	Marcel SIEM	(GER)	(28)	309838.59	246157.62
47	Anders HANSEN	(DEN)	(22)	644153.91	511761.27	97	Marc WARREN	(SCO)	(28)	307396.46	244217.41
48	John BICKERTON	(ENG)	(26)	627816.24	498781.47	98	Gary MURPHY	(IRL)	(30)	301791.91	239764.76
49	Steve WEBSTER	(ENG)	(26)	604181.02	480003.99	99	Paul BROADHURST	(ENG)	(26)	290416.02	230726.96
50	Graeme STORM	(ENG)	(24)	597120.68	474394.75	100	Alvaro VELASCO	(ESP)	(28)	286887.57	227923.71

Pos	Name	Country	Played	€	£
101	Thomas BJÖRN	(DEN)	(21)	285252.10	226624.38
102	Marcus FRASER	(AUS)	(24)	282451.57	224399.44
103	Miles TUNNICLIFF	(ENG)	(26)	282333.38	224305.53
104	Michael JONZON	(SWE)	(25)	280464.75	222820.96
105	Paul WARING	(ENG)	(22)	279871.64	222349.75
106	Phillip ARCHER	(ENG)	(31)	275495.15	218872.76
107	Lee SLATTERY	(ENG)	(28)	275241.76	218671.46
108	Michael LORENZO-VERA	(FRA)	(25)	269091.39	213785.16
109	Alejandro CAÑIZARES	(ESP)	(16)	265000.48	210535.06
110	Benn BARHAM	(ENG)	(29)	262221.75	208327.44
111	Robert ROCK	(ENG)	(23)	258149.27	205091.98
112	Sam LITTLE	(ENG)	(32)	253974.79	201775.48
113	Daniel VANCSIK	(ARG)	(25)	246895.94	196151.54
114	David DIXON	(ENG)	(23)	240031.56	190697.99
115	Peter O'MALLEY	(AUS)	(22)	239023.63	189897.22
116	Shiv KAPUR	(IND)	(29)	233532.03	185534.30
117	Jean-Baptiste GONNET	(FRA)	(29)	231077.36	183584.14
118	François DELAMONTAGNE	(FRA)	(26)	223746.19	177759.75
119	Patrik SJÖLAND	(SWE)	(27)	223413.01	177495.04
120	Garry HOUSTON	(WAL)	(33)	219447.46	174344.53
121	Fredrik ANDERSSON HED	(SWE)	(28)	211958.97	168395.14
122	José-Filipe LIMA	(POR)	(28)	189155.10	150278.15
123	Sam WALKER	(ENG)	(31)	187984.78	149348.36
124	Joost LUITEN	(NED)	(14)	171279.01	136076.12
125	Prayad MARKSAENG	(THA)	(9)	170704.40	135619.61
126	Jean VAN DE VELDE	(FRA)	(24)	170620.25	135552.76
127	Wen-chong LIANG	(CHN)	(13)	167218.38	132850.07
128	Peter FOWLER	(AUS)	(25)	165178.10	131229.13
129	Ariel CANETE	(ARG)	(31)	164839.05	130959.76
130	Carlos RODILES	(ESP)	(31)	162410.89	129030.66
131	Thomas AIKEN	(RSA)	(24)	160775.32	127731.25
132	Peter BAKER	(ENG)	(25)	159093.18	126394.84
133	Scott BARR	(AUS)	(18)	158473.80	125902.76
134	Carl PETTERSSON	(SWE)	(2)	151895.61	120676.58
135	Matthew MILLAR	(AUS)	(21)	151175.73	120104.66
136	Chapchai NIRAT	(THA)	(23)	149307.48	118620.39
137	Iain PYMAN	(ENG)	(28)	146872.07	116685.53
138	James KAMTE	(RSA)	(24)	142061.70	112863.83
139	Anton HAIG	(RSA)	(29)	141579.75	112480.93
140	Sion E BEBB	(WAL)	(25)	138898.38	110350.67
141	Kane WEBBER	(AUS)	(11)	138686.28	110182.16
142	Martin WIEGELE	(AUT)	(25)	138671.98	110170.79
143	Barry LANE	(ENG)	(24)	137184.65	108989.16
144	Henrik NYSTRÖM	(SWE)	(27)	137005.66	108846.95
145	Peter WHITEFORD	(SCO)	(30)	136356.61	108331.30
146	Jan-Are LARSEN	(NOR)	(18)	135588.63	107721.17
147	Edoardo MOLINARI	(ITA)	(26)	135270.14	107468.13
148	Christian NILSSON	(SWE)	(11)	134082.05	106524.23
149	Gareth PADDISON	(NZL)	(26)	132293.60	105103.36
150	Stuart MANLEY	(WAL)	(33)	131902.08	104792.31
151	David DRYSDALE	(SCO)	(24)	131473.39	104451.72
152	Emanuele CANONICA	(ITA)	(28)	128263.64	101901.67
153	Fabrizio ZANOTTI	(PAR)	(27)	127703.11	101456.35
154	Paul SHEEHAN	(AUS)	(7)	127324.76	101155.76
155	Simon GRIFFITHS	(ENG)	(11)	118544.21	94179.88
156	Kyron SULLIVAN	(WAL)	(21)	117723.81	93528.09
157	Simon YATES	(SCO)	(9)	115843.24	92034.04
158	Julio ZAPATA	(ARG)	(26)	107001.75	85009.73
159	Carl SUNESON	(ESP)	(33)	103235.32	82017.41
160	Steven O'HARA	(SCO)	(12)	100752.36	80044.78
161	Julien CLÉMENT	(SUI)	(6)	100609.70	79931.43
162	Chris WOOD	(ENG)	(9)	99705.80	79213.32
163	Sven STRÜVER	(GER)	(26)	96247.50	76465.80
164	Phillip PRICE	(WAL)	(25)	95559.14	75918.91
165	Mardan MAMAT	(SIN)	(22)	94306.08	74923.40
166	Juan ABBATE	(ARG)	(22)	90633.22	72005.42
167	Richard BLAND	(ENG)	(17)	88363.36	70202.08
168	Tom WHITEHOUSE	(ENG)	(34)	88111.34	70001.86
169	Alfredo GARCIA-HEREDIA	(ESP)	(8)	87533.33	69542.65
170	Prom MEESAWAT	(THA)	(10)	86802.39	68961.94
171	Danny WILLETT	(ENG)	(10)	85604.09	68009.93
172	Scott HEND	(AUS)	(9)	82686.01	65691.60
173	Thaworn WIRATCHANT	(THA)	(9)	79361.24	63050.16
174	Per-Ulrik JOHANSSON	(SWE)	(19)	78622.22	62463.03
175	Terry PILKADARIS	(AUS)	(19)	75032.09	59610.78
176	Lee S JAMES	(ENG)	(23)	74377.04	59090.36
177	Mads VIBE-HASTRUP	(DEN)	(26)	71492.71	56798.85
178	David HORSEY	(ENG)	(9)	71358.91	56692.55
179	Keith HORNE	(RSA)	(11)	70452.49	55972.43
180	Santiago LUNA	(ESP)	(15)	70258.83	55818.57
181	David GRIFFITHS	(ENG)	(27)	69502.58	55217.75
182	Pablo MARTIN	(ESP)	(24)	69191.21	54970.38
183	Andrew COLTART	(SCO)	(17)	64342.58	51118.28
184	Steven JEPPESEN	(SWE)	(16)	62711.30	49822.27
185	Gary CLARK	(ENG)	(8)	62661.25	49782.51
186	Craig LEE	(SCO)	(21)	60766.02	48276.81
187	Zane SCOTLAND	(ENG)	(16)	60665.13	48196.65
188	Adam BLYTH	(AUS)	(9)	60130.94	47772.26
189	Jesus Maria ARRUTI	(ESP)	(6)	59393.33	47186.25
190	Darren FICHARDT	(RSA)	(12)	58641.25	46588.74
191	Lian-wei ZHANG	(CHN)	(8)	56790.74	45118.57
192	Joakim BÄCKSTRÖM	(SWE)	(23)	55051.48	43736.78
193	Marco RUIZ	(PAR)	(6)	53685.00	42651.15
194	Alessandro TADINI	(ITA)	(12)	52733.28	41895.03
195	Andrew TAMPION	(AUS)	(7)	51032.37	40543.71
196	Pedro LINHART	(ESP)	(20)	49535.00	39354.10
197	Luis CLAVERIE	(ESP)	(24)	48045.91	38171.06
198	Mattias ELIASSON	(SWE)	(13)	46077.50	36607.21
199	Robert COLES	(ENG)	(6)	45917.09	36479.77
200	Chris RODGERS	(ENG)	(10)	44368.68	35249.61

Flags (K-Z)

Kenya	
Malaysia	
Mexico	
Morocco	
Netherlands	
New Zealand	
Northern Ireland	
Norway	
Paraguay	
Phillipines	
Poland	
Portugal	
Puerto Rico	
Qatar	
Russia	
Scotland	
Singapore	
South Africa	
South Korea	
Spain	
Sweden	
Switzerland	
Taiwan	
Thailand	
Trinidad & Tobago	
Turkey	
United Arab Emirates	
USA	
Wales	
Zimbabwe	

The European Tour International Schedule 2008

Date		Tournament / Venue	Winner	Score	First Prize / Prize Fund
2007 Nov	8-11	HSBC Champions *Sheshan International GC, Shanghai, China*	**Phil Mickelson, USA******	68-66-68-76=278 (-10)	€575,445 €3,450,255
	15-18	UBS Hong Kong Open *Hong Kong GC, Fanling, Hong Kong*	**Miguel Angel Jiménez, ESP**	65-67-66-67=265 (-15)	€255,710 €1,541,160
	22-25	MasterCard Masters *Huntingdale GC, Melbourne, Australia*	**Aaron Baddeley, AUS******	70-66-69-70=275 (-13)	€172,810 €909,430
	22-25	Omega Mission Hills World Cup* *Mission Hills GC, China,*	**Scotland (Colin Montgomerie & Marc Warren)**	63-68-66-66=263 (-25)	€1,092,000 (Team) €3,412,500
	29-2	Michael Hill New Zealand Open *The Hills GC, Queenstown, New Zealand*	**Richard Finch, ENG**	73-65-64-72=274 (-14)	€144,895 €767,990
Dec	6-9	Alfred Dunhill Championship *Leopard Creek, Mpumalanga, South Africa*	**John Bickerton, ENG**	70-69-68-68=275 (-13)	€158,500 €991,600
	13-16	South African Airways Open *Pearl Valley Golf Estates, Paarl, Western Cape, South Africa*	**James Kingston, RSA**	73-69-71-71=284 (-4)	€158,500 €999,200
2008 Jan	10-13	Joburg Open *Royal Johannesburg and Kensington GC, South Africa*	**Richard Sterne, RSA******	71-68-67-65=271 (-13)	€174,350 €1,116,585
	17-20	Abu Dhabi Golf Championship *Abu Dhabi GC, Abu Dhabi, UAE*	**Martin Kaymer, GER**	66-65-68-74=273 (-15)	€225,420 €1,347,500
	24-27	Commercialbank Qatar Masters presented by Dolphin Energy, *Doha GC, Qatar*	**Adam Scott, AUS**	69-73-65-61=268 (-20)	€285,070 €1,713,020
	31-3	Dubai Desert Classic *Emirates GC, Dubai, UAE*	**Tiger Woods, USA**	65-71-73-65=274 (-14)	€283,965 €1,700,700
Feb	7-10	EMAAR-MGF Indian Masters *Delhi GC, New Delhi, India*	**S S P Chowrasia, IND**	70-71-71-67=279 (-9)	€280,560 €1,680,320
	14-17	Enjoy Jakarta Astro Indonesia Open *Cengkareng GC, Jakarta, Indonesia*	**Felipe Aguilar, CHI**	65-62-67-68=262 (-18)	€137,885 €838,360
	20-24	**WGC - Accenture Match Play** *The Gallery at Dove Mountain, Tucson, Arizona, USA*	**Tiger Woods, USA**	def. Stewart Cink 8 & 7	€919,990 €5,451,810
	28-2	Johnnie Walker Classic *DLF G&CC, New Delhi, India*	**Mark Brown, NZL**	71-68-64-67=270 (-18)	€276,390 €1,641,710
Mar	6-9	Maybank Malaysian Open *Kota Permai G&CC, Kuala Lumpur, Malaysia*	**Arjun Atwal, IND******	70-68-68-64=270 (-18)	€219,485 €1,314,510
	13-16	Ballantine's Championship *Pinx GC, Jeju Island, South Korea*	**Graeme McDowell, NIR******	68-64-66-66=264 (-24)	€333,330 €1,988,550
	20-23	Madeira Islands Open BPI - Portugal *Santo da Serra, Madeira, Portugal*	**Alastair Forsyth, SCO******	70-70-66-67=273 (-15)	€116,660 €700,000
	20-23	**WGC – CA CHAMPIONSHIP** *Doral Golf Resort & Spa, Doral, Florida, USA*	**Geoff Ogilvy, AUS**	65-67-68-71=271 (-17)	€865,160 €5,126,875
	27-30	MAPFRE Open de Andalucia by Valle Romano *Aloha GC, Andalucia, Spain*	**Thomas Levet, FRA******	69-68-68-67=272 (-16)	€166,660 €996,270
Apr	3-6	Estoril Open de Portugal *Oitavos Dunes, Estoril, Portugal*	**Grégory Bourdy, FRA******	63-65-68-70=266 (-18)	€208,330 €1,259,345
	10-13	**MASTERS TOURNAMENT** *Augusta National, Georgia, USA*	**Trevor Immelman, RSA**	68-68-69-75=280 (-8)	€857,955 €4,783,275
	17-20	Volvo China Open *Beijing CBD International GC, Beijing, China*	**Damien McGrane, IRL**	68-69-68-73=278 (-10)	€232,120 €1,387,560
	24-27	BMW Asian Open *Tomson Shanghai Pudong GC, Shanghai, China*	**Darren Clarke, NIR**	71-69-67-73=280 (-8)	€243,510 €1,446,410
May	1-4	Open de España *Real Club de Golf de Sevilla, Seville, Spain*	**Peter Lawrie, IRL******	68-70-68-67=273 (-15)	€333,330 €2,011,980
	8-11	Methorios Capital Italian Open *Castello di Tolcinasco G&CC, Milan, Italy*	**Hennie Otto, RSA**	65-66-63-69=263 (-25)	€283,330 €1,707,640

* Approved Special Events   **Play-Off victory   ^ Reduced to 54 holes due to inclement weather

Date	Tournament / Venue	Winner	Score	First Prize / Prize Fund
	15-18	The Irish Open *Adare Manor Hotel & Golf Resort, Co. Limerick, Ireland*	Richard Finch, ENG	71-72-65-70=278 (-10)	€416,660 €2,490,680
	22-25	**BMW PGA CHAMPIONSHIP** *Wentworth Club, Surrey, England*	Miguel Angel Jiménez, ESP**	70-67-72-68=277 (-11)	€750,000 €4,500,000
	29-1	The Celtic Manor Wales Open *The Celtic Manor Resort, Newport, South Wales*	Scott Strange, AUS	63-66-69-64=262 (-22)	€376,670 €2,270,190
Jun	5-8	Bank Austria GolfOpen presented by Telekom Austria *Fontana GC, Vienna, Austria*	Jeev Milkha Singh, IND ^	64-63-71=198 (-15)	€216,660 €1,300,000
	12-15	SAINT-OMER OPEN presented by Neuflize OBC *Aa Saint Omer GC, Lumbres, France*	David Dixon, ENG	77-67-69-66=279 (-5)	€100,000 €604,470
	12-15	**US OPEN CHAMPIONSHIP** *Torrey Pines GC, La Jolla, California, USA*	Tiger Woods, USA**	72-68-70-73=283 (-1)	€858,180 €4,766,395
	19-22	BMW International Open *Golfclub München Eichenried, Munich, Germany*	Martin Kaymer, GER**	68-63-67-75=273 (-15)	€333,330 €1,979,950
	26-29	Open de France ALSTOM *Le Golf National, Paris, France*	Pablo Larrazabal, ESP	65-70-67-67=269 (-15)	€666,660 €3,985,100
Jul	3-6	The European Open *The London GC, Kent, England*	Ross Fisher, ENG	63-68-69-68=268 (-20)	€506,390 €3,032,810
	10-13	The Barclays Scottish Open *Loch Lomond GC, Glasgow, Scotland*	Graeme McDowell, NIR	67-70-66-68=271 (-13)	€631,045 €3,748,320
	17-20	**THE 137th OPEN CHAMPIONSHIP** *Royal Birkdale GC, Southport, Lancashire, England*	Padraig Harrington, IRL	74-68-72-69=283 (+3)	€938,565 €5,335,870
	24-27	Inteco Russian Open Golf Championship 2008 *Le Meridien Moscow Country Club, Russia*	Mikael Lundberg, SWE	67-64-68-68=267 (-21)	€210,240 €1,265,220
	31-3	**WGC – Bridgestone Invitational** *Firestone CC, Akron, Ohio, USA*	Vijay Singh, FIJ	67-66-69-68=270 (-10)	€860,585 €5,022,305
Aug	7-10	**US PGA CHAMPIONSHIP** *Oakland Hills CC, Bloomfield Township, Michigan, USA*	Padraig Harrington, IRL	71-74-66-66=277 (-3)	€867,220 €4,767,715
	14-17	SAS Masters *Arlandastad Golf, Stockholm, Sweden*	Peter Hanson, SWE	66-66-68-71=271 (-9)	€266,660 €1,602,400
	21-24	The KLM Open *Kennemer G&CC, Zandvoort, The Netherlands*	Darren Clarke, NIR	68-64-66-66=264 (-16)	€300,000 €1,793,300
	28-31	Johnnie Walker Championship at Gleneagles *The Gleneagles Hotel, Perthshire, Scotland*	Grégory Havret, FRA	68-71-69-70=278 (-14)	€292,355 €1,747,615
Sept	4-7	Omega European Masters *Crans-sur-Sierre, Crans Montana, Switzerland*	Jean-François Lucquin, FRA**	68-67-69-67=271 (-13)	€333,330 €2,008,990
	11-14	Mercedes-Benz Championship *Golf Club Gut Lärchenhof, Cologne, Germany*	Robert Karlsson, SWE	67-69-68-71=275 (-13)	€320,000 €2,000,000
	19-21	**THE RYDER CUP*** *Valhalla GC, Louisville, Kentucky, USA*	USA	16½ - 11½	
	25-28	The Quinn Insurance British Masters *The Belfry, Sutton Coldfield, West Midlands, England*	Gonzalo Fernandez-Castaño, ESP**	71-70-68-67=276 (-12)	€381,610 €2,296,540
Oct	2-5	Alfred Dunhill Links Championship *Old Course, St Andrews, Carnoustie and Kingsbarns, Scotland*	Robert Karlsson, SWE**	67-70-76-65=278 (-10)	€545,810 €3,284,690
	9-12	Madrid Masters *Club de Campo Villa de Madrid, Spain*	Charl Schwartzel, RSA	69-64-66-66=265 (-19)	€166,660 €1,000,000
	16-19	Portugal Masters *Oceânico Victoria Golf Course, Vilamoura, Portugal*	Alvaro Quiros, ESP	66-68-67-68=269 (-19)	€500,000 €3,000,000
	23-26	CASTELLÓ MASTERS Costa Azahar *Club de Campo del Mediterráneo, Castellón, Spain*	Sergio Garcia, ESP	66-65-66-67=264 (-20)	€333,330 €1,984,350
	30-2	**Volvo Masters** *Club de Golf Valderrama, Sotogrande, Spain*	Søren Kjeldsen, DEN	65-71-69-71=276 (-8)	€708,000 €4,190,600

* Approved Special Events   **Play-Off victory   ^ Reduced to 54 holes due to inclement weather

DIRECTORS

N. C. Coles, MBE, *Chairman*

A. Gallardo, *Vice Chairman*

M. Bembridge

R. Chapman

P. Eales

D. Jones

R. Lee

J. E. O'Leary

M. Roe

D. J. Russell

O. Sellberg

J. Spence

Sir M. F. Bonallack, OBE
(Non Executive Tour Group Director)

P. A. T. Davidson
(Non Executive Tour Group Director, Finance)

B. Nordberg
(Non Executive Tour Group Director)

N. Northridge
(Non Executive Tour Group Director)

K. S. Owen
(Non Executive Tour Group Director, Broadcasting)

CHIEF EXECUTIVE	G. C. O'Grady
DIRECTOR OF INTERNATIONAL POLICY	K. Waters
RYDER CUP DIRECTOR	R. G. Hills
FINANCIAL DIRECTOR & COMPANY SECRETARY	J. Orr
GROUP MARKETING DIRECTOR	S. F. Kelly
DIRECTOR OF CORPORATE AFFAIRS AND PUBLIC RELATIONS	M. S. Platts
DIRECTOR OF TOUR OPERATIONS	D. W. Garland
DIRECTOR OF BROADCASTING & NEW MEDIA	M. Lichtenhein
DIRECTOR OF PROPERTY AND VENUE DEVELOPMENT	D. MacLaren
MANAGING DIRECTOR, EUROPEAN SENIOR TOUR	K. A. Stubbs
DIRECTOR OF CHALLENGE TOUR	A. de Soultrait
CHIEF REFEREE	J. N. Paramor
ASSISTANT DIRECTOR OF TOUR OPERATIONS	D. A. Probyn
SENIOR REFEREE	A. N. McFee
SENIOR TOURNAMENT DIRECTOR AND QUALIFYING SCHOOL DIRECTOR	M. R. Stewart
DIRECTOR OF INTERNATIONAL CHAMPIONSHIPS	P. Adams
DIRECTOR OF CHAMPIONSHIP MANAGEMENT	J. Birkmyre
RYDER CUP MATCH DIRECTOR	E. Kitson
SALES DIRECTOR	T. Shaw
DIRECTOR OF COMMUNICATIONS	G. Simpson

TOURNAMENT COMMITTEE

T. Björn, *Chairman* (DEN)	R. Karlsson (SWE)
D. Clarke (NIR)	B. Lane (ENG)
G. Fernandez-Castaño (ESP)	Paul Lawrie (SCO)
R. Finch (ENG)	P. McGinley (IRL)
J. Haeggman (SWE)	C. Montgomerie, OBE (SCO)
C. Hanell (SWE)	M. Roe (ENG)
R. Jacquelin (FRA)	H. Stenson (SWE)
M. A. Jiménez (ESP)	

Photographers

gettyimages®

Hamish Blair
David Cannon
Cancan Chu
Stuart Franklin
Sam Greenwood
Scott Halleran
Richard Heathcote
Harry How
Ross Kinnaird
Warren Little
Andy Lyons
Ryan Pierse
Andrew Redington
Jamie Squire
Michael Steele
Ian Walton

Additional Contributors
Phil Inglis
Golfing Union of Ireland
Independent Newspapers (Ireland)

Padraig Harrington

The All Time European Tour Winners Country

EUROPEAN TOUR RACE TO DUBAI 2009

1 ARGENTINA
Number of wins: 26
Number of winners: 10
Leading performers:
Eduardo Romero (8);
Vicente Fernandez,
Angel Cabrera (4).

2 AUSTRALIA
Number of wins: 99
Number of winners: 34
Leading performers: Greg Norman (14);
Graham Marsh (10); Rodger Davis (7).

3 AUSTRIA
Number of wins: 2
Number of winners: 1
Leading performer: Markus Brier (2).

4 BELGIUM
Number of wins: 1
Number of winners: 1
Leading performer: Phillipe Toussaint (1).

5 BRAZIL
Number of wins: 1
Number of winners: 1
Leading performer: Jamie Gonzalez (1).

6 CANADA
Number of wins: 3
Number of winners: 2
Leading performers: Mike Weir (2);
Jerry Anderson (1).

7 CHILE
Number of wins: 1
Number of winners: 1
Leading performer: Felipe Aguilar (1).

8 CHINA
Number of wins: 2
Number of winners: 2
Leading performers: Lian-Wei Zhang,
Liang Wen-chong (1).

9 DENMARK
Number of wins: 18
Number of winners: 6
Leading performers: Thomas Björn (9);
Anders Hansen, Søren Hansen,
Søren Kjeldsen, Steen Tinning (2).

10 ENGLAND
Number of wins: 239
Number of winners: 77
Leading performers: Nick Faldo (30);
Mark James, Lee Westwood (18);
Howard Clark (11).

11 FIJI
Number of wins: 13
Number of winners: 1
Leading performer:
Vijay Singh (13).

12 FINLAND
Number of wins: 2
Number of winners: 1
Leading performer: Mikko Ilonen (2).

13 FRANCE
Number of wins: 20
Number of winners: 10
Leading performers: Thomas Levet (4);
Grégory Havret, Jean-Francois Remesy
(3); Grégory Bourdy, Raphaël Jacquelin,
Jean Van de Velde (2).

14 GERMANY
Number of wins: 54
Number of winners: 6
Leading performers: Bernhard Langer
(42); Alex Cejka (4); Sven Strüver (3).

15 INDIA
Number of wins: 7
Number of winners: 3
Leading performers: Arjun Atwal,
Jeev Milkha Singh (3); SSP Chowrasia (1).

16 IRELAND
Number of wins: 45
Number of winners: 13
Leading performers: Padraig Harrington
(14); Des Smyth (8); Eamonn Darcy,
Paul McGinley, Christy O'Connor Jnr (4).

17 ITALY
Number of wins: 11
Number of winners: 6
Leading performers: Costantino Rocca
(5); Baldovino Dassu (2);
Emanuele Canonica, Massimo
Mannelli, Francesco Molinari,
Massimo Scarpa (1).

18 JAPAN
Number of wins: 1
Number of winners: 1
Leading performer: Isao Aoki (1).

MOST VICTORIES BY PLAYER
THE TOP TEN

1. Seve Ballesteros — 50
2. Bernhard Langer — 42
3. Tiger Woods — 36
4. Colin Montgomerie — 31
5. Nick Faldo — 30
6. Ian Woosnam — 29
7. Ernie Els — 24
8. José Maria Olazábal — 23
9. Sam Torrance — 21
10. Mark James — 18
    Sandy Lyle — 18
    Lee Westwood — 18